POSTING IT

UNIVERSITY PRESS OF FLORIDA

Florida A&M University, Tallahassee
Florida Atlantic University, Boca Raton
Florida Gulf Coast University, Ft. Myers
Florida International University, Miami
Florida State University, Tallahassee
New College of Florida, Sarasota
University of Central Florida, Orlando
University of Florida, Gainesville
University of North Florida, Jacksonville
University of South Florida, Tampa
University of West Florida, Pensacola

Posting It

The Victorian Revolution in Letter Writing

CATHERINE J. GOLDEN

UNIVERSITY PRESS OF FLORIDA

Gainesville · Tallahassee · Tampa · Boca Raton
Pensacola · Orlando · Miami · Jacksonville · Ft. Myers · Sarasota

14 13 12 11 10 09   6 5 4 3 2 1

Library of Congress Cataloging-in-Publication Data
Golden, Catherine.
Posting it : the Victorian revolution in letter writing / Catherine J.
Golden.
p. cm.
Includes bibliographical references and index.
ISBN 978-0-8130-3379-2 (alk. paper)
1. Communication and technology—Great Britain—History—19th
century. 2. Postal service—Great Britain—History—19th century.
3. Written communication—Great Britain—History—19th century.
4. Letter writing—Great Britain—History—19th century. 5. Literature
and society—Great Britain—History—19th century. 6. Material culture—
Great Britain—History—19th century. 7. Great Britain—Social life and
customs—19th century. 8. Great Britain—Civilization—19th century.
I. Title.
P96.T422G75 2009
816.'809941—dc22   2009017138

The University Press of Florida is the scholarly publishing agency for the
State University System of Florida, comprising Florida A&M Univer-
sity, Florida Atlantic University, Florida Gulf Coast University, Florida
International University, Florida State University, New College of Florida,
University of Central Florida, University of Florida, University of North
Florida, University of South Florida, and University of West Florida.

University Press of Florida
15 Northwest 15th Street
Gainesville, FL 32611-2079
http://www.upf.com

For the British philatelic community to which
Mr. Robert Johnson kindly introduced me

Contents

Illustrations

Preface

Even though I live in an electronic age and have come to rely on computer-mediated communication, I have a confession to make. I prefer to write and receive traditional, old-fashioned, stamped letters. I am a fan of what enthusiasts of new technology call "snail mail"—a derogatory term that highlights today's fascination with instant communication in the form of e-mail and text messages. I am not unusual in sending cards for special occasions, such as birthdays, weddings, and anniversaries, or in mailing postcards while "on holiday," as they say in the UK. However, I also post thank-you notes after attending a party or dinner at a friend's home. I write cards to acknowledge birthday presents and holiday gifts, even to my closest relatives. I write notes to colleagues and friends when they fall sick or lose a loved one, but I also send notes to these same friends and colleagues when they lose their beloved pets, need a boost, or do something memorable or exciting, like star in a play or get a promotion at work.

Not surprisingly, I come from a long line of letter writers. In my study, I keep several shoeboxes and file folders filled with cherished correspondence. Many handwritten letters bear the traces of beloved family members now gone. I have a whole file of letters from my father, who wrote regularly to me and my twin sons, Jesse and Emmet, even after he adopted e-mail. I still have and occasionally read letters my father's father, Grandpa Poppy, typed on an old-fashioned typewriter; he sent them to me when, as a young teen, I attended a sleepaway camp called Camp Lakeland in western New York. In this treasure trove of letters, I have an unopened, returned letter I sent to my dear Uncle Bob Golden, who died unexpectedly before he received it. I keep childhood correspondence from my lifelong friend Anne Feininger Mulherkar, dating to the fourth and fifth grades. I still chuckle over our audacious autographs, "Cathy the Great," "Anne the Magnificent," and other such epithets. I also have precious cards my sons made me when they were little; thank-you notes from elementary school children when I shared flannel board stories of *Peter Rabbit* and *Caps for Sale* at Lake Avenue Elementary School; cards I received when

I made tenure and promotion to full professor; special notes from my Mom, who really taught me how to write; cheery cards from my sister, Pam—some with a penny enclosed as a symbol of our father's lasting love for us; a separate box filled with all the condolence notes I received when my father died; and a large shoebox of cards that friends and colleagues sent after a bad biking accident derailed me and my sabbatical plans. Clearing out my parents' home as my mother moved into a retirement community, I also came across letters my father had saved from his own parents and siblings, many of which contained family secrets.

My own passion for writing is long standing. Growing up, I wrote books about my childhood adventures, which I vainly called the "Cathy Series." My dad and I regularly exchanged little notes, which we called "Good Words for the Day." In college, I also began to write complaint letters when products fell short of a company's promise—Kellogg's guaranteed two scoops of raisins in every single box of raisin bran, so I felt it my duty to tell Kellogg's that the company must use an awfully small scoop. Writing complaint letters—which I turned into a writing assignment for my English classes at Skidmore College and later, with my husband, Michael Marx, into an article about writing for real audiences—became a profitable venture for me. Not only did the mail bring me coupons for free products from companies and businesses, but I received a full refund from the Buffalo Hyatt when I complained how, on our wedding night, my husband carried me over the threshold into a business suite—not a bridal suite as promised.

Because I like to write and write often, I enjoy shopping in stores that sell stationery, note cards, writing paper, and pens. When I received my PhD, my parents gave me an heirloom fountain pen that had belonged to Poppy; Schaeffer Pens even refurbished it for free. I am particular about the pens and pencils I purchase for teaching and scholarship. I often buy Paper~Mate Sharpwriter pencils that look like real pencils but have retractable lead. I prefer pens with inks in shades of green or purple—Lewis Carroll's ink of choice—over conventional black or blue ink; I strictly avoid red ink when marking papers as that "bloody" color evokes fear in my students. A blotter lined with reproduction William Morris paper graces both my rolltop desk at home and my mahogany desk at work, which I inherited from my father. I have a collection of Victorian pen trays, pens, stamp boxes, letter clips, letter openers, desk sets, and portable writing desks, made of handsome wood and papier-mâché. One treasured clip in my collection belonged to the mother of my dear friends Michael and Diana Fenton.

I take time to pick out stationery—I favor cards with Victoriana and cats, twin passions. I often select museum note cards featuring cats, Victorian woman readers (the topic of a previous book), and Beatrix Potter characters. Each year I design holiday picture cards, which over the years display a record of how our twin sons, Jesse and Emmet, have grown into amazing young men; these cards provide a panorama of highlights of each year, including trips to Israel, Paris, and Bath in England. Personalized postal items also enthrall me—not only address labels, but stationery, and stamps. My specially printed address labels feature a cat logo on a gold foil background. Thanks to my big brother, Grant, and my sister-in-law, Deb, I have personalized stationery with a cat logo, too. For my family and friends, I have turned photos into real United States postage stamps, featuring, for example, Mitzi, my Aunt Esther's beloved dog, and my nephews Alex and Rob during their birthright trip to Israel. I choose my postage stamps with care, selecting designs with flowers, animals, favorite authors, creative artists, and causes I support.

I make this confession at the outset of this book because I am painfully aware that I live in an increasingly paperless society. Today, people favor in-stantaneous and virtual dispatch and delivery of electronic messages and e-cards that arrive with no lag time. Along with certain words like "whom," which I still use and defend, stamped mail—also called paper mail, postal mail, land mail, and snail mail—is behind the times, on the way out. To advo-cates of a green society (an important cause I avidly support), paper commu-nication is not even good for the environment, giving rise to e-mail warnings to think twice before printing out a message. The post has not vanished from our world—"wane" might be a more precise term to describe the diminution of the post to date. Some people find stamped mail endearingly quaint and comforting, but from the vantage point of the twenty-first century, the posted letter appears to be waning in a manner akin to the Cheshire Cat—only its lasting grin alludes to the power of the Victorian post.

The Post Office is no longer our main communications network or a major institution that attracts visiting dignitaries as it did in the Victorian era; none-theless, the postal system, which has been impacted by computer-driven com-munication, plays an important role in society. Its defenders still consider it a remarkable institution; in fact, my fascination not only with letters but with what information technology has inherited from the Victorian letter-writing revolution motivates me to write this book. Somehow, a letter travels from a letter box at one's front door or a street-side mailbox into a vast national and international postal network, and after several days—as opposed to several hours in the Victorian age—it arrives at a home or business in a far-off city, state, or country. *Posting It* returns to a time when stamped mail costing one penny a trip was neither unfashionable nor old-fashioned nor seen as harmful for the environment. Instead, it was miraculous. The Victorians welcomed the Penny Post as a modern, revolutionary form of communication.

ACKNOWLEDGMENTS

I would like to thank the many institutions, libraries, trusts, and archives that opened collections of hard-to-find, out-of-print, and heretofore-unpublished materials, as well as the individuals who helped me to access these materials. Mr. Douglas Muir, curator of philately at the British Postal Museum & Archive, and Louise Todd, archivist, provided entrée to important materials and offered invaluable assistance for my research. My appreciation goes to the Reading and Study Room staff at the National Art Library, the Victoria and Albert Museum, and the staff at the British Library Reading Room. Mr. David Beech, Fellow of the Royal Philatelic Society of London and head of Philatelic Collections at the British Library, and Mr. Paul Skinner, curator, helped me to arrange my visit to the British Library and took time from their busy schedules to show me excellent examples of postal stationery, stamps, and extant correspondence that inform my book.

Mr. Beech introduced me to Mr. Robert Johnson, a fellow British philatelist from Bristol, who provided invaluable assistance on this project. I am grateful to Robert Johnson for sharing his knowledge of all things philatelic, reading draft chapters, and offering a British perspective to my reading of Victorian culture. Robert, in turn, shared my project with his fellow philatelists, Mr. James Grimwood-Taylor and his wife, Pat Grimwood-Taylor, and with Mr. John Forbes-Nixon, who, in turn, directed me to Dr. Adrian Almond. These individuals generously shared their expertise and countless examples of extant and unpublished letters, many of which appear in this book. I dedicate *Posting It* to this group of generous philatelists whose assistance has been invaluable.

Mr. Beech and Mr. Johnson also encouraged me to apply for a grant from the Stuart Rossiter Trust. I am grateful to the Stuart Rossiter Trust for awarding me a grant in 2007 to pay for reproduction costs and rights for several of the illustrations in this book. Named after the late Stuart Rossiter, a leading postal historian of his day, this charitable trust supports research and publications relating to the history of the postal system and communications. It is a registered charity (England and Wales 292076), established with the money from Rossiter's estate and devoted as much to the rapidly changing outlooks in contemporary communications as to those of the past. How people communicated with one another through the ages and across all countries in the world is fundamental to a greater understanding of all types of history. In turn, currently contemplated changes in the British postal system due to regulations within the European community and the impact of computer-driven communication on postal systems will be as profound as nineteenth-century reforms of 1840 and 1875. For more information on the Rossiter Trust, see <http://www.rossitertrust.co.uk/>.

My thanks also go to Janine Marriott, curatorial advisor at Bath Postal Museum, for providing access to the nineteenth-century valentines in the Frank Staff Collection and to Victorian postal products important to my study. Janine Marriott introduced me to Anne Buchanan, local studies librarian, Bath Central Library, who graciously arranged for me to view the Valentine Cards Collection and an extensive holding of extant autograph letters, many of which inform this book. I include Anne and Janine in the philatelic community that greatly benefited my book.

I am grateful to Skidmore College for granting me a sabbatical leave and approving additional Mellon post-tenure sabbatical funding to support my full-year sabbatical to research and write this book. I especially appreciate the support of Charles Joseph, then dean of faculty and vice president of academic affairs, who suggested I apply for Mellon funding. I am grateful, too, to Skidmore for granting me three Faculty Research Grants to help with reproduction rights, the color book jacket, and proofreading services. I would like to thank Linda Simon, recent chair of the English Department, for encouraging me to explore this topic and for her faith in my work. The staff at the Lucy Scribner Library at Skidmore College was incredibly supportive of this book. Special thanks go to Amy Syrell, interlibrary loan supervisor, who facilitated numerous interlibrary loans critical to my research, and to Wendy Anthony, special collections curator, who made available seminal works in the Norman M. Fox Collection. Both greatly supported this project.

There are others at the college I wish to thank. I am particularly indebted to Phylise Banner, a former instructional technologist at Skidmore College, for her willingness to read the conclusion of *Posting It*; she provided incisive responses and helpful suggestions for readings in the area of computer-mediated communication. I am also grateful to Hunt Conard, director of media services, and Steve Otrembiak, senior AV technician of media services, who helped me to produce quality scans of letters and illustrations for reproduction in my book. I also appreciate the insights and support of my colleague

Phil Boshoff, and, in Victorian studies, Phyllis Roth and Barbara Black, as well as those of my excellent students at Skidmore College: David Steinberger (2009), Brooke Cohen (2009), Patrice LaHair (2009), Laurel Boshoff (2009), Heather Moore (2008), Adam Epstein (2008), Ashley Grossman (2008), Melissa Rampelli (2006), Lauren Marder (2006), Justin Coyne (2006), Nicole Zuckerman (2004), Marci Stevens (2004), and Stefanie Vischansky (2003). I thank Mary Frances Johnson (2011) for her assistance in the final stages of production. And I am grateful to my dear friend Norman M. Fox for sharing his personal collection of philatelic materials, including a Mulready envelope featured in this book.

I extend real appreciation to the University Press of Florida. Amy Gorelick, acquisitions editor, guided my writing of a previous book, *Images of the Woman Reader in Victorian British and American Fiction* (UPF 2003). She encouraged me to submit this proposal and was instrumental in shaping my project on a timely topic in Victorian cultural studies. She showed great faith in my work from its start to the finished product, giving unending support on a range of matters that made this project a real success. I am also grateful to my two reviewers, Professor Richard Fantina and Professor Eileen Cleere, both of whom enthusiastically endorsed my book. Richard Fantina intuitively grasped the purpose of my book and gave excellent suggestions on expanding and revising connections among Victorian material culture, literature, history, and politics, along with tips for marketing *Posting It*. Eileen Cleere pushed me to articulate the theoretical underpinnings in *Posting It*, as well as to make explicit the role of sentiment in postal reform. *Posting It* has become a more incisive analysis of Victorian material culture because of the generous and invaluable feedback both reviewers provided. I am grateful for the excellent work of the entire production staff, particularly Stephanie Williams, my publicist, Michele Fiyak-Burkley, my project editor, and Catherine-Nevil Parker, my copy editor, who oversaw the final details of this book.

I value my friends and family for their unconditional support of my academic life. I particularly appreciate Lollie Abramson Stark, Peri Stark, Jo-Ellen Unger, Jeanne O'Farrell Eddy, Ellen Sheets, Robyn Silverman, Susan Pardo, Anna Sugarman, and Suzanne Piekarz, who all cheered me on every step of the way and showed great faith in me and my book. I also am grateful to Holly Grande, Patty Hansen, Joannie Cassick, and Lollie (who vacationed with me in Utah at the very start of this project) for their curiosity, heartfelt support, and pointed questions as I researched and revised this book.

I thank my dear mother, Nancy Posmantur Golden, who taught me "I think I can"; my Mom's belief in my ability has always sustained me, as has her pride in my work. Thanks go to my brother, Grant, who suggested clever titles for book chapters, and to my sisters-in-law, Deborah Goldman and Judy Marx, who showed great interest in my work. I am particularly indebted to my sister, Pam, who was enormously helpful during my research for *Posting It*. Pam, an artist and teacher, traveled with me on a two-week research trip to London and Bath in November 2006 and acted as an informal research assistant. She discussed Victorian paintings with me (although she prefers modern art), purchased materials to aid my research, carried my bags and books (which I could not lift due to a broken arm from a biking accident), helped me to photocopy materials, and endlessly discussed possible titles for my book. I am also grateful for the support of our dear friend Josephine Zilberkweit, who met us during my 2006 research trip and supported this project from its formative stages. In fact, Josephine let us stay in her Rossmore Court flat while I was researching in London and set me straight that, in the United Kingdom, mail is the "post."

I foremost thank my own family for encouragement, support, and patience, as I spent endless hours on *Posting It*. My scholarship took time away from my husband and my sons, not only while I was researching in the UK but, more critically, while I was writing, revising, copyediting, proofreading, and indexing. I spent countless days and evenings in my study, lost in Victorian postal history and the world of my book. At times, they were rightly frustrated. I thank them for loving me, nonetheless, and supporting me throughout this entire project. And where would a writer be without a cat? Our family cats, Lee and Rose, curled up close to my computer and purred me on as I wrote, researched, and endlessly revised. Rose provided a calming presence. No matter the time of day or night I chose to work, Lee, who occasionally jammed my printer and typed extraneous letters and numbers into my text while prancing across the keyboard, was totally devoted to me and my muse.

Introduction

If any person had told the Parliament which met in perplexity and terror after the crash of 1720 that in 1830 the wealth of England would surpass all their wildest dreams, . . . that the post-office would bring more into the exchequer than the excise and customs had brought in together under Charles the Second, that stage-coaches would run from London to York in twenty-four hours, that men would be in the habit of sailing without wind, and would be beginning to ride without horses, our ancestors would have given as much credit to the prediction as they gave to Gulliver's Travels. Yet the prediction would have been true . . .

—Thomas Babington Macaulay, "Southey's Colloquies," January 1830

In August 2005, a Sunderland UK legal firm, Gordon Brown Associates, received a surprise in the post: a letter the firm had sent in 1997 by recorded delivery to a business partner of a deceased client appeared in a routine mail delivery. Fortunately, the letter, which Royal Mail had simply marked "not collected," did not contain pressing information. Someone living in Jane Austen's day expected it to take at least eight hours to travel a distance of eighty miles by stage coach. Gordon Brown Associates was "stunned," however, that it took eight years for a letter meant to travel only a distance of two miles to be returned to sender. "Curiouser and curiouser," how did this letter spend eight years in a postal twilight zone, a realm akin to Lewis Carroll's topsy-turvy wonderland where letters meant to be delivered never are? Where exactly was this letter lying since 1997? Was it wedged behind a piece of processing machinery in a Sunderland post office? Perhaps the letter was stuck to the bottom of a carrier bag or caught in a mail chute? Sometimes letters miraculously appear after long absences because a Good Samaritan or prankster simply finds a lost letter and puts it in the mail. "'To add insult to injury to the eight-year delay, we were charged £1 for the return,'" noted a partner in this firm.[1]

Tales of undelivered or long-lost letters sent by post—a form of communication that today's media enthusiasts disparagingly call "snail mail"—make great news stories. A quick search on the Internet reveals many variations on the story of a letter never reaching its destination, even though Royal Mail claims that the amount of missing mail has dropped dramatically. According to a 2004 statistic, 99.92 percent of mail arrives safely.[2] The Gordon Brown anecdote is humorous; not so, the situation confronting Royal Mail. Post office closures started around 1970, but the number has climbed. The government closed over 4,000 post offices between 1999 and 2007, and the future looks grave. In 2007, the government passed a proposal to close, by 2009, an additional 2,500 post offices or one-fifth of those remaining in the United Kingdom, the birthplace of Rowland Hill, the great innovator of postal reform and creator of the first postage stamp.[3]

In the Victorian age, large numbers of people went to their local post offices not only to send letters but to dispatch books, newspapers, and printed paper of all kinds; to deposit money in the Post Office Savings Bank (from 1861); to purchase money orders and later postal orders as a cheap means of transmitting money; to buy annuities; and, following the Post Office's purchase of private telegraph companies and an act of Parliament which gave the Post Office control of the telegraph service in 1870, to send telegrams and, from 1882, to take advantage of the telephone facilities becoming available in major towns and cities.[4] Local post offices were also public spaces, "special places to see and be seen" and "remarkable places where letters, correspondents, and expectant users of the network all came into contact."[5] In 1914, one third of all British civil servants worked for some branch of the Post Office. Moreover, as C. R. Perry notes in the opening chapter of *The Victorian Post Office: The Growth of a Bureaucracy,* "until the consolidation of the railway companies in 1922 the Post Office, handling a dauntingly wide variety of responsibilities from the management of long distance telephone communication to the sale of licenses for armorial bearings, comprised the largest business operation, public or private, in Great Britain" (3).

From the Victorian era until the eve of World War I, the British Post Office evolved into a major bureaucratic institution. Over 600 post offices, authorized as Post Office Savings Banks, performed transactions from the start of this service in 1861. The number steadily expanded, so people with small means could have the ability to save securely.[6] In turn, the number of persons employed to run Post Office Savings Banks increased—more customers generated greater business for money orders and postal orders.[7] The Post Office also entered into numerous, complicated negotiations with the railway and shipping lines to transport mail at home and abroad and to keep track of postal transmission accounts.

More than the mighty nineteenth-century Ionic façade of the General Post

Office in St. Martin's-le-Grand, London, has fallen. Nineteenth-century inventions in communications, principally the telegraph and the telephone, began to undermine the primacy of the post decades after uniform, prepaid postage became law in Victorian Britain.[8] C. R. Perry pinpoints 1885 to 1895 as the decade when the Post Office refrained from taking on new projects and "started to lose confidence in itself" (266). If today we characterize the post as old-fashioned, slow, and inefficient, in Victorian times, with the introduction of the Penny Post in 1840, it swiftly became synonymous with affordability, social equality, and efficiency—qualities that have changed and diminished as ways of communicating transformed in the twentieth century. The local post office was integral to the daily life of the Victorians, but its presence is dwindling today; according to former Trade and Industry Secretary Alistair Darling, roughly four million fewer people used the post office weekly in 2007 than did in 2005.[9] People in Britain still post stamped letters daily and rely on the Post Office for business and personal uses, paying, for example, a tremendous number of bills through local post offices. However, young and old alike are accessing services formerly performed by Royal Mail by turning, for example, to e-mail, Internet banking, text messaging, landlines and mobile phones, cash point machines, and direct debits to make purchases and pay their bills.[10] Consumers can procure an application for a driving license or passport online or through a retailer as opposed to their branch post office, and pensions and child benefits are now deposited directly into personal bank accounts.[11] A recent cartoon for the comic strip *Grand Avenue*, created by Steve Breen, mocks the plight of the postman: two Yorkshire terriers, dubbed the "evil Yorkies," text the postman about to make a delivery—"Roses are red, Violets are blue, Speedy e-mail & text messaging means no job for you."[12] E-mail, text messages, and mobile phones, now our preferred means of instant communication, impact the post, which requires modernization in the twenty-first century—new products and new services—to remain viable as an institution.

This book returns to the historical moment in Victorian Britain before the invention of the telegraph and the telephone and just at the opening of the Great Western Railway in 1838, a service which sped up mail delivery. To recall the words of Thomas Babington Macaulay, now the post could miraculously "ride without horses," and by 1847, trains replaced mail coaches in all but rural areas.[13] The Penny Post had a tremendous impact on daily Victorian life. It became the number one form of communication, generating a postal network that measurably impacted the economy, reshaped social relations, and arguably stands as a forerunner of computer-mediated communication

(CMC) networks. Historian David Henkin supports this idea, noting that to the Victorians, "the postal system was becoming . . . a network in the most modern sense" (5).[14] Sending letters, newspapers, books, and other information by post was as revolutionary to the Victorians as e-mail, text messaging, and handheld "igadgets" are to us today: G. R. Porter deemed affordable postage a "moral progress" in *The Progress of the Nation* (1847), and Henry Cole heralded the adoption of Uniform Penny Postage as "the glory of England for all time" in *Fifty Years of Public Work* (1884).[15]

Prior to postal reform, members of Parliament had free franking privileges. Postal franking is a system whereby a postmark affixed to the outside of a letter guaranteed its free carriage. The lower and middle classes, by contrast, were burdened by expensive postal charges, which provided the government with revenue. Many could not afford to accept letters without starving or pawning: typically the recipient paid to receive a letter, and the Post Office determined the charge according to the number of letter sheets a writer used multiplied by the distance a letter traveled. Through the Postage Duties Bill of 1839 and the introduction of the Penny Post on January 10, 1840, the post became an inclusive network and a public service, not just a privilege for the wealthy and noteworthy. For a penny, people could send letters to far-flung friends and relations and leave home with the comfort of knowing it was possible to remain connected to family, friends, and communities near and dear to their hearts. The decrease in postage led to an increase in mail, fostering consumerism and giving rise to letters of business, education, condolence, congratulations, and invitation, as well as to a host of postal products demanded by and created for women and men across the social classes. As Ruth Perry points out in *Women, Letters, and the Novel*, letters throughout the century were "a way of being involved with the world while keeping it at a respectable arm's length. Correspondence became the medium for weaving the social fabric of family and friendships in letters of invitation, acceptance, news, condolence, and congratulations" (69).

Britain did not stand alone in postal reform. Anthony Trollope, a long-term Post Office employee and prolific Victorian novelist, looked to France and its pillar boxes (mailboxes) and brought this innovation to Britain. Rowland Hill and other reformers used France's more affordable postage and higher revenues as an argument for lowering British postal charges. America experienced a major communications shift due to westward migration, rising literacy, and key legislations in 1845 and 1851 that resulted in cheaper postage, as David Henkin notes in *The Postal Age: The Emergence of Modern Communications in Nineteenth-Century America*. I am featuring Britain in this book because its prepayment and stamped mail got going sooner. The postage stamp and the scheme of prepayment became a model for other nations. Two Swiss cantons, Geneva and Zurich, quickly issued stamps in 1843, making the area we now call Switzerland the first in Europe to follow Hill's plan.[16] In North America, Brazil (1843) and the United States (1847) quickly followed Britain's example, designing postage stamps with each nation's name blazoned on them. Moreover, by 1860—only twenty years after Hill created the postage stamp—more than ninety countries, colonies, and districts had produced their own postage stamps.

The Penny Post grew out of a letter-writing revolution—hence the subtitle of this book. *Posting It*, in articulating the ideological work of postal reform, considers how the Penny Post sparked other revolutionary events, such as the repeal of the Corn Laws in 1846. If the letter lost its political and familiar edge with the rise of the Post Office as an institution—eclipsing the use of private mail carriers as Mary Favret maintains in *Romantic Correspondence: Women, Politics, and the Fiction of Letters*—the postal revolution and the ephemera it spawned, in turn, arguably teach us about the Victorian "frame of mind," to borrow Walter Houghton's phrasing. The rise of Victorian letter writing in an age of production and consumption led to stamp collecting as a hobby (first dubbed timbromania, now called philately) and stimulated industry, generating a variety of pens, inkwells, stamp boxes, letter holders and clips, wafers and seals, envelopes, scales, writing manuals, and portable writing desks, which today we call postal products, commodities, ephemera, and artifacts. These products were among the industry and wares showcased at the Great Exhibition of 1851—not surprisingly the point at which, as Lara Kriegel points out, "the term *Victorian* was first used as the self-conscious marker of an age" (11).

Over two decades ago in a now-seminal volume entitled *Victorian Things*, historian Asa Briggs established the importance of commodities to learn about nineteenth-century culture and society. Briggs calls for critical inquiry of the things Victorians "designed, named, made, advertised, bought and sold, listed, counted, collected, gave to others, threw away, or bequeathed" (12), setting a precedent for examination of household goods, fashion, song lyrics, manuals, advertisements, newspapers, cookbooks, museum artifacts, and exhibitions, et cetera. Many scholars have since contributed to the growing field of Victorian material culture studies. Most recently, for example, in *Household Gods: The British and Their Possessions*, Deborah Cohen examines objects from British interiors in an age of obsession with home improvement to argue that during this period consumerism cast off its taint of sin to become an expression of individuality—possessions became extensions of their owners. Lara Kriegel in *Grand Designs: Labor, Empire, and the Museum in Victorian Culture* explores connections among markets and museums, economics and aesthetics that shape our perception of British cultural history and art history.[17]

My book also takes its lead from Briggs's *Victorian Things*, specifically chapter 9, "Stamps—Used and Unused," which presents postage stamps and envelopes as key commodities that inform us about culture and society in the long nineteenth century. Taking a Victorian material culture studies approach in *Posting It*, I interpret literature in a historical context and analyze a range of literary and extraliterary sources—principally writing desks and manuals, pens and inkwells, the official catalogue of the Great Exhibition of 1851, extant correspondence, pictorial envelopes, valentines, biographies, diaries, periodicals, book illustration, and narrative painting—to illuminate the lives and values of the Victorians who made and bought these commodities as well as the social, political, and historical contexts in which the Penny Post manifested itself. For example, Mulreadies and their caricatures, the Penny Black, and writing desks transmit information about empire, identity, aesthetics, labor, education, class, and gender.[18] These objects, which have their own histories, tell us what people treasured and commemorated; they help us to remember past events and a former way of life and carry opinions on current events, moral judgments, customs, manners, humor, prejudices, and preferences. Briggs calls such objects, invested with meaning and sentiment, "emissaries" of culture (11). In *Posting It*, I concomitantly argue that objects of postal ephemera, as physical reminders of the past, hold power as "materials of memory" or "material memories," terminology introduced by Ann Rosalind Jones and Peter Stallybrass in *Renaissance Clothing and the Materials of Memory*. Their book explores how "fashion fashions," how "clothing and textiles were crucial to the making and unmaking of status, gender, sexuality, and religion in the Renaissance" (i). In *Posting It*, I am using terms from a seminal text in Renaissance material culture studies alongside terminology from Briggs's landmark Victorian study because the ideas in both sources are relevant to Victorian material culture.

Scholars of literature, focused as we often are on periodization, often lose sight of a profound coherence among the centuries just before and during which industrialization transformed Western culture. Fabric and clothing made in the late sixteenth and seventeenth centuries, which passed from master to servant or between friends and lovers, were powerful forms of material memory that came to be seen as expressions of personal and social identity. These notions are central to an understanding of the Victorian era of production and consumption: what people ate, read, drank, bought, displayed, and wore increasingly became forms of self-expression. In turn, *Posting It* argues that material artifacts of the Victorian revolution in letter writing act not only as emissaries of culture but as "materials of memory"—physical reminders informing our understanding of ideas, values, traits, concerns, and assumptions of the Victorians who commissioned, made, purchased, used, pawned, appreciated, and disparaged these products. Objects of postal ephemera carry with them particular life histories and inform our sense of time and place. They evoke memories of history and society, subordination and authority, nation and identity, class and gender, friendship and love, and aesthetic taste, et cetera. From possessions, objects, and commodities, potent reminders of the past, we gain insight into nineteenth-century society and Victorian notions of nation, gender, social class and status, aesthetics, identity, privacy, public space, and authority—all key concepts in our critical discourse today.

ORGANIZATION

I have organized this book into two parts: "Reforms" and "Outcomes." Chapters in part 1, "Reforms," explore fundamental questions: What was amiss about the postal system in early nineteenth-century Britain? How was it limited? Why did the post have to change, and how did it change? What can we learn about the Victorians by examining a revolution in letter writing that grew out of two earlier information revolutions in writing and printing, which took off in the nineteenth century with the mass production of literature and a great rise in literacy? How do primary materials including nineteenth-century periodicals, letters, pictorial envelopes, caricatures, postage stamps, the Great Exhibition catalogue, diaries, literature, book illustration, and narrative painting illuminate the values, ideas, struggles, and attitudes of the early Victorian era, the boom in letter writing, and the related growth of philatelic materials?

Chapter 1, entitled "Why the Victorians Needed a Revolution in Letter Writing," looks at postal reform stories that appear, for example, in Rowland Hill's pivotal 1837 pamphlet *Post Office Reform: Its Importance and Practicability*, the complete run of *The Post Circular* (a widely distributed propaganda sheet designed to facilitate postal reform), reports from the Mercantile Committee on Postage and the Parliamentary Select Committee on Postage, period books and articles, and Henry Cole's postal reform skit, which casts Queen Victoria as a major proponent of postal reform, a part she, in turn, played in real life. I consider the extravagant claims of supporters alongside the dire predictions of opponents of postal reform. However, I am privileging pre-reform hardship stories—which variously take the form of anecdotes, testimonials, imagined scenes, tales, and narratives of praise—for two reasons. First, they illustrate what was perceived to be amiss in nineteenth-century Britain in the days before Post Office reform. Reading these stories, which make extravagant claims for reform, we come to understand how the nineteenth-century Post Office was limited and why it had to change. In short, we realize why the Victorians needed a revolution in letter writing. Second, these narratives powered reform of the postal service. Tales of Rowland Hill running to the pawnshop and allegedly playing the part of the Good Samaritan in the Lake District, pre-reform anecdotes of isolation and impoverishment due to high-priced mail, and post-reform stories aligning moral, social, and economic improvements with the Penny Post share a key attribute: they moved their audience to take revolutionary action.

Chapter 2, "Signed, Sealed, Delivered: Mulreadies, Caricatures, and the Penny Black," begins on the historic day of January 10, 1840, when the Penny Post was extended to the entire nation. It focuses on the reception and significance of two innovations that accompanied postal reform: prepaid stationery (which took the form of envelopes and letter sheets, dubbed Mulreadies after their designer), and the first prepaid adhesive postage stamps, called the Penny Black and the Two Pence Blue (2d blue). The stamp, Mulreadies, and the caricatures that followed in their wake contain images that tell stories and invite questions. Specifically, what do the stereotypes of home and nation on the officially commissioned Mulready design illuminate about how the Victorians privileged the domestic hearth, engaged in the Opium Wars with China, and viewed former colonies (America, for example) or current British territories abroad (such as India)? While the British coinage had three additional busts for the young head of the Queen, and the penny stamp changed color—from black to red—why did it and the 2d blue retain the youthful profile of Queen Victoria, whose image was displayed on every letter that entered nearly every British home throughout her entire reign?[19] Although the public rejected the Mulready, a commissioned design, the highly popular Mulready caricatures and the "Queen's head" (as the stamp was nicknamed)—which the Victorian public seemingly approved by buying in droves—more reliably stand as material memories, showing how correspondence became a way to convey ideas. These postal products are emissaries of nation, of national pride and values on a broad scale: they tell us something of Britain's imperial identity, its trade relations, military and naval operations, and its conception of foreign lands and British territories abroad; they convey information about Victorian aesthetics and humor and other relevant issues of the age. I close this chapter with George Elgar Hicks's painting *The General Post Office, One Minute to Six* (1860) because it showcases how twenty years following the introduction of the Penny Post, the reformed postal service became emblematic of Britain as a nation. Through Hicks's canvas of Victorian life, we come to know the needs and fascinations of the Victorians, their love affair with progress, and their pride in the nation; we also glimpse the legacies postal reform created, leading to advances, trends, and problems still with us today.

Part 2, entitled "Outcomes," explores the negative and positive repercussions of postal reform. The three chapters in this section analyze at times extravagant predictions postal reformers made about the Penny Post in relation to the outcomes of reform. Chapter 3, "'Why is a Raven . . .?': The Rise of Postal Products from *Alice's Adventures in Wonderland* (1865) and *Vanity Fair* (1848) to the Pages of the Great Exhibition Catalogue (1851)," looks at an arguably unexpected outcome of postal reform—the production and consumption of materials that accompanied the Victorian revolution in letter writing. Did the Victorians anticipate that in passing Uniform Penny Postage they would foster postal products and innovations, a new field of industry? Suddenly, a stamp box was needed to hold a stamp. Slots cut in front doors or personal letter boxes were needed to facilitate mail delivery. (Gone were the days when the postman had to ring the doorbell and await payment before handing over the mail.) Demand grew for writing desks to keep stationery, sealing wax, and a host of postal products. Chapter 3 uses as a focal point the massive *Great Exhibition of the Works of Industry of all Nations, 1851. Official Descriptive and Illustrated Catalogue*, which describes and illustrates postal ephemera among other symbols of progress featured at the Great Exhibition of 1851. Envelopes, pens, inkwells, stamp boxes, letter holders, wafers and seals, letter clips, scales, manuals, and portable writing desks present the post as a growing commercial enterprise, invite classification and analysis, and, in turn, educate consumers today. Functioning as material memories of the age to which they belong, pictorial envelopes, letter-writing manuals, and, in particular, writing desks evoke a former way of life, conveying information about social class and status, gender, and aesthetics, as well as about Victorian preoccupations with etiquette, privacy and personal values, such as love and duty. The *Official Descriptive and Illustrated Catalogue* (as I have abbreviated it) and Thackeray's *Vanity Fair* demonstrate how the writing desk proved indispensable for travel, security, privacy, secret keeping, and writing.

While many Victorians supported Uniform Penny Postage for trade, commerce, and education and believed in its utopian promises of moral and social reformation, opponents presented dire predictions, and a small but vocal minority emerged in the first five years following the Penny Post. To the disgruntled, Hill's plan would facilitate unwanted or superfluous missives, vice, threats, fraud, blackmail (that might ruin a reputation), and ultimately fostered danger and discontent. The negative impact of increased cheap correspondence forms the focus of chapter 4, "Unwanted Missives and the Spread of Vice—'Curious Things,' Slander, and Blackmail from *Household Words* to the Fiction of George Eliot, Charles Dickens, Wilkie Collins, and Anthony Trollope." How did postal reform encourage unsolicited mass mailings for services and products and become an emissary of useless items that today we refer to collectively as spam and junk mail? Harmful outcomes include the rise of unwanted and clandestine missives and indecent, indecipherable, and inappropriate mailings, ranging from threats of arson to live snakes, leeches, and lucifer matches. Contrary to pre-reform predictions that lowering postal rates would improve public morality, it actually worked instead to more glaringly expose preexisting problems and to facilitate the spread of certain vices. While twentieth-century critics align the Victorians with a heartless and unforgiving attitude toward sexual transgression and a commitment to almost puritanical standards, a different story emerges from objects of material culture: in making it affordable for the masses to use the mail, the Penny Post ironically turned the reformed Post Office into a mechanism for distributing curious missives, unwanted mail (that is, junk mail), immorality, slander, and blackmail—problems that carry into information technologies today.

Chapter 5, "Benefits and Blessings: Letters Home, Friendship, Death Notices, Courtship, and Valentines by Penny Post," considers, in contrast, beneficial types of communication that we can trace to the Victorian letter-writing boom following postal reform. Staying connected with friends and relatives across the new class society—a motto that resonates in our modern, global world of computer-mediated communication—was a central reason why the Victorians believed they needed Post Office reform. Accordingly, letters of mourning, advice, friendship, health, courtship, law, business, as well as valentines, although in use prior to Uniform Penny Postage, rose in popularity following reform, offering evidence that the reformed Post Office enabled many more Victorians to reach out to others and stay connected, much as postal reformers had hoped. Calling upon a range of visual and textual sources, this chapter examines postal commodities that carry memories of Victorian mourning, family and friendship ties, and courtship rituals during a period where home and family were sacrosanct, romantic love increasingly affected marriage choices, and death palpably informed daily life. What does it say about the Victorians that they edged their condolence letters in black? How do love letters illuminate Victorian etiquette, courting rituals, and morals? How might a letter safeguard a reputation, circumvent disapproving parents, or enable a suitor to craft an idealized self to impress a lover? I also feature two collections of Victorian valentines, popular post-1840 missives that carry knowledge of Victorian conceptions of love, humor, and aesthetics.

Motivating this book are the following questions that inform, in particular, the conclusion: how did the institution of the Penny Post, which ostensibly was a democratic victory, both improve the lives of the Victorians and create a host of challenges and complications that we have inherited from the Victorians? What is the connection among objects of material culture, literature, history, and politics? What does the Victorian revolution in letter writing teach us about Victorian culture as well as about our own fascination with technological progress in the field of computer-mediated communication? In what ways do many of our new technologies arguably extend, rather than simply replace, the Victorian invention of the Penny Post by attracting an increasingly larger global community of readers and writers? In *The Victorian Internet*, Tom Standage posits, for example, that the Internet is an extension of the Victorian telegraph. What other potent parallels exist between Victorian letter-writing practices and products and late twentieth- and twenty-first-century modes of communication? In teaching us about how the Victorians responded to great innovations of their time, this book equally informs us about how people respond to innovations that are new and revolutionary to our own time. Have we inherited our skepticism, excitement, and fascination with innovation from our Victorian ancestors, who reacted to the adhesive postage stamp and prepayment of mail with both joy and suspicion? How different is our twenty-first-century obsession with progress and instant communication from the Victorians' pride over "sailing without wind," "beginning to ride without horses," and the technological wonders exhibited in the first World's Fair, the Great Exhibition of 1851?

The conclusion, entitled "Looking Forward from the Victorian Revolution in Letter Writing to Information Technologies Today," addresses these very questions by using details from George Elgar Hicks's 1860 painting *The General Post Office, One Minute to Six* as a lens through which to explore how epistolary communication of the nineteenth century and information technologies in the later twentieth and twenty-first centuries interweave in integral ways. I cite the relevance of four clusters of details and figures in the painting—a lady holding a letter with stamps, signaling innovation; a lost child and four patrons rushing to make the last post, symbolizing bewilderment and anxiety;

a pickpocket, an image of criminality; and a policeman, standing for law and order—to illuminate what our current information revolution has inherited from the Victorian revolution in letter writing.

METHODOLOGY

This book is not a history of the Victorian Post Office. Howard Robinson in *The British Post Office: A History* and more recently M. J. Daunton in *Royal Mail: The Post Office Since 1840* and C. R. Perry in *The Victorian Post Office: The Growth of a Bureaucracy* have already admirably accomplished this task. It is also not a straightforward analysis of the postal reform scheme, such as Douglas Muir ably provides in *Postal Reform and the Penny Black* or Gavin Fryer and Clive Akerman masterfully compile in their two-volume collection of primary materials entitled *The Reform of the Post Office in the Victorian Era*. Rather, I explore this social reform from the vantage point of a literary critic deeply interested in Victorian studies, material culture, literature, and the visual arts, which I here define as illustration, painting, and objects of postal ephemera that we can appreciate for their aesthetic, commemorative, and narrative value. In *The Postal Age*, David Henkin sets out to show how in America, a "postal network that became popular during the middle of the nineteenth century laid the cultural foundation . . . for the experiences of interconnectedness that are the hallmarks of the brave new world of telecommunications" (ix). My study of the British postal system similarly aims to demonstrate how the Penny Post and the prepaid postage stamp in Britain in 1840 (which America and other nations swiftly emulated) allowed Victorians to post letters, books, newspapers, and other information across the nation, initiating a communications revolution that laid the foundation for computer-mediated communication. I find particularly useful Henkin's application of the modern meaning of "network" to frame how "a critical mass of Americans began reorganizing their perceptions of time, space, and community around the existence of the post" (3). The concepts of time, space, and community in *The Postal Age* inform my analysis of the emerging nineteenth-century British postal network.

Relevant to *Posting It* is the work of Eileen Cleere, who argues in *Avuncularism* that the 1837–40 campaign for Uniform Penny Postage is "a site of Victorian social reform that has been virtually ignored by historians and literary critics" (29). While the Penny Post has not been ignored by historians, I concur with her claim that literary critics have not sufficiently tapped this area of social reform that took root in Victorian culture. *Posting It*, in some respects,

builds upon Cleere's presentation of "the question of postal reform as an affective dilemma rather than a political challenge" (173), which forms the focus of
her chapter 5, entitled "'Send the Letters, Uncle John': Trollope, Penny-Post-
age Reform, and the Domestication of Empire." Cleere's well-researched book
combines psychoanalytic and economic theory with close readings of primary
texts to explore how novelists, essayists, economists, and propagandists used
metaphors of the extended family and kinship to manipulate developing commercial theories of industrial England. Cleere uses the concept of the avunculate to unsettle prevailing notions of the Victorian family as a fixed nuclear
one with a central patriarch at its head. The term "avunculate" comes from the
area of cultural anthropology concerned with kinship, where it often describes
a shift in authority, primarily through control of wealth and inheritance, from
inside the family to outside of the family in the figure of the uncle. The vernacular "my Uncle" referred, during the Victorian period, to a "pawnbroker,"
an ambivalent, outsider figure embodying both beneficence and deceit. Like
other sociopolitical trends of the period that indicate a moving away from domestic and national insularity—land privatization and colonialist expansion,
for example—the Victorian Post Office represents in institutional form this
movement toward a new political economy—one that locates authority outside the demesnes of the nuclear family and, by extension, the nuclear island
nation, to a broader global theater and its commercial institutions. Like the
figure of the pawnbroker, this movement held promise and engendered anxiety at the same time. Analyzing the "anthropological architecture of Victorian
postal reform in a variety of cultural materials" (30), Cleere likewise considers
periodicals, pamphlets, and novels—in particular Trollope's fiction—to show
how the Penny Post, a welcomed reform, offered a means for social control by
manipulating a metaphor of the extended family.

I share Cleere's interest in how postal reform, with its emphasis on kinship and moral and intellectual improvement, became a seeming solution for
Victorian Britain's social and economic problems; but my analysis, with its
emphasis on material culture, more closely resembles the approaches of Briggs
and of Jones and Stallybrass. Postal artifacts carry meaning about political,
economic, cultural, and national issues at stake in the Victorian communications revolution similarly to the way spectacles, cameras, home furnishings,
household goods, and commemorative artifacts provide a panoramic view
of Victorian culture in Briggs's *Victorian Things* or that clothing and fashion
trends illuminate Renaissance culture in Jones and Stallybrass's work. I analyze the Penny Post and its outcomes from the vantage point of social history
and as a window onto Victorian society. I adopt a material culture studies ap-

proach to look at the sentimental, historical, and political value of Victorian objects, documents, literature, and paintings as emissaries of culture or as material memories that carry knowledge of the opinions, prejudices, and ideas of the society to which they belonged.

Posting It also situates the sentimental story of postal reform within the larger methodology of Peter Brooks's *Reading for the Plot.* My plotting of postal reform aims to move the reader through a series of pre-reform deprivation tales and post-reform fulfillment stories in a fashion akin to that of Victorian postal reformers, who privileged the sentimental story. Affective narratives, stories, anecdotes, and tales—terms which I use interchangeably— also form a consistent thread in scholarship and biographical accounts of postal reform. Literature, ephemera, extant correspondence, periodicals, and pamphlets carry knowledge of the positive and negative impact of the Penny Post and inform the "plot" of postal reform. Brooks defines "plotting" as "the activity of shaping . . . that which makes a plot 'move forward,' and makes us read forward, seeking in the unfolding of the narrative a line of intention and a portent of design that hold the promise of progress toward meaning" (xiii); he points out that plot forms an essential part of nineteenth-century narratives written in an age when "men and institutions are more and more defined by their shape in time" (xii). Given my conviction that postal reform narratives helped to usher in the Penny Post scheme, I foreground stories of pre-reform hardship and post-reform satisfaction that "unfold" how postal reform swiftly became aligned with moral, social, scientific, and intellectual progress. I also privilege anecdotes that offer "a line of intention" as to why the Victorians needed postal reform and plotlines from Victorian novels that, in turn, "hold the promise of progress toward meaning" in our understanding of why the Victorians needed letters and how letters and commodities functioned in a postal age. Second, this book proposes that akin to illustration and narrative painting, pictorial envelopes, stamps, and postal ephemera, in turn, are narrative in nature, informing today's readers about Victorian values, practices, beliefs, and dreams.

Material culture studies and plotting, interpretive approaches and activities, have guided my consideration of social history, literature, periodicals, literary criticism, illustration, art, and a range of cultural objects. Thus, my examples draw from catalogues, pamphlets, propaganda for and against postal reform, histories of the post, biographies and autobiographies, extant period correspondence, conduct manuals, diaries, multivolume editions of letters by leading nineteenth-century figures, and critical studies of Victorian culture, as well as of nineteenth-century British fiction (including Dickens, Trollope,

Eliot, and the Brontës), illustration (Hablot Knight Browne, John Leech, and Sir John Everett Millais, for instance), and narrative painting (for example, George Elgar Hicks, Richard Redgrave, and Augustus Egg). I diverge from previous studies of the British post to examine side by side this variety of historical, literary, and visual sources; stories found in these sources; ephemera, including antique writing implements, writing desks, stamps and stamp boxes, and pictorial envelopes; writing manuals and conduct manuals; diaries; extant correspondence; and valentines. In the chapters that follow, I also foreground key events, for example Parliamentary approval of the Penny Post; period letters and documents, including Rowland Hill's 1837 pamphlet and the complete run of *The Post Circular*; seminal figures in Victorian postal history, such as Rowland Hill and Henry Cole, as well as Trollope, whose autobiography and prolific fiction provide an insider's look at the General Post Office.

Popular writing guides and conduct manuals present the Victorian commitment to self-help, illuminating the cultural customs, practices, and values that produced them and identifying those who bought and conscientiously adhered to them. Diaries offer a glimpse of life as Victorian women and men actually lived it. Diary entries by Rowland Hill, for example, offer an intimate look at postal history as it unfolded. The biographies of Rowland Hill and Cole, among others, are chock-full of narratives, and postal artifacts are narrative in nature. The iconography on the officially commissioned Mulreadies and on their highly popular caricatures tell us, directly and indirectly, about the beliefs of the Victorians who designed and purchased them: their views of British supremacy, for example, or their attitudes toward the Irish and the Chinese, and so on. Extant letters are key contemporary sources since they were written person to person, often naively, without thought of public consumption. In "Editions of Letters in the Age of the Vanishing Text," Norman Kelvin praises the "voice" of the letter writer and notes how the letter offers a source of cultural history: we reconnect with "the letter-writer in all the complexities of the cultural moment" (589–90).

Although I recognize distinctions between actual letters and fictional letters that are written for public viewing, I agree with Ruth Perry, who maintains in *Women, Letters, and the Novel* that the difference "comes to feel pretty slippery when reading through the volumes of posthumously printed correspondence of real people, for these often read like fiction" (79). The similarities between fictional letters and those written for a private audience but subsequently published in an edition (a genre highly popular in the eighteenth century) bolsters the legitimacy of analyzing art and fiction alongside authentic correspondence to illuminate postal reform in its heyday.

Writing and receiving letters forms an integral part of the nineteenth-century novel, which—unlike the epistolary novels of letters more readily associated with the eighteenth century—includes the letter as a device to develop plot and characterization. Typically written as a series of letters sent and received, the epistolary novel (a genre which also includes diary entries and newspaper accounts) gained prominence in the eighteenth century with the success, in Britain, of Samuel Richardson's *Pamela* (1740) and *Clarissa* (1749) and later Fanny Burney's *Evelina* (1778); in France with Pierre Choderlos de Laclos's *Les liaisons dangereuses* (1782); and in Germany with Johann Wolfgang von Goethe's *The Sorrows of Young Werther* (1774). In her early career, Jane Austen attempted to write in epistolary form in her novella *Lady Susan* (composed circa 1795–1805; published 1871), but she gained prominence for novels in two or three parts in which she incorporated a large number of letters sent and received. Novels written throughout the long nineteenth century from Austen to Thomas Hardy brim with letters and with descriptions of handwriting, spelling, sealing wax, stationery, local post offices, and mail deliveries and illustrate the importance of letters in daily life. Business letters, legal letters, banknotes, and wills appear in novels as frequently as personal letters. The fiction of Austen, Dickens, the Brontë sisters, Elizabeth Gaskell, William Makepeace Thackeray, Hardy, Eliot, Trollope (whom I treat as a man of letters as well as a Post Office reformer), and Wilkie Collins among others offers a key source for this book since these nineteenth-century authors, who were prolific letter writers themselves, incorporate letters into their fictions, describe letter-writing practices and letter-writing etiquette (such as proper handwriting), and include postal ephemera (for example, portable writing desks) to move the plot along or to illuminate theme and character.

Austen uses the Highbury Post Office in *Emma* (1815) as a means by which the engagement of Jane Fairfax and Frank Churchill remains a secret: Jane secretively sends and receives Churchill's letters by insisting she collect the post while visiting her grandmother and aunt (Mrs. Bates and Miss Bates, respectively). In an evening excursion to post a letter in *Jane Eyre* (1847), Charlotte Brontë engineers a first meeting on the moors between Jane and Mr. Rochester when Jane is walking to post a letter in nearby Hay just as "the moon was waxing bright" (96)—Rochester falls from his horse, startled by the figure of Jane, who, for the first of many times, comes to his aid. Eliot views the post as a means to present matrimonial discord in *Middlemarch* (1872): Rosamund Vincy writes secretively to her husband's wealthy uncle/guardian, Sir Godwin Lydgate, hoping he will send money to get them out of debt; this move embitters her husband and rocks their marriage when an angry Sir Godwin writes to Lydgate: "Don't set your wife to write to me when you have anything to ask. It is a roundabout wheedling sort of thing which I would not have credited you with" (715). Dickens includes over fifty notes and letters in *Bleak House* (1853), some essential to the plot. For example, Captain Hawdon's distinctive handwriting on a series of law documents prompts Lady Dedlock's ultimately fateful query, "'Who copied that?'" (11), to Sir Leicester Dedlock's cunning legal advisor, Mr. Tulkinghorn.[20] Likewise, Robert Audley's recognition of Lady Audley's "so charming and uncommon a hand" (141) in Mary Elizabeth Braddon's *Lady Audley's Secret* (1862) helps him to puzzle out his step-aunt's true identity and to disclose her adulterous past. Hardy complicates the plot in *Far from the Madding Crowd* (1874) when Bathsheba Everdene sends an anonymous valentine to Farmer Boldwood, unknowingly setting madness and murder in motion. Gaskell also uses letters for many purposes in *North and South* (1855), including late in the novel when a lawyer's letter informs a recently orphaned Margaret Hale of her good fortune in becoming an heiress.

These fictional examples and the copious others that stand alongside them lead me to join Alexander Welsh in questioning "whether a literary fashion is ever merely literary" but rather "a phenomenon of general historical significance" (4), as he concludes in *George Eliot and Blackmail*. Briggs goes so far as to argue that "Novels and poems do not simply illustrate or decorate: they compel attention through their insights, and they frequently point to explanations" (18–19). I acknowledge the fine line between fiction and history, taking care not to misconstrue fiction for life or represent a book as a historical document. Nonetheless, I recognize that novels and the visual arts, if read in context of Post Office reform, have historical value and speak to the challenges and excitements surrounding the coming of the Penny Post. Victorian novelists wanted to use contemporary developments familiar to their readers, and their references to the post and other innovations in communications and technology—such as railways, steamships, and telegrams—that now seem quaint, commonplace, or outmoded show how authors and artists were responding to their changing world. When revising *Sense and Sensibility* for publication in 1811, Austen added in the London Twopenny Post to bring up-to-date a novel that she had composed over a decade earlier (Shields 144).

Certain parameters of social class and gender are implicit in the nature of the material I am studying. Although many arguments powering reform of the postal service focus on the working class, the written and visual texts I have considered were ostensibly produced by and designed for a white middle- and upper-class readership. The prominent postal reformers and opponents were men—principally Rowland Hill, but also Henry Cole, W. H. Ashurst, and John Wilson Croker. However, when possible, I include the voices of women, such as Rowland Hill's daughter, Eleanor Smyth, and Harriet Martineau, a highly esteemed, liberal Victorian journalist (she supported women's rights and abolitionism as well as Post Office reform). I feature Martineau throughout this book since, to quote A. N. Wilson, "she was one of the most popular interpreters of the English-speaking nineteenth century to itself" (152). I have made an effort to examine the letter-writing practices and oeuvre of nineteenth-century women authors (including Eliot, Gaskell, and the Brontë sisters) alongside works by nineteenth-century male authors (such as Trollope, Thackeray, and Dickens) that point to, weigh, endorse, or challenge the post as a new information technology. I also consider issues of social class and gender in relation to postal materials and propaganda, which were used to forecast opposite outcomes depending on which side of the reform issue a spokesperson stood. Many postal reformers argued, on the one hand, that affordable postage would usher in a more moral nation. By enabling young people to benefit regularly by letter from their parents' sage advice, for example, affordable postage would help them avoid the pitfalls and snares awaiting innocents away from home. Reform opponents predicted, on the other hand, a rise in women's impropriety. Trollope, for example, feared the anonymity afforded in posting a letter at a pillar box would encourage clandestine relations.

While the designation of "Victorian" typically covers the years of Queen Victoria's reign, for the purposes of this study, I include material from the early nineteenth century (for example, Austen) up to 1914. Pre-reform materials prior to 1837 allow us to glimpse problems resulting from high-priced mail, such as illicit letter-writing practices, and thus to envision a status quo that had to change. The Victorian way of life arguably continued into the early Edwardian period; thus, the onset of World War I offers a useful marker for this book since it denotes a significant change in British life. Although I occasionally make transatlantic parallels to further my analysis, I have included only brief discussions of transatlantic mailings, a movement referred to as "Ocean Penny Postage," and postcards, an Austrian invention dating to 1869; these topics are worthy of sustained and separate investigation.

The following two sections in this introduction—"Context" and "Postal Reforms, Terms, and Reformers up to 1840"—facilitate an understanding of how Victorian innovations in communication responded to prior developments and anticipate our current information revolution. Above all, these sections provide a background for how postal reform came to be seen as a much needed, welcomed Victorian progress and achievement.

CONTEXT

We live in an age where we have increasingly more ways to communicate without posting letters. Many people still use the post to renew a driver's license, take out a subscription to a magazine, or enroll in a course, but even in these instances, companies and educational institutions provide options for swifter processing through online applications. While it is customary to send thank-you notes, letters of condolence, and formal invitations, unlike our Victorian ancestors, we rarely write a letter to a friend in the same town to announce an intention to pay a call. Except for formal occasions like weddings, we do not typically respond to an invitation with a written reply, situations we commonly find when perusing nineteenth-century collections of letters by, for example, Carroll, Trollope, or Thackeray.[21] Wouldn't it seem preposterous to post a letter to a relative living in a distant location to urge him or her to come home to pay last respects, as Gaskell does in *North and South* when Margaret Hale implores her brother to journey home from Spain to see their mother before she dies? We might use the telephone to call a close friend to share sad news about the death of a close relative or sibling rather than compose a letter as Charlotte Brontë did upon the losses of Branwell, Emily, and Anne in rapid succession.[22]

I begin with these scenes from Victorian life and fiction to establish that every time we pick up the telephone—a landline or a mobile phone—or send an urgent e-mail or text message, we must remind ourselves that if we were living in the late eighteenth or nineteenth century (especially in the days before telegrams were invented or affordable), we would take pen in hand, write a letter, and send it either by post or an irregular means of transport. Letters were knit into the fabric of the lives of ordinary citizens and famous Victorians. The sheer volume of collections of letters to and from Dickens, Carroll, and Thackeray, among others, speaks to the importance of the post in daily Victorian life. There were letters of introduction and invitation, thank-you notes, travel updates, job inquiries, cartes de visite, confessions, love letters, and, in time, telegrams. The British in the late eighteenth and early nineteenth centuries also relied on the post to correspond with absent family members who left home for a career or to pursue their education: for example, in 1788, the Rev. George Austen (Jane's father) sent a farewell letter to his son Francis, departing for service to the East Indies, to offer practical and moral advice (prudence in spending and time management, for example).[23] Charlotte Brontë wrote a weekly letter home to Haworth Parsonage while studying at Roe Head School in 1832. Through letters, the Victorians transacted business, communicated with family and friends, sought employment, and announced births and deaths. They also expressed gratitude for receiving condolences, as indicated in an extant letter dated August 23, 1853, in which a resident of Bath named W.G.R. Cockburn thanks his friend "most sincerely for your very kind letter, which you were so kind as to address to me upon this, as upon so many similar sad bereavements."[24]

Throughout the nineteenth century, people wrote for advice, employment, friendship, courtship, and consolation. Charlotte Brontë corresponded with Robert Southey, poet laureate, in March of 1837, to inquire whether she should pursue a career as a writer; happily, she did not heed the disparaging advice he offered via the post that "Literature cannot be the business of a woman's life: & it ought not to be."[25] Brontë—who used the post to find a situation as a governess and, along with her sisters, advertised a school in Haworth (which never came to fruition)—recognizes the value of the post in *Jane Eyre*: even though Jane is living in relative isolation at Lowood, she advertises for a position and accepts a place as governess at Thornfield Hall by post. Anne Brontë, who served as governess much longer than her sisters, knowingly incorporates the sending and receiving of letters into her governess novel, *Agnes Grey* (1847), to ease the trials of her fictional governess's life. Some people proposed marriage by letter and, in turn, accepted proposals by letter, as Eliot shows in the romance between Rev. Edward Casaubon and Dorothea Brooke in *Middlemarch*. Moreover, letters loomed large for those emigrating to a new world, as well as for their loved ones who remained behind. In his painting *A Letter from Abroad* (1834), Thomas Webster shows a rural postal carrier delivering a letter to a cottage family gathered to receive news, presumably, from a son who has emigrated. Likewise, Gaskell ends *Mary Barton* (1848) with Jem Wilson and Mary Barton, now living in Canada, rejoicing over the post that brings news from their former home in Manchester. An extant letter sent from Liskey, Ireland, to James Robinson of Boston from his mother Narthew Robinson, dated April 2, 1847, tells of the potato famine and urges her son to send for her: "I long to get out of this country, from among these poor people, for starvation is pictured almost in all countenances. Your affectionate Mother to death."[26]

Uniform prepaid postage was a welcome measure in Britain. In the early nineteenth century, postal charges grew high due to the inflationary pressure of the Napoleonic Wars; the government regarded postage as a form of taxation that provided a ready source of revenue. Postage, not reduced after the Battle of Waterloo (1815), remained a heavy burden on the middle and working classes. Prior to nationwide cheap postage that went into effect on January

10, 1840, inequities abounded in the post, which did not serve all social classes. For example, around 1830, someone with an income of £1,000 a year could easily afford to pay postage, but if that person happened to be a member of Parliament (a Common or a Lord), he was exempt from postal charges that a poor laborer could not afford to pay. In contrast, a member of the working class might pay a day's wage to receive a letter.[27] In large cities like London, there were local postings that cost 1d or 2d for delivery. However, prior to the Industrial Revolution, Britain was primarily an agrarian society; for those who lived in towns or rural areas without a Penny Post, expensive postage became an intolerable hardship and a communications barrier.

Before the interim uniform 4d measure of December 5, 1839, the Post Office calculated postage according to the distance a letter traveled times the number of letter sheets a writer used. Because an envelope and an "enclosure" (something tucked into a letter) were charged as extra sheets, it cost twice as much to send a letter composed of two letter sheets or a single sheet placed in an envelope than to post one folded, sealed letter sheet. The Post Office did not calculate cost by the actual distance between the place of posting and the place of delivery, but, in the words of prominent Tory John Wilson Croker, "the distance through which the post-office may, for its own convenience, cause the letter to pass" (515). Croker well recognized that changes were necessary even if he objected to Hill's particular plan for postal reform. He cites the following example in an 1839 article in *Quarterly Review* (to which he was a frequent contributor): "letters addressed in a town thirty miles from London on one road to another only five miles distant on a parallel road, would be sent up to London and down again, and, in addition to the vexatious delay, would be charged with sixty miles of postage instead of five" (515). Some charges seemed capricious and inconsistent. In 1830, a letter traveling from London to Edinburgh typically cost 1s ½d, but the cost could be as low as 8d if it traveled partway by coastal steamer; if that same letter traveled a far shorter inland route from London to Brighton, the postal charge also was 8d (Allam 3).

In his two-volume memoir, *The Life of Sir Rowland Hill*,[28] Rowland Hill offers other examples of unpredictable postal charges that irritated the British public: if a person posted two letters at the same time from the same place, one directed to Highgate and another to Wolverhampton, the missive to Wolverhampton, a distance of 120 miles further than Highgate, cost less than the letter sent to Highgate (1: 282). Prior to reform, sending parcels was more affordable than sending letters: Smyth records how someone mistakenly posted a packet of papers (addressed to Sir John Burgoyne) from Dublin to another Irish town as a letter rather than a parcel; as a result, it received a charge of

£11: "For that amount the whole mail-coach plying between the two towns, with places for seven passengers and their luggage, might have been hired" (44). Although the number of sheets led to double and triple postage, the Post Office granted leniency on the size of each sheet when assessing charges (Staff 81). Since it was not uncommon for standard postage to triple, the system burdened the public, and the public, in turn, sought ways to evade high postal charges.

Despite a host of factors that plausibly should have led to an increase in revenue from postage—such as rising literacy rates, growth in the general population, more and more people writing letters, and high postage rates themselves—Post Office revenue in early nineteenth-century Britain fell steadily (Staff 76), a situation opposite to that in nineteenth-century France, which had cheaper postage rates. Robert Wallace and Rowland Hill speculated that due to high postage, people avoided the post and abused it along with the franking system. Even if it was desirable to write weekly correspondence home, prior to postal reform, it was not feasible for members of the working class to do so, nor was it readily affordable for members of the middle class. Perhaps the poor suffered the most from high postage. Gaskell illustrates this situation in her industrial novel *Mary Barton* through the character of poor Alice Wilson, who lives in squalid Manchester circa 1840. Alice essentially leaves her family behind—and never sees her mother again—when she moves from her home in the country to go into service in Manchester. Those of the lower reaches who migrated for employment rarely heard from their families until a death notice arrived, which they often could not afford to accept. Sometimes a kindly postmaster or postmistress paid out of his or her own pocket, receiving goods as security, until an impoverished family could raise the necessary funds to learn the fate of a loved one.

Some refrained from writing letters, dashing off notes only when it was essential, "crossing" their lines to save space and money, while others sent letters by illicit means, inserting them into merchandise on the way to market, bribing a carrier to smuggle letters at a cheaper cost, or writing a code on the outside of a letter, which the receiver could decipher and then refuse to accept. Sir Rowland Hill reports that the number of letters sent by irregular means of transport in Birmingham, for example, "very greatly exceeds ... the number distributed within the same district by the Post Office."[29] People of all social classes resorted to illicit means, engineering scams and employing privately paid, independent mail messengers to avoid high postal charges, leading to an amazing loss in revenue for the British government. If people refused mail rather than pay high postage, then the government's carriage of these letters became completely unprofitable. The reduction of the Stamp Tax on newspapers in 1836, allowing a newspaper to travel for one penny, offered a ready model for the Post Office to emulate during an era when sons and, increasingly, daughters attended boarding schools and unmarried middle-class women left their family hearths for employment—typically as private governesses or to teach in schools, both of which Charlotte Brontë illustrates in *Jane Eyre*.

Agitation for postal reform began in earnest in 1837, the year Queen Victoria came to the throne and Rowland Hill published *Post Office Reform: Its Importance and Practicability*. Between 1837 and 1838, Hill printed four versions of his enormously popular pamphlet that scrutinized why the Post Office needed reform and suggested a feasible solution.[30] Postal reform eventually carried because of the swelling insistence of merchants and businessmen. In July 1839, Parliament passed Rowland Hill's postal reform plan to create a nationwide penny postal rate that went into effect on January 10, 1840. The post at once became unvarying and cheap: For one penny, a letter weighing up to half an ounce could travel anywhere in Britain regardless of the distance; one could purchase either a prepaid adhesive postage stamp (a Penny Black or Two Pence Blue) to affix to a letter, a prepaid envelope, or a prepaid letter sheet, similar to an aerogram today.

Prior to reform, it was a social slur to send a prepaid letter, a visible presumption that the receiver did not possess adequate funds to accept it; in addition, prior to reform, some wealthy individuals preferred to use private means to carry their letters rather than resort to the regular post. Robert Surtees makes these very points in his 1858 novel *"Ask Mama"; or, The Richest Commoner in England*:

> The two-penny post used to be thought a great luxury in London, though somehow great people were often shy of availing themselves of its advantages, . . . The Dons, never thought of sending their notes, or cards of invitation by the two-penny post. John Thomas [a horse] used always to be trotted out for the purpose of delivery. Pre-paying a letter either by the two-penny post or the general used to be thought little short of an insult. Public opinion has undergone a change in these matters. Not paying them is now the offence. (342)

Prior to 1840, the letter carrier, who was essentially in debt to the Post Office, had the time-consuming task of collecting funds for letters at the time of delivery, a situation that led to delays in mail service (ready cash was not always on hand or the recipient was not at home, necessitating multiple return visits); if the recipient could not afford to pay for the letter, it was returned to sender. One had to be rich enough or at least financially solvent to receive a letter. However, with postal reform, the sender, not the receiver of the letter, paid the cost of mail, reversing the common practice of the recipient paying on delivery. "Not paying [postage] is now the offence," to recall Surtees.

What were the conditions that made nineteenth-century England ripe for postal reform? A compelling combination of social issues primed Britain for this ostensibly democratic measure, which, in turn, led to an information revolution and a new branch of industry. The years leading up to reform witnessed dramatic social change and a tumultuous political climate, including a shift in sovereigns from Victoria's uncles, George IV (1820–30) and William IV (1830–37), to Queen Victoria (1837–1901). At the turn of the nineteenth century, Britain, which had long been an agrarian society, was undergoing rapid industrialization, leading workers to leave the countryside for manufacturing centers such as Manchester and Birmingham. As war heated up with France, sons routinely joined army and naval regiments, leaving their families, friends, and country behind for long stretches at a time. In fact, two of Austen's brothers, Francis (who earlier served in the East Indies) and Charles, entered the Royal Naval Academy, served in the British navy during the Napoleonic Wars (1805–15), and became admirals. Letter writing was their only means of staying in contact with the close Austen family. In the early nineteenth century, more people began to travel, seek education, and gain employment, all of which created greater necessity and demand for written correspondence. Visits to family and friends, which lasted weeks or even months, also made more urgent the need for reliable and affordable communication with loved ones. Austen, for example, spent two months in London in 1811 with her brother Henry and his wife while preparing the proofs for *Sense and Sensibility*, and her letter to her beloved sister, Cassandra, conveys the importance of letter writing to sustain their closeness during her long absence: "'I have so many little matters to tell you of, that I cannot wait any longer before I begin to put them down.'"[31]

This was an era of mounting population, expanding literacy, ever-increasing mobility, and rising emigration, accompanied by rapid expansion of the British Empire, industrialization, innovation in transportation, and by an information revolution in printing. Population grew despite high infant mortality rates, because people began to live longer. Improved life expectancy came in response to progress in health care and nutrition, cleaner drinking water, and better sewage removal. Young men left Britain, traveling overseas either for advancement opportunities—such as gold mining in Australia or investment and trade in India (service in the East India Company, for example)—or for new homelands in America, Canada, Australia, and New Zealand (countries to which many British emigrated in the nineteenth century). These conditions, in turn, created a surplus of single unmarried women. A daughter of a working-class family might find employment in a mill town, while an unmarried daughter of a middle-class family of slender means could seek employment as a private governess or teacher in a school. If a young woman from the country went into domestic service or took a job at a school in far-off London and eventually married, would she ever return home again?

Other factors contributed to the overwhelming support for postal reform. With the Industrial Revolution—coupled by King George III's 1803 pronouncement that all members of his kingdom should be able to read the Bible—literacy was on the rise in nineteenth-century Britain, even if not all factions universally endorsed it. Mechanics institutes, initiated in the 1820s, offered adult education and libraries for the working class. The 1826 founding of the Society for the Diffusion of Useful Knowledge, a movement associated with publisher Charles Knight (who published Hill's famous pamphlet), promoted literacy and inexpensive reading matter. By 1900, 97 percent of the population of England and Wales was literate; however, because the Victorians based this figure on the number of people aged 16 to 25 who could sign the marriage register, Richard Altick cautions that there were older men and women entered as "illiterate" at the time of their own marriages whose literacy status presumably had not altered. Nonetheless, Altick credits this rise in literacy to the Penny Post and the cheaper price of attractive reading matter (172). With serial publication, books and periodicals targeted for a range of audiences—men, women, young adults, and children—grew more affordable.

Beginning in the 1830s and routinely by 1847 in all but rural areas, the carriage of mail "without horses" made the Penny Post feasible nationwide, as Surtees observes in *"Ask Mama"*: "We need scarcely expatiate on the boon of the penny post, nor on the advantage of the general diffusion of post-offices throughout the country, though we may observe, that the penny post was one of the few things that came without being long called for; indeed, so soon it was practicable to have it, for without the almost simultaneous establishment of railways it would have been almost impossible to have introduced the system" (342). This was an age of penny magazines and penny newspapers as well as the Penny Post. At the same time, as literacy, women's education, and travel increased so did demand for writing products that could be mass produced and sold at a price affordable to the middle class. Industrialization, cheaper printing, and a growing cultural interest in self-help sparked creation of writing manuals. In part owing to the Great Exhibition of 1851—also known as "The Great Victorian Collection" (Briggs 52)—innovations in postal products (for example, steel-nibbed pens, envelope machines) became equated with social progress and influenced consumerism, fostering demand for a wider range of writing desks and tools (stamp boxes, pen trays, and so on).

Two Sides to a Penny . . . Post

Just as there are two sides to a penny, there are two sides to the complicated history of the Penny Post and, ultimately, what it tells us about the Victorian age. Those eager to diffuse rigid class demarcations embraced what they perceived as a democratization of the post; concomitantly, those who saw nationalization as an end to the familiar letter (written by one person and sent privately to another) opposed it, as well as what it came to represent. Some supporters of postal reform championed it for social and humanitarian reasons, while others recognized that the post could be advantageous for trade and commerce, as well as for education. Would cheap postage put a stop to illegal mail carrying, commonly called "irregular postal usage"? What some lauded as a democratic measure for all social classes seemed, to others, a ludicrous venture, doomed to fail or bankrupt the British government. Some conjectured that people would write so many letters that the Post Office could simply not handle the demand. Others viewed the prepaid postage stamp with suspicion, preferring the time-honored method of paying for mail on delivery, which the Post Office essentially curtailed by charging double postage for letters not prepaid.[32]

Even though many people had felt burdened by heavy postage, some considered prepayment "un-English." Others thought prepayment unreliable since, prior to reform, the carrier was responsible for a certain number of letters and had to either recover payment for each letter at the time of delivery or bring back an uncollected letter. This provided a system of accountability which, many contended, checked dishonesty. As William Lewins notes in *Her Majesty's Mails: A History of the Post Office* (1864), "with prepaid letters, it was said, there was great temptation, unbounded opportunity for dishonesty, and no check" (209). With prepayment, how could one be sure that a letter, especially one containing coin or jewelry, was actually delivered? Still others argued the opposite side of this debate. Account keeping, tedious under the old system of payment on delivery, tempted letter carriers to commit fraud. As Smyth explains, "when a weak or unscrupulous man found a supply of loose cash in his pocket at the end of his delivery, his fingers would itch—and not always in vain—to keep it there" (63). Smyth also points out that an honest carrier traveling on an ill-lit street could be robbed or even murdered for his earnings. Post Office practices such as candling (holding a letter up to the light) also led to letter opening and discovery of banknotes that tempted clerks to commit robbery (Hill and Hill 1: 283). Fears also sprang up around the postage stamp (Allam 25): would it be fodder for forgery or, more terrifyingly, through the licking of a stamp to affix it, could the postage stamp become an agent of the dreaded cholera, which killed thousands in the epidemics of 1849 and 1853–54?

Contradiction even emerged among postal reform supporters: what some embraced as a measure to bring equality to a class-based postal system was, to others, a means to keep the lower reaches in line. Early nineteenth-century England witnessed an increasing fear of revolution: would England follow in the footsteps of revolutionary France, as Karl Marx and Friedrich Engels predicted? Although sentimental stories made a case for postal reform, we cannot underestimate the political concerns that fueled the ideological work of Post Office reform. Postal reformers and parliamentary supporters who ultimately recommended reform of the postal service recognized that small measures of progress might ease the political unrest between "the masters and the men," quelling political revolt, which never came to pass in England. A poor young man in the Manchester mills who could maintain ties with his family living in the country might be less likely to revolt against the British status quo. As Ashurst convincingly argues in *Facts and Reasons in Support of Mr. Rowland Hill's Plan for a Universal Penny Postage* (1838), "the strikes that have taken place between masters and men have been shown to result from causes which would not have existed if the men could have communicated freely with each other, so as to have ascertained the rates of wages at different localities" (91). Ashurst goes on to conclude in praise of cheap postage: "if the men had had the opportunity of writing to their friends and acquaintances of their own grade, . . . and the stream of facts had had its free course, as it would have had at a cheap postage, . . . the error as to facts would not have existed, and the strikes would not have resulted" (92). Ashurst's incisive comments encourage us to ask which group postal reform was really designed to benefit—the masters or the men?

POSTAL REFORMS, TERMS, AND REFORMERS UP TO 1840

The contributions of earlier postal reformers paved the way for Victorian innovations that, in turn, pioneered methods for safe, swift, and cheap carriage of mail. The nineteenth-century post grew from developments in the Middle

Ages, but the concept of a post dates to antiquity. Although in the advent of reform, advocates sometimes spoke about the post as if it were a new invention, to the Victorians the post was an ancient system of communication that fascinated nineteenth-century historians. For example, William Lewins in *Her Majesty's Mails* traces the first documented letter to the ancient Hebrews. King David, lusting after Bathsheba (wife of Uriah the Hittite), put in Uriah's hands a letter to Joab, his commander, directing Joab to send Uriah into the thick of the battlefield. The letter became Uriah's own death warrant—testimony that he, in fact, delivered the letter (2). Lewins also includes the oft-quoted example of Persian King Ahasuerus, who proclaimed that "'every man should bear rule in his own house'" (4) when he banished Queen Vashti for alleged disobedience; his "'letters were sent by posts into all the king's provinces.'"[33] Although we commonly equate the word "post" with mail, it originally applied to messengers carrying letters into vast ancient worlds: by camel or mule in Persia; by horseback, vessel, or cart in the Roman Empire, where, under the rule of Octavius, the Romans created an elaborate system of post roads.[34] Lewins distinguishes the Persian king Cyrus the Great for organizing a regular and reliable system of postal riders. Of Cyrus's posts, it was said that "'neither rain nor snow prevented them from carrying out their appointed task'"—a still-famous postal creed.[35] A post for royal, official use dates to antiquity, although remarkably there is no evidence of "carriage by the government of its own mail and that of the public."[36]

During the Middle Ages, various types of posts existed throughout Europe: royalty sent documents by messenger; merchants engaged in trade with foreign countries; monks exchanged letters among monasteries; and lawyers and judges issued decrees by post. At the end of the fifteenth century, King Edward IV set up a temporary system of postal riders to Scotland during a period of war.[37] However, progress in the development of an efficient post was neither steady nor continuous: first because the British government discontinued some notable innovations, such as Edward IV's postal riders, and second because the English Civil War (1642–51) disrupted progress of many measures generally regarded as democratic. Improvements to the Post Office, first under Henry VIII and later under Charles I, which led to a public running post in 1635, actually insured the Crown a monopoly on courier service.[38]

Following the English Civil War, postal reform resumed in earnest with the establishment of the General Post Office and a postmaster general, recognized by a statute under Cromwell. In 1660, Parliament passed a second Post Office Act to grant the statute credibility after The Restoration. With the return of Charles II in 1660 came improvements for safe and swift deliveries, including weekly postal services from London to Dublin and London to Edinburgh; the creation of an organized system of six mail post roads; and introduction of a postmark (date stamp) in 1661 (a divided circle with date and month on either side) for tracking speed of delivery. The subsequent General Letter Office, a chartered national postal service, predates and paved the way for Royal Mail today.

Douglas Muir maintains that economics, more than anything else, motivated the opening of the post to the public in the seventeenth century: "profit to the Revenue was the prime consideration" (14). Wars in the eighteenth and early nineteenth centuries made postal service an increasingly costly tax on the British public. Prime Minister William Pitt, also first lord of the Treasury beginning in 1783, attempted to reduce the British national debt accrued during wars with America and France by raising taxes on many items, including the post (Muir 11). The economic and class-based arguments that motivated postal reform in the nineteenth century had thus already taken root in the seventeenth and eighteenth centuries and gained force over the intervening years.

The late seventeenth and eighteenth centuries brought three key improvements to the postal system—penny posts, cross posts, and mail coach delivery—and laid the foundation for Victorian reforms. A penny post began in London in 1680, offering mail service to private homes in London and Westminster. Historians generally credit to William Dockwra the innovation of a cheap penny post with delivery service to private residences.[39] Under this scheme, all mail cost one penny, and people no longer had to travel, send servants, or hire messengers to go to the General Letter Office to collect their letters. Dockwra added hundreds of receiving houses and sorting stations and charged a uniform price of 1d for citywide delivery to be prepaid for a parcel or letter up to one pound weight. Under Dockwra's scheme, letters received, in turn, a postmark as receipt of payment, which has led some philatelists to argue that this seventeenth-century postmark should be considered Britain's first postage stamp.[40]

Though the London Penny Post turned out to be a popular and profitable service, in 1682 the government closed it down on the grounds that it was illegal and reopened it under government control. The Penny Post under Dockwra's management allegedly infringed on the General Letter Office under the Charter of 1660, which made the General Post a monopoly. Muir suggests, too, that the post provided valuable revenue for the Duke of York, who "saw in Dockwra's Penny Post a loss of earnings" (17). Under the name London District Post, the city postal system operated relatively unchanged until 1794, at which point prepayment became an option; in 1801, it became the Twopenny Post (Robinson 72–75). An act of 1765 legalized penny posts in cases where the Post Office found them "necessary and convenient."[41] Dock-wra's innovations—charging by weight (instead of number of letter sheets), prepayment, and a uniform low rate of postage—long predated and provided a successful local-scale model for Victorian postal reform.

Cross posts and mail coach delivery affected the entire nation in the late seventeenth and eighteenth centuries and set the stage for nationwide postal reform between 1837 and 1840. The establishment of cross posts to connect nearby towns on the six major post roads cut delivery time, as not all letters had to enter London. A "bye letter" traveled along the main post road but did not enter the London Post Office; it stopped short of London or traveled only part of the main road to its destination. A cross-post letter—written in Bristol and sent to Exeter, for example—no longer had to travel to London, only to be redirected to Exeter, but could travel along a cross-post road to its destination. The cross-post system, while ingenious, was largely in a state of disarray until 1720 when Ralph Allen, who became postmaster of Bath in 1712, took under contract, oversaw, and developed an extensive and well-organized bye-road and cross-post-road system in England and Wales. Allen set out to ensure that bye letters and cross-post letters followed the swiftest route possible, were accounted for, and not miscarried.[42]

A key change also occurred in the eighteenth century both in how mail traveled and how fast it traveled: mail coaches replaced messengers or posts. In 1780, a parcel that went by coach traveled to London from Bath in sixteen hours at the speed of almost seven miles per hour. By contrast, a letter travel-ing the same distance by horse post could take over forty hours to reach the same destination, if the postboy did not fall prey to highway robbers first. (When postage was paid on delivery, postboys carried substantial sums of money.) John Palmer achieved "mail-coach fame" by recognizing during his frequent trips along the London–Bath road that coaches and diligences to transport passengers (and, probably, illegal letters as well) traveled far faster than idle and unpunctual postboys.[43] Palmer not only suggested moving mail by coach but also recommended arming mail coaches with guards—an imple-mentation that virtually eliminated highway robbery (Robinson 132).

In a 1784 trial run, the first mail coach traveled from Bristol to London. By 1785, stage coach routes multiplied to connect major British cities: Manchester, Liverpool, Leeds, Birmingham, Chester, Portsmouth, Holyhead, and Swansea. Coach service in Britain remained the preeminent form of mail carriage until postal transportation took another quantum leap in speed and efficiency: beginning in the 1830s, trains began to carry mail. Sorting carriages on trains allowed for organization of the mail by city and district while the train was moving, further cutting delivery time and increasing reliability of delivery. The post soon began riding without horses and was so successful that trains had almost completely replaced coaches for mail delivery by 1847 (remote or rural areas were at length serviced by train delivery in the second half of the nineteenth century).

Originally a theater proprietor, John Palmer went on to become comptroller general of the mails in 1786. In fact, Palmer appointed Francis Freeling to help enact the first cross-post coach mail service, connecting Bristol and Portsmouth via Salisbury. Freeling, in turn, assumed the position of Post Office secretary, briefly with Anthony Todd in 1797, and then independently from 1798 until his death in 1836 (Robinson 152). During Freeling's administration, agitation for the Penny Post began to grow as a result of his readiness to raise postal charges. Freeling, whom Robinson describes as an "autocratic Secretary," ran the Post Office with "meanness and parsimony" (249); he essentially "believed in high rates of postage" (Muir 21). An 1801 postal increase, followed by another even greater increase in 1812, helped finance Britain's wars with Napoleon. A letter traveling from London to Edinburgh cost 6d in 1765, but that same letter traveling the same distance in 1812 cost 1s 2d (more than double), leading Howard Robinson to conclude that war "made the Post Office an instrument of taxation" (157). Freeling, with his exemplary organizational and administrative skills, was not without supporters, including Croker, who reminded his followers in an 1839 *Quarterly Review* article that Freeling was "in early life, a post-office reformer, and to his last hour professed to be" (514). While Croker largely blamed high postage on the Treasury, which viewed the Post Office as a key source of revenue, he also admits of Freeling that "At length, however, it began to be suspected that the administration of that excellent public servant had, perhaps, lasted too long" (514).

A major source of controversy was inconsistency in who paid postage: some people paid huge sums for the privilege of accepting letters, others paid minimally, and still others sent and received mail for nothing at all. Beginning in 1795, soldiers and seamen on active duty could post a letter for a penny, if it were prepaid. Starting in 1836, after rigorous campaigning, the government dropped the newspaper Stamp Tax, and newspapers could pass through the Post Office for one penny (Robinson 246; Hill and Hill 1: 270). No postage was necessary for franked mail, including franked newspapers, which traveled at no cost. (A "frank" is a printed postmark applied to the outside of a letter that indicates free carriage.) Like other letters, however, franked letters had to be weighed, counted, checked, and carried by post. Franks began by ordinance in 1654 under Cromwell: letters written by members of Parliament (MPs), both Commons and Lords, received an official frank postmark, allowing letters or packets in service of the state to travel for free. This practice, which came to be called "franking," was ripe for abuse from the very start. An MP (and other persons holding government offices beginning in the eighteenth century) could extend this privilege to friends, relatives, or even employees as a favor. We might recall, as an example, Austen's Sir Thomas Bertram in *Mansfield Park* (1814), an MP who can frank his niece's letters as a favor. Edmund Bertram assures his cousin Fanny that her letter to her brother William can travel by post: "'as your uncle will frank it, it will cost William nothing'" (33).

Employers sometimes handed out franks for wages, and an illiterate servant could, in turn, sell the franks, leading Smyth to conclude that franking "was an easy, inexpensive way of making a present, or of practising a little bribery and corruption" (45). Various measures had been enacted to check abuses of the franking system: a limit was set on both the number and weight of franked letters that could be sent and received, and in an effort to stop the counterfeiting of MPs' names, the use of false franks was closely monitored. At the time of postal reform, an MP could send out ten letters a day and receive up to fifteen for free, as long as none exceeded one ounce in weight. Still, as Rowland Hill notes in his memoir, "there were franks of another kind which served for unlimited weight, and were said to have been actually used to free a greatcoat, a bundle of baby-linen, and a pianoforte" (Hill and Hill 1: 241). More egregiously, franks covered the free carriage of cows, horses, and even maidservants.[44] The franking system, as Smyth notes, became "a hoary iniquity" (42), a "growing burden," according to Robinson, that grew into an "evil" of "intolerable proportions" (118) until postal reform of 1840 largely curtailed it.

Not surprisingly, franking became a platform on which postal reformers based arguments for Universal Penny Postage, as witnessed in Henry Cole's cartoon of March 2, 1838, with the clever caption, "Great Weight and No Price! Little Weight and All Price!!" (see figure 1). In this comic illustration, included in issue 12 of *The Post Circular* (1839) and published as a single sheet, Cole filled the roof of an Edinburgh mail coach with 273 pounds of newspapers, forty-seven pounds of franked mail, and Stamp Office parcels, all traveling for free. The small bundle of chargeable letters—normally carried in the hind boot of the coach under the guard's foot—balances precariously on top of the

FIGURE 1. "Great Weight and No Price! Little Weight and All Price!!" From *The Post Circular* 12, Tuesday, April 30, 1839. Reproduced by kind permission of the British Postal Museum & Archive.

roof. Weighing a mere thirty-four pounds, the taxable bundle carries a £93 charge, while the rest of the carriage travels for free. As the cartoon shows, the middle and working classes literally paid for the entire load that the Post Office transported.

More than the franking system was in need of reform. A decade prior to postal reform, London's Post Office hub was a complex and unwieldy enterprise of three overlapping systems or offices: the urban Twopenny Post; Inland Service for letters throughout the kingdom; and the Foreign Branch. All three were located at the new central headquarters north of St. Paul's on St. Martin's-le-Grand, and each office operated as a system in itself with its own receiving house and letter carriers and its own methods for processing letters and assessing charges. Postal terms, many now antiquated, allow us to imagine what it meant to process a letter in the early nineteenth century. Once letters arrived at St. Martin's-le-Grand, clerks had to check that the deputy postmaster from a receiving house had correctly assessed charges on every letter. Thus, well before the introduction of postage stamps, letters were "faced." That is, workers placed each letter on a huge table side by side with other letters and made sure the addresses and postal charges appeared in the uppermost corners. In turn, before assessing them for charges and sorting them for delivery, officials postmarked or stamped letters, "an operation which results in the imprinting upon each the date, hour, and place of posting" (Lewins 267).

To charge letters fairly, many had to go through the candling process. To determine whether the charge should be single, double, triple, or even higher, a clerk held a letter up to the light of a candle or lamp (often in a darkened room) to see if it contained the extra sheets or enclosures that were subject to extra charges (Muir 25; Hill and Hill 1: 283). In some cases, the sealing wax was softened to open the letter. According to Hill in his memoir, this process also "exposed the clerks to needless temptation, led to many acts of dishonesty, and brought much loss to correspondents" (Hill and Hill 1: 283). Candling could also lead to capricious charges. Smyth recalls how one clerk, after candling a letter to be sent from London to Wolverhampton and discovering an enclosure to which a small piece of paper was attached, charged triple for the post (52). Writers did not generally use envelopes, also called "little bags," "wrappers," or "covers," because the cost of a "wrapped letter" (one sheet placed in an envelope) was double that of a single sheet fastened with a waxed seal or a gummed wafer. If a letter arriving at a receiving house had by chance traveled a circuitous route, it not only took longer to get to its destination, but it cost the recipient more to accept it.

Since postal officials determined charge according to the number of letter sheets, some people adopted the method of "cross writing" to save on postage. Rather than continuing a letter on a second page, a writer, after composing the letter in standard, vertically-aligned top-to-bottom format, turned the sheet horizontally and "crossed" (or wrote over) the original text at a right angle. Austen offers a good description of this technique in *Emma*, when Miss Bates tells Emma Woodhouse about a letter she has received from her niece, Jane Fairfax:

> "I really must, in justice to Jane, apologise for her writing so short a letter—only two pages you see—hardly two—and in general she fills the whole paper and crosses half. My mother often wonders that I can make it out so well. She often says, when the letter is first opened, 'Well, Hetty, now I think you will be put to it to make out all that chequer-work'—don't you, ma'am?—And then I tell her, I am sure she would contrive to

make it out for herself, if she had nobody to do it for her—every word of it—I am sure she would pore over it till she had made out every word." (157)

Cross writing guaranteed privacy. It took great effort to decipher "chequer-work," as Austen aptly calls cross writing. It also allowed the writer to convey a great deal of information on one sheet of paper if the writer "crossed and crossed again," as Dickens shows in *Oliver Twist* (1838) in describing the confessional letter Oliver's dying father leaves behind, offering "prayers to God to help" Oliver's unwed mother and their unborn child (418).

Throughout the Victorian era, it was not unusual for an address to include only a person's name, occupation, or county. These letters, called "stone-blind" letters, were "hopelessly incomplete" (Lewins 271). The Blind Letter Office regularly received "illegible, misspelt, misdirected, or insufficiently addressed letters or packets" (Lewins 270). Poor handwriting or misspelling might also require extra attention, causing a letter to be directed to the Blind Letter Office. Lewins offers the following humorous example of a "stone-blind" letter that the Post Office eventually deciphered and delivered: "Coneyach lunentick a siliam" actually meant "'Colney Hatch Lunatic Asylum'" (271–72). In addition to the Blind Letter Office, the Dead Letter Office handled letters that were missent, uncollected (or unpaid), and hence undeliverable. Beginning in 1811, this office aimed to return letters marked "address illegible" to their senders. To do so, clerks often opened undeliverable letters in order to learn the sender's address, as it was Victorian practice for the sender to include his or her address in full inside the sealed letter (as opposed to printing it on the outside of the envelope as commonly practiced today). The address typically appeared either under the signature or, as Carroll advises in *Eight or Nine Wise Words About Letter-Writing* (1890), at the top of the sheet (3).[45] Returning letters became profitable when, beginning in 1811, the Post Office charged the sender the cost of receiving an undeliverable letter back. Recognizing this profitability, the Dead Letter Office, established in 1784, took the name Returned Letter Office in 1813, but the name changed again to Dead Letter Office in 1833 and underwent further variations throughout the century (Gotland and Armstrong 91). This office, now called the Return Letter Centre, has continued because some late Victorians, such as the notorious Reginald Bray, deliberately sent letters or postcards all over the world to arcane addresses that postmen could not easily or possibly deliver to. For example, Bray addressed a postcard (stamped November 21, 1899) to "Miss Ramsay Daughter of the Postman who has walked 232,872 miles Kirremuir Post Office Forfarshire." Not surprisingly, it ended up in the Returned Letter Office. Following in Bray's footsteps, in 1998, Harriet Russell, inspired by the decorated envelopes of her great great grandfather, Henry Ponsonby, private secretary to Queen Victoria, challenged Royal Mail in Glasgow by embarking on a project of envelope art, posting to herself 130 wittily addressed envelopes (for example, with addresses written backwards, spelled badly, conveyed pictorially or via crossword puzzle). Remarkably, 120 of the letters arrived at their destination.[46]

THE BEGINNINGS OF REFORM

Above all else, the years between 1836 and 1840 marked a time of transition in the Post Office, which was primed for change. By 1836, Freeling had died, and Colonel William L. Maberly took on the position of secretary to the Post Office. A year prior, in 1835, the Earl of Lichfield became postmaster general, and "both men have been stigmatized for their opposition, in whole or in part, to Rowland Hill's scheme of uniform penny postage" (Muir 39). Victorians and twentieth-century postal historians charged Lichfield and Maberly with inexperience in postal matters. Writing in the *Quarterly Review* in 1839, Croker lamented that the General Post Office fell into the "utterly inexperienced hand of *Lieutenant-Colonel Maberly*, who was so strangely selected to succeed Sir Francis Freeling in this very peculiar and technical department" (514). Lichfield was interested in an efficient post but preoccupied elsewhere. How curious that in 1836 Lichfield was writing pressing memoranda about the need for snowplows to ensure prompt mail delivery in winter (Muir 39–40) at the very same time that Rowland Hill was working to revolutionize the British Post Office for all four seasons.

Hill's work in Post Office reform built specifically upon the contributions of Wallace, MP of Greenock. A newly elected member of Parliament, Robert Wallace, in 1832, began to investigate postal irregularities, including the violation of seals. Wallace recorded in a printed address dated 1845 that he encountered "'apprehensions of friends and the sneers of opponents'" when he brought to light copious instances of postal irregularities and abuse.[47] In the nineteenth century, biographers began to champion Wallace's efforts. Writing in 1887, for example, Rowland Hill's son, Pearson, praises Wallace's "series of bold attacks upon the postal administration" (15). Wallace did not receive universal applause, however. Croker disparaged Wallace's work as "of that kind of random motion with which a member *fishes for abuses*, but is still more anxious *to catch notoriety*," concluding that Wallace succeeded in "deluding" the government that there was "really 'something rotten in the state of' St.

Martin's-le-Grand" (515). Lord Lowther, who eventually became postmaster general, supported Wallace's efforts to limit Freeling's power to open letters suspected of containing more than one sheet, and Parliament set up a commission in 1835 to inquire into the general state of St. Martin's-le-Grand. The resulting Parliamentary Select Committee on Postage, comprised of fifteen members and over which Wallace presided, did not begin its meetings until February 1838. For sixty-three days, the committee met and listened to testimony from all the senior officials of the Post Office as well as eighty-three witnesses from various occupations, including Rowland Hill himself.

Rowland Hill, like two previous postal reformers—John Palmer and Robert Wallace—was an outsider of the Post Office. Hill's father was a liberal and a forward-thinking schoolmaster. In 1819, Thomas Wright Hill founded Hazelwood, a school progressive by the standards of any era. In an age notorious for public school brutality, Thomas Hill, whom Fryer and Akerman call "a sincere Victorian—a man of ideas and high ideals" (1: xxiii), allowed his pupils to participate in self-governance and instruction.[48] Rowland Hill, who became a teacher at Hazelwood at the age of twelve, centered his own reform efforts on the Post Office. As early as 1826, Hill began suggesting improvements in the equipment and operations of the British mail system. Hill's relationship with Wallace, whom he met in 1836, spurred his plan for reform. Hill records with gratitude how Wallace used his franking privilege to send to his home "an additional half hundred weight of raw material" in the form of official government and General Post Office blue books that were heavy and unwieldy to carry (Hill and Hill 1: 246). Because the load traveled free, Wallace cleverly used the franking system to help the postal system reform itself. In turn, Hill analyzed the material systematically and produced a pamphlet filled with facts and figures to make a convincing case for postal reform (Hey 67). Following parliamentary approval of Uniform Penny Postage, Hill initially earned an appointment to the Treasury to oversee the introduction of his penny postage plan. After his service to this office ended in 1842, he became secretary to the postmaster general in 1846 and, in 1854, secretary to the Post Office, a position he held until he retired in 1864.

Hill was not universally popular. Among those who disliked him was Trollope, an admitted "anti-Hillite" who relished his "delicious feuds" with Hill and maintains in his autobiography, "I think in all such differences I was right" (246). Trollope was well established in the Post Office by the time Hill began his mission for postal reform. I include Trollope in this list of postal reformers because in his thirty-three years in the Post Office, many in a senior position, Trollope made contributions to the distribution of mail in rural areas

(C. R. Perry 265–66), and postal historians credit him with promoting stand-ing pillar boxes to collect the mail in Britain. Trollope's *Autobiography* (1883) provides a window onto the workings of the nineteenth-century Post Office and its chief players, both before and after postal reform. A prolific Victorian novelist, Trollope wrote fiction while traveling in the capacity of surveyor for the Post Office. His fiction offers insight into the impact of postal reforms on the lives of upper- and middle-class Victorians. In *Can You Forgive Her* (1865), Trollope even mentions Rowland Hill by name.

∗   ∗   ∗

Today "post" as a concept and a word remains part of our vocabulary and our collective consciousness, even if we do not rely on it as our Victorian ances-tors did. We use the term "posthaste" to convey urgency, although we may not know the term originates from the expression "'Haste, post haste,'" which in the Middle Ages directed a messenger to ride with the greatest speed to ensure a swift delivery of a message.[49] We no longer use the word "post" to convey urgency, as Robert Louis Stevenson does in *Treasure Island* (1883) when Squire Trelawney instructs Doctor Livesey and Jim Hawkins to join the Hispaniola to begin to hunt for treasure: "'come post; do not lose an hour'" (43). Nonethe-less, we still believe letter carriers can deliver the post through rain and sleet and snow because of a motto that dates to King Cyrus of ancient Persia.

The term "post" also resonates in twentieth-century pop culture. If we turn on the radio and tune it to an "oldies" station, we might catch the tune "Please Mr. Postman," which twice made it to #1 on the pop charts: first in 1961 with the Marvelettes and again in 1975 when the Carpenters recorded it. The expression "going postal," a relatively new American English slang term for workplace rage, stems from incidents of violence that began in 1986 when United States Post Office employees shot and killed citizens and fellow postal workers. Terry Pratchett further popularized this term in his thirty-third Discworld novel called *Going Postal* (2004), which spins a story about a dysfunctional postal service at Ankh-Morck that runs amok when its transdimensional letter-sort-ing machine sorts letters that have never actually been written.

What people experienced during the information revolution that took off in the England of the Victorian age is far removed from our concept of "going postal," but was no less prophetic. The Penny Post launched an information network, which, in turn, became not only a hallmark of a postal age but a forerunner of new technologies.[50] Today, we take postage stamps and prepaid stationery for granted and are surprised that neither of these now common-place inventions caught on before 1840.[51] Behind this book lies my conviction that while the products that captivate us have changed over the last 170 years, we have inherited from the Victorians a desire for innovation and progress in modes of communication which, as it did them, likewise motivates and sustains us. By examining the Victorian revolution in letter writing, readers of this book will hopefully gain insight into our current love affair with innovative information technology, as well as into the complications and challenges such innovation inevitably brings.

1

REFORMS

Chapter 1

Why the Victorians Needed a Revolution in Letter Writing

—what a wonderful liberty our Rowland Hill has given to British spir-
its, . . . we "flash a thought" instead of "wafting" it from our extreme south
to our extreme north, paying a penny for our thought, and for the electricity
included. I recommend you our penny postage as the most successful revolution since the "glorious three days" of Paris.

—Elizabeth Barrett Browning, Letter to Cornelius Matthews, April 28, 1843

In 1803, receiving a letter was not an everyday occurrence for middle- and
working-class English families, nor was it a welcomed event. Postage was high.
Prepayment, often considered an indirect social slur on the recipient, was possible but uncommon. Typically, postage was due when the recipient collected a
letter at a local post office or, for those living in London or within recognized
"free delivery" areas (usually cities or towns), when the letter was delivered to
one's home by a postman.[1] Such was the situation eight-year-old Rowland Hill
faced when he answered a knock at his door in Kidderminster, near Birmingham, and found a postman standing there. The "letter-carrier," as he was called
in the early nineteenth century,[2] requested payment for a letter for the Hill
household. Rowland's father, the progressive schoolmaster Thomas Wright
Hill, was not at home when the postman called. His mother did not have
enough money to accept the letter. Although it was quite common for a family
not to have sufficient funds to pay for postage—and a schoolmaster's family
in the year 1803 was far from wealthy—this was a situation Rowland's mother
had long feared. Sarah Lea Hill gathered up a few family possessions and sent
Rowland, her third child, into town to raise money for postage. He soon returned with three shillings, more than enough to pay the letter carrier.[3]

I have come across a canon of such anecdotal and domestic tales that explain Rowland Hill's calling to reform the nineteenth-century postal service,
that dramatize the consequences of high postage, and that urge revolution-

ary change. In this chapter, I focus on these written anecdotes, testimonials, scenarios, stories, and narratives for two reasons. First, stories that appeared in periodicals and propaganda pamphlets of the day, as material products of Victorian culture, are emissaries of the time and place in which reform gained force. They illustrate what the British perceived to be amiss in the early nineteenth century before the coming of the Penny Post on January 10, 1840. From stories of pre-reform deprivation, we come to understand why the British were dissatisfied with the Post Office in the early nineteenth century and why they believed it had to change. Second, these narratives, which still resonate in biographies about Rowland Hill and books about the Penny Post, suggest how stories became a persuasive tool for powering reform of the postal service in the years 1837 to 1840. I have clustered these stories thematically to consider tales that present Rowland Hill as a major figure in the democratization of the Post Office, along with those featuring economics, kinship ties, morality, perceived blessings, and utopian aspirations as signal issues in postal reform. All of these stories—the lore of Hill's reformist vocation, pre-reform tales of isolation and impoverishment linked to high postage, post-reform accounts that pin social, economic, and moral improvements on the Penny Post—cumulatively shaped what cultural critic Eileen Cleere calls "the question of postal reform as an affective dilemma rather than a political challenge" (173).

In the 1830s, the General Post Office was still aligned in the public consciousness with political espionage and censorship, and "its obvious relevance to trade and society" was, as David Allam points out, largely overlooked (3). Those in favor of cheap postage ran their campaign by arguing that reform was not a matter of party politics. Rowland Hill insisted in his preface to *Post Office Reform: Its Importance and Practicability* (1837) that "Fortunately this is not a party question" (iv). Rowland Hill, Henry Cole, and W. H. Ashurst amassed facts and figures to bolster their claim that England would benefit economically from a reduction in postage because, presumably, the smuggling of letters would decrease and more people would write letters. More persuasive, however, was the way these and other postal reformers skillfully used stories that moved readers by emotional appeal, arousing the public (particularly merchants and businessmen) and ultimately carrying the tide of postal reform.[4]

Some critics suggest that artfully constructed pre-reform anecdotes created discontent with the General Post Office by "taxing" family sentiment with poignant scenarios of families torn asunder by high postage. In *Administration of the Post Office* (1844), the anonymous author explains how pitiful tales made Uniform Penny Postage "a case, not of mere business, but of *feeling*, and won immediate access to the heart of a large class of people. . . . [With] what dexterity," he complains, "the snare of cheap postage was spread" (20). Our anonymous author implies here that postal reformers not only manipulated the public with the lure of cheap postal charges but, worse, that they may have deliberately masterminded public dissatisfaction with the post. According to David Allam in *The Social and Economic Importance of Postal Reform in 1840*, this may indeed be the case, as "there appears to have been surprisingly little open dissatisfaction expressed by the public with the condition of the Post Office or its high charges before 1837" (3). Eileen Cleere interprets Allam to speculate that propaganda by Hill and Cole "constructed a retrospective narrative of family disaffection that reformers and parliamentarians alike seem to have accepted as historical fact" (178).

Reconstructing the history of dissatisfaction with the British postal system during the rise of cheap postage is complicated, as much of the material in *The Post Circular* (subtitled *Or, Weekly Advocate for a Cheap, Swift, and Sure Postage*) is undoubtedly propaganda. Many nineteenth-century books about postal reform are by Hill himself or by Hill's close kin: his daughter, Eleanor Smyth; his son and private secretary, Pearson Hill; and his nephew, George Birkbeck Hill. Following his 1864 resignation from the Post Office, Hill spent much of the final fifteen years of his life "given over to the preparation of an elaborate autobiography—the apologia," in Howard Robinson's view, "of his efforts and of his place in postal reform" (366). M. J. Daunton likewise concludes of Hill: "The truth is that the development of the Post Office is now viewed almost entirely through the distortions of Hill's own voluminous writings, works of self-justification which do not provide an objective view of the reforms introduced in 1840" (3–5).

Factual evidence does exist, however, that postal evasion, arguably proof of dissatisfaction, was widespread during the 1830s. By July 1839, the Mercantile Committee on Postage presented to Parliament about 2,007 petitions for postal reform bearing 262,809 signatures. Granted, the Mercantile Committee on Postage initiated the *The Post Circular* as a vehicle for postal reform propaganda and was busily organizing meetings, circulating fliers, printing news, and stirring up agitation for cheap postage in the late 1830s. Even so, the committee collected an impressive number of signatures in favor of reform, including one petition with 12,500 signatures gathered in one day. Census figures show that, as of June 6, 1841, the population of England and Wales was 15.9 million. Given that 36 percent of the people represented by this figure were under age fifteen (and thus ineligible to sign a petition),[5] the number of adult petitioners for reform suggests that dissatisfaction with the British postal system was real and wide open by 1839.[6] Moreover, Allam's analysis does not preclude the possibility that rather than constructing "a retrospective narrative of family disaffection" (Cleere 178), postal reformers were making public existing but largely unvoiced disaffection, probably embellishing it in the process.

In his critique of postal reform published in 1839 in the *Quarterly Review*, John Wilson Croker—one of the *Quarterly* founders and "a brilliant Tory both with tongue and pen" (Robinson 295)—argues this point. Embellished as they were for affect, pre-reform tales of the hardship of high postage on the poor became, in Croker's view, "a mere *ad captandum* exaggeration" (529), a specious and seductive form of argument designed to win over a crowd. That many of the same stories appear in a range of publications advocating reform suggests a strategic maneuver on the part of postal reformers to dramatize existing discontent. Tales about economic hardship and depravity resulting from high postage take the form of testimonials, letters to the editor, and articles in journals, pamphlets, and the complete run of the *The Post Circular*, demonstrating that Hill, Cole, and other reformers intuitively recognized the power of pathos in narrative to stir reformist sentiment and spur reform.

Secretary to the Mercantile Committee on Postage, Henry Cole founded and became editor of *The Post Circular*. In addition to publishing Hill's views on the British postal system, including extensive material from *Post Office Reform: Its Importance and Practicability*, *The Post Circular* reprinted evidential summaries from the Parliamentary Select Committee on Postage, supplementing them with stories and, in some cases, refutations of presented evidence. Henry Hooper, a publisher whom Gavin Fryer and Clive Akerman call "the propaganda and proselytizing arm of the Mercantile Committee on Postage," published this "newspaper-cum-newsletter/propaganda sheet," which had a run of sixteen issues, from March 14, 1838, until November 20, 1839 (2: 717).[7] Cole speculated that simply by adding some advertisements, death notices, and city news, *The Post Circular* could be registered as a newspaper and bring its reformist message to the masses for only a penny, in essence making the General Post Office a medium for its own reformation.

It is my contention in this chapter that postal reformers made touching stories the very heart of postal reform materials printed in *The Post Circular* and other publications to align the existing postal system with family disaffection. Cheap postage, in turn, purportedly fostered family and friendship ties and surmounted boundaries of time and space by bringing letters within economic reach of the poor and middle class. Widely publicized and arguably exaggerated pre-reform stories project a rosy future of heightened communication and moral reformation of isolated groups (apprentices, governesses) and potentially degenerate social groups (discontented workers, unruly soldiers). Narratives offered hope for restoring family unity and safeguarding morality during an industrialized era riddled with broken kinship ties due to war, limited work opportunities (requiring relocation), and emigration. In addition, well after 1840, heartrending tales that retroactively argued for the necessity of postal reform and promoted its success continued to shape how the public viewed the social and moral condition of England before cheap postage unburdened the nation.

WHY ROWLAND HILL AGITATED FOR POSTAL REFORM

The story of Rowland Hill going to the pawnshop to raise money to pay high postal charges regularly appears in postal histories and biographies of Rowland Hill, although some of the particulars vary. In *Sir Rowland Hill and the Post Office*, Alan James describes the articles eight-year-old Rowland's mother sent him to pawn as "bits and pieces" (36), while Colin Hey in *Rowland Hill: Genius and Benefactor 1795–1879* suggests Hill's mother gave him "a bundle of old clothes" and does not specify how much money he received for them (30). In *Sir Rowland Hill: The Story of a Great Reform Told By His Daughter* (1907), Smyth embellishes the story with poignant details. Rowland Hill is a "weakly" child, having a "fragile form [that] held a dauntless little soul" (8). To "Rowland Hill's parents, and to many thousands more, in those days of slender income and heavy taxation, the postman's knock was a sound of dread" (44). We imagine Sarah Lea Hill with profound worry on her face. Rowland, a pale, thin child carrying clothes or, perhaps, a prized family spoon, is being hurried out the door, panicked by the postman's dreaded knock. All the while, an impatient letter carrier is tapping his foot at the Hill doorstep, awaiting payment.

The word "dread" appears throughout retellings of this pre-reform hardship story. To Pearson Hill, "the visit of the postman, so far from being welcomed, was, as a rule, dreaded" (3). Pearson Hill associates dread with the postman's visit whereas in her retelling, Smyth associates dread with the sound of the postman's "knock." In *Social Reformers*, Norman Wymer locates dread in Hill's mother's reaction to the postman: "Though both Mr. and Mrs. Hill did their best to make light of their problems in front of their children, Rowland could not fail to notice his mother's dread of the postman or her relief when she sent him along to the rag-and-bone merchants with a bundle of old clothes to sell and he had returned with a shilling more than she had expected" (5). Even Fryer and Akerman, in their two-volume documentary history published by the Royal Philatelic Society of London in 2000, use the word "dread" to describe Rowland Hill's childhood remembrance of seeing "his mother's dread of a letter coming with a high postage charge to pay at a time when she had insufficient money in the house" (2: 1187). "Dread" in these four examples— a word that conveys anxiety, dismay, terror, and trepidation—subsumes not only the Hill family but all those with slender means who, prior to postal reform, had insufficient funds to pay for a letter.

Hill's biographers have also privileged this incident as a formative one in his development, particularly in his decision to reform the Post Office. In *Social Reformers*, Wymer opens his chapter on Hill by surmising, "If Rowland Hill, as a very small boy, had not noticed his mother's worried look whenever the postman knocked at her door to demand a shilling or so for the letter he brought her we might never have been able to collect postage stamps" (3). Similarly, Hey calls it "a strange trick of fate" that led Hill "at a very early age to reflect on the shortcomings, and indeed evils, of the existing postal system"; he concludes that an "ordinary domestic incident made a big impression on [Hill's] childish mind and undoubtedly sowed the seed of his ideas for establishing a cheap, nation-wide postal service; it proved to be the main trigger-point of his whole career" (29–30). Moreover, Hey refers back to this incident midway in his biography (67–68) when describing what "triggered" Hill to write his famous 1837 pamphlet.

Biographers, including Smyth, favor a second oft-told story—Samuel Taylor Coleridge paying a shilling, so a poor cottager could receive a letter—as the impetus behind Hill's later plans for postal reform. Hill probably contributed to this association by including the tale both in *Post Office Reform* and in his memoir, *The Life of Sir Rowland Hill* (1880), posthumously completed by his nephew George Birkbeck Hill. The incident occurs in the context of Coleridge's 1822 walking tour through the English Lake District. In a letter dated Saturday, March 22, 1822, Coleridge records, "'One day, when I had not a shilling which I could spare, I was passing by a cottage not far from Keswick, where a carter was demanding a shilling for a letter, which the woman of the house appeared unwilling to pay, and at last declined to take.'" Describing an act of kindness in response to the situation, Coleridge adds, "'I paid the postage; and when the man was out of sight, she told me that the letter was from her son, who took that means of letting her know that he was well: the letter was *not to be paid for*. It was then opened, and found to be blank!'"[8] The blank letter was, by a prearranged agreement between mother and son, simply a way to convey the son was alive and well. In some retellings of this anecdote, the letter writer differs—he is an absent father, husband, or brother. In other versions, both players change—for example, a poor barmaid lacks the money to accept a letter from her brother. And some versions identify the deliverer as a postman or letter carrier, rather than a "carter," that is, a driver not employed by the Post Office (although carters followed certain regulations so as not to offend the Post Office monopoly on carrying letters).[9] Hill includes this tale about Coleridge in his 1837 pamphlet and concludes, "This trick is so obvious a one that in all probability it is extensively practised" (107).

Harriet Martineau reports that Rowland Hill volunteered the shilling that, in fact, Coleridge paid during his 1822 walking tour.[10] This apocryphal version, mistakenly casting Hill as the Good Samaritan, bears repeating. In volume 2 of *The History of England during the Thirty Years' Peace* (1850), Martineau records that during a tour of the Lake District as a young man, Rowland Hill saw a cottager examine a letter but return it to a postman, declaring that she could not pay the heavy postal tax. Overhearing that the letter came from the woman's brother, Hill paid the postman. Once the postman was gone, the cottager "showed Mr. Hill how his money had been wasted, as far as she was concerned. The sheet was blank. There was an agreement between the woman and her brother that as long as all went well with him, he should send a blank sheet in this way once a quarter; and she thus had tidings of him without expense of postage" (2: 425).[11] In her subsequent analysis of the story, Martineau—anticipating the analyses of later critics, including Wymer and Hey—foregrounds this incident as pivotal in Hill's developing moral consciousness: "Most people would have remembered this incident as a curious story to tell: but Mr. Hill's was a mind which wakened up at once to a sense of the significance of the fact. There must be something wrong in a system which drove a brother and sister to cheating, in order to gratify their desire to hear of one another's welfare" (2: 425). Here Martineau erroneously suggests that Hill was "wakened up at once" to reform the General Post Office, and she even concludes her discussion of postal reform by giving Hill credit for a noble action he did not actually perform: "The neighborly shilling given in the Lake district was well laid out" (2: 431).

As Cleere notes in *Avuncularism*, "the desire to keep Hill the central figure of reform efforts and to locate him at the origins of reform led some psychobiographical historians to insist that the true alpha of penny postage was in Hill's childhood and in the bonds of family affection that made him so sensitive to issues of domestic harmony" (179). The Good Samaritan story and the anecdote of young Rowland pawning family goods for postage locate Hill at the very "origins" of postal reform. Of considerable significance, in the apocryphal version, Hill takes on the role of the Good Samaritan, a figure revered in Victorian culture. This was an age when images of the Good Samaritan tending the wayfarer adorned the walls of Victorian homes as moral examples. Illustrations accompanying Victorian novels demonstrate this point: in the illustration captioned "Oliver Recovering from a Fever" for Charles Dickens's *Oliver Twist* (1838), George Cruikshank includes a picture of the Good Samaritan tending a wayfarer in the parlor of Mr. Brownlow's Pentonville home to indicate his caring nature toward orphan Oliver. Likewise, William Makepeace Thackeray places the Good Samaritan figure behind a sickly and quaking Jos Sedley in his final illustration for *Vanity Fair* (1848), entitled "Becky's Second Appearance in the Character of Clytemnestra." This picture reflects on the kindness of Jos's visitor, William Dobbin, who has journeyed far to inquire after his brother-in-law's declining health under Becky Sharp's dubious care. Like honest Dobbin, the character closest to being a hero in Thackeray's "Novel without a Hero," and good Mr. Brownlow, who adopts Oliver at the end of Dickens's tale, Hill in the apocryphal version of the cottager's letter emerges as a valiant, sensitive, and selfless citizen, single-handedly challenging the brutish Post Office, which was notorious for taxing sentiment and kinship ties.

What was Rowland Hill's reaction to the apocryphal story? He explains in his memoir how Martineau's "blunder" came to pass. On Martineau's request, Hill sent her a copy of his pamphlet, which, he laments, she read "'carelessly'" (1: 239). (Hill correctly attributed the cottager's letter story to Coleridge in his pamphlet.) What was the Victorian response? According to his memoir, a *Notes and Queries* article "'attacked'" Hill for making a false claim of charity (1: 239–40). The story, in turn, gained mythic proportions. A savvy innkeeper—eager to cash in on Hill's alleged tour of the Lake District, where he supposedly devised the scheme of Uniform Penny Postage—went so far as to advertise a room at an inn where Hill stayed when he had this epiphany to reform the Post Office. Stories invariably change over time. But both versions of this story, the correct and the apocryphal, widely appear in books about Hill and Uniform Penny Postage and still inform public perception about the origins of postal reform. In fact, the apocryphal version of the Good Samaritan story garners equal if not greater attention than the actual version.[12]

In *Postmarks, Cards and Covers: Collecting Postal History*, Prince Dimitry Kandaouroff repeats a variation of the apocryphal story printed in Martineau's work, admitting it may be false. In his account, the letter comes from a poor village girl's fiancé who lives in London. When Hill valiantly intervenes and pays the charges, the embarrassed village lass explains to Hill a stratagem the lovers devised to cheat the post: "By means of various simple signs and marks drawn on the covering of the letter, the young man was able to let her know that he was keeping well and that he still loved her" (48).[13] Also employing the approach of psychobiography, Kandaouroff quickly moves from incident to problem to solution:

> Rowland Hill was profoundly disturbed by this story and he pondered on the problem. He concluded that there was a vicious circle in which high postal charges caused a diminution in the number of letters carried and this, in turn, forced the rate up in order to make the postal services pay their way. One way of breaking the cycle would be to introduce pre-payment of postage and thus eliminate the current cumbersome methods of accounting for postage. From this he deduced that a uniform rate of postage would make accountancy even simpler. (48)

In making the Penny Post scheme a direct outcome of Hill's charitable action, Kandaouroff whisks away his earlier qualification that this story may, in fact, be apocryphal, as we now know it to be today. Time and again, postal collectors and historians trace and attribute Hill's on-the-spot inspiration to an incident that never actually occurred. This incident is even repeated on several current Web sites. Mike Mills's *Glassine Surfer*, a stamp-collecting site for philatelists, includes a section called "Rowland Hill and The Penny Black," which gives the apocryphal version of the cottager's letter story (with a few variations): "as the story goes, the reform-minded Hill with his sterling reputation and access to the government, happened to witness a distressing event that spurred him into action."[14]

HILL, A MAN WITH AN OPEN HEART

Analyzing the British postal system from the vantage point of an enlightened outsider, Rowland Hill published four editions of his epic *Post Office Reform: Its Importance and Practicability*. The first (printed by William Clowes and Sons) came out in early January 1837, marked "private and confidential." A second edition for the general public (published by Charles Knight) appeared on February 22, 1837. A third version came out later in 1837 and the fourth in 1838.[15] The pamphlet and Hill's two-volume memoir (1880) prove good reading today because of Hill's ability to tell an engaging story. His pamphlet and memoir, more importantly, offer a window onto why the British in the early nineteenth century believed they needed postal reform. These products of Victorian culture through which the revolution in letter writing manifested

itself encode memories of collective hardship, discontent, moral consciousness, optimism, and an emerging notion of public service.

In the appendix of *Post Office Reform*, Hill tells of a postal evasion scheme
involving a "friend of mine" posting a bundle of old newspapers to his family. The postmark and date of the mailing showed the friend's location, while
the frank, the name of a specific peer or member of the House of Commons,
informed the traveler's parents of his health "without putting them to the expense of postage" (91). In his memoir, Hill presents a more detailed version of
this same story, admitting that he, not a friend of his, practiced it while traveling from the Lake District to Scotland in 1823. Hill sent old newspapers to his
family, printing names of conservative Tories, like Lord Eldon, to indicate he
was poorly, and names of Liberals, such as Sir Francis Burdett, to signal he was
in robust health.[16] Moreover, in his memoir, Rowland Hill points to his previous deception in a footnote: "In 'Post Office Reform' this anecdote is given as
of a friend, but in truth I was my own hero" (1: 240). This was a bold move,
even in a footnote, given that in the 1820s specimen signatures were held at the
General Post Office in London and checked, as were the number of privilege
letters sent by MPs each day. Not the Good Samaritan that Martineau imagined, Hill, by his own admission, was actually in the Lake District a year later
than she thought, carrying out a mild form of postal evasion common in the
early nineteenth century. (According to Hill, "any one was at liberty to use the
name of any Peer or Member of the House of Commons without his consent"
[1: 240].)

The significance of this confession is its disclosure of a personal flaw. The
same Rowland Hill, who at age eight pawned family belongings to pay the
postman, humanized his mission for cheap postage and humbled himself in
his 1880 memoir by admitting that as a young man, he, like so many of his contemporaries, felt compelled to be his "own hero" and falsely frank newspapers
to stay in touch with his close and affectionate family. Even the man the Queen
knighted for his efforts to reform the General Post Office—a reformer who, if
not uniformly liked, was publicly heralded "Sir Rowland Le Grand" (see figure
2) in a John Tenniel cartoon on the occasion of his 1864 retirement as secretary
of the Post Office—felt compelled to use franks illicitly to stay connected with
his loved ones.[17]

Hill's method of franking newspapers as a health bulletin, though not ingenious, was a viable way of communicating in an age of high postage, as Harriet
Martineau observes in *The History of England*: "Parents and children, brothers
and sisters, lovers and friends, must have tidings of each other, where there is
any possibility of obtaining them; and those who had not shillings to spend in

FIGURE 2. "Sir Rowland Le Grand." Illustration by John Tenniel for *Punch*, March 19, 1864. Reproduced with permission of Punch Ltd., www.punch.co.uk.

postage . . . would resort to any device of communication, without thinking there was any harm in such cheating" (2: 425). A variety of newspaper scams were routinely practiced during the early nineteenth century, as indicated in issue 9 of *The Post Circular* (July 5, 1838): "Newspapers are an obvious means of evasion. They are written on, pricked, dotted, invisible inks are used, systems of cipher employed, marks are agreed upon" (26). In addition, people regularly sent letters via workmen and friends traveling to a specific location. For example, a folded letter to George Hodgkinson Barrow, Esq., at Southwell, sealed with a gummed wafer and dated April 12, 1809, records on its cover the following instructions for delivery: "To be sent by the carrier with a haunch of venison from the Maypole Inn, Nottingham."[18] A Mr. John Wright gave testimony at the Parliamentary Select Committee on Postage that his blacking manufacturing firm of Warren, Russell, and Wright (located on the Strand, London) sent no more than one invoice a week by post; the firm enclosed the rest in the casks it sent out to its customers.[19] Postal reformers, in turn, seized on such means of irregular mail transport as an argument for cheap postage: with postal rates at a penny, the same as the Stamp Tax on newspapers, British manufacturers and citizens, including Rowland Hill, wouldn't need to resort to irregular means to evade the post.

Despite her initial blunder in presenting Hill as the Good Samaritan of the Lake District, Martineau later correctly identified Coleridge when she revised her work in 1877–78 (without acknowledging her earlier error).[20] However, in the original version of *The History of England*, published in 1850, she insightfully introduces Hill first and foremost as "a man of an open heart, who could enter into family sympathies," before she describes him as "a man of philosophical ingenuity, who could devise a remedial scheme—and a man of business who could fortify such a scheme with an impregnable accuracy—to achieve such a reform" (2: 427). Martineau recognized that Hill combined heart and ingenuity to present touching stories, which he placed strategically within the appendix of his 1837 pamphlet.

The opening pages of Hill's pamphlet show tables, facts, and figures. Hill argues by analogy for a reduction in postal tax by citing the outcomes of cuts in taxes for leather, malt, soap, and coffee. A 50 percent reduction in the coffee tax, for example, actually resulted in more than a 50 percent increase in coffee production (1). Hill raises the conundrum as to why, during the years 1817–37, postal revenue diminished slightly instead of keeping pace with the growth of population (3). He also presents a compelling rational metaphor to suggest the importance of the post in an increasingly industrialized age:

When it is considered how much the religious, moral, and intellectual progress of the people, would be accelerated by the unobstructed circulation of letters and of the many cheap and excellent non-political publications of the present day, the Post Office assumes the new and important character of a powerful engine of civilization; capable of performing a distinguished part in the great work of National education, but rendered feeble and inefficient by erroneous financial arrangements. (8)

Logically, the mismanagement of the Post Office made the "engine" inefficient and, at times, unproductive. If letters could travel "unobstructed," Hill argues, then the Post Office would transform into a locomotive for ethical and moral change to improve religion, morality, education, and civilization. Even if postal historians like Daunton conclude that Hill "fundamentally miscalculated the economics of his scheme for a Penny Post" and was quarrelsome and "obsessive about 'my plan'" (5), these same parties recognize Hill's ambition and achievement.

Touching stories fueled Hill's mission to make the Post Office an "engine of civilization" to benefit "all sects in politics and religion . . . and all classes from the highest to the lowest" (*Post Office Reform* 66). Two stories of pre-reform deprivation bear repeating. The shorter of the two shows Hill's reasoning that cheap postage would make "many a heart gladdened" in an age where friends and family lost touch for long periods of time due to marriage, apprenticeships, employment, and education (*Post Office Reform* 92). Hill tells how a brother and sister, one living in Reading and the other in Hampstead, had not communicated at all during a span of thirty years. The General Post Office destroyed the bonds of family affection until one of the siblings met a "fairy godmother," a kindly MP. According to Hill, "that they were deterred solely by considerations of expense is proved by the fact, that, on franks being furnished by the kindness of a member of parliament, a frequent interchange of letters was the immediate consequence" (*Post Office Reform* 93–94). This story has a happy ending because a Good Samaritan shared his allotment of franks. Strategically locating this story in his pamphlet after an extended discussion of widespread pre-reform deprivations suffered by domestic servants and laborers separated from their families, Hill leaves the reader pondering: how many more brothers and sisters, parents and children, lovers and sweethearts were *not* lucky enough to receive tokens for free carriage of correspondence and remained isolated from family and friends?

The longer and more dramatic of the two tales offers an example of egregious postal fraud as an impetus for reform. In 1834, a Liverpool merchant named Mr. Duncan posted a Bank of England note for £50 sterling to his mother, who resided in Broughty Ferry, Forfarshire. Mrs. Duncan did not receive her son's letter, and efforts to trace the letter—which was to have traveled from Liverpool to Edinburgh, to Dundee, to Broughty Ferry—proved futile: "All that could be learned was, that the letter containing the bank note had been put into the Liverpool Post Office and had not reached its destination" (*Post Office Reform* 72–73). In what seemed like an unrelated incident, a bank teller at the Commercial Bank of Edinburgh happened to notice a man at the theater and the next day, at his bank, saw the very same individual, in a disguise of green spectacles and a large fur cap and cloak, attempting to cash a Bank of England note for £50 sterling. The teller, curious as to why someone would adopt a disguise to cash a banknote, made some inquiries and learned that this very note was the one that had been stolen from Mr. Duncan's letter. Because the man in disguise had written a false name on the stolen note when presenting it to the bank, the teller wondered whether the man was a dishonest Post Office employee. In a lineup of Post Office employees, the bank teller eventually identified the criminal as James Wedderburn Nicol. The spectacles and cap, as well as a number of banknotes, turned up in a search of Nicol's residence. Had the case against Nicol not been so strong, he would have likely gone free, as he had an alibi—he was allegedly on shift at the time he cashed the stolen check. Nicol apparently stole the note during a routine candling of a letter to determine whether it was single or double charge. The incident led Hill to conclude that "Nicol, who was well connected, and it is understood of previously good character, was tempted to abstract the letter" (*Post Office Reform* 74). For his crime, Nicol received "transportation for life"—the same fate that befalls Dickens's Artful Dodger at the end of *Oliver Twist*.

This narrative—complete with false identities, disguises, and detective work—reads more like a Sherlock Holmes story than a Dickens novel. More than entertaining, it makes two compelling points: temptation to fraud in the Post Office was great, and detection was left to chance. Candling often led to the discovery of jewelry and banknotes ripe for stealing. Had postal charges been lower, Hill surmises, Mr. Duncan could have sent his banknote in two pieces, each under separate cover, thus eliminating the temptation for stealing. Moreover, if the Post Office charged by weight and not by number of sheets, then postal employees would not have had to candle the letter, a daily practice leading otherwise honorable employees into temptation. Second, had the teller not happened to observe the thieving Post Office employee in the pit of an Edinburgh theater the night before he entered the bank, the teller might not have been suspicious of Nicol's costume, and the theft would likely have gone undetected. In this tale, the General Post Office emerges as more villainous than Nicol, the actual thief. Ashurst makes this same point in his 1838 *Facts and Reasons in Support of Mr. Rowland Hill's Plan for a Universal Penny Postage*. Reprinting a figure from the "Eighteenth Report of Commisioners of Revenue Inquiry" that each evening in St. Martin's-le-Grand as many as 40,000 letters are candled to determine whether or not each should receive a single or double charge, Ashurst offers a warning in emphatic capital letters: "THE EXAMINATION OF EACH LETTER BY A CANDLE, BY REVEALING THE CONTENTS, CREATES TEMPTATIONS TO THEFT, WHICH HAVE TOO OFTEN BEEN IRRESISTIBLE" (19–20).

Elucidating the Victorian frame of mind, Martineau explains that cheap postage freed scores of lovers, friends, parents, and children "of previously good character" from having to "resort to any device of communication, without thinking there was any harm in such cheating" (*History* 2: 425). That there was harm in such cheating, Martineau, Ashurst, Hill, and other postal reformers knew well, especially as scams often involved numerous postal workers, as indicated in another tale that appeared in issue 9 of *The Post Circular* (July 5, 1838). A letter posted in Greenock, passing through the Post Office in Glasgow, arrived at its destination minus a £10 note from the Bank of England that the writer had enclosed within it. Another letter containing a £10 note from the Royal Bank and a £6 note from an undisclosed bank happened to pass through the Glasgow Post Office on route to Dumbarton at around the same time; while this second letter reached its destination, it was missing the £6 note and curiously contained the £10 note from the Bank of England included in the letter posted from Greenock. This theft and mix-up of banknotes resulted in suspension of six clerks and stampers; one went to prison. Not all cases of postal theft ended so neatly. Postal workers who candled letters continuously fell into temptation; thieves went undetected and unpunished. As Hill and other postal reformers brought more and more stories of pre-reform postal evasion and illicit practices into the open, a vote for postal reform came to be seen as a vote for moral reformation.

NOT A SHILLING TO SPARE

The post was expensive prior to 1840 unless one could frank a letter, that is, send it for free. Indeed, Thackeray, who sets his monumental *Vanity Fair* in Regency times, uses the price of postage to prove the popularity of his alleged heroine, Amelia Sedley. Miss Schwartz, an heiress of considerable fortune, insists to Amelia on her leaving Miss Pinkerton's Academy, "'Never mind the postage, but write every day, you dear darling'"; however, even Thackeray acknowledges that Miss Schwartz seems "impetuous" in making this rash request to pay high postage daily just to receive a letter from little Emmy Sedley (8). Not surprisingly, financial hardship dominates pre-reform stories promoting the Penny Post as well as post-reform stories retroactively constructing its necessity. Potent reminders of the past, these stories materially represent the longing experienced by far-flung friends and family in an increasingly mobile society. From them we can extrapolate what many early Victorians wanted, as well as what countless believed postal reform would and, to an extent, did bring.

Tales of hardship due to high postage emphasize the depth of suffering of the poor. In an 1840 *Edinburgh Review* article called "Post-Office Reform," the author records, "It would be easy to fill pages with instances of pain and misery which result from there being no post-office for the poor" and offers "*pregnant* facts, drawn from the evidence" (M. D. Hill 554). This "evidence" consists of anecdotes, mainly relayed second hand: a needle manufacturer tells of an indigent man who did not know of a relative's death for six to eight months because he could not pay the postage. A postmaster in the town of Congresbury relates that a poor laborer refrained from paying eight pence for a letter from his daughter for fear "'it would take a loaf of bread from his other children'" (M. D. Hill 555). Recounting this same story, Smyth adds that in the early nineteenth century, a time worse than the "'Hungry Forties,'" a person sometimes spent "more than eightpence—more occasionally than double that sum—on his children's loaf" (61).[21] A pauper living in Rosser could not raise the postage to receive her granddaughter's letter, and when a kind person gave her a shilling to pay for it, the local post office had already returned the letter to sender.

Many pre-reform hardship stories focus on wretched or desolate females. One tells of an impoverished mother entreating her local post office to act as a pawnshop: she offered a silver spoon to the postmistress to hold until she could raise postage for a letter from her husband in prison; she was caring for six children on her own and could not easily spare the money. This story, credited to Mr. Emery, commissioner of taxes and deputy lieutenant for Somersetshire, also appears in Pearson Hill's *The Post Office of Fifty Years Ago* (1887). In this narrative, appearing in publications published over forty years apart, the postmistress refused to take the spoon but held the letter until the poor woman could return with the fee. A similar tale appears in W. H. Ashurst's 1838 pamphlet among a collection of anecdotes Ashurst gathered from a kind magistrate in a western county while working as solicitor and parliamentary agent of the Mercantile Committee on Postage.[22] In this version, the Post Office, acting as a pawnshop, accepted the silver teaspoon as a "pledge" of payment: the woman whose husband was in prison faced a terrible dilemma since her family was "*without bread*," and she "'was compelled to leave a silver tea spoon, by way of pledge to the post-mistress, for the payment of the postage, and thereby obtained the long-wished-for letter from her incarcerated husband'" (68). This widely reprinted pre-reform tale of hardship is one of many that made postal reform an affective dilemma: reformers envisioned cheap postage as a welfare measure, a "beneficent legislation," to recall Martineau's retrospective estimation (*History* 2: 426).

Reformers likely seized on the analogy between paying high postage and pawning because pawnshops were so widespread. In 1844, four years after the coming of the Penny Post, in Manchester alone there were sixty pawnshops frequented by workers who pawned their possessions, mostly clothes, on a Monday in the hope they could redeem their clothes by repaying the loan and the interest on the money they had borrowed when payday arrived on Saturday.[23] Henry Cole cunningly opened his 1838 skit, "A Report of an Imaginary Scene at Windsor Castle Respecting the Uniform Penny Postage," with a fictional Queen Victoria—the Mother of the Nation—lamenting, "Mothers pawning their clothes to pay the postage of a child's letter! . . . such things must not last."[24] Smyth concurs with Cole: "mothers yearning to hear from absent children would pawn clothing or household necessaries rather than be deprived of the letters which, but for that sacrifice, must be carried back to the nearest post office to await payment" (61). Stories of "sacrifice" grow even more desperate: Ashurst reports that a pauper widow in Somersetshire, who could not afford to pay for a letter from her daughter, used one third of her weekly allotment from the relieving officer to accept it (68)—she probably had nothing to pawn.[25]

THE VIRTUES OF STAYING CONNECTED

Staying connected became a paramount concern to members of an increasingly mobile British society where war, as well as trade and industry, removed the possibility of verbal communication for months, years, and at times longer.[26] Postal reform stories, in preserving memories of hardship and longing, teach us that in the midst of changing times and "family dispersion," to use Harriet Martineau's term,[27] countless Victorians wanted to stay connected. Although the Internet, e-mail, and igadgets would surely amaze nineteenth-century time travelers to the twenty-first century, community building and staying connected with family and friends—which the Victorians sought to achieve via letter writing—would certainly seem comfortingly Victorian.

Modern forms of transportation have placed within easy reach distances which seemed insurmountable in the early to mid-nineteenth century. Those living in rural towns without a district post office felt, to recall the words of one postal reformer, "as much isolated in this respect as if they lived at Timbuctoo."[28] Letters were a crucial form of contact in an age of industry and expanding empire, but high postage often severed kinship ties. Only when the Post Office could provide what Hill called an "unobstructed circulation of letters" could members of the working class and middle class easily and affordably send letters offering advice, guidance, information, and comfort. Preserving kinship ties became a strong selling point for cheap postage; as Hill advocates in his 1837 pamphlet, "to the poor it [the Penny Post] will afford the means of communication with their distant friends and relatives, from which they are at present debarred" (67).

The opening "address" in the first issue of *The Post Circular* (Wednesday, March 14, 1838) raises these same points: "That the masses of the rising generation are necessarily obliged to go forth from the family roof as apprentices, clerks, shopmen, travelers, teachers, domestic servants, and labourers of all kinds; that they often settle in marriage in places distant from their parents and relations; and that, to immense numbers of these, the present rates of postage prevent communications with relatives and friends" (1). Set against the collective citizenry or "masses" are words of coercion and oppression: "obliged" and "prevent." Countless people were forced to leave their homes for employment and, in turn, lost contact with their families because the government-controlled Post Office hindered kinship ties with high costs. In an age when home and family were sacrosanct, the emotional rhetoric in this passage positions the disenfranchised "masses" of teachers, apprentices, and clerks, already uprooted from the safety of their domestic circles, against an unwieldy, unfeeling Post Office, which "debarred" a rising generation from remaining in close contact with friends, families, and communities, making them feel as if they lived in Timbuktu (an expression we still use today).

Praising postal reform for restoring "access to home" in an 1843 letter to Thomas Wilde, MP, Martineau highlights the widespread benefits of cheap postage to conclude, "Far more important is the opening of the Post Office to hundreds and thousands of these industrious workers than an increase of earnings would be; for the restoration of access to home, which might then be an expensive indulgence, is now a matter of course for all; a benefit enjoyed without hesitation or remorse."[29] Martineau's position on the Penny Post became a widely accepted view.

Nonetheless, it seems important to qualify that even 1d was a large amount to some people living in early to mid-nineteenth-century England. In London around 1840, with 1d one could buy many commodities far more precious to the poor than a postage stamp. As Nicholas Bentley notes in *The Victorian Scene*, "Bread was the staple of the working-class diet, but some could afford only stale bread, which was sold in the streets for as little as a penny or sometimes even a halfpenny for a four-pound loaf" (102). The notion of a working-class family forsaking bread to pay postage still remained a consideration in 1840, as a penny stamp cost approximately the same as a loaf large enough to feed a whole family. Coffee stalls in London in 1842 sold ham sandwiches, baked potatoes, and slices of cake or bread and butter for no more than 2d, and a steaming mug of coffee, tea, or cocoa cost 1d. A city clerk might purchase an ample lunch at a London chophouse for 1s 6d. The rent for a model flat in London was 4s a week in 1842, more than most working men could afford (Bentley 102). On the other hand, in 1844, a professional such as a middle-class bank clerk typically allotted 25 GBP (Great Britain Pound) a year for rent, 2s 6d per week for beer, and 6d a week for eggs.[30] Although I offer these figures to put readers in touch with the economic realities of Victorian times at the beginning of postal reform, clearly the price of a penny to post a letter made communication affordable and put the Post Office in reach of the masses eager to remain connected.

Staying connected also informs the contents of a widely circulated petition for Uniform Penny Postage that the Mercantile Committee on Postage produced in black and white and in color, as well as in small and large formats, and regularly printed in *The Post Circular*.[31] The petition's opening three lines (under a lengthy salutation) lure the reader with pre-reform scenarios of separation: "MOTHERS AND FATHERS that wish to hear from their absent children! / FRIENDS who are parted, that wish to write to each other! / EMIGRANTS that do not forget their native homes!" Words in capital letters and bold print cumulatively carry knowledge of the widespread longing experienced by those mourning loved ones they left behind. Also printed in bold is the motto, "THIS IS NO QUESTION OF PARTY POLITICS!"—one of the key axioms of the postage reform movement that resonates in Hill's pamphlet and in articles and messages in *The Post Circular*, such as this one: "Postal Reform is not a question of politics, but of the pocket, the home, the heart: Tory, Whig, Radical, and even 'Precursor,' may unite for 'a long pull, a strong pull, and a pull altogether."[32] That the petition urges "every one in the Kingdom sign a Petition with his name or his mark!" suggests literacy was on the rise but not widespread in the 1830s. In fact, consistent in the reform literature is a belief that a reduction in postage would motivate the illiterate to gain literacy to take advantage of cheap postage and stay connected with loved ones.

A large version of the placard published March 28, 1839, in issue 10 of *The Post Circular* has a brilliant orange border surrounding green and orange type and even comes with directions on how to display it. The editors call attention to "a handsome placard inside the paper. When contents of the paper have been digested, we trust this placard will be exhibited in the market-place, public rooms, or some shop-window, in a good thoroughfare; and when it has served the turn of one town or village, the Post-office will have the honour of conveying it, gratis, to serve the same good end in another spot, if the possessor will but take the little trouble of directing it to some friend" (51).[33] Displayed in shop windows, marketplaces, and other public places, passed from one Victorian to another, this widely circulated placard reached out to farmers, merchants, and tradesmen who might benefit from cheap postage, to mechanics and laborers who might use the post to learn about work opportunities, and to parents separated from their absent children.

Although Ashurst titled his pamphlet *Facts and Reasons in Support of Mr. Rowland Hill's Plan for a Universal Penny Postage*, he, too, relied on emotional appeal in his arguments:

> If a law were passed forbidding parents to speak to their children, till they had paid sixpence to government for permission, the wickedness would be so palpable, that there would be an end to the tax, in that form of exaction, in twenty-four hours. Yet what difference is there in principle when parents are prohibited from writing to their children, and children to their parents, nay, when ALL who are beyond verbal reach of each other, are prevented from communicating their wants, their sympathies, their anxieties, and desires, unless they pay that amount of tax under the name of postage. (1)

In this scenario, high postage becomes an affective dilemma, a tax on parental affection, a "wickedness" that causes anxiety among "ALL." The capitalization of "ALL" makes typographically omnipresent the pre-reform hardship of those who merely want to stay connected to absent loved ones.

Here and throughout his ninety-two-page pamphlet, Ashurst skillfully maintains his affective rhetoric, using terms of coercion, such as "prevent" and "prohibit," to convey how poor families suffer "under the name of postage." In one of Ashurst's many examples, the father of a young man from the north of England, who had written to his poor father of his safe arrival in a new country, admitted that he had no funds to accept more letters from his son, even though this one brought him great joy. Ashurst generalizes that this plight, which affected 50,000 Irish laborers in Liverpool and the same number in Manchester, amounted to "a sentence of transportation" (66). He maintains that "Unless the social and domestic affections exist amongst the poor, the world to them is a blank":

> Every poor man's child is obliged to go forth from home into servitude or labour of some kind, and this is right; but from the time the child leaves home, the postage-tax works a sentence of banishment upon it from its parents and kindred; and let it be remembered, that this is an act of the government; not merely negative, that is, omitting to do that for the people which the people could not do for themselves, but it is a positive infliction of evil, for it prohibits the people from doing that which they could have done for themselves, for a cost less than that which it is now proposed to give to government. (76)

In Ashurst's document, high postage is not merely a cause of separation but a permanent verdict of excommunication. Ashurst does not question the larger social conditions that required the children of the poor to leave home and often emigrate for employment. Instead, punctuating his rhetoric with parallelism and repetition to make a memorable point on behalf of the poor, he places blame on the Post Office for economically disenfranchising those whose "blank" and monotonous lives would be relieved by something as simple as an exchange of letters with loved ones. In other words, the unreformed Post Office hinders those who wish to help themselves.

Arguably the most woeful propaganda story of separation is "ONLY A POSTAGE. [A TALE ILLUSTRATIVE OF THE EFFECTS OF HIGH POSTAGES.]" First printed in the *Brighton Herald*, it appeared in issue 12 of *The Post Circular* (Tuesday, April 30, 1839). In this story, composed of five sections, the outcome of high postage is death. The tale begins melodramatically: "It was a sad day when Rose Maydew left her father's cottage. There were tears on the cheek of her mother, and a cloud on the old man's brow, for though they both strove to look cheerful, they could not disguise their grief, which was too strong to be put aside" (60). Like many country girls from large families, Rose enters domestic service in London, leaving behind eight brothers and sisters and loving parents, who urge her to be good and to write, especially in times of trouble: "'thou wilt find none in the world who will counsel and guide thee like thy parents'" (60). Initially, Rose sends happy letters home from London, and her parents possess the funds to accept them, but in the second part of the story, Rose's father experiences hardship, and his income drops to 6s 6d a week, barely enough to feed the ten family members remaining at home. When Rose's next letter arrives, Mrs. Maydew cannot pay the ninepence to receive it, because she needs the money to feed her other children. The letter waits at the shop unclaimed, and when no payment comes at the end of a week, the postmaster returns it to London.

The third part of the tale treats the consequences of that fateful, returned letter. Rose, deprived of the parental guidance and strength that letters might have imparted, is now a "fallen" woman: "Young and inexperienced, was it wonderful that she should fall—that she should have been allured in wiles which her innocence dreamt not existed,—that she should have learnt only her error when redemption was too late" (60). Rose confesses her sin in a letter to her parents, who the author tells us are "stern in their ideas of virtue" (60). She begs their forgiveness and anxiously awaits it by post. As the week passes without word from her parents, Rose thinks "to herself that death were preferable to such a degraded state of existence" (60).

The fourth section of the story turns our attention away from suicidal Rose to the Maydews, who resolve to "'go without a meal or two'" to pay for that selfsame letter already sent back to London unpaid. Here the anonymous author makes a pitch for Uniform Penny Postage: Rose's mother proclaims, "'postages are all so dear—suppose they were only a penny, now what a thing it would be for us poor people. . . . I should like to write to her every day'" (60). Immediately following her pronouncement, a postman brings the Maydews another missive posted in London, this time in an unknown handwriting, at the sight of which Mrs. Maydew "whose heart grew sick . . . sunk senseless on the ground" (60). The letter, from a London police officer, tells of a young woman found drowned, the only clue to her identity being the letter, now enclosed, and penned by Rose. Believing herself disowned by her parents, Rose in this letter begs God to forgive her for her sins. At this point in the melodrama, we plainly see that the fateful letter the Maydews could not afford to accept in the second part of the tale is, in fact, the very confession that Rose sent home in hope of forgiveness. The tale concludes, unsurprisingly, with the Maydews' observation that "'if we had a penny postage, . . . then this would never have happened'" (60).

A critical reader might wonder how the Maydews have funds to accept the policeman's letter—especially as it contains an enclosure and so likely incurred double charge (there is no mention it was prepaid). But logic is not the strength of this story. Pathos drives the pre-reform hardship tale. Different from other postal reform stories, this one, laden with sentimental despair, reads like a Victorian cautionary tale. In its finality and dire outcome, this narrative also recalls propaganda from the heated nineteenth-century debate over women's reading: antifiction critics warned young women not to read romance and sensation fiction for fear they would be led morally astray. An 1855 article published in the *Wesleyan-Methodist Magazine*, "What Is the Harm of Novel-Reading," follows a young woman who becomes hooked on rubbishy novels, loses her virtue, and passes "into eternity without hope, in what might have been the very bloom of her days, leaving behind her two unhappy infants, to perpetuate her shame" (78). Sensation fiction was considered a controlled substance as addictive as opium. The culprit of "ONLY A POSTAGE," by contrast, is not a perceived vice, but the government-controlled Post Office that taxes communication.

Rose Maydew experiences two deaths—the death of her virtue and her literal death—and this tale of pre-reform tragedy places both deaths at the door of the Post Office, an institutional Grim Reaper. Had Rose benefited from more frequent communication with her parents, would she have erred while in service in London? Alas, "From the expense attendant on a letter, her communication with home had been limited, and little opportunity had been offered her to receive that good counsel which cannot be too often repeated" (60). Further, the suicide letter reveals that Rose considered herself "disowned by her parents, on whose good name she had brought down shame" (60). Had she received forgiveness from her stern and virtuous parents, who simply could not afford to accept her letter, would she have refrained from taking the final desperate act of "self-murder," a Victorian term for suicide?

"ONLY A POSTAGE" appeared in an age when a dichotomy of two classes of women existed—the virtuous and the fallen—as George Watt articulates in his introduction to *The Fallen Woman in the Nineteenth-Century English Novel*. An element of Victorian society did not distinguish between a prostitute and a virtuous woman who made one mistake. The loss of Rose's virtue might well be the more significant of her two deaths to a nineteenth-century reader. Dickens illustrates this very point in *David Copperfield* (1850) through his chapter titles and David's reflective commentary on Emily Peggotty's fall. Chapter 30, "A Loss," details the death of Clara Peggotty's husband, Barkis, but chapter 31, "A Greater Loss," chronicles Emily's fall and resulting disgrace. Foreshadowing the death of Emily's virtue twenty-eight chapters earlier, David speculates that Emily's near death by drowning as a child "would have been better for little Em'ly" than her actual fate of becoming a fallen woman (39). Moreover, those who sinned sexually regularly faced banishment or death (at least in Victorian fiction). Dickens punishes his fallen Emily by sending her to Australia. George Eliot allows her fallen Hetty Sorel of *Adam Bede* (1859) to escape the gallows for the infanticide of her illegitimate child, but Hetty dies during transportation after suffering mightily. Elizabeth Gaskell, who granted her fallen heroine Ruth Hilton of *Ruth* (1853) a second chance, has Ruth pay the ultimate price, although she dies a Good Samaritan. Had high postage robbed Rose Maydew only of her virtue and not led her to commit self-murder, we can imagine she would have lived out her life in seclusion like Emily Peggotty and another of her fallen sisters, Gaskell's Lizzie of "Lizzie Leigh" (1850), who ends her days in near isolation in the English countryside.

Imagined or metaphoric deaths resonate in other pre-reform stories of separation. In *The History of England*, Martineau compares the struggles of crusaders setting off on long voyages to "a separation almost like a death": "We look back now with a sort of amazed compassion to the old crusading times, when warrior-husbands and their wives, grey-headed parents and their brave sons, parted with the knowledge that it must be months or years before they would even hear of one another's existence" (2: 426, 425). Martineau strategically aligns crusading times with 1830s England by claiming, "till a dozen years ago, it did not occur to many of us how like this was the fate of the largest classes in our own country" (2: 425). Until the postal reform of 1840, "hundreds of thousands of apprentices, of shopmen, of governesses, of domestic servants, were cut off from family relations as if seas or deserts lay between them and home" (2: 426). The Penny Post, by contrast, saved the virtuous from moral peril and helped "to throw down old barriers" as previously impenetrable as a vast raging ocean or a windswept desert (2: 426).[34]

MORALITY, LITERACY, AND NO REVOLT

Postal reform propaganda quickly aligned a reformed postal service not only with "the interchange of domestic affections" but with improved morality. In fact, those praising the early outcomes of postal reform between 1840 and 1842 suggest cheap postage "almost entirely prevented breaches of the law" (Lewins 198). Just three years after passage of the Penny Post, Harriet Martineau, in her May 15, 1843, letter to Thomas Wilde, MP, enumerated the benefits that had so far accrued to postal reform, along with those yet to come. It had turned idleness to action, comforted "rising" industrious young men, and cheered the sick. Anxious children, rich in morals but poor in funds, could dutifully send a "daily bulletin" when "families must remain asunder," heartening the "infirm father, the blind mother, whose pleasures are becoming fewer and fewer" (46, 47). With prepaid postage only a penny, expense was "no longer the irritating hindrance of speech, the infliction which makes the listening parent deaf, and the full-hearted daughter dumb" (45). Freed from such "infliction," one's daughters, Martineau retrospectively argued, would readily spill out their woes on paper; likewise, "the moral dangers of a young man's entrance upon life" were "incalculably lessened," as he, too, could "pour out his mind" to family and friends (45). Cheap postage, in Martineau's view, benefited Britain, at home and abroad, in the "rectitude and purity of its rising citizens": "that it encourages the enterprising, rouses the indolent, and, in short, brings all the best influences of the old life to bear upon the new, it is clear that the State must be better served in proportion to the improved power and comfort of the rising race of men" (45).

As Martineau's letter to Wilde reveals, the stories that agitate for postal reform and retrospectively praise its enactment turned the Penny Post into a measure to preserve innocence and upright behavior, spread literacy, and ensure widespread benevolence. Pre-reform tales predict that mothers and their daughters will sleep better, knowing they have unburdened their hearts. Similarly, soldiers with improved behavior will gladly accept franks for letters from their commanding officers. Ashurst's pamphlet features the report of a Lieutenant Ellis of the Royal Navy to the Mercantile Committee on Postage that his sailors are desirous of communication: those who can write act as scribes for those who are illiterate, with the result that "'bags and bags of letters go away'" (70). A story by Captain John Bentham of the 52nd regiment, presented as testimony to the Parliamentary Select Committee on Postage, found its way into *The Post Circular*, Ashurst's 1838 pamphlet, and an 1840 article in the *Edinburgh Review*, gaining force with each retelling. Bentham reports in the latter that his soldiers wrote seven and a half letters yearly and "appeared to value the privilege most highly—that an anxiety to write their own letters, led them zealously to profit by the regimental schools—and that the acquirement of the art of writing conduced to their respectability and good conduct."[35] In Ashurst's pamphlet, Bentham is given out as stating that soldiers who corresponded most with their families were "well-behaved men in a military point of view" (70). That these particular soldiers managed to write in army barracks led Ashurst to conjecture that the letter writing of those living in conditions more conducive to writing would increase "fifteen fold" (70) if cheap postage were passed. Issue 7 of the *The Post Circular* (May 11, 1838) includes this same story and notes Bentham's opinion that many soldiers "learn to write in the prospect of promotion, but I am very aware that it is considered by them a matter of importance to be able to write their own letters, on account of the privacy and the credit of it" (38).

Conjecture about an emerging class of well-behaved, literate, letter-writing sailors and soldiers quickly became fact. In her retrospective justification of postal reform, Martineau asserts the "well-known fact, that in regiments where the commanding officer was kind and courteous about franking letters for the privates, and encouraged them to write as often as they pleased, the soldiers were more sober and manly, more virtuous and domestic in their affections, than where difficulty was made by the indolence or stiffness of the franking officer" (*History* 2: 426). We find evidence of this view in *Mansfield Park* (1814), where the narrator commends William for his "excellence as a correspondent" (69), writing long missives to his beloved sister Fanny Price while serving in the King's service at sea (as two of Austen's own brothers did).

Would all members of the British armed services rise to the occasion to write long letters? Croker in his 1839 antireform article published in the *Quarterly Review* includes a story told by the Duke of Wellington about a regiment in Scotland in which soldiers did not write more letters when they had access to penny postage. Despite their location in a region known for family sentiment and education, the soldiers scarcely used the letter-writing privilege. In 1838, over a period of six or seven months, 700 men wrote a scant 63–64 letters (528–29). Even if Croker included this story to call into question Captain Bentham's report that his soldiers used the penny privilege to each write seven and a half letters a year (as widely circulated in postal reform materials), Croker recognized the importance of using stories to effect. Despite his antireform bias, Croker is almost certainly correct that reformers were prone to use stories to "exaggerate the importance" of postal reform as a means to "improve the education, and to promote the domestic morals of the people" (530).

More critical than the extent to which the penny rate increased the number of letters posted is to what degree householders around 1840 could read the letters that soldiers or sailors sent home. Literacy in the nineteenth century is hard to ascertain. Because the only criterion for literacy used in the Victorian census was the ability to sign a marriage register, there is no way of knowing how many ostensibly literate individuals could actually read or write anything other than their own names or how many illiterate older men and women were living alongside a rising generation of more literate citizens. In any case, census figures show a gradual rise in literacy. The first nationwide report on literacy in nineteenth-century England, published in 1840, covers the year ending on June 30, 1839, and notes that 67 percent of males and 51 percent of females were literate. The same census conducted in 1851 indicates that 69.3 percent of males and 54.8 percent of females in the whole nation were literate. Following passage of the 1870 Forster Act, a landmark legislation that mandated a national system of education, the literacy rate for males and females increased more dramatically: by 1900, 97.2 percent of males and 96.8 percent of females in England and Wales were considered literate.[36] Richard Altick singles out the reduction in cost of printed matter and the Penny Post as key to Victorian literacy: "the gradual cheapening of printed matter attractive to the common reader; and (never to be underestimated) the introduction of the penny post in 1840, which gave an immense impetus to personal written communication—these together were responsible for the growth of a literate population outside the classroom" (172).

Postal reform stories likewise linked cheap postage with literacy. Issue 14 of *The Post Circular* (June 28, 1839) reports the testimony of a Mr. Thomas Hopkins, a witness to the Parliamentary Select Committee on Postage: "He did not know any indirect means of promoting the spread of education, likely to be so effectual as leading people to the practice of writing letters. It taught them to think; . . . The very effort to write a letter must improve the mind" (64). Mr. Alderman Kershaw, whose testimonial appears in this same issue, argued that penny postage "would be a stimulus for those who at present scarcely knew how to write, to learn to do so" (64). Hill presents similar evidence from the Parliamentary Select Committee on Postage in his memoir, noting that those who did learn to write in school could not previously afford to exercise the privilege: "The consequence of the high rates, in preventing the working-classes from having intercourse by letter, is, that those who learned at school to write a copy have lost their ability to do so" (1: 309).

Why did so many postal reformers focus on literacy as an argument for the Penny Post? A more literate working class might arguably be more accessible to rational argument and therefore less likely to revolt. Among their political subtexts, postal reform stories and propaganda evince the potent fear of revolution that characterized nineteenth-century England. The same year that Hill published his Post Office reform pamphlet, Thomas Carlyle's *French Revolution* (1837) appeared in book form. Fear of revolution was very much a part of the early to mid-nineteenth-century British consciousness. Long after the defeat of Napoleon, the British still feared invasion by France. Moreover, as historian A. N. Wilson points out, the British regarded France as "the very object lesson of what could happen if a society imploded" (17).

Much was undemocratic about British government in the early nineteenth century. Harsh working conditions, rampant child labor, workhouses (which Dickens targets in *Oliver Twist*), a huge gap between the rich and the poor, and grinding poverty all fueled economic arguments for postal reform. Chartism was growing in the late 1830s, resulting in the People's Charter and National Petition of 1838, an attempt to demand political representation for the disadvantaged poor. Despite efforts for peaceful activism, the Chartist movement, which Wilson describes as a "collectivist-socialist trumpet" (45), gave way to violent blasts: riots and angry mobs fed Whig government fears that violent revolution was imminent. Strikes in Britain also fed fears of uprising and revolution. Gaskell aptly illustrates labor tensions between masters and men and the British preoccupation with home control in *Mary Barton* (1848). Set in the lean years around 1840, the novel follows the rise and defeat of the Chartist movement through John Barton, a Chartist representative from Manchester. *North and South* (1855) reads more squarely as an industrial novel than does *Mary Barton*. In *North and South*, Gaskell paints poignant images of starving workers who are misinformed and strike for wages that masters cannot afford to pay. At the peak of their misery, angry mill workers storm the factory of a decent master, John Thornton, to protest his desperate measure of importing Irish hands to complete a shipment of work that is overdue. The workers become a "troop of animals," then "an angry sea of men," flinging their heavy wooden clogs at the mill owner whom they perceive as "their enemy" (162).

No one addressed the role of cheap postage in circumventing revolution more boldly than Ashurst, who argued that reduction in postage would lead to improved labor relations and prevent strikes between masters and men. Although he doesn't present a strike in such chilling terms as Gaskell, Ashurst spins a tale of how strikes occur and how they can be prevented: "disputes do arise, from ignorance of facts" (91). High postage shuts out workers from evidence that might show them their opinions are based on "erroneous statements of fact" (91), and with "cheap postage, . . . the error as to facts would not have existed, and the strikes would not have resulted" (92). Cheap postage, in turn, would lead to a "stream of facts . . . current among the masses" (92), much correspondence, happy workers, and, in essence, home control.

Members of Parliament concurred, as evidenced in a third report the Parliamentary Select Committee on Postage issued in August 1838: high postage kept workers "ignorant of the state of wages in different parts of our country, so they do not know where labour is in demand. This state of ignorance has a tendency to promote strikes and trade unions among them."[37] Martineau confides in a letter to an American friend that penny postage may be the solution to avoiding revolution, much feared in Britain in the lean years around 1840: "I question whether there will be now time left for the working of beneficent measures to save us from violent revolution, but if there be, none will work better than this."[38] Writing from retrospection, Elizabeth Barrett Browning calls postal reform a "successful revolution" in a letter to an American friend: "I recommend you our penny postage as the most successful revolution since the 'glorious three days' of Paris" (142). Browning here refers to the July 1830 revolution, commonly known as Three Glorious Days, which instituted a constitutional monarchy in France. Uniform Penny Postage brought a "social change" equivalent to a revolution in a society already undergoing social, political, and economic change—hence the subtitle of this book. As historian Howard Robinson explains, "The change was, in truth, a revolution, not a political one such as that of 1830 in France, but a social change that fittingly followed British political revolution wrought by the Great Reform Bill" (302). Thus postal reform was both revolutionary and antirevolutionary at the same time: it ultimately appeased the masses, quelled fears of revolution, and maintained the status quo.

POSTAL BLESSINGS

With cheap postage, reformers predicted, England would become a safer, more moral, and a more blessed nation. Not surprisingly, the word "blessing" frequently appears in narratives promoting postal reform. A Glasgow banker reported to the Mercantile Committee on Postage that if the post can be an entitlement for the poor, not just a luxury of the rich, letters will promote "philanthropy and civilization" and "the better feelings and tastes that would ensue could not fail to prove an inestimable blessing."[39] Issue 14 of *The Post Circular* (June 28, 1839) reports that "Petitions praying for a uniform penny rate of postage were presented by several noble lords, and by the Duke of Richmond" (61) to Parliament. It was routine to write a petition in the form of a prayer, a term that had two meanings in the nineteenth century: a religious request and a polite civil request. Interestingly, the reminder at the bottom of the widely circulated petition that appeared in *The Post Circular* and as part of an appendix to Henry Cole's postal reform skit (also known as "Queen Victoria and the Uniform Penny Postage—A Scene at Windsor Castle") includes the following passage after the word "pray": "Remember the 4,000 petitions [that] last year emancipated the slaves. Let there be the same number this year to emancipate the POSTAGE" (Fryer and Akerman 745). These lines set the idea of praying in a religious and civil context simultaneously. The petition, which invokes ideas of enslavement and liberation, powerfully envisions the high-priced British postage system in chains, waiting for emancipation.

This analogy seems all the more vivid in context of 1839. The antislavery movement was very much part of the collective British consciousness of the 1830s. On August 1, 1834, the British freed all slaves throughout the British Empire. The British also advocated economic and moral emancipation that they believed would accompany cheap postage: no more pawning or starving to pay the post; no more youth going astray due to a lack of guidance or unemployment—"it was obvious that information would be flying about as to where work could be had" (*The Post Circular* 14: 63). From these postal reform materials, cheap postage emerges as an emissary of morality, leading to many blessings and social improvements: manly and sober soldiers; virtuous domestic servants; parents and children unburdened of their cares; emigrants heartened by frequent messages of mother love; well-informed and conscientious workers.[40]

Some postal reformers called the Penny Post a "godsend" and "birthright,"[41] as well as a "blessing." The opening page of issue 15 of *The Post Circular* (published October 11, 1839, after cheap postage was passed) includes the banner line, in capitalized and boldfaced letters—"NATIONAL TRIBUTE TO MR. ROWLAND HILL"—to praise "the merits of Mr. Hill's invention," along with testimonials of "his indefatigable exertions for the public good" (34, 35). In *Her Majesty's Mails* (1864), Lewins reprints period testimony that uses the word "blessing" to characterize Hill's success in legislating cheap postage as a "public good." In *Notes of a Traveller* (1842), Scottish travel writer Samuel Laing proclaims, "'This measure will be the great historical distinction of the reign of Victoria,'" adding "'Every mother in the kingdom who has children earning their bread at a distance, lays her head on the pillow at night with a feeling of gratitude for this blessing.'"[42]

The Victorian public revered Rowland Hill as the one who bestowed "The blessings which have thus accrued [and] are too vast for estimate" (Martineau, *History* 2: 431). In her memorable 1843 letter to Sir Thomas Wilde, MP, Martineau transforms Rowland Hill into a wise parent, physician, minister, and ruler, who stands for all the blessings he has conferred on the British nation:

The personal obligations of every one of us are heavy, but when we think of the amount of blessing he has conferred on the morals and affections of a whole people, of the number of innocent persons and sufferers cheered by the knowledge spread abroad and human happiness promoted by his single hand, we are led to question whether any one member of society ever before discharged so much of the functions at once of the pulpit, the press, the parent, the physician, and the ruler—ever in so short a time benefited his nation so vastly, or secured so unlimited a boon to the subjects of an empire; and when other nations shall have adopted his reforms, there may be an extension even of this praise. (48)

Even *Punch*, on the occasion of Hill's death on August 27, 1879, left satire aside to wax emotional about the "Originator of Cheap Postage" in a lengthy seventeen-stanza poem, "In Memoriam," that lauded his visionary accomplishments and "far-seeing fighting with the blind":

> Breaking the barriers that, of different height
> For rich and poor, were barriers still for all,
> Till "out of mind" was one with "out of sight,"
> And parted souls oft parted past recall;
>
> Freeing from tax unwise the interchange
> Of distant mind with mind and mart with mart;
> Releasing thought from bars that clipped its range;
> Lightening a load felt most i' the weakest part.[43]

Hill's plan not only bridged geographical distances that had left the poor "cut off from family relations as if seas or deserts lay between them and home" (Martineau, *History* 2: 426); in the words of "In Memoriam," the Penny Post broke "through life's web dark and wide" and "barriers" of time and space, laying the foundation for modern day telecommunications.

POSTAL UTOPIA?

Postal reformers projected an ideal world, as well as a blessed one. As a result of Uniform Penny Postage, the British would have a greater volume of legally carried mail (and thus, eventually, a higher revenue), a morally upstanding nation, and much more: there would be a variety of trade circulars (advertisements), mail order catalogues, more insurance benefits, well-informed investors, better written novels, greater philanthropy, fewer epidemics, and important medical discoveries. Some claims make more sense than others. Commerce would naturally increase, because insurance companies could afford to make more inquiries for their clients, and stock companies could communicate freely and affordably with their shareholders. Charitable societies would benefit because they could afford to communicate directly with potential benefactors, and scientists and doctors would have ready access to facts and information to advance their research and benefit the lives of their patients.[44]

Some amazing testimonials about the outcomes of the Penny Post are almost certainly exaggerated. New postage stimulated trade, according to Charles Knight (who spearheaded the Society for the Diffusion of Useful Knowledge); but were country booksellers in constant communication with London houses? Did literary societies and educational establishments, including night schools, seemingly spring up overnight as Lewins claims in *Her Majesty's Mails* (199)? The secretary to the Parker Society, founded to reprint ecclesiastical literature, claimed the organization "could never have come into existence but for the penny postage" (Lewins 199). Moreover, the benefits seemed unbounded. For example, books would theoretically be better written under cheap postage, reformers claimed, because authors would not have to beg for franks to pay to receive the proofs that publishers sent through the post. Both Lewins and Martineau recount an anecdote about eighteenth-century poet William Cowper, who complained that he had to spend much of his precious writing time obtaining franks for his manuscripts and page proofs, in what Lewins calls the "'Prerowlandian days'" (198). According to Martineau, the success of Cowper's edition of Homer was regrettably dependent on somebody else's "good offices!" (*History* 2: 426).

Some claims of the benefits postal reform brought about are well grounded. The letter-writing revolution sparked other revolutionary events, notably the dismantling of the Corn Laws. Designed to protect the crops and profits of wealthy British landowners, the Corn Laws imposed hefty taxes on less expensive, imported grain. While the higher price of corn did not raise the wages of laborers, it did raise the cost of a loaf of bread, which, prior to reform, could not be spared to pay for postage. The Anti–Corn Law League, an organized labor movement, created a mini revolution, arguably an echo of the Victorian revolution in letter writing. Smyth reprints the rumor that when postal reform passed in the House of Lords, "Cobden is said to have exclaimed: 'There go the Corn Laws!'" (141). In 1843, Richard Cobden, the radical leader of the Anti–Corn Law League, wrote Hill a letter calling the reformed Post Office "a terrible engine for upsetting monopoly and corruption: witness our League operations, the *spawn of your penny postage!*" (Hill and Hill 1: 478). In 1843, Cobden circulated 40,000 Anti–Corn Law League pamphlets and "gave it as his opinion, that their objects were achieved *two years earlier* than otherwise would have been the case, owing to the introduction of cheap postage" (Lewins 200).

Most postal historians concur that though fears surrounding increase in foreign exportation of grain proved to be exaggerated, the abolishment of import tariffs helped to move the repeal of the Corn Laws and stimulated the rise of free trade (Bentley 110). The allegedly glowing benefits to science attributed to cheap postage are probably based more in the Victorian imagination than in actuality. Ashurst predicted in 1838 that "To open the post-office is to bring forth the stream of intellect, . . . [which] will be to science what light and air are to vegetation" (53). In *History of England*, Martineau applauds the "curious specimens passing between men of science" following penny postage (2: 426). In his memoir, Rowland Hill even advances that the Penny Post led to a decline in smallpox: "Who would now divine that high rates of postage could have any relation to the prevalence of small-pox?" (1: 305). Prior to postal reform, rural doctors, Hill laments, "and others in the country do not apply for lymph, in the degree they otherwise would do, to the institutions formed in London for the spread of vaccination, for fear of postage" (1: 305). Clearly, the early nineteenth-century medical system suffered under high postage. One need only think of Eliot's harsh critique of antiquated country medical practices in *Middlemarch* (1872), set in the early 1830s prior to both the Reform Bill and the Penny Post. But it may well be overstating the case to claim that a dreaded disease grew to epidemic proportions in early nineteenth-century Britain because physicians feared amassing high postal charges.

Ashurst concurs that high postage hindered science and the humanities: "the present rates of postage shut up the sources of discovery in science and the arts" (1). Worse, "It prevents men of science from collecting the facts from those who principally possess them—the operatives and labouring men of the country; the mine of facts which is now locked-up in *them*, cannot be brought forth; the results of past, and the seed of future scientific, mechanical, and moral fruit is wholly unproductive" (2). Prophesying new vaccinations and cures from frequent communication by post, postal reformers wrapped science in a utopian vision of Britain, projecting that a cheap postage would allow medical research to become wholly *productive* and bear fruit. The same benefits were said to accrue to agricultural science. Lewins prints testimony from Professor Henslow of Suffolk, who certifies: "'To the importance of penny postage to those who cultivate science, I can bear most unequivocal testimony, as I am continually receiving and transmitting a variety of specimens by post. Among them, you may laugh to hear that I have received three living carnivorous slugs, which arrived safely in a pill-box'" (200).

Across a wide range of documentary resources, and even in fiction, postal reformers essentially reconstructed the necessity for postal reform and celebrated its achievement. Cheap postage became an integral part of an exciting new world of railways, steamships, and telegraphs, with its beneficiaries lauding much more than the safe passage of a species of terrestrial mollusk still widely found in central England. Benjamin Disraeli includes the reformed Post Office as part of the utopian world he envisions in his novel *Endymion* (1880): "It is difficult for us who live in an age of railroads, telegraphs, penny posts, and penny newspapers, to realize how uneventful, how limited in thought and feeling, as well as in incident, was the life of an English family of retired habits and limited means only forty years ago" (48). Maria Edgeworth, author of *Moral Tales for Young People* (1805) and *Practical Education* (1798), wrote to Hill in 1840: "I truly think that the British nation, the united empire, owes you millions of thanks for the improvements that have been made in social intercourse—in all the intercourse of human creatures for pleasure or business, affection or profit; including the profits of literature and science—foreign and domestic" (Hill and Hill 1: 421). Lauding postal reform at the occasion of its golden jubilee, Pearson Hill recalls how, before 1840, poor cottagers had to choose between buying a loaf of bread for their starving children or paying for a letter from an absent child. "In these days," he continues, "when postal facilities have so enormously extended, and cheap and rapid communication by letter has become so completely a part of our every-day life, like the air we breathe or the water we drink, few persons ever trouble themselves to think how it would be possible to exist without them" (2). As this touching anecdote conveys, the reformed Post Office came to connote the sustenance of life itself.

CLEVER HENRY COLE

Henry Cole, a key proponent of postal reform, engineered several clever schemes to show the absurdities of postal rates and to campaign for postal reform. A fine piece of propaganda, Cole's skit (sometimes called a "play" or a "playlet") stands as a material memory of Victorian frustrations related to high postage and reveals how reformist attitudes were cleverly engendered and spread. In *Fifty Years of Public Work* (1884), Cole explains how he showed the absurdities of pre-reform postal charges by crafting two types of letters. The first, a large sheet, measured 35 × 23 inches and weighed under one ounce. The second—described in Hill's memoir as a "letter for Lilliput" (1: 295)—measured 4 × 2½ inches and was comprised of two thin sheets, weighing only seven grains total. Cole sent fifty large and fifty tiny letters to a clerk with a good sense of humor who worked at the Charing Cross Post Office. Candling revealed that the large letter was a single sheet, and the clerk marked it single rate, although Cole notes that had the letter gotten wet, the post office would have charged fourfold. Assessing the second letter, "the Postal Official turned crimson," according to Cole, "became furious, and cursed a little, but he could not help marking it *double* postage. Roars of laughter came from the crowd" (*Fifty Years* 1: 45). Laughter continued, Cole recounts, as the postal official repeated the process for each of the 100 letters, and "No less amusement was produced in the House of Commons when Mr. Wallace exhibited the big and little letters" (1: 45). Cole appended to his examples a caption that reads: "Specimen of Postage Charges in 1839. *To be Preserved among the Curiosities of any Museum, &c.*" (Muir 58).[45] As historian Frank Staff concludes, "This sort of propaganda had a telling effect, and together with cartoons, posters, and placards, displayed in shop windows, Henry Cole's campaign was highly successful" (81).

The same clever reformer who used comparative letter size to show the folly of postal rates to members of Parliament also keenly recognized that fiction could power reform of the postal service. A quintessential example of period propaganda is Cole's 1838 playlet, "A Report of an Imaginary Scene at Windsor Castle Respecting the Uniform Penny Postage," widely circulated from 1838 to 1840. More an object of material culture than literature per se, it carries political meaning, revealing how Cole attempted to script Queen Victoria's approval of Uniform Penny Postage years before it actually came to pass. Cole cast major players of the British government of the 1830s—Lord Melbourne, then currently prime minister; Lord Lichfield, postmaster general; Rowland Hill; and the newly crowned Queen Victoria. Cole also included as minor players Lord Lowther, member of the Parliamentary Select Committee on Postage; Lord Ashburton, a wealthy conservative in favor of postal reform; and Mr. Francis Baring, the chancellor of the exchequer (in the skit, Queen Victoria bemoans Baring's illegal posting activities). Making a strategically calculated political pitch for postal reform, Cole included and footnoted quotations from Lord Lichfield's actual speeches presented to the House of Lords up to mid-December, 1837, leading Fryer and Akerman to conjecture that Cole wrote the skit and Henry Hooper printed it in 1838.[46]

From here, Cole moved into invention. Queen Victoria rivals Rowland Hill in her understanding of the problems of high postage. According to the stage directions, she is in "deep study" of Rowland Hill's pamphlet on postal reform.[47] Surrounding her are reports on postage, leaflets on French and American post offices, and copies of *The Post Circular*, one of the publications which, in turn, strategically circulated this skit, creating what we now call a "Quaker Oats effect." As keen as Victoria is about postal reform, Cole's bumbling prime minister admits to knowing only "something about it," to which Cole's royal mouthpiece sharply replies, "So I suppose has every one, from the Land's End to John O'Groat's house." Memorable also are the lines of Lord Lichfield, who tells Hill, "Of all the wild and visionary schemes which I have ever heard or read of, it is the most extravagant"—this, a direct quote from the *Mirror of Parliament* of June 15, 1837.[48] The Queen ignores Lichfield, and Lord Melbourne concurs: "My dear Lichfield, I fear the Queen has found you in a scrape." Following Lichfield's polite request, "With your Majesty's leave I will retire," Queen Victoria cleverly retorts to Lord Melbourne that Lord Lichfield should "retire" altogether from the Post Office. The prime minister replies in agreement: "he has not realized the fond hopes we cherished of him." At this point in the skit, Cole's Queen Victoria boldly declares, "It appears to me, my Lord, that the loss of Colonel Maberly to the Post-Office would be another great gain to the public." Clearly, Cole wanted to emancipate not only postage but the Post Office: in the play, Queen Victoria dismisses both officials who, in actuality, opposed Hill's plan.

Stressing home, heart, and virtue, Cole fills Victoria's dialogue with exaggeration and exclamation points to bemoan poor mothers running to pawnshops to pay for postage and "Every subject studying how to evade postage, without caring for the law!" Victoria supports Penny Postage, as it "appears to me likely to remove all these great evils." Speaking in an "emphatic tone," Queen Victoria makes postal reform a vote for educational and moral reform, commercial prosperity, and welfare for the poor: "I am sure it would confer a great boon to the poorer classes of my subjects, and would be the greatest benefit to religion, to morals, to general knowledge, and to trade—that uniformity and payment in advance would greatly simplify the Post-Office, and get rid of their troublesome accounts—that it would effectually put down the smuggling postman, and lead my people to obey and not disobey the law." Of course, British subjects could write petitions and addresses to the Queen free of postal charges, but Cole likely omitted that detail for effect. Here we see how Cole artfully employed his Queen to convey what he and his fellow postal reformers fervently hoped would happen in Britain with the coming of postal reform, and he lends insight into the social, economic, and political persuasions that motivated many to clamor for it. Postal reform would "put down" immorality, bring an end to the "smuggling postman," and curtail the lawlessness of British subjects of all social classes by promoting morality. In turn, the British public would rise up to "obey," and "the nation will owe you [Hill] a large debt of gratitude."

Queen Victoria did not dismiss her joint secretary of the General Post Office or her postmaster general as Cole's skit envisions. Following Sir Francis Freeling, William Maberly served in his secretarial post from 1836 to 1854, while Lichfield served in his postmaster general's post from 1835 to 1841, followed by Lord Lowther (1841–45). However, Queen Victoria supported postal reform, so in this respect an imagined proclamation in a skit preceded actual law. As Cole also predicted, the British people, in gratitude for Hill's Penny Post plan, granted him countless honors including knighthood, an honorary degree from Oxford, the designation of Freeman (from the city of London), and burial in Westminster Abbey.

In his memoir, Hill declares that the Queen was "graciously pleased (and here the words were no mere form) to abandon her privilege of franking, thus submitting her letters to the same rule as those of her humblest subject" (1: 388). I do not wish to suggest that Queen Victoria simply acted according to Cole's script. The Queen's journals reveal she did not readily relinquish her franking privileges, "'but Lord M. advised me as everybody gave it up, to do so also.'"[49] Early in her reign, Victoria was particularly open to influence from Lord Melbourne, who as prime minister reported matters to the Queen. As postal historian Douglas Muir notes, "Politically this was astute. . . . This decision was later portrayed as Victoria's enthusiastic endorsement of penny postage, and proved a popular action" (104). Smyth explains the situation this way: "the agitation in favour of the postal reform was in full movement, and in the midst of it the old king, William IV, died. His youthful successor was speedily deluged with petitions in favour of penny postage" (119).

In his biography of Queen Victoria, Stanley Weintraub makes clear that postal reform came to the fore just when King William IV's "youthful successor" was beginning to "establish her identity as sovereign": "Educating herself in the business of government was the Queen's highest priority" (101, 105). One of the first things Victoria did was to appoint a Select Committee on Postage, chaired by Robert Wallace, which she charged to look into the present condition of the post with a view to postal reduction. In the midst of dealing with troubles in Ireland, concerns in Canada, and a deadlock over the abolition of slavery in Jamaica, Queen Victoria impressively ushered in postal reform only three years into her reign, with a short transition of uniform 4d postage from December 5, 1839, until January 10, 1840, when 1d postage was extended nationwide.

Regardless of any influence Cole's skit may have had on Queen Victoria, we cannot underestimate the power the play had on the public and, potentially, on her ministers. As Martin Meisel notes in *Realizations: Narrative, Pictorial, and Theatrical Arts in the Nineteenth Century*, audiences of the period considered drama a mimetic art (52). To a nineteenth-century public, Cole's invention would have been perceived as imitative of real life, as domestic melodrama—represented across both textual and visual narrative genres—commonly brought real social issues to public notice. To this end, one need only think of the many domestic dramas of the period: Douglas Jerrold's play *The Rent Day* (1832), based on Sir David Wilkie's famous 1807 picture of the same title, or dramatizations of George Cruikshank's temperance series, *The Bottle* (1847), and its sequel, *The Drunkard's Children* (1848).

The opening scene of Queen Victoria exclaiming over endless postal reform materials mimics a tableau vivant, a staple of domestic melodrama. That some of Lichfield's dialogue is drawn from actual speeches likely made the play seem realistic. Cole included the royal insignia of the lion, unicorn, and British crown as a header on the printed skit, giving his playlet an authoritative look. Moreover, that the Queen calls Rowland Hill "the ingenious author of the Universal Penny Post Plan" (742) and sanctions reform, if only in a play, may have blurred the line between fiction and reality, suggesting that life could, indeed, imitate art. In his analysis of acting and action in Becky Sharp's impersonation of the murderess Clytemnestra in a theatrical scene in *Vanity Fair*, Meisel concludes, "The performer and the role have become one" (335). It is likely that for nineteenth-century audiences, a similar coalescence occurred between the real Queen Victoria and the character of Queen Victoria as an advocate for Uniform Penny Postage.

We also cannot minimize the power of fiction and newspapers in giving Cole's postal propaganda play widespread visibility. Fryer and Akerman estimate that Henry Hooper printed and distributed over 140,000 copies: 2,000 went to members of Parliament; 100,000 were sold or circulated across Britain; and 40,000 copies were bound into part 13 (April 1839) of Dickens's serial *Nicholas Nickleby*, the best-selling novel of 1839.[50] *Nicholas Nickleby* came out in nineteen monthly numbers (installment 19 was a double number). Each number included two illustrations by Hablot Knight Browne (also known as Phiz) and cost a shilling (except for the last number, which cost two shillings). Dickens launched the serial in April 1838, so by April 1839, *Nickleby* had a vast and steady following whose members eagerly read Cole's play along with their latest installment of Dickens.

Cole's choice of *Nicholas Nickleby* as a vehicle for postal reform seems ingenious. First, having already published *Sketches by Boz* in 1836 and *Oliver Twist* in 1838, Dickens had earned a reputation as a writer who championed the righting of social injustices and the remediation of conditions of London's poor. Dickens's fiction was enormously popular, suggesting a ready audience for Cole's play. Although Dickens did not record how he felt about including the skit in an installment of *Nickleby*, a remark published many years later in *Household Words* (August 1, 1857) suggests that Dickens was a supporter of postal reform. Recalling conflicts among members of the Parliamentary Select Committee on Postage, Rowland Hill, and the Circumlocution Office, Dickens notes, "'it invariably turned out that Mr. Rowland Hill was right in his facts, and that the "Circumlocution Office" was always wrong.'"[51]

The plot of *Nicholas Nickleby* also makes it a fitting vehicle for powering reform of the postal service. The death of Nicholas's father at the opening of the novel leaves our hero penniless, so Nicholas Nickleby, a naïve and, at times, violent but ultimately worthy hero, must scramble to find a way to support his mother and sister. Dickens takes a stab at greed, as well as the cruelties of education in his depiction of the brutal, one-eyed schoolmaster Wackford Squeers of Dotheboys Hall (under whom Nicholas serves). Nicholas goes to Dotheboys at the command of his uncle, Ralph Nickleby, the antagonist of the novel and a usurer who cares only about money. In fact, Ralph Nickleby's actions parallel those of Francis Freeling, secretary to the Post Office from 1787 until his death in 1836, known for crippling the poor through high postage. Freeling wrote the following just before he died: "'Cheap postage—what is this men are talking about? Can it be that all my life I have been in error?'"[52]

Dickens created in Nicholas Nickleby a hero who readily comes to the defense of the downtrodden—Nickleby beats Squeers in retaliation for his cruel treatment of the pathetic Smike, a perpetually ill cripple (who turns out to be Ralph Nickleby's son). If Nicholas Nickleby were a man and not a literary character, we can imagine that he, like his creator, would have supported postal reform, a measure designed to unburden an entire nation. Moreover, Dickens makes constant mention of letter writing in his novels, and *Nicholas Nickleby* is no exception. Dickens opens this novel with the arrival of a death notice and refers to letters in thirty-seven of the sixty-four chapters. In chapter 42, one of the chapters in part 13 into which Cole's skit was bound, Nicholas Nickleby even makes mention of writing a letter to John Browdie, a character originally from near Dotheboys Hall who helps Nicholas escape from Yorkshire following his altercation with Squeers and who, in turn, frees Smike from Squeers's cruel control. We can easily imagine that the struggling Nicholas Nickleby—as skilled a correspondent as any Dickensian hero—was himself in sore need of Hill's plan for a Universal Penny Post.

*　*　*

The Postage Duties Bill gained parliamentary assent on July 29, 1839, and royal assent on August 17, 1839. It granted the lords of the treasury until October 5, 1840, to abolish franking and to design prepaid stationery (envelopes and letter sheets) and stamps (to affix to letters). There were a number of interim measures, as well. From December 5, 1839, to January 10, 1840, there was a short transition to the new postage system with letters uniformly charged 4d. The fourpenny rate applied to letters sent outside of London, while letters sent within the London area and weighing less than a half ounce cost 1d if prepaid and 2d if not prepaid.[53] Uniform Penny Postage went into operation nationwide on January 10, 1840. The elimination of franks—even for the Queen— also chipped away at the rigid class system in England, a source of discontent among the working class and an impetus for emigration. The Penny Post, heralded as a much-needed equalizing measure, transformed the post from a privilege for the wealthy to a civic service extended from "the peer to the peasant."[54] All letters weighing up to half an ounce cost the same and could travel anywhere in the United Kingdom, even to those regions that seemed as far off as Timbuktu.

We cannot underestimate the power of carefully crafted pre-reform hardship tales to the cause of postal reform. Likely exaggerated and often reprinted, pre-reform postal reform stories moved the public with scenarios of widespread hardship and affliction, of kin torn asunder, and of widespread cheating, at which, to use Robinson's words, "everybody had more or less winked in the past" (285). Cole's skit solved the problem of high postage, and Dickens's fiction promoted the solution. Women saved from degradation, reformed and literate soldiers, unrebellious mill workers, and home control—these are just some of the imagined benefits that moved the early Victorians to support a postal reform movement that went on to have widespread social, economic, and political repercussions. Fiction, drama, cautionary tales, testimonials, stories, and anecdotes together form a canon of postal reform narratives that kept cheap postage ever in the public consciousness and made powerful "a case of feeling," rousing the public to agitate for, and ultimately receive, revolutionary reform.

Chapter 2

Signed, Sealed, Delivered

Mulreadies, Caricatures, and the Penny Black

a bit of paper just large enough to bear the stamp, and covered at the back
with a glutinous wash, which the bringer might, by applying a little moisture,
attach to the back of the letter . . .

—Rowland Hill, *Post Office Reform: Its Importance and Practicability*, 1837

On January 10, 1840, post offices were bustling all across England. "'Penny
Postage extended to the whole kingdom this day,'" notes a triumphant Rowland Hill in his journal on that historic date (Hill and Hill 1: 390). The number of stamped letters posted on January 10, 1840, was 112,000. This figure,
which surpassed Hill's expectation, was nearly four times the typical number.
In addition, all but 13,000–14,000 of the letters postmarked January 10th were
prepaid.[1] Although postal reformers had pondered how to determine prepayment, the solution came in two inventions attributed to Rowland Hill—prepaid postal stationery, which took the form of letter sheets and envelopes, and
an adhesive postage stamp, which Hill curiously describes as "a bit of paper
just large enough to bear the stamp, and covered at the back with a glutinous
wash, which the bringer might, by applying a little moisture, attach to the back
of the letter" (*Post Office Reform* 45). William Mulready designed both types of
prepaid stationery, which were subsequently named after him. On the design,
Britannia is mounted on a lion and surrounded by four winged messengers
sending news to lands across the globe.[2] The Penny Black (1d stamp) features
on a black background a bust of young Queen Victoria (modeled after William Wyon's 1837 City Medal) while the Two Pence Blue (2d stamp) has a blue
background and uses the same bust of the Queen.

Prepaid stationery and stamps arose in an era of visual literacy: it was common to read images on broadsides and in illustrations accompanying serial
fiction and to derive meaning from them. Pictorial journalism also gained

footing in the 1840s: May 1842, for instance, witnessed the launching of the *Illustrated London News*, the first journal entirely devoted to pictorial journalism. In fact, one of the stated aims of this journal—"to keep continually before the eye of the world a living and moving panorama of all its actions and influences"—applies to the officially commissioned stationery and the Penny Black, which brought "before the eye of the world" a sanctioned image of Britain as a nation, a British view of foreign lands and British territories abroad, and the visage of the Queen.[3]

Although in "Reforms," I am foremost explaining why the British in the early nineteenth century believed they needed a revolution in letter writing, this chapter considers and attempts to resolve several related questions. Specifically, what messages did Mulreadies, Mulready caricatures, and the postage stamp communicate to their first audiences, and what do these innovations in communication and the caricatures they spawned teach us about early Victorian views? As I argued in chapter 1, narratives shaped by the rhetoric of emotional appeal moved the British in the 1830s to adopt postal reform. In turn, Mulreadies, Mulready caricatures, and the postage stamp—as tangible objects of material culture—persist as material memories of early Victorian politics, economics, and culture, carrying meaning about British national identity and political tensions, as well as about Victorian prejudices, family ties, social customs, aesthetics, ideas of authority, pride, humor, and values.

To some early Victorians, prepaid postage and the postage stamp seemed like the greatest new ideas of their time. The Penny Black, also called a "Queen's head," won instant popularity. The Victorians welcomed the concept of a prepaid envelope (which lends insight into a developing Victorian standard of privacy). Even so, it appears that Mulready's design scarcely represented the British psyche circa 1840. Caricatures and plans to withdraw the Mulreadies appeared within the first week of their introduction. That the design was lambasted, lampooned, and abandoned—"vast quantities of the Mulready envelope and lettersheets remained unsold" (Muir 180)—suggests it may have been not only irrelevant but contrary to the way the British public wished to communicate at the time. Nonetheless, Queen Victoria, as well as members of the Royal Academy, approved the design, which leads me to propose that, even if the Mulready was not uniformly accepted or publicly liked, it still stands as an endorsed and valuable sign of Victorian Britain's place in a larger political world. This seems especially true if we view the design in light of the Treasury Commission's and Mulready's own descriptions of the intended meaning of its iconography. Mulready caricatures and the first postage stamp, which the public approved by buying in large numbers, arguably serve as reliable indicators of how Victorians communicated ideas via correspondence. This chapter also considers anecdotes about the reception of Mulreadies and the Penny Black and concludes with an analysis of George Elgar Hicks's narrative painting *The General Post Office, One Minute to Six* (1860), which illustrates how twenty years following the introduction of the Penny Post, the reformed Post Office became emblematic of the Victorian way of life.

OPENING DAY OF THE PENNY POST

For some Victorians, like Samuel Lines, Uniform Penny Postage became official during the wee hours of January 10th. Eager to be the first in Birmingham to use the Penny Post, Samuel Lines, who was Rowland Hill's boyhood drawing master at Hill Top and Hazelwood, reportedly stood outside a Birmingham post office on the evening of January 9th to post a letter of congratulation to his former pupil. Waiting for the stroke of midnight, Lines listened intently as the town clock chimed loudly twelve times. At the very last stroke of twelve, Lines rapped on the post office window, woke up an astonished, sleepy postal clerk on duty, handed him a penny, and said, "'It's a penny today, I believe.'"[4]

Lines may well have been the first person in the nation to usher in the new system, but on this historic day, thousands across the United Kingdom prepaid a letter for a penny.[5] Hill was not among them. As he notes in his journal at the time, "'I have abstained from going to the Post Office to-night lest I should embarrass their proceedings,'" and adds later to his memoir, "I learnt that on the first evening of the penny rate, notwithstanding the crush and inconvenience, three hearty cheers were given in the great hall for Rowland Hill, followed by three others for the officers of the department" (Hill and Hill 1: 390, 391).[6] Was the excitement worth the "crush and inconvenience"? Did Hill and the Post Office each receive three cheers and a "hip-hip-hurrah!" as Norman Wymer describes it (23)? Or was there one "great cheer" each for Hill and the Post Office as Eleanor Smyth reports in her rendition of opening day (165)?

Smyth so vividly describes closing time at St. Martin's-le-Grand on opening day that we tend to assume she was there.[7] Her narrative moves us inside the famous building, designed by architect Robert Smirke and completed in 1829. This neoclassical structure, with its stone façade and Ionic columns (resembling Smirke's famous British Museum façade), attracted the notice of Londoners and foreign visitors and dignitaries, such as the Queen of Saxony, who toured postal headquarters (C. R. Perry 3). On this historic day, the crowd gathered in the large center entryway of St. Martin's-le-Grand from 5:00 to 6:00 p.m. This was typically the most crowded time of the General Post Office anyway, but many more people were rushing to prepay their letters in time for the last posting on the first day of nationwide penny postage. Six windows were open for business, instead of the usual one. In the final minutes before six o'clock, the head of the circulation department opened a seventh window to help with the crowd, which Smyth calls "good-tempered"; in her view, the people "evidently enjoyed the crush" (164). Just before closing time, "the last letters and accompanying pennies were thrown . . . [into the windows], sometimes separating beyond hope of any reunion" (Smyth 164–65). Not all customers were able to reach the window by closing time, a moment Smyth portrays with drama: "When the last stroke of the hour had rung out, and the lower sash of every window had come down with a rush like the guillotine, a great cheer went up for 'penny postage and Rowland Hill,' and another for the Post Office staff who had worked so well" (165).

As Eileen Cleere aptly notes, "Hill's daughter described the scene of the Post Office on the first evening of the reform in an idiom that domesticates even the most pernicious emblem of the French Revolution" (187). The guillotine metaphor builds on Smyth's earlier description of General Post Office practice to shut its windows suddenly with ferocity at closing time, "sometimes with a letter or newspaper only half-way through" (163). Amidst the crush of people and the hail of flying pennies, we can now imagine at least a few "severed" letters and newspapers scattered on the floor. The sashes of the windows at the General Post Office also caught the attention of Charles Dickens, who, ten years later, with W. H. Wills, personified them in the opening issue of *Household Words* (March 30, 1850): "Here huge slits gape for letters, whole sashes yawn for newspapers, or wooden panes open for clerks to frame their large faces, like giant visages in the slides of a Magic Lantern" (6). Clearly the sashes and panes framing the faces of postal workers were capable of executing far more than an occasional letter or newspaper, but on January 10, 1840, postal employees were busily and energetically executing the mail, delivered by the "good-tempered" crowd.

Referring to a *Globe* article, Rowland Hill focused in a journal entry on the volumes of people streaming into St. Martin's-le-Grand, which "'has been quite besieged by people prepaying their letters'" (Hill and Hill 1: 391). The word "besieged" again invites comparison between the Penny Post and French revolutionary activity, an association Elizabeth Barrett Browning made explicit in calling "our penny postage . . . the most successful revolution since 'the three glorious days' of Paris."[8] In a May 1840 article on uniform postage published in *Westminster Review*, Henry Cole adds in the element of spectators—not readily associated with execution of the post but common enough

for an execution by guillotine: "'The great hall was nearly filled with spectators, marshalled [*sic*] in a line by the police to watch the crowds pressing,
scuffling, and fighting to get first to the window.'"9 Postal reform carried the
fervor of revolutionary activity: just days after Uniform Penny Postage went
into effect, people came in droves to prepay their letters or simply to watch
the proceedings at St. Martin's-le-Grand. But the Penny Post had a pacifying
effect, as well: as postal reformers predicted, the "pressing, scuffling, and fighting" crowds were not protesting the government, but demanding to be first in
line to receive a remarkable and welcomed government service, which postal
workers performed with enthusiasm. Spectators at St. Martin's-le-Grand were
under the command of the police in an orderly queue. Cole's description of
opening day at St. Martin's-le-Grand offers a picture of home control: "'the
mob, delighted at the energy displayed by the officers, gave one cheer for the
Post Office, and another for Rowland Hill.'"10 Though "delighted mob" sounds
like an oxymoron—given that we associate mobs with violence and political
unrest—Cole's "mob" is, in fact, an energetic multitude, arriving at the General Post Office not to protest but to receive the benefits of an information
revolution and to celebrate a remarkable achievement.

THE SCHEME OF PREPAYMENT

Much behind-the-scenes work took place to prepare for this historic day. The
Postage Duties Bill gave the Department of Treasury, the governing body of
the Post Office, "'a power of carrying into effect the reduced and uniform rate
of Postage contemplated by Parliament either according to the present mode
of collecting the Postage or by prepayment by means of Stamps Compulsory
or optional.'"11 The Treasury essentially adopted the main prepayment ideas
Hill had elucidated in *Post Office Reform: Its Importance and Practicability*
(1837): (1) a postmark "stamped" on a letter to indicate payment; (2) "stamped"
covers or envelopes and "stamped" sheets of papers sold at a price to include
the postage ("Letters so stamped," Hill had explained, "would be treated in all
respects as franks, and might, as well as franks, be put into the letter-box, as at
present, instead of being delivered to the Receiver" [42]); and (3) bits of paper
"covered with a glutinous wash" affixed to a letter or envelope (45). The third
proposed method of prepayment describes a postage stamp, of course, which
quickly caught on and inspired the hobby of stamp collecting, also called "philately." Of note, Hill and Cole used the word "stamp" broadly in their postal reform pamphlets. That is, "stamp" means a postmark that is stamped onto a letter, as well as a printed or stamped label (what we now call a "postage stamp")

affixed to a letter. In his pamphlet, Hill also credits publisher Charles Knight with inspiring the idea of a prepaid envelope, since Knight had suggested that postage for newspapers might be collected by selling stamped wrappers or covers when, prior to 1836, lowering the Stamp Tax on newspapers from 4d to 1d was under discussion (41–42).

Although not a Post Office employee, Rowland Hill was intimately involved in the process of "carrying into effect" Uniform Penny Postage. Hill received a two-year appointment for "an ill-defined post"[12] at the Department of the Treasury under the new chancellor of the exchequer, Francis Baring.[13] Fittingly, Cole, editor of *The Post Circular*, became Hill's assistant for the Treasury position. It was up to the Treasury, in conjunction with the Board of Stamps, to choose and oversee the production of new stationery and postage stamps. Today, of course, the Post Office governs these activities, but in Rowland Hill's time, the government Stamp Office and its licensees minted, distributed, and controlled new stationery and stamps. There was much to consider—design, color, printing, gumming. Acting almost immediately on its mandated charge, the Treasury, on August 23, 1839, announced a competition to determine the best ideas for prepaid stationery and postage stamps.[14] The Treasury invited "all artists, men of science, and the public in general" as well as "people in any part of the civilized world" to submit designs.[15] Submissions for labels, seals, postal stationery, and stamps came flooding into the Treasury. The best design was to receive £200 and the second best, £100. Hill and Cole estimated the Treasury received between 2,600 and 2,700 submissions, although only a small portion of these has survived.[16] Foreign and British artists could participate, so entries came from overseas, particularly France.[17] Colored and black-and-white designs ranged from practical to ornamental, beautiful to crude, embossed to plain. Not surprisingly, some designs featured national symbols, such as the Royal Arms and the Union Jack. The committee evaluated all submissions against the following criteria: convenience to the public, security from possible forgery, ease of checking the design, and expense of production and circulation.[18]

The preferred designs, however, did not end up coming from the Treasury competition.[19] In December 1839, the chancellor of the exchequer authorized Hill to approach two individuals: William Wyon to draw up plans for postage (stamps minted or embossed) and William Mulready to create stationery (envelopes and letter sheets). On January 4, 1840, six days before Penny Postage went into effect across the nation, the chancellor of the exchequer approved Mulready's design. John Thompson, recognized as the leading wood engraver of his day, engraved the design, and William Clowes printed it. Mulready received £352 10s on June 17, 1840, by which time the public had roundly ridiculed the work.[20] During this same period, Wyon was at work designing a silhouette of Queen Victoria for official Post Office stationery, and this image (based on the 1837 City Medal) also became the design for the 1d and 2d postage stamps.[21] Penny postage went into effect on January 10, 1840, but these items were not available for purchase until May. Stamps and postal stationery went on sale May 1, 1840. May 6, 1840, was the first legal date for mailing, but some people posted Mulreadies and stamped letters on May 5, 1840. Perkins, Bacon & Petch engraved, trademarked, and printed the 1d and 2d stamps of a design based on Wyon's Queen's head.

MULREADIES AND THE STORIES THEY SPIN

Envelopes, now standard fare for letter writing, were a class marker before 1840. Prior to postal reform, an envelope was a separate sheet of mail, and a letter placed in an envelope incurred a double charge. Thus, an envelope was a luxury, except for people of means (Rigo de Righi 25). A far more economical letter-writing practice held sway: a writer folded one single sheet, wrote an address on the outer face, and sealed the letter with wax. Not surprisingly, William Thackeray's cunning Becky Sharp of *Vanity Fair* (1848), set in the Regency period, knows the art of folding and sealing. Even in her rush to depart from Miss Crawley's employment, she leaves behind a letter of elopement bearing a "neat seal" that Thackeray sees fit to illustrate in "The Note on the Pincushion" (194–95). With cheap postage, however, envelopes "became extremely popular almost overnight" and quickly replaced folded letters, as Thomas De La Rue, a prominent London publisher, reports in a March 11, 1841, letter—presumably to Henry Cole: "'previously to the Reduction of Postage very few envelopes were in use—since then our consumption goes on increasing—latterly we sell about 40,000 per day—we can hardly however supply regularly our demand or we should be selling more.'"[22]

Mulreadies took the form of envelopes—also called wrappers, pockets, and covers—as well as letter sheets, which resemble what today we call air letters in the United Kingdom and aerograms in the United States. Laid flat, the Mulready envelope resembled a large diamond, with four angled corners. A writer could fold the four corners of the Mulready envelope around a letter and seal it that way, or the writer could fold three of the envelope corners together, slide the letter inside the pocket, and then fold down and seal the fourth flap, much as we do with envelopes today. The Mulready letter sheet, by contrast, worked like current airmail stationery. A writer composed a message on the inside of the square letter sheet, then folded its top and bottom and sides together before sealing it to post. When folded, the letter sheet side panels displayed printed information about prices and posting regulations. The Mulready envelope, by contrast, showed on its back face the word "Postage," printed across a rectangular engine-turned background, with a stereo number above it. The outsides of surviving envelopes and letter sheets often contain printed advertising.[23] As with air letters today, the Mulready envelope and letter sheet did not require an additional stamp, because the design itself made clear the item was prepaid (Muir 131). Moreover, Hill instructed the secretary of the Post Office to have clerks place a postmark, which Hill called an "obliterative stamp," on top of the icon of Britannia to prevent a writer from attaching a stamp to the outside and using the envelope or letter sheet again (Lowe 84). The Maltese cross cancel (in red ink for the Penny Black and black ink for the Penny Red) offered proof of cancellation.

Prior to his postal commission, Mulready, an Irish-born academy-trained artist, had earned a reputation as a Romantic painter. Many of his paintings of English life hang in the Victoria and Albert Museum (*The Sonnet* [1839] and *First Love* [1839], for example) and in the Tate Britain (*The Last* [1835]).[24] A versatile artist, Mulready also designed portraits and book illustrations, including plates for Oliver Goldsmith's *The Vicar of Wakefield* (1766), which many critics consider his best illustrative work. Philatelists, however, think of Mulready as the creator of what Henry Cole dubbed a "highly poetic design" for the penny postage envelope.[25] Mulready included the following note with the proof of his design, which the Treasury sent to Queen Victoria: "'This Design is intended to convey the idea that the measure it assists in carrying out, emanated from Great Britain, and that it is a very wide spreading benefit, facilitating our friendly and commercial intercourse with remote lands, and bringing, in a manner, our separated brethern [*sic*] closer to the sick beds and cheerful firesides of home.'"[26] Hill took a copy of the design to the National Gallery on April 10, 1840, and recorded in his diary that it was "enthusiastically approved 'by the R.A.s who were met in Council.'"[27]

The bottom half of the Mulready design represents the domestic front, while the top half represents the global arena. The sentimental scenes of hearth and home on the lower left and right sides of the Mulready design illustrate the argument that the Penny Post would support and strengthen familial relationships in Victorian England (see figure 3). These clichéd images idealize the Victorian family and embody the idea of the importance of maintaining close family bonds through the post, or, in Mulready's words, of "bringing,

FIGURE 3. Mulready envelope, posted from Taunton, Somerset, UK, with "26 JU 1840 BY POST" postmark. From the collection of Norman M. Fox.

in a manner, our separated brethern [*sic*] closer to the sick beds and cheerful firesides of home."

The bottom left sickbed scene shows a son (or daughter?) reading a letter to a dying woman, presumably the mother. The ailing woman, hands clasped in prayer, gazes heavenward. Is this long awaited missive "bad news," as E. B. Evans suggests in his 1891 analysis of the design (4)? Martineau reads the iconography differently, arguing that the design shows "the uplifted hands and eyes of the widowed mother who is receiving a letter from an absent son" (*History* 2: 430), perhaps the last she will receive before her imminent death.

On the bottom right, a young mother is reading a letter to her children, who cluster around her. To the Victorian viewer, the Mulready envelope showed five angels: four winged angels surrounding Britannia at the top of the design and one "angel in the house" at the bottom—a pretty, modest mother in demure high-necked, long-sleeved gown, her hair gathered into a bun. This figure embodies qualities Coventry Patmore immortalized a decade later in his sequence of poems entitled *The Angel in the House* (1854–63): faithfulness, love, earnestness, devotion, patience, and unselfishness. Mulready's angel in the house also embodies learning and literacy.[28] The eldest child peers over her mother's shoulder, eager to read the letter independently; the younger of the two children begs to see the letter, signaling a desire to learn to read, one of the reasons Victorians supported the Penny Post. As in the sickbed scene opposite, Mulready leaves the contents of the letter undetermined. Is it good news, as Evans suggests (4)? If Evans is correct, Mulready's domestic figures, flanking the opposite lower right and left corners of his design, express the oppositions governing human experience—youth and age, health and sickness, joy and sorrow, good news and bad. These albeit cloying domestic scenes encapsulate the main reasons the early Victorians advocated cheap postage: staying connected with friends and family in an increasingly mobile Victorian society; heartening the "infirm father, the blind mother, whose pleasures are becoming fewer";[29] and spreading the benefits of literacy.

Grouping visual stereotypes of nation and race, the top of Mulready's design signals the world of politics and commerce and reminds us of the nativist attitudes that accompanied British national identity and pride. Mulready's central figure, Britannia, sends forth four winged angels to bring news of postal innovation to the far reaches of the earth.[30] Britannia, as the national figurehead, has a rich history dating to the Romans, who personified Great Britain as a goddess in armor. In fact, Britannia made her way onto official coinage over a century and a half before she entered the postal domain (she appeared on the farthing as early as 1672). Akin to other artists' depictions of Britain's female figurehead, Mulready's Britannia's arms are raised above shoulder level and outstretched to dispatch her angelic emissaries. Enthroned on a rock that appears to rise from the water (a visual allusion to her island nation and perhaps to King Arthur's Excalibur), Britannia is clad in armor and a victory helmet, a large lion lying contentedly at her feet and a Union Jack shield resting against her knee.

Flanking Britannia's island and separated from it by sea, iconic representations of Eastern nations on the top left side of the envelope and of Western nations on the top right indicate British colonial holdings or interests: India, China, Lapland (behind Britannia's right shoulder), North America (including Canada), and the partially British-controlled West Indies. Cargo-laden camels and elephants, saronged natives, naked to the waist and bent beneath the weight of bundled wares, Chinese officials in Manchu robes with queues down their backs—these stereotypical images signal countries of the Asian continent. The turbaned scribes in the far left foreground of this group may represent India but could also signal Turkey or Persia.

Moving from the top left to the top right of the envelope (and across the sea as it were), we see what appears to be a fleet of British sailing ships behind Britannia's left shoulder and behind her right the sled rider and reindeer that may represent Lapland (a remote area that today encompasses the northern parts of Norway, Sweden, Finland, and the Kola Peninsula in Russia) or another northern locale, such as the arctic region of Canada.[31] Far to the right, Indians in feathered headdresses and loincloths represent North America, while slaves toiling over rum casks in front of a palm tree probably emblematize the West Indies.

By twenty-first-century standards, Mulready's design verges on the politically incorrect and arguably reflects what A. N. Wilson calls "the natural xenophobia of the English" (143). It also encapsulates the English perception of what Trollope calls in *The Warden* (1855) the "kingdoms of Queen Victoria" (195). As Britannia confers "her" glorious outreach to peoples of far-off or "uncivilized" lands, Mulready's now-dated visual stereotypes of race—a headdress for the Native American, a pigtail for the Chinese—register as residues of racial supremacy, cultural bias, and colonial exploitation. Such nativist stereotypes were common in the Victorian era.[32] Today, we read in the Mulready envelope a depiction of the geographical range of British political authority in 1840 that forecasts the increasingly aggressive expansion of British imperialism after the death of Prince Albert in 1861.

Mulready's attested aim in his design was to show Britain conferring "a very wide spreading benefit, facilitating our friendly and commercial intercourse with remote lands." But Britannia's victory helmet, her shield, and the fleet of British ships assembled behind her also speak to Britain's sense of expanding dominion and authority in 1840. Britain was the first Western country to industrialize and readily disseminate its views and achievements—a set of circumstances that culminated in the Great Exhibition of 1851. Though remote to travelers, some of the lands depicted on the Mulready design were, at the time of its debut, British holdings not unfamiliar to the public. In the early 1840s, Britain was keenly aware of its power to colonize and confident of its economic prowess. Granted, the British were not alone in their efforts at empire building. The French resembled their English neighbors in their rival efforts to colonize the West Indies and Africa, and the two Boer Wars are enough to remind us that the Dutch, aided by the Germans, fought Britain over possession of South Africa.

So, while the action of empire building describes many nineteenth-century European powers, the 1840 Mulready transmits knowledge about specifically British national dominance and preserves an early Victorian view of "un-English" lands. We might recall that in an effort to rally participants to its postal design competition, the Treasury issued an invitation "to people in any part of the civilized world." In the nineteenth century, the terms "civilized" and "uncivilized" automatically evoked other dichotomies, such as "explored" versus "unexplored" worlds or "cultured" peoples versus "primitive" or "wild" peoples. The Asian figures assembled to the left of Mulready's Britannia suggest that Britain viewed postal outreach as a means of sharing its achievements with less Westernized and therefore relatively unexplored countries, among which it included India and China.[33]

The British presence in India, the most precious jewel in Queen Victoria's crown, began in the early seventeenth century when British merchants for the East India Company traveled there first to trade with and, in the mid-eighteenth century, following the 1757 British victory at Plassey, to war with and eventually rule over this vast and largely unknown country. In the late eighteenth century, Britain began to annex more Indian territories, and by 1840 the government was aggressively acquiring still more Indian territories to add to British India.[34]

When the Mulready stationery made its public debut, the British colonial presence in India was nearing its apogee, and Britain was entering into the first of two Anglo-Chinese wars. The three Chinese figures in Mulready's design—they are talking with an Anglo gentleman (as indicated by his broad-brimmed hat)—recall the First Opium War, which erupted over British-controlled opium traffic into China. Despite China's drug laws prohibiting the importation of opium into the country (it was plagued by addiction), the British continued an illicit trade and profited enormously by it. (Opium was grown in India, then under British rule.)[35] When the Qing government confiscated and destroyed about 20,000 chests of illegally imported British opium, Britain charged China with destroying private property. Just one month after Mulreadies went on sale, Britain, in June 1840, sent warships, soldiers, and a British-Indian army to China. The British victory led eventually to the Treaty of Nanking in 1843, a peace measure which marked the end of the First Opium War between the British and Qing Empires (1839–42). Set in its cultural moment, then, Mulready's design documents Britain's active involvements in the East in 1840, specifically in India and China.[36]

Like the images that point in Mulready's design to Victorian-era British attitudes toward the East, his iconography also encapsulates British attitudes toward the West. In his depiction of North America, Mulready shows William Penn talking to the Delaware Indians along the banks of Chesapeake Bay. This iconography likely indicates how North America still figured in the collective consciousness of many Victorians. Douglas Muir suggests that Mulready probably based his representation on Benjamin West's popular 1772 painting, *William Penn's Treaty with the Indians* (121). An American neoclassical painter, West, in this painting, represents a 1682 verbal treaty between Penn and the

Indians involving exchange of goods and money for the province of Pennsylvania.[37]

Mulready embodies the West Indies in figures of bare-chested black laborers, rolling and repairing rum casks at a sugar plantation, while a white overseer directs their labor. Slavery was abolished across the British Empire between 1833 and 1834, with full emancipation going into effect in 1838. Though the peculiar institution, as it was called, was still going strong in the antebellum South at the time Mulready's design greeted the British public, the images of palm trees, bare-breasted slave women nursing their babies, and rum casks make it less likely that the artist was depicting the American South than an emancipated sugar plantation somewhere in the British West Indies, like Trinidad, Barbados, or Jamaica. In 1840, British antislavery legislation had not long been law.[38] The West Indian colonies did not quickly acquire democratic self-government but remained under the British Crown Colony system with appointed governors well into the twentieth century. This situation led to political unrest, the Eyre controversy being a prime example.[39] It is in hindsight, then, from a twenty-first-century critical historical perspective that the Mulready design stands as a material memory of British colonial influence in the West Indies.

A TALE OF RIDICULE

Rejection of Mulready stationery was immediate, forceful, overwhelming, and universal. As Muir aptly concludes, "Derision was the common response to the Mulready design. It was caricatured in words and imitative drawings" (176). Hill quickly realized the failure of the design; he records in his diary entry of May 12, 1840, only eleven days after Mulreadies went on sale: "'I fear we shall be obliged to substitute some other stamp for that designed by Mulready, which is abused and ridiculed on all sides. In departing so widely from the established "lion and unicorn" nonsense, I fear that we have run counter to settled opinions and prejudices somewhat rashly. I now think it would have been wiser to have followed established custom in all the details of the measure where practicable'" (Hill and Hill 1: 395). The design was, in Hill's view, "'swimming against the tide,'" although he did not regret "'our attempt to diffuse a taste for fine art.'"[40] Some Victorians cared enough about the design to hand color it.[41] However, the design was quickly withdrawn, as Hill predicted. In January 1841 the 1d Mulready envelope disappeared, and by April 1841 the 2d envelope was abandoned. William Wyon's embossed design of Queen Victoria first replaced Mulready's design on the envelope and, by 1844, on the letter sheet so that prepaid stationery matched Wyon's stamp. The large stock of withdrawn Mulready envelopes and letter sheets was destroyed in 1862.[42]

Responses vary as to why the design invited instant scorn, but many of them center on a disjunction between form and function. Ridicule was immediately forthcoming from businesses, which "preferred simplicity to this work of art which left little room for the address" (O'Keefe 66).[43] Writing in the 1890s, E. B. Evans concludes that Mulready's design, "however beautiful as a work of art, was altogether unsuited to the prosaic purpose for which it was intended," adding that it was "unbusinesslike," which "to 'a nation of shopkeepers,' was doubtless enough to condemn it" (4). The format of the envelope was also one of Martineau's objections to the design, which had "two great defects:— it did not leave space for a long address, or one made long by the scrawling of the illiterate; and it rendered stale some signs of emotion which should never be made irreverently familiar" (*History* 2: 430). Although Henry Cole did not object to the placement of the domestic scenes on the stationery, he expresses a complaint similar to Martineau's: "After forty years' additional experience, I agree in the soundness of the public opinion expressed, that this fine design was quite unsuitable for its purpose. . . . The postage cover was for a dry commercial use, in which sentiment had no part. The merchant who wishes to prepay his letter rejects anything that disturbs his attention. I now think that anything, even a mere meaningless ornamental design, would have been out of place" (*Fifty Years* 1: 63–65).[44] Cole goes beyond purely practical concerns, however, to bring the issue of artistry into play: "Had an allegorical fresco for any public building been required to symbolize the introduction of the universal penny postage, nothing could have been better than Mulready's design, and I still hope to see it perpetuated in some fine work of art where it would not be impertinent" (*Fifty Years* 1: 65). Was this hypothetical "allegorical fresco" a "fine work of art," to recall Hill's and Cole's views? Or did the Victorian public ridicule Mulready's design because they viewed it as bad art?[45]

The reaction of the press in 1840 to Mulready's design suggests that some Victorians objected to the allegorical-pictorial-historical approach altogether,[46] leading Asa Briggs to conclude that "For once symbolism—or at least Mulready's brand of symbolism—was out-of-fashion" (343). Similar criticism appears in London papers of the time. In the *Times* of May 2, 1840, and the *Morning Herald* of May 25, 1840, reviewers deemed the design the work of a caricaturist, not an artist. Hill includes in his memoir a review from an unnamed London city paper: "'this is a wondrous combination of pictorial genius, after which Phiz and Cruikshank must hide their diminished heads.'"[47] An 1840 reviewer for the *Times* quipped, "'Cruikshank could scarcely produce anything so laughable,'" adding that the envelope showed "'sundry figures, who, if they were to appear in the streets of London or on any of our highways, would be liable to the penalties of the Vagrant Act for indecent exposure.'"[48] Likewise, a reviewer for an 1840 edition of *The Tablet* criticizes

> "the infinite drollery of the whole, the curious assortment of figures and faces, the harmonious *mélange* of elephants, mandarin's tails, Yankee beavers, naked Indians, squatted with their hind-quarters in front, Cherokee chiefs, with feathered tufts, shaking missionaries by the hand; casks of Virginia threatening the heads of young ladies devouring their love letters, and the old woman in the corner, with hands uplifted, blessing Lord Lichfield and his Rowland for the saving grace of 11 *d.* out of the shilling, and valuing her absent husband's calamity or death as nothing in comparison with such an economy."[49]

Earlier, the reviewer even more fiercely lampoons the domestic scene—sacrosanct to some Victorians, like Martineau—in suggesting a "dutiful boy, [is] reading to his anxious mama an account of her husband's hapless shipwreck, who, with hands clasped, is blessing Rowland Hill for the cheap rate at which she gets the disastrous intelligence."[50]

Racial and ethnic epithets—"mandarin's tails," "Cherokee chiefs, with feathered tufts"—figure prominently in reviews of the Mulready, including one in poem form that appeared in an 1840 newspaper: "The picture's completed by well-tailed Chinese / A-purchasing opium and selling of teas"; "There a planter is giving and watching the tasks / Of two worthy niggers, at work on two casks."[51] This anonymous verse review, which Hill includes in his memoir, indifferently fuses four Eastern nationalities, dismissively characterizing the figures to Britannia's left as "'some Hindoo, Chinese, Arabic, or Turkish merchants,'" who have "'closed their bargains and correspondence'" (Hill and Hill 1: 394). A reviewer writing in the *Morning Herald* on May 25, 1840, also uses a string of now-offensive terms to describe human figures in the design: "'Red Indian'"; "'Chief Cut-and-come-again, of the Splitskull Tribe'"; and "'Hong merchants.'"[52] In our age of political correctness, such terms may shock, but their prevalence in Victorian reviews, as well as their visual approximations in the Mulready design and its caricatures, suggest that in a nineteenth-century context, they were in no way exceptional. As materials of memory, such rhetoric—both textual and visual—conveys the climate of an age where stereotypes and caricatures dominated the field of political satire and illustration, where it was common to typecast nations and races in pictures and words.

MULREADY CARICATURES: A NATIONAL LAMPOON

As soon as the Mulready design appeared, caricaturists lampooned it. Whereas the Mulready was an officially commissioned design that the British public ridiculed and refused to purchase, the public bought the highly popular caricatures in droves. The caricatures arguably reveal more widely held views of pressing mid-nineteenth-century issues, prejudices, preferences, and preoccupations than the officially commissioned design. Mulready caricatures ridicule the monarchy, the postal system, the Opium Wars, the Irish, social practices, and major politicians of the day. My aim here is not to elucidate all the caricatures that the Mulready spawned—in 1891, E. B. Evans admirably undertook that task when compiling *The Mulready Envelope and Its Caricatures*—but to identify some of the series and summarize trends that carry meaning about how early Victorians communicated ideas and current events via correspondence.

Though in the original design, the one-legged angel is a result of error, caricaturists commonly joked about the missing leg and, in turn, created one-legged postmen, cherubs, et cetera. They mocked Mulready's name, signing their satires Mul-led-already, Mullheaded, and Mull-rooney (a dig at Mulready's Irish origins). Britannia herself was prime for caricature: she grows stouter and fatter in some imitations, bolder and more masculine in others; she dons a jester's cap and bells or transforms into a literary figure (her shield, a writing desk); she poses as a washerwoman, a one-eyed fiddler, a fisher and a hunter, as well as a pipe smoker (is she smoking opium?). In turn, her tame lion wears an eye patch; closes its eyes and sports a spotted nightcap (the accompanying inscription reads, "The British Lion Asleep"); wears spectacles; bares its rump to the viewer; and turns into a menagerie of other animals, including a donkey, a letter-reading poodle (the letter begins, "Dear Pug, I wish to cur tail your") and a lamb sporting then British prime minister Lord Melbourne's head.

Caricaturists copied and changed the design to advance a host of political and social ends. A series of six envelopes published by J. W. Southgate mocks Victorian women's affinity for letter writing, evincing a vivid misogyny and classism. In caricature 2 of the Southgate series, Britannia is "sending out letters to the gentler sex of all ranks" (Evans 82), including, on the one hand, a gaggle of girls at a "LADIES SCHOOL" (reminiscent of Miss Pinkerton's Academy in *Vanity Fair*) all rushing to receive their precious letters and, on the other, a washerwoman too busy with laundry to accept a letter from the letter carrier. This latter image was probably intended to ridicule and undercut arguments that the Penny Post would benefit all classes, by insinuating that the working class would not have access to such benefit anyway.

Numerous caricatures comment on compelling issues of national policy and make much of Mulready's Irish origins, which he downplayed. Mulready's family came to England in 1792 during the great Irish immigration. This wave of cheap Irish labor led to tense Anglo-Irish relations fueled by British intervention in Irish government that increasingly met with resistance and anti-British rebellion. Thus, the Irish as well as the Chinese (an association Mulready likely invited by including stereotyped mandarins in his original design) became prime topics for caricature. Number 4 in the Southgate series uses the Mulready as a template to mock heated political matters in Ireland and China, as well as to lampoon the Queen. The pedestal rising out of the water is now labeled the "BLARNEY STONE" (known to bestow eloquent speech on all who kiss it). The lion takes the visage of Daniel O'Connell—Ireland's preeminent political leader in the first half of the nineteenth century and a champion of the downtrodden. Here, however, O'Connell is smoking opium, a direct allusion to the First Opium War then raging in China. Britannia is transformed into Queen Victoria, weighted down by a necklace featuring a miniature of Prince Albert (a visual dig at Albert's influence on the Queen). Worse, she is shooing away her ministers, positioned around her like the winged messengers in the original design.[53] On the far left of the caricature, a fierce-looking, queued "Chinaman," with a pronounced Fu Manchu mustache, spears with a red-hot poker Lord Palmerston of the Foreign Office, who has been caught in the act of packing a case of opium.

The second in a more extensive series of fourteen envelopes published by William Spooner and signed "W. Mulheaded, R.A."[54] shows Britannia smoking a long pipe and watching an exploding barrel of gunpowder that has been ignited by sundry Chinese. Stereotyped images of "Chinamen" predominate in Mulready caricatures, showing that the First Opium War was foremost in the British public consciousness around 1840. Other visual stereotypes of race, ethnicity, religion, and national identity crop up, too: images of black Africans in livery (Britain had only recently emancipated its slaves) and Britannia as the Pope, a dig at Catholicism; India represented by elephants, Turkey by turbans, China by mandarins with queues. Clearly, visual stereotyping was an easy and popular route of political satire in the 1840s.

Arguably one of the cleverest Mulready caricatures (see figure 4) is by John Leech, who, along with Cruikshank and Phiz, created memorable illustrations for Dickens's fiction.[55] Leech—who signed his caricature "Mul-led-already"—features instead of Mulready's stately Britannia, a dumpy one with a silly grin

FIGURE 4. Mulready caricature by John Leech, 1840. Reproduced by kind permission of the British Postal Museum & Archive.

and a fleshy nose, who directs a multitude of uniformed Penny Postmen, one of them missing a leg. The lion, standing rather than lying down, wears a patch over its eye and has a string of letters tied to its tail. Leech simplified Mulready's original design, choosing to portray only the British West Indies and China. To the right, a white planter thumbs his nose at Britannia as he oversees a black laborer repairing a cask. Here, Leech may lampoon the Crown for denying slave labor to British plantation owners (a move which left some planters scrambling to hold onto the fortunes they had amassed). He may also satirize the limited reach of British authority, indicating by the planter's disrespectful gesture that this class of citizens—at a convenient remove from England—will do exactly as it pleases regardless of government edict. On the left, four Chinese—one in a straw "coolie hat," three wearing queues, and a central, fat one with an enormous Fu Manchu mustache—sit atop a large bale labeled "OPIUM" in capital letters. Mirroring the gesture of the planter figure, one of the mandarins on the left (holding what appears to be an opium pipe) thumbs his nose at Britannia. Although one is never sure of a master caricaturist's political views (Cruikshank mercilessly ridiculed both sides of the Queen Caroline and King George IV scandal), Leech here playfully illustrates, perhaps mocks, Chinese discontent with British trade policy. (The proprietary positioning of four men atop the drug cargo suggests that Chinese opposition to opium trade within China may have more to do with economics than concern for public welfare.) In any case, this masterful comical design probes the efficacy of British imperialist ideology, while at the same time calling into question the popular motives ascribed to political stances of the day.

THE PENNY BLACK, OR THE QUEEN'S HEAD

Although Hill believed that the public would prefer postal stationery to stamps when he proposed both methods of prepayment, the adhesive postage stamp quickly became the far more popular invention of the two. Asa Briggs notes in *Victorian Things* that in May 1840 demand far exceeded the number of available postage stamps (331). As historians have repeatedly noted, Rowland Hill underappreciated the significance of the postage stamp, viewing the "small stamped labels" as "almost an after-thought" (Briggs 328). A. G. Rigo de Righi makes the same case in *The Story of the Penny Black and Its Contemporaries*: "Hill himself only produced it [the postage stamp] as an after-thought" (5).[56] The "demand" for stamps surprised Hill, who notes in a journal entry of May 10, 1840, (only nine days after the Penny Black went on sale): "'the demand for labels is such that the contractors (Perkins Bacon), though they have five presses, are obliged to work night and day; they are now producing 600,000 (stamps) daily.'"[57] Hill's curious description of an adhesive postage stamp in *Post Office Reform: Its Importance and Practicability* is often quoted. "Glutinous wash" or "cement," as it was also called in 1840, allowed the writer to fix the stamp onto the envelope; period terms for a stamp include "essay" (a crude label), "label," "letter seal" or "seal," and "sticking-plaster." Perkins Bacon suggested black as the stamp's color because of its suitability for steel plate engraving, but the Penny Red replaced the Penny Black in 1841, in part because the red Maltese cross cancellation symbol was hard to discern on a black stamp.[58] The Two Pence Blue, also introduced on May 6, 1840, for letters exceeding one-half ounce but not exceeding one ounce, features the same bust of the Queen's head and remained on the stamp and on postal stationery throughout Victoria's reign.

Of the 2,600 entries in the Treasury competition, fewer than fifty were for stamped letter seals or postage stamps. Although Hill awarded four prizes of £100 each to entries by Benjamin Cheverton, Charles Whiting, Henry Cole, and the joint team of James Bogardus and Francis Coffin, none of these prize-winning designs graced the stamp or the stationery (although Hill did use Cheverton's suggestion to put the sovereign's head on the stamp in a design modeled after Wyon). Hill selected a leading printing firm, Perkins, Bacon

& Petch, which commissioned Henry Corbould, a well-known illustrator and miniaturist, to make a drawing of Queen Victoria's profile after William Wyon's 1837 City Medal for the first adhesive postage stamp, called the Penny Black.[59] Wyon, the premier engraver and medalist of his age, created the City Medal to commemorate Queen Victoria's first visit to London in November 1837 (Briggs 339). Wyon, who at the time was designing an embossed die of Queen Victoria's head for stamped paper, created many images of royals (including King George IV and William IV) for coinage. Because Wyon began drawing Princess Victoria when she was only thirteen, the image that graces the Penny Black incorporates Wyon's impressions of the young princess who became England's longest reigning queen.

Wyon knew the Queen's face intimately. For her eighteenth birthday, he designed a medallic portrait of Victoria, which led to the creation of two medals: a portrait in lower relief for use on the new home coinage (which began its circulation in the summer of 1838) and a diademed portrait commemorating the Queen's first visit to London in November 1837 and called the City Medal. Although Wyon went on to produce images of Queen Victoria as she matured into womanhood and married glory—including portraits of Victoria and Albert for the Great Exhibition of 1851 (completed just before Wyon's demise)— the image of youthful Victoria, created in 1837, endures as the face of the Penny Black.

The image on the first postage stamp (see figure 5) is in neoclassical style. Neoclassicism, a 1765 art movement that reacted to the heaviness of baroque and rococo styles, aimed to return art to the perceived purity of the classical arts of Greece and Rome by creating idealized, controlled, and inspired designs. Wyon wanted the portraits he created of Victoria to be balanced, uncluttered, pure, even beautiful. Thus, it is not surprising that the Queen's medalist found favor with the Queen. Wyon's depictions of the young head of Queen Victoria for the stamp and coinage show classically beautiful features: "'You always represent me favourably,' she is reported to have told Wyon, while he, for his part, is said to have found the Queen an excellent sitter."[60] Besides the young head, three additional busts of the Queen adorned coins during Victoria's reign: one on the 2s 0d piece, minted when Britain attempted to move to a decimal coinage in 1848–49;[61] the 1887 Jubilee head of the Queen (showing her at middle age); and the 1895 older head of Victoria wearing a diadem and veil. The commissioned postal stationery shows minor variations on Wyon's original Queen's head design, as do stamps from some of the British colonies.[62] However, Wyon's neoclassical portrait of a young Victoria remained a constant on the postage stamp during Queen Victoria's entire reign: "At no

FIGURE 5. Penny Black, posted May 6, 1840. From the collection of James Grimwood-Taylor.

point in the Victorian age were British users of stamps to see anything else but the head of Victoria. There was, after all, only one side to the stamp, unlike the coin" (Briggs 339).

The decision to put the Queen's head on the first postage stamp follows the longstanding practice of placing a sovereign's head on a coin. It may also have arisen in response to "a very practical philosophy of the eye" (Briggs 339) that was marshaled to avoid forgery. Cheverton included in his winning entry not only a wish that the stamp be based on Wyon's head of the Queen, but a persuasive argument that, because the eye is trained in discerning details of the face, detection of a false copy of a familiar face would occur more easily than it would for an ornamental design.[63] I am particularly interested in what the Queen's head came to symbolize to the Victorians. What does this object of material culture tell us about the values, traits, ideals, and assumptions of the Victorians who designed, commissioned, made, purchased, and used postage stamps? How did the public react to seeing the Queen's head on a stamp? Why did the stamp never change—a point that fascinated French historian Élie Halévy in his study of French versus British coins and stamps under contrasting regimes?[64] Did the postage stamp make Victoria, and the values she came to embody to her empire, an increasingly visible and palpable symbol of Victorian times and shared values?

In his memoir, Hill prints an 1840 review from a leading London paper, noting the "'unlucky perversion of the royal features'" on "'bits of "sticking plaster,"' with a head upon it which looks something like that of a girl, but nothing of a Queen'" (Hill and Hill 1: 393, 395). An 1842 illustration for *Punch* entitled "HORIGINAL OBSERWATIONS" perverts the features of Wyon's design: in the caricature, Queen Victoria has a distinctive frown on her face and a sad expression, conveyed through a downward slant of the eyes. The caricature apparently enraged the commissioner of stamps, leading *Punch* to publish a humorous article entitled "Punch on the Queen's Head," which laid to rest the commissioner's alleged fear that *Punch* would help "reduce the postage from one penny to nothing at all . . . by enabling people to cut the Queen's head out of the periodical, and use it to place upon their letters."[65] Some Victorians were "'rather proud of sticking the Queen's head on their letters'" (Hill and Hill 2: 91). In the words of one Victorian schoolboy, who did not "'fancy making my mouth a glue-pot,'" licking a stamp, nonetheless, provided the "'satisfaction of kissing or rather slobbering over Her Majesty's Back. This, however, I should say is about the greatest insult the present Ministry could have offered the Queen.'"[66] An amusing rhyme entitled "Lines on the Post Office Medallion," which appeared in the weekly sheet *The Town*, puns that the dampening of the back of the postage stamp places a kiss on the Queen's "behind":

You must kiss our fair Queen, or her pictures, that's
   clear
Or the gummy medallion will never adhere;
You will not kiss her hand, you will readily find
   But actually kiss little Vickey's behind.[67]

"Little Vickey" was no beauty. As Briggs concludes in *Victorian Things*, "It was paradoxical for Hill, therefore, that many contemporary art critics, who were uneasy about Mulready envelopes, or hostile to them, accepted with enthusiasm the penny black stamp, which Hill cared little for, and that it figures prominently in most late-twentieth century histories of design" (343). Even if Hill conceived the stamp as an "after-thought" and cared little for it, by the end of the 1840s the Penny Black (replaced by the Penny Red in 1841) ushered in stamp collecting, a hobby which became more popular than rock or coin collecting and sparked a Victorian craze—timbromania—that eventually came to be called "philately." The placement of a stamp on an envelope even evolved into a "language." The specific positioning of the stamp (that is, tilted right or placed upside down) typically in one of six sections of an envelope (top left corner, top right corner, left of surname, right of surname, bottom left corner, or bottom right corner) conveyed a hidden message to the receiver, such as "I love you," "I think of you," "Yes," "No," or even "Goodbye, Sweetheart."[68]

Material objects that carry meaning and sentiment naturally arise in the making of culture. If we think of a design on a postage stamp not only as a work of art but a record of history that projects a material memory of Victorian national identity, then it seems significant that the postage stamp essentially bore the same face of the United Kingdom from 1840 until the dawning of the twentieth century. The image of young Queen Victoria stood for the United Kingdom for sixty-one years of Victoria's sixty-four-year reign. This longstanding image became, for some Victorians, an issue of national pride, leading Frederick Philbrick and W. A. Westoby to claim in 1889 that "stamps of no other country in the world save Great Britain will be able to show an unbroken line of representations of its sovereign during fifty years from their first issue."[69] Significant also is what the twenty-first-century eye perceives as absent from the first postage stamp: the country of origin. The name "England," "Britain," "Great Britain," or "United Kingdom" was not on the stamp for two reasons: Britain was the first country to launch the postage stamp, and the stamp was, in its first years, mainly for domestic use.[70] The only words that appear on the Penny Black and 2d blue are "Postage" (on top) and "One Penny" or "Two Pence" (on the bottom).

Ironically, while the postage stamp was an egalitarian measure to bring an affordable post to all social classes (with it, the Queen gave up her own franking privilege), the stamp simultaneously magnified and made more visible the power of the Queen, whose death in 1901 marked the end an era. Telling is the nickname for the stamp—"Queen's head." Given the growing need for communication by letter, the stamp put Victoria's image and royal authority into nearly every home in her entire kingdom on an almost daily basis. By virtue of its ubiquity, equity, stability, and longevity, the "Queen's head" stamp may be said to embody what today we call Victorian values—moral propriety, domesticity and family affection, duty, and tradition—while at the same time standing as a national symbol of the British Empire and a personal symbol of the Queen's "longevity as well as personal morality" (Arnstein 836–37).

Noteworthy to a twenty-first-century audience is the long reign of Victoria's youthful image on the postage stamp. The coronation of Queen Victoria had symbolized a movement away from the corruption, injustice, and disease long associated with the England of her predecessors, George IV and William IV—often called the "wicked uncles." From 1840 to 1901, while the same philatelic image of a young Queen entered homes, businesses, and philanthropic and religious organizations throughout Great Britain, Queen Victoria and her nation underwent major life and political changes. The young, diminutive monarch, who came to the throne during the agitation for Uniform Penny Postage, became a blushing bride (she married her beloved Prince Albert on February 11, 1840), a devoted wife, a mother of nine children and (with Prince Albert) a proponent of family values, a grieving widow, a doting grandmother, an old woman, and, ultimately, a firm, demanding, and increasingly reclusive and unpopular monarch. Victoria and the entire nation suffered considerably from the loss of Prince Albert, leading many scholars to speculate how history might have been different had typhoid spared him. The Prince Regent had brought to England a patronage of the arts, an attention to charity, and a valuable European perspective on British politics. Was it a mark of vanity, then, that the youthful Queen's head stamp persisted for so many decades, or did the choice to maintain this image instead point to an effort to keep alive in the national consciousness the sense of hope and promise that had accompanied Victoria's coronation and married life?

We now regard Victorian England as an age of contradictions, major innovations, dreadful mistakes, and continuous revolutions in industry, education, transportation, communication, and gender roles. The country engaged in numerous wars: the first and second Opium Wars, the Crimean War, and the Anglo-Boer War. The government righted many social abuses: the Ten Hours Bill of 1847, for example, limited women's and children's workdays to ten hours, and the 1872 Infant Protection Act regulated baby farming. Important reforms were likewise passed: the 1870 Foster Act established government responsibility for education, and the Married Women's Property Acts (of 1870 and 1882) granted married women the right to hold property. Of course, British colonialism—especially the empire's incursions into India and Africa—also planted the seeds of a host of political and social problems that plagued Britain well into the twentieth century. During this period, too, Britain experienced an enormous increase in literacy. The literacy rate in England and Wales reached 97 percent by 1900, and more and more Victorians communicated by letter across both the private and public spheres.[71] In the midst of all this urgent and irrevocable change, Queen Victoria's youthful image—with its aura of grace, calm, and authority—remained static and unwavering, reigning "continually before the eye of the world" (King and Plunkett 385).

The relationship between a static representation and a changing human life recalls Oscar Wilde's *The Picture of Dorian Gray* (1891). Dorian remains ageless and beautiful while his portrait, painted by artist Basil Hallward, develops the outward signs of debauchery brought on by his undisciplined life. Of course, the Queen did not possess the beauty of a Dorian: she was known to be comely but not beautiful, always watching her weight and aging rather ungracefully. Neither did she lead her empire into the hedonistic pleasures and sins that Dorian pursues. Nonetheless, an analogy drawn between the two relationships—Queen Victoria's relation to the Queen's head stamp and Dorian's relation to his portrait—foregrounds the disjunction between life and a representation of life. Beautiful Dorian never changes, though his portrait grows bloated and twisted. As the real woman changed with her life's progress and the personal and political exigencies that left indelible marks on the Queen and her nation, her silhouette on the postage stamp remained fresh and youthful, unblemished by pain, struggle, trouble, or time.

THE GENERAL POST OFFICE, ONE MINUTE TO SIX

Twenty years after Uniform Penny Postage went into effect on January 10, 1840, George Elgar Hicks chose this historical moment as the setting for his monumental canvas entitled *The General Post Office, One Minute to Six* (1860), first exhibited at the Royal Academy Summer Exhibition of 1860 (see figure 6). I close this chapter with Hicks's painting because it showcases how the reformed Post Office became, for many Victorians, emblematic of life in industrialized Britain. The painting draws its inspiration from contemporary life. This was the vogue in visual arts in the Victorian era, famous for its love of taxonomies and classification. Hicks's painting presents visual vignettes of Londoners of many different ages, classes, occupations, and life situations, who all gather in the General Post Office, which, by 1860, had become a core social institution, a public curiosity and site of human interest (like a living museum), a hub of social and economic activity, and, of course, the brunt of satire. The reduction and eventual removal of the Stamp Tax on newspapers in 1836 and 1855, along with the introduction of the Penny Post in 1840, greatly encouraged the growth of a cheap and reliable daily postal service that became indispensable to Victorian life. The Victorians depended on getting to their local post offices before the 6:00 p.m. closing time—even after the advent of the telegraph—in order to prepay and post a whole range of printed materials, including books, newspapers, death notices, urgent letters home, love letters, and other more curious items that I discuss in chapters 4 and 5.

Different from today, Victorian cities around 1860 had six to twelve daily postal deliveries, as well as frequent daily collections from letter boxes.[72] The directive "return of post" instructed the receiver to answer a letter by the next

FIGURE 6. *The General Post Office, One Minute to Six*, by George Elgar Hicks, 1860. ©
Museum of London.

collection of any given day. Victorians expected that a letter might arrive two
to three hours after posting, although to the dismay of many patrons, it often
took eight or nine hours (still far speedier than mail service today). As one
Victorian complained to the *Times* in 1861: "'If there is any good reason why
letters should not be delivered in less than eight hours after their postage, let
the state of the case be understood: but the belief that one can communicate
with another person in two or three hours whereas in reality the time required
is eight or nine, may be productive of the most disastrous consequences.'"[73] By
1861, one year after Hicks displayed his painting at the Royal Academy exhibition, patrons had come to depend on their local post offices as places where
they could deposit money in a Post Office Savings Bank. Eventually, they also
came to rely on the purchase of postal orders to transmit money inexpensively.
In 1869, the Post Office purchased the telegraph companies, and in 1882, telephone facilities became available through the Post Office. The ever-expanding
scope of communications technologies over which the Post Office presided
indicates why the Victorians regularly used and relied upon the post.[74]

Hicks visually guides us into the massive entryway of St. Martin's-le-Grand,
just one minute before the six o'clock closing. Here, twenty years earlier, crowds
had given one cheer—or possibly three—for Rowland Hill and his invention
of Uniform Penny Postage. Young and old, rich and poor, man and woman,
thief and policeman, human and canine all form a "crush" on canvas remi-

niscent of Hill's, Cole's, and Smyth's descriptions of thousands of Londoners crowding into St. Martin's-le-Grand on January 10, 1840, to prepay letters or simply watch the crowd. There is one big difference, though: a viewer looking closely at the painting can discern in the hands of Post Office patrons envelopes bearing Penny Red and Two Pence Blue stamps. On opening day of cheap postage, stamps were not yet available for public purchase. Amidst the chaos at one minute to closing, we see a whistling newsboy, a pickpocket, a policeman, prosperous patrons, an office boy carrying business posts, a kindly man leading a lost girl, a well-dressed woman rushing to post a personal letter, and many other individuals. Fittingly, all eyes look toward the postal windows (outside the actual boundaries of Hicks's picture) that seized the imaginations of Hill, Cole, Smyth, and, of course, Dickens and Wills, who describe closing time at the General Post Office in the 1850 opening number of *Household Words*.

What came of the rosy postal-age utopia that postal reformers predicted? Much happened across England's vast empire in the twenty years intervening between the time postal stationery and stamps became available for public purchase and the time that Hicks painted his canvas. Britain had witnessed, for example, the Crimean War crisis; the dawning of the Pre-Raphaelite Brotherhood; the publication of Charles Darwin's controversial *The Origin of Species* (1859); an increase of religious doubt; the craze of sensation fiction; expanding imperialism and ensuing conflicts in India, Africa, China, Canada, and the West Indies; communication by telegraph; and travel by steamships and railways (Palmer's mail carriages were obsolete except in rural areas).[75] And, as we might expect, there were still fallen daughters, degenerate soldiers, and indolent apprentices even though mail could now travel throughout England for a penny, and people of all classes and circumstances could more easily stay connected with family and friends.

Hill himself underwent many career changes during this same twenty-year period. Initially appointed a member of the Department of Treasury on September 16, 1839, and unseated in 1842 with the election of the Conservative Party, Hill was by 1846 secretary to the postmaster general of the Post Office and, by 1854, secretary of the Post Office, a position he held until he retired in 1864. Hill seems to have had his share of critics, as well as supporters. Anthony Trollope found Hill an autocratic leader, and even his fellow postal reformer, Henry Cole, complained of the "peremptory and highhanded" leadership style that prompted Hill to quarrel with successive competent postmasters general.[76] On the other hand, in 1861, one year after Hicks painted *The General Post Office, One Minute to Six*, Queen Victoria knighted Hill for his efforts to bring an affordable post to the masses. That same year, an outbreak of typhoid fever killed Prince Albert, who, only a decade earlier, had brought great optimism and pride to England when he ushered in the Great Exhibition of 1851. Albert's brainchild, this first world's fair attracted an unprecedented number of visitors from the Continent and Great Britain and exhibited among its featured technological innovations an envelope-folding machine, portable writing desks, and other postal paraphernalia, the commercial production of which boomed following the postal reform of 1840.

All narrative paintings tell stories, and in this respect Hicks's work is unexceptional. What *is* exceptional about *The General Post Office*, even if, as Mark Bills points out, "Hicks was no Hogarth" (550), are the number of stories Hicks tells within the limited extent of one canvas. In fact, Victorian art critics compared aspects of Hicks's work to Hogarth in their assessments of *The General Post Office*. Despite a generally unfavorable view of the work, Frederick George Stephens considered Hicks's subject "a task worthy of Hogarth" (688), and W. Thornbury conceded in his 1860 review for *The May Exhibition: A Guide to the Pictures at the Royal Academy* that Hicks's choice of painting recalls "'Hogarthian scenes of London life . . . if [rendered] less powerfully than our great satirist, [then] certainly more genteely.'"[77] "Hogarthian" Hicks certainly made his reputation painting diverse London crowds and scenes in *Dividend Day at the Bank of England* (1859), *The General Post Office, One Minute to Six*, and *Billingsgate Market* (1870) (a still-famous London fish market).[78]

There are three focal points that range from left to right in Hicks's canvas. The first is comprised of five figures at the far left of the picture. A young girl lost in the bustle of the crowd is being helped by a kindly gentleman in a red coat and top hat. Close behind this pair, a police officer catches a young thief in the act of picking the pocket of a respectable young woman, who is wholly unaware of the filching about to take place. The second focal point, in the central foreground of the painting, is also comprised of five figures. Two female customers wait impatiently in line to post their letters: a young woman wearing a brown dress and dark tartan shawl, accompanied by her little dog, and a little girl in a red plaid dress and brown cloak. A whistling office boy, probably a delivery boy, stands facing them to the right, while another youth crouches to pick up newspapers that have fallen to the floor. In the third focal scene, located at the far right middle of the picture plane, men and boys appear to push into the canvas from a side door, clamoring under the weight of bundles of newspapers in the depicted rush of activity accompanying their daily distribution. Papers fly through the air and litter the ground.

Hicks took pains to accurately render the postage stamps on the letters the patrons hold. A Two Pence Blue stamp appears on the letter held by the young woman in brown, while a Penny Red shows on the letter held by the little girl standing next to her on the right. Behind and to the left of the woman in brown, a delivery boy carries two stacks of letters, one labeled with Penny Reds and another with Two Pence Blues. By 1860, Mulreadies had long been withdrawn, and the Penny Black had long since given way to the Penny Red. The Queen's head on the 1d red and 2d blue postage stamps, however, was still very much in the public eye.

There was a lot of buzz about Hicks's painting. Critics were quick to dismiss it. Frederick George Stephens, one of the founders of the Pre-Raphaelite Brotherhood, who went on to become a leading Victorian art reviewer and official critic for the *Athenaeum* from 1860 to 1900, notes in a May 19, 1860, review, "There is hardly a more hopeless and meretricious picture in the Royal Academy than that by Mr. G. E. Hicks, (No. 367); indeed, but for its prominent position, we should pass it over in silence, content that mere mechanism could not do much harm. Placed as this work is, we have no other choice than to point out the poor and machine-like character of a picture which, by its showy and pretentious execution, is sure to find observers" (688). An anonymous art critic for *Fraser's Magazine* observes in "The Exhibitions of 1860," that Hicks "has given way to the too common weakness for making things comfortable, a weakness which does more towards producing real vulgarity in art than any other. The haste and confusion are admirably given, but the crowd is evidently a select crowd; and from its general cleanness and neatness might pass for a set of persons in good society performing the final scene in the charade of 'Post-office'" (688).

Despite its detractors, the painting was wildly popular among Victorian viewers—perhaps because it conveyed "a striking statement about the pace of activity in the city, about the behaviour of the crowd and the role of the centralised post and press system at the heart of a vast empire," as Mark Bills notes (550). Some Victorian critics, such as Thornbury, concur: "'The last moment of posting time is a scene expressing the ardour and abundance of our national life, and well worth perpetuating.'"[79] Something akin to "ardour" was apparently experienced by viewers who crowded to see *The General Post Office* at the 1860 Royal Academy Summer Exhibition. (It was displayed in the west gallery of the National Gallery in Trafalgar Square.) Public clamor was great enough to catch the attention of *Punch*, which reported in its June 16, 1860, article "The Royal Academy" that "the crush represented in MR. HICKS'S picture gives only a faint idea of the crowd around it. The glimpses which you catch of it, between hats, over shoulders, and under arms, increase the reality of the scene" (246). Indeed, Hicks's canvas captures the nineteenth-century

British Post Office as a center of "ardour and abundance" that reflected the vitality of London as "the heart of a vast [and rapidly growing] empire" (Bills 550). Through the urgency and pathos of his subject, Hicks portrays how revolutionary innovations in postage had become integral to the fabric of daily life, even if the Penny Post had not created the utopia that reformers had predicted it would. In 1860, the year Hicks exhibited this monumental canvas, the public was still rushing to make the last posting at St. Martin's-le-Grand, and communication by post was central to the Victorians and their way of life.

2

OUTCOMES

~

Chapter 3

"Why Is a Raven . . . ?"

The Rise of Postal Products from *Alice's Adventures in Wonderland* (1865) and *Vanity Fair* (1848) to the Pages of the Great Exhibition Catalogue (1851)

Mechanical reproduction of art changes the reaction of the masses toward art.
—Walter Benjamin, "The Work of Art in the Age of Mechanical Reproduction," 1935

Two landmarks frame postal reform in nineteenth-century Britain in part 1 of *Posting It*: on January 10, 1840, cheap, affordable mail extended across England; in May, 1860, George Elgar Hicks exhibited *The General Post Office, One Minute to Six* at the Royal Academy Summer Exhibition, commemorating St. Martin's-le-Grand as an institution integral to Victorian life. Part 2, "Outcomes," takes as its starting point these twenty intervening years (1840–1860) in which Britain experienced an arguably unexpected outcome of postal reform—a steady rise in postal products that accompanied the advent of cheap postage. Did the Victorians anticipate that in this age of mechanical reproduction, the passing of Uniform Penny Postage would foster a new field of industry? Cheap postage and the ushering in of prepaid stationery and postage stamps led to the creation of jobs, hobbies, innovative postal practices, and telling material objects.

Modern day consumerism has its roots in the Victorian age of production and consumption. The Industrial Revolution led to an increase in speed of work and production and granted opportunities for leisure, choice, shopping, and collecting. Britain was the undisputed leader of the Industrial Revolution; the Great Exhibition of 1851, the first World's Fair held in London at the Crystal Palace, showcased technological, economic, and military achievements of the civilized world and, in turn, created a demand for more consumer products. The Victorians manufactured and imported a range of materials for consumption, including fiction, food, drink, clothing, and postal ephemera. Once connected with sin and indulgence, consumerism and, in turn, consumption became forms of self-expression. Victorian identity became intertwined with the books readers chose for their libraries, the foods people ate, the beverages they drank, the fashions they wore, and, post-1840, the goods they increasingly bought for the activities of daily life, including correspondence. A bewildering array of high-end and mass-produced postal products were among the emissaries of progress exhibited in the Great Exhibition of 1851. Pillar boxes, envelopes (plain and pictorial), pens, inkwells, stamp boxes, letter holders, wafers and seals, letter clips, scales, writing manuals, and portable writing desks, in turn, represent the post as a growing commercial enterprise.

This chapter lays out this array of postal products included in the Great Exhibition of 1851 and features material objects in which the Victorians invested meaning and sentiment. Pictorial envelopes, letter-writing manuals, and, in particular, writing desks are material memories—physical reminders of the past that transmit knowledge of decorum, social class, political views, gender, and aesthetics of the period. Sources as diverse as temperance envelopes, Lewis Carroll's *Alice's Adventures in Wonderland*, the *Official Descriptive and Illustrated Catalogue* of the Great Exhibition (1851), and William Makepeace Thackeray's *Vanity Fair* illuminate a commercial boom accompanying the Victorian revolution in letter writing, informing us about the Victorian age and the Victorians who created, bought, collected, and used these products. Writing desks, which we might aptly call Victorian laptops, tell us about privacy, security, and portability at a time when heating was inefficient, houses were not yet electrified, and people of the upper reaches made long visits to friends and family lasting weeks and months. While the outside of the box carries meaning about aesthetics, gender, and social class, the inside, including the key lock and hidden drawers, reveals the importance of privacy; in making this valuable item of furniture a plot device in *Vanity Fair*, Thackeray, in turn, illustrates how the writing desk functioned as a private, transportable space to save and safeguard possessions, billets-doux, and secrets.

PILLAR BOXES AND LETTER BOXES

We can trace roadside pillar boxes—a now standard fixture in British cities and the countryside—to Uniform Penny Postage of 1840. As more people took advantage of the post, and letter writing continued to rise, the pillar box offered a convenient way to send letters. Not a British invention, pillar boxes appeared on the Continent in Paris as early as 1653.[1] However, we can credit pillar boxes in Britain to Anthony Trollope, who—though known today as a leading Victorian novelist—spent thirty-three years of his life in the Post Office, many in the capacity of surveyor.[2] Familiar with the convenience of pillar boxes in France, Trollope takes credit for originating "pillar letter-boxes" in the "streets and ways of England": "I was the originator, having, however, got the authority for the erection of the first at St. Heliers in Jersey" (*Autobiography* 246). The Channel Islands formed part of Trollope's district, and upon Trollope's recommendation, four red-painted hexagonal boxes arrived in St. Heliers, Jersey, on November 23, 1852, followed by three more pillar boxes in Guernsey in February 1853.[3] The iron pillar box stamped with the initials "V. R." became a welcome convenience,[4] even if some like Jemima Stanbury, Trollope's formidable spinster aunt in *He Knew He Was Right* (1869), placed little confidence in them: "she had not the faintest belief that any letter put into one of them would ever reach its destination. She could not understand why people should not walk with their letters to a respectable post-office instead of chucking them into an iron stump,—as she called it—out in the middle of the street with nobody to look after it. Positive orders had been given that no letters from her house should ever be put into the iron post" (69).

What Trollope dubbed "iron stumps" in *He Knew He Was Right* came to the mainland of Britain in September 1853, arriving in London on April 11, 1855.[5] Eleanor Smyth offers one humorous story in which Trollope's Jemima Stanbury's most paranoid fears come true. Shortly after the introduction of pillar boxes in 1855, a London merchant grew angry that not all his letters were being delivered. Periodically, he wrote furious letters to the postmaster general, lambasting the Post Office for its poor delivery service and demanding to know why his letters did not always reach their destinations. When the Post Office searched for the letters without success, the merchant wrote letters to the press, trumpeting the "stupidity" of the Post Office. During city improvements, the missing letters turned up in an ancient pump missing its handle. The explanation resides in the novelty of the pillar box: "An errand-boy had, at odd times, been sent to post the Firm's letters, and had slipped them into the narrow slit where once the vanished pump-handle used to work. The introduction of street letter-boxes was then recent, and their aspect still unfamiliar. The boy had therefore taken the venerable relic for one of those novel structures, and all the missing letters lay therein" (Smyth 146–47). Not just children made this common mistake, as one English postmaster reported in 1877: "'There is hardly any opening onto the street that is not occasionally mistaken for the slot of a mailbox by some uninformed person.'"[6]

Popularity of the pillar box rapidly grew: by the time of Queen Victoria's death, there were over 30,000 letter boxes in England (Briggs 335). Some now-longstanding changes in postal delivery came much sooner than pillar boxes. In 1840, with postmen leaving prepaid letters at a person's door (rather than ringing and waiting for payment), many Victorians, like Harriet Martineau, rushed to create slits in their doors or to put up letter boxes for their post to facilitate rapid delivery. Martineau describes this flurry of activity in a letter of 1840: "'We are all putting up our letter-boxes on our hall doors with great glee, anticipating the hearing from brothers and sisters,—a line or two almost every day. The slips in the doors are to save the postmen's time—the great point being how many letters may be delivered within a given time, the postage being paid in the price of the envelopes, or paper. So all who wish well to the plan are having slips in their doors.'"[7] Not all Victorians responded to this development as eagerly or "gleefully" as Martineau, however. In 1848, Rowland Hill asked the postmaster general to issue a notice asking Londoners to provide their own letter boxes. Notable is the resistance of the late Marquis of Londonderry, who, Hill reports, "'indignantly demanded whether the Postmaster-General actually expected that he should cut a slit in his mahogany door!'"[8] Official Post Office notices—such as "Rapid Delivery of Letters. Street Door Letter Boxes," distributed in Whitby in 1885—suggest that some people resisted letter boxes well into the century, although this particular notice states, "Already in many localities these Boxes are extensively used."[9]

POSTAL PRODUCTS

As letter writing and the number of daily postal deliveries increased, savvy manufacturers and designers created a host of new products to make writing a convenience and an aesthetic pleasure. A pen needed a pen rest as well as a pen wiper to clean it and, in the case of a quill pen, a pen knife to sharpen it. Inkwells grew in popularity; given an increasingly mobile Victorian society, traveling inkwells also became a common item. Stationery came in a range of sizes and colors to suit the occasion—courtship, business, mourning—and gave rise to matching envelopes and stationery cases, designed for the convenience of the writer, although some Victorians preferred to house their stationery in a writing desk. A letter needed a letter tray or a letter rack to hold it, as well as a letter opener to unseal it and a scale to weigh it (manufacturers designed small versions of scales for personal use). Another common item for letters was a paper clip or holder, often made of brass or tin and typically shaped like a gloved hand. National emblems, like the lion and the unicorn, adorned some paper clips, while others took the shape of ivy, fruits, flowers, hearts, butterflies, and shells or catered to a specific consumer (for example, a horseshoe for the equestrian, a cameo for a lady). The Victorians used paper clips to gather letters to take to the local post office or to clip the post when it arrived at the home or workplace.

Pictorial Envelopes

Following Uniform Penny Postage, envelope production soared. Anticipating the picture postcard (invented in Austria in 1869), tourist envelopes showed picturesque sites from the United Kingdom and other countries that readily interested the Victorian public. "Curiously enough," as Asa Briggs suggests, "the failure of the Mulready envelopes may have given an impetus to the popularity of other envelopes bearing views of places and sketches of people and things" (343). The public taste for illustrated envelopes became something of a vogue, even a "craze" (Lowe 90), that peaked in 1841 and resurged in the late 1840s and 1850s. The pictorial envelope, like other forms of illustrated stationery of the period, became a ready vehicle for circulating commercial advertising and social propaganda, for documenting key historical events, and for pressing social and political reforms. While today a Victorian time traveler might be surprised to find people standing on street corners, holding protest signs, and conducting rallies, over 150 years ago, this Victorian might have expressed his or her views by purchasing and posting pictorial envelopes advocating causes, such as affordable transatlantic postage, peace and brotherhood, and temperance.

Elihu Burritt, United States consular agent in Birmingham, spearheaded the movement for Ocean Penny Postage. Although Burritt idealistically argued that cheap overseas postage would promote global peace and brotherhood, this movement was also pragmatically motivated by the high cost of overseas mailing. In 1852, for example, it cost 1s od to send a letter from Iona (an island off the coast of Scotland) to the "Collector, Controller, & Surveyor of Customs, Boston, North America." The face of this letter bears twelve individual Penny Red stamps, plainly pointing to the high cost of transatlantic postage. Since the post office in Iona was remote and inhabitants rarely sent letters abroad, the post office simply did not have 2d, 6d, or 1s stamps to sell. The letters of soldiers stationed abroad could travel overseas for 1d as opposed to 1s od. A postal charge of 1d appears on an extant 1841 letter from "Hospital Sergeant Duran of the 66th Regiment in Portsmouth to J. S. Cartwright, Esq., in Kingston, Upper Canada, British North America." In it, Duran asks for a refund on a land purchase or a better plot (a fellow officer already stationed in Canada had apparently seen the land and told Duran of its poor quality).[10] With the exception of the concession for the military, given the high cost of overseas postage, it is not surprising that Ocean Penny Postage followed on the tail of Uniform Penny Postage. Interestingly, Rowland Hill opposed it, arguing that land transport was not equivalent to ocean transport of mail.[11]

Many extant Ocean Penny Postage envelopes date to the years between 1849 and 1854. Designed around 1854, one peace envelope shows in the upper left-hand corner an image of Mercury in his winged cap positioned above an overseas vessel. The words "Ocean Postage" and diverse visual symbols—of peace, transportation, and postal service—adorn the envelope: the clasped hands of individuals of different races; a dove holding an olive branch; a railway train, a canal boat, and mail packets. A pair of scrolls unfurl along the top and bottom of the design, bearing in bold, block letters, "BRITAIN! FROM THEE THE WORLD EXPECTS AN OCEAN PENNY POSTAGE—TO MAKE HER CHILDREN ONE FRATERNITY."[12] The Valentines of Dundee, personal friends of Elihu Burritt, printed numerous pictorial envelopes dedicated to universal brotherhood, peace, and abolition (one depicts Britannia as the defender of the liberated slave). In similar spirit, an 1850 Victorian Peace Society envelope announces in bold, block letters: "WHEN ALL THE WORLD IS PREPARED FOR WAR, WAR BECOMES ALMOST INEVITABLE" and "BLESSED ARE THE PEACEMAKERS."[13]

Pictorial envelopes became a powerful propaganda tool in the temperance movement's effort to get abstinence pledges from the citizenry by preaching the dangerous consequences of drink: poverty, crime, moral degeneration, sickness, and death. George Cruikshank, a reformed drinker, depicts these tragic outcomes (adding suicide and madness) in his highly popular series of prints entitled *The Bottle* (1847) and its sequel series, *The Drunkard's Children* (1848), both of which he designed on behalf of the Victorian temperance movement. Pictorial envelopes promoting temperance likewise show scenes of inebriation in the home, pub, and street and include boldfaced, block letter captions, such as "INTOXICATING DRINKS—ARE THE BANE & CURSE OF SOCIETY" and "INTEMPERANCE IS THE BANE OF SOCIETY." Still other envelopes preach the positive side of abstinence with the Goddess of Temperance flanked by flag-bearing delegates from Europe, Asia, Africa, and America, all paying her homage.[14]

While clearly the purpose of some pictorial envelopes was to persuade, agitate, or sermonize, others were created simply to entertain. Beginning in 1840,

Richard and James Doyle created covers for Fores's Comic Envelopes that offered a comical view of daily Victorian activities—musical soirées, dancing, hunting, horse racing, shooting, courting, and Christmas celebrating.[15] Scenic or tourist envelopes showcased picturesque Victorian locales—scenes of Oxford, Windsor Castle, and Castle Walks (Stirling Hume's home), for instance. In addition to envelopes, pictorial stationery of tourist sites was also highly popular in the 1850s: a letter dated December 7, 1850, from Rev. Richard Warner to Sir George Burrard, is written on a pictorial letter sheet featuring a magnificent façade of the Bath Abbey with the caption, "West Front of the Abbey Church."[16] Envelopes of a celebratory nature commemorated the marriage of Victoria and Albert (1840), the Great Exhibition of 1851, the genius of Shakespeare (an 1852 design shows his birthplace, characters, and portrait), and, much later, in 1890, the Jubilee of Penny Postage itself.[17]

The booming commercial success of the envelope had as much to do with practical security as it did with the item's usefulness in promoting tourism, commemorating public events, agitating for reform, or proselytizing and propagandizing in the service of causes: it provided an extra layer of protection, safeguarding its enclosure.[18] Some people worried that an envelope might be thrown away and the sender's address permanently lost to its receiver. When envelopes for business correspondence quickly became popular, many offices made a practice of attaching a letter to the envelope in which it arrived. By replacing the folded, sealed letter, the envelope became aligned with ideas of progress, as well as with a developing Victorian notion of privacy in public and private spheres. An untidy or poorly sealed letter was, in contrast, linked to "old-fashioned" ways, as Thomas Hardy illustrates in making a cracked wax seal a plot device in *The Mayor of Casterbridge* (1886). Susan Henchard, "though more patient than her husband, had been no practical hand at anything": on her deathbed, "in sealing up the sheet, which was folded and tucked in without an envelope, in the old-fashioned way, she had overlaid the junction with a large mass of wax without the requisite undertouch of the same. The seal had cracked, and the letter was open" (127). This letter, "'Not to be opened till Elizabeth-Jane's wedding day,'" reveals to Michael Henchard his daughter's real identity—she is not Henchard's biological child—and Henchard's unintentional eavesdropping leads to dire consequences in true Hardy fashion.[19] Disdain for an untidy, "old-fashioned" letter with a cracked seal—so unlike the neatly folded letters that Jane Austen wrote regularly and took pains to seal so carefully[20]—speaks to this emerging Victorian regard for privacy, bolstered by a belief that an envelope granted both privacy and confidentiality.[21]

Wafers and Stamp Ephemera

Before widespread use of envelopes, wafers offered a ready means to seal a folded letter. They grew in popularity alongside envelope production, because envelopes initially did not have a gummed flap and required a wafer for sealing. Wafers, thin slips of paper with gum or wax on the reverse side, came in a range of shapes—circles, ovals, and lozenge-shaped shields. Especially popular were wafers with initials, designs (cameos, for instance), or with English and French sayings, such as "Answer quickly," "Time explains all," "Faithful to the end," "*Chacun à son goût,*" and "God is love."[22] Like pictorial envelopes, wafers could also be used as emissaries of social and political change or of protest, as in the case of the Corn Laws. In 1844, wafers arose in response to the prying of British Home Secretary James Graham, whom the public lambasted for opening private letters—written by or to suspected political dissidents—in an inner, secret office of St. Martin's-le-Grand. Although Robert Wallace, MP, among others believed prepaid uniform postage would eliminate the need to candle letters to determine the number of sheets and thus ensure privacy, the practice of letter opening continued in the Post Office and, when discovered, was an indignity, to quote Thomas Carlyle, "of kin to picking men's pockets."[23] In turn, savvy advertisers created "anti-Graham" wafers to protest the activities of the home secretary, whom *Punch* in 1844 caricatured as the intrusive Paul Pry. This character from John Poole's popular play *Paul Pry* (1825) was known to come into a room at an inopportune moment, umbrella under his arm, saying, "'I hope I don't intrude.'"[24]

Postage stamps sparked the creation of a host of products as well as a craze. A stamp required a shop to sell it in and a stamp case or a recess in a writing desk to hold it in (prior to 1840, such a recess might hold wafers).[25] Stamp collecting as a hobby speaks to the Victorian desire to list, name, count, contain, organize, collect, display, advertise, and bequeath things. "A philatelist," as Asa Briggs notes, "was far more than a stamp collector. He had to study stamps at least as carefully as the numismatist studied coins or the geologist fossils" (348); to Briggs, stamp dealers and stamp collectors became a "new breed" (344). By 1842, *Punch* mocked the fad of stamp collecting—it had taken on such proportions. A "'new mania,'" *Punch* notes, has "'bitten the industriously idle ladies of England . . . they have been indefatigable in their endeavors to collect old penny stamps; in fact, they betray more anxiety to treasure up Queen's heads than Harry the Eighth did to get rid of them.'"[26] One such "industriously idle" young lady even took out a personal advertisement in the *Times* in October 1842, soliciting "'good-natured'" souls to send her these "'otherwise useless, little articles'" to "'assist her in her whimsical project'" of papering her entire dressing room with cancelled postage stamps. At the time of posting, she had already received 16,000 Queen's heads from friends and well-wishers, but she still needed far more cancelled postage stamps to complete her mission.[27]

Letter-Writing Manuals

While today we can purchase books on how to construct a business letter or write a resumé, Victorian letter-writing manuals include dozens of model letters that carry knowledge of the lives of the Victorians who created, purchased, and followed the prescriptions these books offered.[28] More specifically, letters on how to send condolences, offer congratulations, declare a long undisclosed passion, propose, accept an offer of marriage or cordially reject it, accept or reject a job applicant, et cetera, are material memories of friendship, love, business decorum, good manners, and bereavement in the Victorian age. For example, *The Wide World Letter Writer* (n.d.) advises that in the case of condolence letters—"the most trying of all letters to write or receive" and "of vast importance in friendship"—it is "best to make your letter short, but earnest and sincere" (92). While the "wounds" of death necessitated earnestness in the Victorian letter writer, courtship required restraint. A lady, this same manual recommends, must adopt "a quiet, affectionate dignity in writing" even to her betrothed and not "put too much of the most sacred of feelings upon paper" (130).

Letter-writing manuals emerged in an age where people considered penmanship a mark of good breeding and where the language and contents of a letter determined one's character. Period letter-writing manuals also give insight into styles of communication, values, and decorum of a bygone era. These and other prescriptive manuals—part of a genre which today we refer to as "self-help"—were fueled, in part, by the Society for the Diffusion of Useful Knowledge, which, between 1826 and 1848, published pamphlets for members of the working or middle classes who were interested in self-education (some of whom were unable to afford schooling). Some letter-writing manuals alleged to help writers take advantage of the opportunities for frequent communication now affordable by the larger public. In fact, the preface and introduction to *The Wide World Letter Writer* state that the manual is dedicated to the "vast numbers of people who seldom write or read a letter" (vii). According to the first nationwide census of 1840, 67 percent of males and 51 percent of females in England (most of whom were between the ages of 16 and 25) were literate (based on the ability to sign the marriage register that year);

these figures increased to 69.3 percent of males and 54.8 percent of females in the 1851 census, offering testimony that there was a ready and growing market for newspapers, books, writing implements, and letter-writing manuals.[29]

The large, receptive audience for writing manuals suggests that merely lowering postage was not enough to promote literacy as reformers had prophesied. Since free franks were believed to be an incentive for literacy among the military and navy, reformers had argued by analogy that cheap postage would offer the general public a similar incentive. The opening pages of *The Wide World Letter Writer* promote this book with the very same arguments that postal reformers used for why the early Victorians needed postal reform in the first place: writing manuals would help Victorians stay connected with friends and family, since "It is a rare exception in our nation when families remain together after the children have arrived at years of maturity" (vii). In an increasingly mobile Victorian society, these self-help books were seemingly designed to help friends stay in touch as they moved from country to city or emigrated to a new world, such as Canada, America, or Australia. The rhetoric of emotion that dominated the campaign for postal reform resonates in *The Wide World Letter Writer*, as it addresses the "Many who handle the saw or hammer daily" but "will shrink from attempting to wield the pen" (vii). Letters will "bind these hearts closely together, though faces and loving eyes are far asunder" and "keep alive the warm home love" (vii); "the wide ocean, the vast prairie, the lofty mountain, the stronger bar of years of time, may stretch between loving hearts, yet a letter will speed from one to the other, keeping alive the tenderest emotion" (x).

Likewise, in *The Universal Letter Writer* (c. 1850), Rev. T. Cooke proclaims, "Letters are the life of trade—the fuel of love—the pleasure of friendship—the food of the politician—and the entertainment of the curious" (vi).[30] The frontispiece to this book features a young woman posed at her writing desk, quill in one hand, her other reaching toward her heart, writing what we presume is "the fuel of love," an intimate billet-doux (see figure 7). A familiar handwriting was not only reassuring but an emissary of love, as Edward Bulwer-Lytton expresses in *Eugene Aram* (1832), when the postman, "that most welcome of visitants to a country place," brings joy to Madeline Lester via a letter from her lover, Eugene Aram: "one letter—for Madeline—Aram's handwriting. Happy blush—bright smile! Ah! no meeting ever gives the delight that a letter can inspire in the short absences of a first love" (115). Handwriting, as David Henkin points out, formed "the essence of personal correspondence" since "handwritten letters bore the trace of physical contact and not simply the recognizable imprimatur of individual identity" (55–56)—a point Charles Dickens illus-

FIGURE 7. Frontispiece to
The Universal Letter Writer
by Rev. T. Cooke, c. 1850.

trates in *Bleak House* (1853): Lady Dedlock startles at the recognition of the distinctive penmanship of her longed-for lover, believed dead, on some law papers the family lawyer, Mr. Tulkinghorn, brings to Chesney Wold.

Handwriting could impress, as well as delight or alarm a reader. According to *The Companion to the Writing Desk* (small enough to fit easily into a ladies' writing desk), a "slovenly and negligent manner of writing argues a want of due respect" (103). Tidy, careful, attractive writing, in contrast, garnered "due respect," as Austen illustrates in *Emma* (1815). Frank Churchill impresses the neighborhood of Highbury and, in particular, his new stepmother, Mrs. Weston—all of whom he has never met—by writing a "'handsome letter'"; from this "highly-prized letter," notes Austen, "Mrs. Weston had, of course, formed a very favourable idea of the young man"(18). Penmanship was a skill that a lady and gentleman cultivated through practice if it did not come naturally. In the days before typewriters, penmanship was part of the school curriculum, and people understood the importance of good handwriting not only to court

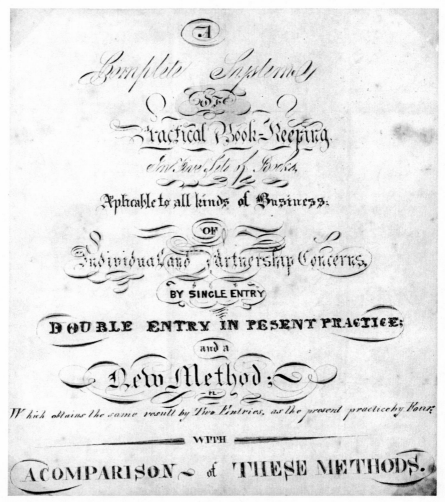

FIGURE 8. Scottish schoolboy's handwriting, 1842. From the collection of James Grimwood-Taylor.

but to garner a position. One extant prepaid letter posted from a schoolboy in Dumbarton, Scotland, to his brother in Liverpool, dated "15th/20th Apr. 1842," features colored inks and a range of calligraphy styles (see figure 8). Was the lad boasting of his abilities or perhaps hoping that his brother could show this letter to a prospective employer to help him to secure a job?[31]

In George Eliot's *Middlemarch* (1872), the upstanding Caleb Garth tells the aspiring but fallible Fred Vincy that he must improve his handwriting if he is to remain in his employ: "'Why you must learn to form your letters and keep the line. What's the use of writing at all if nobody can understand it?'" (611). Eliot's advice about handwriting as a representation of one's personal author- ity comes straight from the writing manuals of the day. *The Wide World Letter Writer* insists: "If you write what cannot be read, why write at all? It is surely a waste of time, pen, ink, and paper to make marks that are absolutely useless to a reader, or that are to consume perhaps valuable time to decipher what ought to be perfectly plain at sight" (xii). The Dumbarton schoolboy and Eliot alike recognized the Victorian view that a well-written letter "stamps a man's capac- ity" and advanced all people, "from the Premier in his cabinet to the labourer in the streets; from the lady in her parlour to the servant in her kitchen; from the millionaire to the beggar; from the emigrant to the settler" (*Wide World* xi).

LEWIS CARROLL: INVENTOR OF POSTAL MATERIALS

Charles Lutwidge Dodgson, better known as Lewis Carroll, was barely eight years old when Britain ushered in Uniform Penny Postage. Carroll, who grew up in an age of affordable postage, was a prolific letter writer; he kept an accu- rate register of all the letters he wrote and received during his lifetime. Among Carroll's abundant correspondence are letters to the Post Office regarding delivery service—in one, for example, he recommends that a postman wear a special cape to protect letters from rain—and ideas about registering let- ters or parcels.[32] Although Queen Victoria's head (in various colors) graced the stamps that Carroll knew and used his entire life, it seems fitting that in 1979, eighty-one years after his death, the British Post Office issued a set of four stamps commemorating his creations—Alice, the Mad Hatter, and the Cheshire Cat.

An inventor of word games, puzzles, charades, riddles, and acrostics, Car- roll devised two postal products that piggybacked on the popularity of his enduring *Alice's Adventures in Wonderland*—what he called "The Wonderland Postage-Stamp Case" and a short manual about letter writing marketed with it, entitled *Eight or Nine Wise Words About Letter-Writing* (1890). They sold together for one shilling in stationers' shops in 1890, the jubilee of Uniform Penny Postage. Desire for enduring fame arguably motivated Carroll to invent a Wonderland stamp case. Toward the twilight of his career, following the dis- appointing reception of *Sylvie and Bruno* (1889) and its 1893 sequel, Carroll, according to his biographer Morton Cohen, "could find consolation in the flourishing Alice industry" (*A Biography* 491). By 1891, over 100,000 copies of *Alice's Adventures in Wonderland* and *Through the Looking-Glass* (1871) had sold; translations of Carroll's works flourished, and the *Alice* books sparked a range of commercial enterprises (a biscuit tin in 1890, for example) as well as imitations and parodies. Motivated perhaps by *Alice's* commercial success, Emberlin and Son of Oxford in 1890 manufactured the Wonderland stamp case, along with the miniature pamphlet *Eight or Nine Wise Words*. Macmillan, Carroll's lifelong publisher, on the other hand, declined to market it.

The slipcase features on its front and back, respectively, Tenniel's illustrations of Alice holding the Duchess's baby and the Cheshire Cat grinning broadly. In a transformation befitting Wonderland, when the stamp case is pulled from its covering, the illustrations have changed: the front shows Alice holding a pig, and the back shows only the Cheshire Cat's enigmatic grin. The stamp case contains twelve pockets for various denominations of postage stamps ranging from ½d to 1s (each pocket holds up to six stamps). Akin to the Lilliputian-sized letter that Henry Cole created to promote Uniform Penny Postage, Carroll designed a letter the size of a postage stamp, which he tucked into one of the pockets of a prepublication copy of *Eight or Nine Wise Words* for his child friend Mary Jackson. Different from other manuals on the market, Carroll's is, as Cohen aptly puts it, "practical, sensible, and tongue-in-cheek" (*Biography* 493). Carroll advises the writer to reread a letter before answering it; to put the stamp and address on the envelope before writing to avoid the "wildly-scrawled signature—the hastily-fastened envelope, which comes open in the post—the address, a mere hieroglyphic" (*Eight or Nine* 2–3); to write legibly; to avoid extensive apologies for not writing sooner; to use a second sheet of paper rather than to "cross"—"Remember the old proverb '*Cross-writing makes cross reading*'" (16–17); to avoid the "headlong rush to the Post Office, arriving, hot and gasping" (3)—a scene Hicks shows in *The General Post Office, One Minute to Six*; to carry letters to the post in one's hand and not one's pocket, as the writer might arrive home with letters still in his or her pocket (something Carroll often did); and so on. Carroll even advises where to keep the stamp case: "*this* is meant to haunt your envelope-case, or wherever you keep your writing-materials" (37).

It seems curious that Carroll did not designate the writing desk as the logical depository for his postage stamp case. Most Victorians kept their writing materials in a portable writing desk. Moreover, much earlier in his writing career, Carroll created a riddle about a writing desk in what is now arguably the world's most famous tea party scene. In *Alice's Adventures in Wonderland*, the Mad Hatter asks Alice: "'Why is a raven like a writing-desk?'" (97). Much folly ensues among the Mad Hatter, the March Hare, the Dormouse, and Alice in "A Mad Tea-Party." Alas, "Alice thought over all she could remember about ravens and writing-desks, which wasn't much" (98). In the midst of the mayhem, the Mad Hatter abruptly queries, "'Have you guessed the riddle yet?'" (100), but when Alice gives up and demands the answer, the Mad Hatter admits, "'I haven't the slightest idea'" (101). Carroll enthusiasts have tried to solve the riddle—responses include "Edgar Allan Poe wrote on both" and "both ravens and writing desks come with inky quills."[33] The riddle still entertains even if we don't know much about writing desks, one of the commodities on display at the Great Exhibition of 1851.

THE GREAT VICTORIAN EXHIBITION: CELEBRATING POSTAL INNOVATION

Inkwells, letter openers, stamp boxes, pens, stationery, stationery boxes, envelopes, envelope cases, and writing desks listed in the *Official Descriptive and Illustrated Catalogue* are emissaries of Victorian culture and civilization. The massive three-volume catalogue with steel engravings offers a record of the Great Exhibition (also called the Crystal Palace Exhibition and the Great Victorian Collection [Briggs 52]), the first-ever world's fair of culture and industry held in Hyde Park, London, from May 1 to October 15, 1851. There were fairs for centuries before this one, and national exhibitions of commerce date to earlier nineteenth-century England and France, but none were so monumental.[34] Over six million visitors came to London to see the Great Exhibition, which contained more than 13,000 exhibits from Britain and from foreign countries across the globe. Prince Albert, Henry Cole, and other members of the Royal Society for the Encouragement of Arts, Manufactures and Commerce conceived of the international exhibition as a way to celebrate economy, industry, technology, and design. If to radicals such as Karl Marx the exhibition became "an emblem of the capitalist fetishism of commodities,"[35] to those who attended, including leading literati like Charlotte Brontë, it was a wonder to behold.

Brontë notes in a letter to her father, dated June 7, 1851, upon seeing the Crystal Palace for a second time:

Whatever human industry has created—you find there—from the great compartments filled with Railway Engines and boilers, with Mill-Machinery in full work—with splendid carriages of all kinds—with harness of every description—to the glass-covered and velvet spread stands loaded with the most gorgeous work of the goldsmith and silversmith— and the carefully guarded caskets full of real diamonds and pearls worth hundreds of thousands of pounds. It may be called a Bazaar or a Fair—but it is such a Bazaar or Fair as eastern Genii might have created. It seems as if magic only could have gathered this mass of wealth from all the ends of the Earth—as if none but supernatural hands could have arranged it thus—with such a blaze and contrast of colours and marvellous power of effect.[36]

Brontë's response encapsulates an innocent and sentimental gaze on commodities that Marxist philosophers politicize in their critiques of capitalism. Marx critiqued the capitalistic mode of production, bemoaning what he saw in Victorian London, according to Asa Briggs, as "capital accumulation and the spread of commodities," which led to "'a mania for possessions,' a 'fetishism' which 'clung to the products of work once they became wares'" (15). Nonetheless, even those who criticize a culture often partake of it. Marx owned a writing desk, a highly displayed commodity at the Great Exhibition. Moreover, Marx spent the greater part of his life in London, either in the reading room of the British Museum or at his own writing desk, a product of the fancy goods trade much in demand following the Great Exhibition.[37]

To Prince Albert, this World's Fair was more than a fetishistic obsession with commodities as Marx theorized it or a spectacle of color and magic that so mesmerized Charlotte Brontë and countless other Victorians. (Queen Victoria visited the Great Exhibition over forty times.) It was an exposition with a humanitarian vision, foreseeing "'the realization of the unity of mankind'"; "'the products of all quarters of the globe are placed at our disposal, and we have only to choose which is the best and cheapest for our purposes,'" Albert declared. "'THE EXHIBITION of 1851 is to give us a true test and a living picture of the point of development at which the whole of mankind has arrived in this great task, and a new starting point from which all nations will be able to direct their further exertions.'"[38]

The Great Exhibition was foremost an exposition of the power of British industry, fueled by the Industrial Revolution, which transformed western culture. Tourists from many nations flocked to London to see art and architectural history, exhibitions of animal and plant life, geological displays, and a range of commodities including nautical items, a reaping machine, steel-making equipment, new kitchen appliances, and inventions or improvements of other kinds, including those integral to the Victorian post—for example, an envelope-folding machine, new grades of stationery, the latest wafer seals, steel-nibbed pens, envelopes with innovative gummed flaps, and papier-mâché portable writing desks. I am interested in the written narratives that exhibitors provided for the *Official Descriptive and Illustrated Catalogue* that describe these "wonders of Art and Industry which man, taught by God, has been by Him enabled to accomplish."[39] The descriptions accompanying each entry contain the exact wording Victorian manufacturers, inventors, and designers provided to the compilers of the catalogue, who printed them verbatim. The compilers of the official catalogue seem to have anticipated the importance of these narratives, noting in the preface that "the great spectacle it illustrates will pass away" (v), but the catalogue will become "a record of the most varied and wonderful collection of objects ever beheld, and as a book of reference to the philosopher, merchant, and manufacturer, it will constantly prove both interesting and instructive to the reader" (v). Important to *Posting It*, these "instructive" and surprisingly "interesting" narratives about postal products enhance the economic, social, and political meaning that the commodities themselves carry as materials of memory: narratives transmit knowledge of gender, social class, aesthetics, and the fancy goods trade in Victorian England as well as the importance of travel, security, and the developing notion of privacy.

POSTAL INNOVATION

The pages of the Great Exhibition *Official Descriptive and Illustrated Catalogue* contain copious listings of writing accoutrements, stationery, and writing boxes, offering evidence that postal products became a thriving industry but one decade after Uniform Penny Postage.[40] According to its introduction in volume 2 of the *Catalogue*, exhibition class 17, "Paper, Printing, and Bookbinding," includes "Paper of every description, printing and bookbinding, with the miscellaneous articles connected with correspondence, and useful and ornamental stationery, for the subjects of the present Class. The manufacture of these articles—ministering not to the personal or domestic wants of mankind, so much as to their intellectual requirements—is one the annual increase of which is coextensive with the diffusion of knowledge."[41] In turn, the Great Exhibition of 1851 (and subsequent expositions) stimulated even greater demand for postal products, manufactured as commercial items and fancy goods.[42]

Amidst printing machines, microscopes, talking and printing telegraphs, carriages, photographic equipment, and steam turbines, we find a lengthy description of an envelope-folding machine as well as narratives about pens, stationery, and the newest rage in envelopes—covers with a gummed or adhesive flap (which made wafers ornamental, no longer necessary for fastening). For example, "Smith, Jeremiah, *42 Rathbone Place*— Inventor and Manufacturer"

lists "Adhesive envelopes (requiring neither wax nor wafer), and note and letter papers, embossed with emblazoned arms, crests, mottoes, initials, &c."[43]
Jeremiah Smith also provides an exposition on papermaking among European nations, comparing English papers with Belgian, French, and Swedish
types. Of interest is not only the range of paper this manufacturer offers—for
example, brown wrapping paper, handmade drawing paper, "bibulous plate
paper for engravers' use"—but the suggestion that the new postal regulations
following cheap postage influenced production: variations exist among "substantial English writing papers and the thin post papers of France and Bel-
gium, whose different qualities arise from the difference of postal regulations
in those countries."[44]

In this same class of items, manufacturer H. Penny boasts of "Metallic
pocket-books, with pencils composed of various metal. The writing cannot
be obliterated by the friction of the leaves, or by the use of India-rubber."[45]
Spicer Brothers, which published the *Official Descriptive and Illustrated Catalogue*, lists an array of colored papers (blue, cream, yellow) and types of paper
for writing (wove post, laid post, wove bank post), accounting (laid imperial,
royal, demy or foolscap), and printing (superfine demy foolscap, superfine
royal, etc.).[46] Manufacturers' descriptions also feature inks, wafers, and sealing
wax in "various colours and quantities," to recall the words of manufacturer
George Waterston of Edinburgh.[47] Many manufacturers catered to women:
telling is a narrative advertisement by Eliza Byam of Soho Square for a "Com-
pound stationery case: traveling, writing, working, dressing, and refreshment
case; lady's carriage companion."[48] This description equates letter writing with
gentility, making it an essential part of a lady's day: the Byam case meets a
lady's needs by allowing her to write in the parlor, bedchamber, or carriage.
Narratives by Byam and other manufacturers present the importance of writing in a lady's life and the growth of the stationery industry, particularly for
women.

The word "pen" derives from the Latin "penna," meaning feather, and although the quill changed but little over the ages, it received a major upgrade,
acquiring a steel nib during the Victorian age of steam and industry.[49] While
H. Penny lists pencils in class 17, "Papers, Printing, and Bookbinding," many
more writing tools appear under class 22, "General Hardware, Including Locks
and Grates." The inventors Knight & Foster of Eastcheap, for example, registered a variety of pens, including "Steel pens, of various designs, in boxes.
Bank of England pens. Swan pens. Correspondence pens. Anti-corrosive
pens."[50] Swan pens and Waterman pens remained popular brands of fountain

pens throughout the Victorian age and came in various shapes, sizes, and colors. Designers changed the pen holder as well as the nib: holders were made of wood, ebony, gold, and glass and even carried inscriptions or trademarks.[51]

Joseph Rodgers & Sons of Sheffield presents "Pen-machines, for making pens at one stroke," alongside scissors, razors, cutlery, and various "Specimens, showing the several stages of manufacture of the different articles, from the raw material to the finished goods."[52] The word "specimens" appears throughout the *Official Descriptive and Illustrated Catalogue*, transmitting the idea of scientific acumen. Moreover, borrowing the language of taxonomy, the compilers arranged items including pens, papers, wafers, sealing wax, inks, book bindings, pressboards, and writing desks into "classes." These terms speak not only to the Victorian propensity to collect and classify, arguably driven by a desire for self-education, but to the burgeoning interest in science and natural history in the mid- to late nineteenth century, reaffirmed by Darwin's publication of *The Origin of Species* in 1859 and reflected in literature of the age. Elizabeth Gaskell's *Wives and Daughters* (1866), for example, features a naturalist (Roger Hamley) as Molly Gibson's love interest.

"SOME OF THE MOST INGENIOUS MACHINERY RECENTLY INVENTED"

Among the specimens of postal ephemera is an envelope-folding machine invented in 1845 by Edwin Hill (Rowland Hill's brother) and Warren De La Rue. It went on display during the Great Exhibition as an example of "some of the most ingenious machinery recently invented."[53] The envelope-folding machine—which could fold and gum at least 45 envelopes a minute and had the distinction of being a favorite of Queen Victoria's—appears as entry 76 in class 17 of volume 2 of the *Catalogue*, along with a drawing of two workers, one a feeding-boy and the other an attendant, jointly operating the machine (see figure 9).[54] The lengthy narrative explains the intricate workings of the machine, detailing the mechanics of the feeding, folding, gumming, and taking-off apparatus, followed by a "final squeeze," after which the attendant helped fetch away the envelopes. According to the compilers of the catalogue, the machine folded 2,700 envelopes per hour,[55] while, prior to this invention, it took an experienced worker an entire day to fold 3,000 envelopes by hand with use of a rudimentary "folding-stick." Although the British used envelopes prior to 1840,[56] the catalogue credits this astonishing rise in envelope use and production to Uniform Penny Postage: "It is to the stimulus created by the adoption, in 1839, of Mr. Rowland Hill's system of postage reform, and the

FIGURE 9. "Edwin Hill and Warren De La Rue's Envelope-Folding Machine." Illustration in the *Official Descriptive and Illustrated Catalogue* of the Great Exhibition, 1851.

consequent increased demand for envelopes, that their manufacture owes its rank amongst the arts" (542).

In 1840, envelopes accompanied about half of all posted letters; by 1850, five-sixths of all posted letters were in envelopes, which amounts to 347,000,000 envelopes a year or about 1,000,000 a day.[57] Fascinated by the contents of this enormity of envelopes, the compilers query in their narrative: "What does this million of envelopes contain?" (542). Such a quantity of envelopes likely contained love letters, family correspondence, valentines, receipts, invoices, bills, wills, and official documents. Moreover, the popularity of the envelope tells of a growing concern for privacy in the public and private spheres, even though, as the Graham controversy confirms, envelope use did not curtail the intrusive practices of a Paul Pry. Synonyms for envelope—such as cover or wrapper—indicate how the envelope, as opposed to a folded letter with a wafer or wax seal, came to signal an extra level of security, as well as protection from the elements (rain and snow). For reasons of privacy and confidentiality, as well as practicality, another popular commodity—the portable writing desk—also became a favorite of the growing Victorian middle class.

THE LOOK AND USE OF A WRITING DESK

The *Official Descriptive and Illustrated Catalogue* and Thackeray's *Vanity Fair* stand as benchmarks from which to view the rise of the writing desk, a product which carries meaning about Victorian aesthetics, gender, social class, and privacy—notions critical to current discourse. Often made by the same manufacturers that created dressing cases, jewelry cases, and pocketbooks, portable writing desks were classified as furniture and, therefore, mainly appear in class 26 of the *Catalogue* (volume 2, section 3), "Furniture, Upholstery, Paper Hangings, Papier Maché, and Japanned Goods." Victorian companies and consumers variously refer to the writing desk as a writing box, lap desk, writing slope, writing table, table desk, dispatch box or case, portable or traveling writing desk, or simply a box or a desk. The writing desk, which likely grew out of the medieval lectern,[58] paved the way for subsequent innovations in writing that have replaced it: the briefcase, the laptop, the Palm Pilot, the BlackBerry, and the iPhone. From writing desks—which anticipated laptop computers in their portability and usefulness for storage and security—we learn how the Victorians wrote for business and pleasure at a time when heating was inefficient, buildings were not routinely electrified, and people of the upper and middle classes made long visits to friends and family; recall how Elizabeth Bennet spends several weeks with Charlotte Lucas following Charlotte's marriage to Mr. Collins in Austen's *Pride and Prejudice* (1813).

David Harris credits not only the growth of literacy, but the rise of Uniform Penny Postage as a key factor leading to more letters being written, improved postal service (even in remote areas), demand for portable writing desks, and, in turn, greater variety of desks (for example, as commercial items and fancy goods). The Victorian age witnessed the creation of more writing desks than any other period, and Harris's *Portable Writing Desks* (23–24) illuminates innovations in design and raw materials in desks for members of the middle and upper classes that date to this period.[59] There were four types of writing desks—the most basic being a box with a sloping lid hinged at either top or bottom (the top of the box served as a writing slope if the box were hinged at the top, but the open lid acted as the writing surface if the box were hinged at the bottom); elaborate desks contained multiple storage compartments and recesses;[60] and some fancy ones that were combination desks—for example, writing desk/workboxes, and writing desk/dressing cases, such as the "lady's carriage companion" by Eliza Byam.[61] Most extant desks have a writing slope, typically lined with velvet, leather, or baize (a woolen cloth similar to felt); storage for stationery, blotting paper, envelopes, wafers, sealing wax, and small writing manuals; a pen rest for quill pens or steel nib pens (as the century progressed); a stamp compartment or slope (for wafers before the invention of stamps); one or two ink bottles (one likely for pounce, a chalky substance to blot ink, before the invention of blotting paper); a key lock.

The desk importantly teaches us about the importance of portability and security to the Victorians. The portability of the writing desk allowed the writer to move it to the warmest and brightest part of the house. Many owners kept candle sconces in their desks for writing in the later afternoon or evening. The desk was typically small enough to fit into one's luggage, making it popular for travel. Moreover, it offered a handy place to stow away a passport, and by 1820 roughly 150,000 British travelers regularly went to the Continent for health or pleasure.[62] The portability and size of the desk also facilitated confidentiality since a writer could move it to a private study or bedchamber to write undisturbed. Moreover, writing desks have key locks, and some also have hidden chambers, called secret drawers—places to protect or hide important letters, valuables or any information that the owner did not wish anyone to know about. Some dressing and jewel cases also contain secret drawers. Duplicitous Lady Audley of Mary Elizabeth Braddon's *Lady Audley's Secret* (1862), for example, hides a lock of her child's "pale and silky yellow hair" (30) in the secret drawer of her jewel case, and Luke Marks, who blackmails her, takes it, recognizing it is more valuable than the diamond bracelet her maid would have liked to steal. The writing desk, likewise, became the depository of things personal and precious: money, accounts, jewelry, passports, love letters, special treasures, even incriminating evidence. Phineas Finn, a rising Irishman serving in Parliament in Trollope's *Phineas Finn* (1869), uses his writing desk to hide from his London friends (who anticipate a match with wealthy Madame Max Goesler) his engagement to Mary Flood Jones, his Irish sweetheart from Killaloe; Phineas locks Mary's love letters in his desk but privately withdraws "Mary's last letter and read[s] it again" (2: 304).[63] Trollope wrote many of his novels—including *The Warden* (1855), *Barchester Towers* (1857), *Framley Parsonage* (1861), and *Orley Farm* (1862)—"with much train traveling" and the aid of his traveling writing desk of his own design (Harris 4);[64] his frequent train journeys for his job as a Post Office official took him throughout England and Ireland and to faraway places including the Continent, the Middle East (including the Holy Land), and the West Indies.[65]

Well before Trollope, Austen used her writing desk to write letters and novels and to store her valuables. Just like her character Catherine Morland of *Northanger Abbey* (1818), Jane Austen nearly lost the mahogany writing desk that her father gave her on her nineteenth birthday to encourage her talent.[66] Staying in Dartford at the Bull and George Inn in 1798, she recorded the following mishap: "my writing and dressing boxes had been by accident put into a chaise which was just packing off as we came in, and were driven away towards Gravesend in their way to the West Indies. No part of my property could have been such a prize before, for in my writing-box was all my worldly wealth."[67] While the table on which Austen set her writing desk remains part of the Jane Austen House Museum in Chawton, the desk itself—which she used to revise *Sense and Sensibility* (1811) and *Pride and Prejudice* and to write *Mansfield Park* (1814), and *Persuasion* (1818)—is on display at the British Library. Austen's hardwood desk appears more functional and plain than many ladies' desks of the era: it has a leather slope and room for two inkwells (likely one held pounce); roughly the size of a portable typewriter, it came equipped with a drawer and a glass inkwell and has a sturdy handle for travel as well as plenty of room for manuscripts.

With the rise of industry and mass production in Victorian Britain, a plain, utilitarian desk such as Austen's became affordable for members of the rapidly increasing middle class. It was possible for a governess, a doctor's wife, a clergyman, and a clergyman's wife to own a modest desk to safeguard cherished things and for writing, as the fiction of Elizabeth Gaskell and the Brontë sisters illustrates. In Gaskell's "Mr. Harrison's Confessions" (1851), Mrs. Rose offers to retrieve from her writing desk a prized possession, the medical "'dognoses'" of her departed physician-husband's illness, in case Dr. Harrison would like to write it up for a medical journal (218). Charlotte Brontë describes how "the inmates of Moor House" in *Jane Eyre* (1847)—Jane, Diana, and Mary—read, sketched, and studied while St. John Rivers, more reserved than Jane and his sisters, "sat at the window, his desk and papers before him" (298, 299). In chapter 19 of Anne Brontë's *Agnes Grey* (1847), entitled "The Letter," Mrs. Grey receives a letter from her wealthy father, offering to reinstate her in the family if, upon her clergyman husband's death, she will now repent her "'unfortunate marriage'"; she replies by calling for her writing desk: "'Get my desk, Agnes, and send these things away: I will answer the letter directly,'" and "the letter was quickly written and dispatched" (214–15). During her own trials as a governess for the young Bloomfield children at Horton Lodge, Agnes Grey just barely rescues her valuable writing slope from her naughty charges: young Tom Bloomfield, the most malicious of the children (he also tortures innocent dogs and birds), instructs his sister, "'Mary Ann, throw her desk out of the window!' . . . and my precious desk, containing my letters and papers, my small amount of cash, and all my valuables, was about to be precipitated from the three-story window. I flew to rescue it" (94).

The Brontë sisters recognized the worth of a writing desk for possessions, privacy, and correspondence: each of the three surviving daughters of Reverend Patrick Brontë owned one. Their writing desks are on display at the Brontë Parsonage Museum in Haworth, where, in the evenings in 1846, they sat in the small family parlor and wrote their novels, all published in 1847: Charlotte's *Jane Eyre*, Anne's *Agnes Grey*, and Emily's *Wuthering Heights*. Charlotte Brontë's relatively plain writing slope has some inlaid brass decoration on the front and top. It bears a brass nameplate simply engraved C. Brontë and stores her surviving writing materials, including bits of sealing wax, a seal with an ivory handle, two glass inkpots, blotting paper, a sheet of hand-ruled paper, one quill pen, 114 steel nib pens, enameled wafers bearing inscriptions ("In answer to yours"; "All's well"; and a commemorative of the "Prince of Wales, born Nov 9 1841"), a tiny devotional with a page for each day of the year, Charlotte's wire-rimmed glasses, and an invitation from the mayor and mayoress of Oxford to attend a reception in the Town Hall on June 22, 1854.[68]

Manufacturers' Narratives

It is hard to determine the exact number of Victorian manufacturers promoting writing desks at the Great Exhibition given the variety of ways to list a writing desk. Not every manufacturer offered a description for inclusion in the *Catalogue.*[69] Nonetheless, 6 percent of the manufacturers' narratives in volume 2, section 3, class 26 makes explicit reference to writing desks, suggesting their importance as postal products. In addition, many manufacturers list related items, such as workboxes, some of which were combination workboxes and writing desks. Inkstands and desk sets regularly appear as items of furniture, further testimony to the importance of writing accoutrements following Uniform Penny Postage. Often in what appear to be relatively straightforward narratives, telling details emerge about raw materials or the designated gender of a writing case owner; Thompson & Worthy of Durham, for example, stipulate the company is displaying a "Ladies' writing desk."[70] Men's and women's desks carry memories of the dichotomy of separate spheres in an age with a marked division between the public space of work—where Victorian gentleman used their writing desks—and the private sphere of the home—where genteel Victorian women kept up their correspondence or wrote fiction in well-appointed parlors. Although George Eliot (née Mary Ann Evans) and the Brontë sisters felt compelled to publish fiction under pseudonyms, women of the period were acknowledged as capable of writing pleasing correspondence; manufacturers' narratives reveal there was a ready market for writing desks, inkwells, desk sets, and other postal ephemera designed especially for women. Moreover, the Great Exhibition of 1851, in showcasing new products, significantly impacted the fancy goods trade, creating a demand for women's desks far more elaborate than the relatively simple ones Austen and the Brontë sisters used earlier in the century.

Men's and women's desks differed in size, raw materials, and degree of decoration. A man's writing desk tended to be handsome, though relatively plain, and large (typical dimensions are 14" × 10" × 6"). A wealthy gentleman had servants to load his desk and other belongings into a train or carriage; in *Vanity Fair*, for example, Captain George Osborne instructs his servant to put his writing desk and dressing case in his carriage the morning of his wedding to Amelia Sedley (262). Perhaps it is with this very desk that George writes his infamous note urging Becky to run away with him just before his death at Waterloo? It would not have been surprising if Osborne brought his desk to the Continent. Military officers brought portable desks and diverse items of traveling furniture for their extended military service during the Napoleonic Wars. The writing desk offered a gentleman not only a means to communicate with home but a place to lock away letters and valuables, including money; again in *Vanity Fair*, Rawdon Crawley, when tricked into a debtors' prison, writes to Becky to "'Please send me my desk . . . I've seventy in it'" (671).

The large size of a man's traveling desk speaks to its serviceability and usefulness, but its quality determined the social class of its owner. Manufacturers and designers made gentlemen's desks of mahogany, walnut, ash, or rosewood, with superior veneers of good grain, color, and patina. Some craftsmen, taking pride in their work, chose a single piece of wood for the front, sides, and back of the desk so that the grain continued, without interruption, from one side to the next. However, men's desks were also made of leather, as Dickens indicates in his description of Mr. Dick, the wise fool of *David Copperfield* (1850), who "never travelled without a leathern writing-desk, containing a supply of stationery and the Memorial" (which he is forever writing, but making little progress on) (215). The slopes typically have leather or felt linings, and many men's desks are "brass bound," meaning that they have brass bindings on the corners and edges for stability. Some styles feature brass mounts and medallions on the top and sides, such as a matching escutcheon (nameplate) and cartouche (decoration around a lock), giving grace to the design. Frederick Waller, a manufacturer from Fleet Street, advertises a "Commercial and diplomatic despatch writing-desk; the open paper-rack and folding slope being combined, so as to form a portable appendage to the writing-table. The annexed cut represents this writing-desk."[71] The accompanying drawing (see figure 10) shows a large, practical writing desk for work in a commercial setting. The generous paper rack has five standing trays to hold paper and stationery. In addition to the slope, there is a pen tray and space for stamps or an ink bottle. The narrative does not identify the type of wood, which, from the drawing, appears plain. The desk has a bit of detail on the inside of the right lid, but essentially this commercial desk has clean lines and no ornamentation: it is designed for men of business. Together, commercial and fancy writing desks for men provide material reminders of Victorian taste and gender: the Victorian gentleman favored clean lines, quality materials, simple but tasteful decoration, and in writing desks that were not industrial in nature, an understated elegance.

In contrast, ladies' desks appear smaller and daintier than gentlemen's desks (10" × 8" × 3"), but they are sumptuously decorated. For ladies, Frederick Waller advertises a "Small, rosewood, open desk . . . containing various sizes of note paper and envelopes."[72] Here the manufacturer includes the size and quality of wood to appeal to women consumers and notes the desk comes with stationery and envelopes—the lady could conceivably take the desk right into her parlor or bedchamber to write her daily correspondence, as was the fashion of the era. Many of the manufacturers' narratives include words like "enrichments," "rich," "highly decorated," "fancy edges," "highly ornamented," and "fitted with every requisite" to describe ladies' writing desks of quality, or they emphasize rare woods, including rosewood, ebony, Spanish

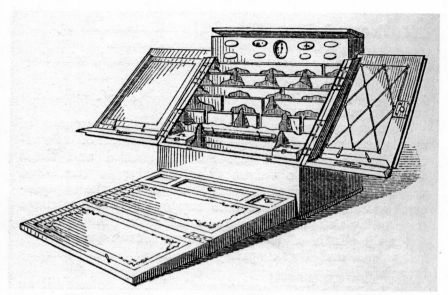

FIGURE 10. "Waller's Commercial Writing Desk." Illustration in the *Official Descriptive and Illustrated Catalogue* of the Great Exhibition, 1851.

mahogany, New Zealand totara wood, and zebra wood, as well as boulle or buhl (an elaborate inlay made of tortoiseshell and engraved brass) and a high grade of papier-mâché.[73] The manufacturers' narratives indicate that designers gave special attention to the lids of ladies' writing desks, workboxes, and hand screens, which often feature scenes from well-known myths, musical performances, or tourist sites, including the opening of Pandora's box; a portrait of Jenny Lind, the famous nineteenth-century opera singer known as the Swedish Nightingale; a view of Windsor Castle; a view of Das Königliche Schloss in Charlottenburg, a famous German chateau near Berlin.[74] Lithographed pictures and transfer prints also proved popular as decorations for writing desk lids through 1880.

Narratives about ladies' writing desks and accompanying accessories carry knowledge of the growing Victorian fancy goods trade, as well as what was in vogue for females.[75] Rare and, at times, dazzling materials used in the crafting and manufacture of ladies' writing desks transmit knowledge of Victorian preferences, aesthetics, and luxury. Fabric also added to the quality of a writing desk: slopes of many extant ladies' writing desks are lined in rose or lavender silk velvet, although some slopes have felt or leather linings. The materials comprising the outside and inside of ladies' desks transmit knowledge of female taste: we find a preference for exquisite design—fine woods with

mosaic and marquetry inlays or adorned by means of engraving, embossing, painting, and piercing; some lids show topographical views or elaborate
designs of fruits, flowers, birds, hearts, and gardens, exquisitely ornamented
with pearls, gold, silver, precious gems (diamonds, pearls, rubies, lapis lazuli),
sea shells, tortoiseshell, and china. For example, McCallum & Hodson, a well-
regarded Birmingham manufacturing firm, lists "writing desks, [with] inlaid
pearl flowers and shells."[76] Period inkstands for women, often made of high-
grade papier-mâché, are also highly ornamented with gold, pearl, silver, jewels, and mother-of-pearl inlays, with quality veneers, and with mosaic embel-
lishments.

Although ornamental, the ladies' desk still had to be serviceable, since
women used them for teaching, household matters, and writing. In *David
Copperfield*, for example, we find David's mother, Clara Copperfield (Murdstone), "ready . . . at her writing-desk" to tutor her young son (52); the onerous
Miss Murdstone "busy at her writing-desk, which was covered with letters
and papers" (116); and angelic Agnes Wickfield "sitting by the fire, at a pretty
old fashioned desk she had, writing" (478). Dickens equips another Dickensian angel, Esther Summerson, with a desk for her household accounts in
Bleak House. Intelligent, sweet, and self-effacing Esther informs the reader,
"As it was the day of the week on which I paid the bills, and added up my
books, and made all the household affairs as compact as possible, I remained
at home while Mr. Jarndyce, Ada, and Richard, took advantage of a very fine
day to make a little excursion" (98). Interrupted by the lovelorn, ridiculous
Mr. Guppy (a law clerk who woos Esther unsuccessfully), Esther turns him
down and continues at her desk: "I sat there for another hour or more, finish-
ing my books and payments, and getting through plenty of business. Then, I
arranged my desk, and put everything away" (102). Phiz's illustration likewise
depicts Esther, acting in her capacity as housekeeper of Bleak House, seated
at her writing desk (see figure 11). In "In Re Guppy. Extraordinary Proceedings," Phiz shows Esther's disregard for Guppy, but highlights her dedication
as housekeeper. Bills, a writing desk, and what appears to be a letter rack or
stationery box surround her as she assiduously uses her quill pen to keep neat
household accounts for her guardian, Mr. Jarndyce.

Writing desks for men and women also carry meaning about economics
and social class. Savvy manufacturers catered to consumers across the upper and middle classes. Beginning in the 1830s, a writing desk came within
economic reach of members of the middle class who could now afford to
purchase luxury items, such as a writing desk, fancy pen tray, or envelope
case, as a Christmas gift for a friend or relative, as well as for their own use.

FIGURE 11. "In Re Guppy. Extraordinary Proceedings." Illustration by Hablot Knight Browne for Charles Dickens's *Bleak House*, 1853.

Accordingly, some descriptions of writing boxes and other postal products drip with glitter (but offer no substance), such as those by Charles Stocken, manufacturer of Regent Street, which advertises a "Papier maché stationery-case and blotting-book *en suite*, inlaid with gems in imitation of diamonds, rubies, pearls, &c."[77] Different from McCallum & Hodson, which advertises a desk adorned with authentic pearls, here we find a nod to the increasing popularity of writing slopes for members of the emerging middle class, who could only afford desks made with simulated diamonds and pearls. Ladies' writing desks for the upper reaches are products of skilled handwork; they are comprised of quality woods and adorned with gemstones and precious materials.

In contrast, writing boxes for middle-class men and women, built with lower quality woods and less generously adorned (or perhaps adorned only with imitation materials), tend to be machine-made and plain commercial items rather than fine crafts. By the second half of the nineteenth century, Harrods and the Army and Navy Cooperative began to sell writing desks, showing how the writing desk came to be viewed as an item that one could purchase in a department store (Harris 28).

The trend of papier-mâché desks provides further understanding of how the writing desk became both a classed and gendered item. The *Official Descriptive and Illustrated Catalogue* reveals the popularity of papier-mâché in 1851. Harris notes that the Great Exhibition "marked the high point for papier maché" (34), and some manufacturers like Spiers & Son of Oxford offered a range of items made exclusively of papier-mâché: "Specimens of decorated papier maché, consisting of tables, cabinets, fire and hand screens, albums, writing-portfolios, desks, envelope-cases, work-boxes, card-trays, panels for internal decorations, &c."[78] Of particular interest, one of the compilers of the catalogue (whose initials are W.C.A.) inserted a bracketed paragraph following an entry by Halbeard & Wellings (a Birmingham manufacturer) to explain grades of papier-mâché and "different stages of manufacture from the raw material to the finished article":

> There are two varieties of papier maché: the best is produced by pasting together, on an iron or brass mould, a number of sheets of paper of a spongy texture, allowing them to dry between each addition. In the common variety, the paper is reduced to a pulpy substance, and the form is given by pressure into matrices of metal. Papier maché may be formed into any desired article by means of the lathe, the plane, or the rasp; it is several times varnished; and the irregularities of surface are removed by scraping and rubbing with pumice-stone. The artist then introduces the design; it is again varnished, polished with rotten-stone; and its final brilliancy is given by rubbing with the palm of the hand.[79]

In a different instance, the picture accompanying a Spiers & Son entry for an "ornamental fire-screen of papier maché, with a view in Oxford, the Martyrs' Monument" suggests a high-grade product, as it features birds, cherubs, flowers, and elaborate scrollwork and inlays.[80] Jennens & Bettride, a leading Birmingham designer and manufacturer, created two grades of papier-mâché as evidenced by this explanation: "Four tea-trays, exhibited for their cheapness, being of the second quality papier maché (or 'pulp')." An illuminating parenthetical remark follows this Jennens & Bettride entry: "There are two modes of manufacturing 'papier maché' articles: the first is by pasting paper in sheets upon models, and the second by pressing in dies, the pulp of paper. The former produces the best quality, and the latter the least expensive and inferior kinds. The specimens above-named as 'exhibited for their cheapness,' are of the latter description, and the rest are of the former."[81] In business from 1815 to 1864, Jennens & Bettride earned a reputation, however, as "makers of best-quality British papier mâché, and articles made by them were generally marked with their name" (Harris 33). Ornamentation with mother-of-pearl was a particular specialty of this manufacturer, known as "Makers to the Queen" (Harris 33–34).[82]

Although papier-mâché was exceedingly popular in the Victorian period, along with Tunbridgeware it fell out of fashion in the later Victorian period due to mass production. The plethora of items described as made from papier-mâché in the *Official Descriptive and Illustrated Catalogue* points to a fashion trend in its heyday. The connection between mass production and declining popularity of papier-mâché writing desks also pertains to the fate of the writing desk per se: "Excessive mass production led to a cheapening of items of all kinds and, as they were no longer quality pieces, they became less desirable"(Harris 30).[83] As it became more and more remote from a hand-crafted decorative arts prototype, the portable writing desk suffered depreciation similar to that described by Walter Benjamin in his 1936 "The Work of Art in the Age of Mechanical Reproduction": "Mechanical reproduction of art changes the reaction of the masses toward art" (234). Due to mechanical reproduction of lower quality products (as illustrated by the two grades of papier-mâché), the writing desk lost what Benjamin calls its "aura" or authenticity, a quality only an original art work possesses. This loss of aura, in part, accelerated the devaluation of the portable writing desk, which led eventually to its discontinuation.

An Inside Look: Becky's Writing Desk as a Motif in *Vanity Fair*

Thackeray recognized the usefulness of a desk for storage, privacy, secrecy, and personal advancement when creating the work that brought him distinction as a major novelist. Numerous nineteenth-century authors show writing desks indispensable for men's and women's correspondence, social interactions, secrecy, and travel. In *Emma*, Austen complicates the Churchill-Fairfax love plot when Frank Churchill locks his letters addressed to Jane Fairfax in his writing desk but forgets to post them. Wilkie Collins quite self-consciously refers to the writing slope at the start of *The Moonstone* (1868) by having his first narrator, head servant Gabriel Betteridge, announce his intention to use his writing desk to compose the very story—about a large and mysterious stolen Indian diamond—that we are in the process of reading: "I went to my writing-desk to start the story" (10). But perhaps no author more artfully turns the inside of a writing desk into a crucial plot element than Thackeray in *Vanity Fair*. Through Thackeray's treatment of Becky Sharp's most prized possession, we come to see how the Victorian writing desk became a portable, private space to save and safeguard valuables, letters, passions, and secrets.

Set in the Regency period, *Vanity Fair* satirizes Victorian society and its social practices and institutions to inspire a remodeling of a more moral world. As John Sutherland notes, the novel "follows, through their turns of fortune, the careers of two women. One is good, stupid, bourgeois and (initially) rich; the other is clever, selfish, bohemian and (initially) poor"; as the novel progresses, Becky rises, Amelia falls, and then "there is a turn of the wheel; Becky is plunged into (deserved) ruin, Amelia comes into (deserved) good fortune. But with an ironic twist, Thackeray brings both heroines into final equilibrium."[84] Thackeray—as master puppeteer and "Manager of the Performance" (as he refers to himself in his "Before the Curtain" preface)— maneuvers his characters (or puppets) to disclose the hypocrisy and deceit of Victorian society that he depicts as a cracked looking glass, an image that symbolizes the many imperfections of "VANITY FAIR; not a moral place certainly; nor a merry one, though very noisy" (1). Of interest to *Posting It*, Thackeray recognizes that "Perhaps in Vanity Fair there are no better satires than letters" (229). Among the many motifs in the novel that form the subject of scholarly inquiry (for example, the jester, the looking glass, the mermaid, Napoleon, and reading), I add a small but critical detail of the plot that rarely receives the critic's gaze: the writing desk on which clever Becky composes her sharp "satires" in the form of letters.[85] Major and minor characters own a writing desk,[86] and throughout the novel, Thackeray elaborates upon its contents and manifold uses. Becky Sharp quintessentially uses her writing case to advance in the corrupt world of Vanity Fair while Major William Dobbin and Amelia Sedley use their writing boxes to safeguard their deepest emotions.

Rebecca's desk comes as a gift from her school chum, Amelia Sedley. Thackeray continually refers to Becky's writing slope as "an old desk, which Amelia Sedley had given her years and years ago" (603) or "the little desk which Amelia had given her in early days" (676) to maintain the connection between them, but he does not pinpoint when Amelia gives Becky the desk.[87] Just when Becky loses Jos Sedley as a beau and succumbs temporarily to the fate of becoming a governess, she receives many *cadeaux* from Amelia, so the

FIGURE 12. "Miss Sharp in Her Schoolroom." Illustration by William
Makepeace Thackeray for his *Vanity Fair*, 1848.

desk, originally Amelia's own, may have been a consolation for Becky's disap-
pointed expectations. A seemingly incidental gift becomes a key plot element
well into the novel, although even in chapter 10, Thackeray depicts Becky
seated at this very writing desk in her schoolroom at Queen's Crawley in the
full-page engraving entitled "Miss Sharp in Her Schoolroom" (see figure 12).
Thackeray sets the novel in the early nineteenth century (before the impact of
the fancy goods trade), so it is not surprising that the desk looks plain (there is
a slight suggestion of decoration on the side). It seems larger than many ladies'
desks of the period but appears to be functional for teaching, should Becky

actually wish to use it for that purpose. Becky largely ignores the education of Miss Rose (the elder) and Miss Violet Crawley, "thin insignificant little chits of ten and eight years old" (91), who, in this illustration, are squabbling over a book. Turning her head away from her bickering charges, Becky sneers in a kind of theatrical aside to the reader-viewer. Unlike David Copperfield's mother who uses her writing desk to teach young Davy, Becky values her desk solely as a means for her own advancement and personal profit. Moreover, as the novel continues, the size of Becky's desk clearly proves useful for her own ends.

Thackeray asks a telling question about Becky two-thirds of the way into the novel but refrains from answering: "Was she guilty or not?" (677). This question specifically pertains to whether Becky commits adultery with Lord Steyne. The night in question, Rawdon Crawley escapes from the debtors' prison into which he has been tricked, noting later, "'It was a regular plan between that scoundrel and her.' . . . 'The bailiffs were put upon me'" (683). Rawdon returns to his home in Curzon Street to find his wife decked in brilliants, entertaining wealthy Lord Steyne, the servants sent away. Becky is "in a brilliant full toilette, her arms and all her fingers sparkling with bracelets and rings; and the brilliants on her breast which Steyne had given her" (675). This is not the first time Rawdon has seen Becky wearing at least some of these "brilliants," however. Several chapters earlier, on the way to Becky's presentation at Court, an astonished Rawdon remarks, "'Where the doose did you get the diamonds, Becky?' . . . admiring some jewels which he had never seen before, and which sparkled in her ears and on her neck with brilliance and profusion" (602). Becky blushes as does Rawdon's wealthy brother, Sir Pitt Crawley, who has surreptitiously given Becky "a very small portion of the brilliants" (603), but Lord Steyne "knew whence the jewels came, and who paid for them" (604). Becky declares she hired the jewels from a Mr. Polonius of Coventry Street, but Thackeray tells us, "The diamonds, which had created Rawdon's admiration, never went back to Mr. Polonius, of Coventry Street, and that gentleman never applied for their restoration; but they retired into a little private repository, in an old desk, which Amelia Sedley had given her years and years ago, and in which Becky kept a number of useful and, perhaps, valuable things, about which her husband knew nothing" (603).

Here Thackeray uses the words "private repository" as a synonym for writing desk, suggesting that, for Becky, the desk is not primarily valuable for writing, although she writes clever letters under her own name, a pen name (Eliza Styles), and Rawdon's name (to try to get him back into wealthy Matilda Crawley's good graces). Functioning as a hideaway for money and jewels that

Becky's husband knows nothing about (until Rawdon discovers Becky tête-à-tête with Lord Steyne), the writing box is material evidence of Becky's use of secrecy and deception in her social ascent and is, likewise, a silent but material medium of her power and agency. Thackeray also uses this moment to talk in general about husbands kept in the dark—"O ladies! how many of you have surreptitious milliners' bills? How many of you have gowns and bracelets, which you daren't show, or which you wear trembling?" (603). In these questions, Thackeray indirectly implicates the locked desk and the hidden key.

Rawdon immediately demands Becky's keys when he confronts her entertaining Lord Steyne. Crafty "Rebecca gave him all the keys but one: and she was in hopes that he would not have remarked the absence of that. It belonged to the little desk which Amelia had given her in early days, and which she kept in a secret place" (676). The clandestine location of the desk suggests it has seemingly lost its value for correspondence, while it has exquisitely maintained its usefulness for "all hopes, schemes, debts, and triumphs" (677). While "flinging" about Becky's boxes, Rawdon "at last found the desk. The woman was forced to open it. It contained papers, love-letters many years old—all sorts of small trinkets and woman's memoranda. And it contained a pocket-book with bank-notes. Some of these were dated ten years back, too, and one was quite a fresh one—a note for a thousand pounds which Lord Steyne had given her" (676). Earlier Thackeray tells us that after receiving a large sum from Lord Steyne, allegedly to pay off Briggs (since Becky "'ruined her'" [608]),[88] Becky "paid a visit upstairs to the before-mentioned desk, which Amelia Sedley had given her years and years ago, and which contained a number of useful and valuable little things: in which private museum she placed the one note which Messrs. Jones and Robinson's cashier had given her" (611). In calling Becky's writing desk a "private museum," Thackeray reveals how commodities invested with meaning and sentiment are not only physical reminders of individuals to whom they belonged but emissaries of culture. The inner arrangement of Becky's desk resembles a building designed to hold and exhibit valuable historical, scientific, or artistic objects. Just as a museum preserves items worth keeping, treasuring, and displaying, Becky's private museum, in turn, displays the nature of its owner, but only to those who possess the key.[89]

Of all the "useful and valuable little things" that Becky keeps in her locked "repository," the miniature of Jos Sedley riding an elephant and George's adulterous love note prove the most "useful and valuable" in her final maneuverings to secure a stall in the shallow world of Vanity Fair. With the elephant picture, Becky finally "hooks" Jos Sedley, just as old Mr. Sedley predicts she will in chapter 4: "'Here is Emmy's little friend making love to him as hard as she can; that's quite clear; and if she does not catch him some other will. That man is destined to be a prey to woman, . . . mark my words, the first woman who fishes for him, hooks him'" (36). Maintaining this piscatorial metaphor throughout the novel, Thackeray confirms in the final chapter, entitled "Births, Marriages, and Deaths," that Becky "had cast such an anchor in Jos now as would require a strong storm to shake. That incident of the picture had finished him. Becky took down her elephant, and put it into the little box which she had had from Amelia ever so many years ago" (864).[90]

From her locked writing desk, Becky also retrieves an adulterous note, which confirms George Osborne's infidelity and fully awakens Amelia to the unworthiness of her dead husband, leaving Jos to become Becky's "prey." Thackeray highlights the love note in a full page engraving entitled "The Letter Before Waterloo." A weeping Amelia cannot deny the written proof of George's callous, unworthy nature, evidence of which Dobbin also holds in his own writing desk where he keeps "Osborne's accounts, and a bundle of I O U's which the latter had given, who, to do him justice, was always ready to give an I O U" (495). It is likely that Becky wants to get Amelia out of her way, even as she alleges that Emmy must get over her idolization of dead George and "'marry the bamboo-cane'" (865), as Becky calls honest Dobbin, since Emmy needs Dobbin to protect her. However, Amelia (whom Thackeray calls a heroine and a "tender little parasite" [871]) remarkably uses her writing desk to help herself for once: she confides to Becky that "a letter about which she did not speak a word to anybody, which she carried to the post under her shawl" (865) has already gone out earlier the same day. George's love letter to Becky becomes, for Amelia, a material memory of George's infidelity that allows Amelia, at long last, to fully love Dobbin and to marry him.

Through the contents of their respective desks, Thackeray artfully links the lives of Becky, Amelia, and Dobbin and shows how a Victorian commodity can materially attest to values of privacy and means of self-advancement, while revealing its owner's true nature. George's note that Becky conceals for years in her locked desk[91] frees Amelia to love Dobbin "'with all my heart now'" (869), but the motivation for Amelia's uncharacteristically bold move to declare her love for Dobbin (who has finally left her) resides in the hidden recesses of her desk: "And the major, on going away, having left his gloves behind him, it is a fact that Georgy, rummaging his mother's desk some time afterwards, found the gloves [of Dobbin] neatly folded up, and put away in what they call the secret drawers of the desk" (859). For privacy and concealment, the Victorians prized secret compartments, typically placed under the desk lid (Harris 15). The owner released the drawers by inserting a tool into a small hole or by releasing a catch on a small removable partition (often part of an inkwell compartment). In *Vanity Fair*, Thackeray well recognizes the use of secret drawers: in the secret recesses of her desk, Amelia places not only Dobbin's gloves but her repressed love for him, which young Georgy, playing the part of Paul Pry, discloses to the reader.

For Dobbin and Amelia, the writing desk expresses what each represses. In *Repression in Victorian Fiction*, John Kucich describes "repression" as a "nineteenth-century cultural decision to value silenced or negated feeling over affirmed feeling"; he continues, "refusals mark a general Victorian tendency to make matters of intense feeling—primarily, but not exclusively, sexual feeling—matters of secrecy and self-reflexiveness, and to withhold them from speech and action" (3). Amelia hides her affection for Dobbin by stowing away his sacred gloves. Dobbin displays his love for Amelia only within the recesses of his private desk. Despite Peggy O'Dowd's plot to entice Dobbin with the vision of "Glorvina O'Dowd in pink satin" (549), "there was but this image that filled our honest major's mind by day and by night, and reigned over it always. Very likely Amelia was not like the portrait the major had formed of her: there was a figure in a book of fashions which his sisters had in England, and with which William had made away privately, pasting it into the lid of his desk, and fancying he saw some resemblance to Mrs. Osborne in the print" (549). Were Amelia to have opened Dobbin's desk to find proof of George's debts and Dobbin's undying love for her, or Dobbin—rather than Georgy—to have peeked into Amelia's secret desk drawers, would Dobbin ever have left Amelia for a second time, only to return again?

Becky Sharp's writing desk, alternately—at once embodying her means to deceive, to protect, and to advance—conveys the potency of this object in the Victorian age, especially as a tool of female agency. Thackeray—who refuses to condemn his real heroine in this "novel without a hero"—has granted Becky a writing desk in which she can hide her illicit activity below the novel's "water line" (812). Thackeray warns the reader, "Those who like may peep down under the waves that are pretty transparent, . . . but above the water line, . . . has not everything been proper, agreeable, and decorous, and has any the most squeamish immoralist in Vanity Fair a right to cry fie?" (812–13). Thackeray makes no mention of whether or not Becky's desk, like Amelia's, has secret drawers, but if it does, we can only imagine what Becky might keep hidden deep within them.

*   *   *

From the pages of the Great Exhibition catalogue to *Vanity Fair*, from Lewis Carroll's riddles to copious Victorian novels, commodities like the writing desk, which grew out of a communications revolution and the fancy goods trade, transmit meaning from without and within. If the outside of the desk carries material memories of Victorian fashion trends, as well as gender and class identifications, the inside, in turn, illuminates personal habits and conveys knowledge of privacy, authority, agency, secrecy, deception, and desire. A lover's gloves, banknotes, spectacles, love letters, IOUs, locks of hair long faded, miniatures—these are some of the items Victorian men and women, real and fictional, locked in their "private repositories" and which, to recall Thackeray's metaphor of the "private museum," give us an understanding of their owners, who used their writing desks to create letters and novels and safeguard possessions. Extant letters—ranging from billets doux to blackmail and junk mail, letters of mourning to missives of friendship and courtship— are also emissaries of Victorian culture and society and form the subject of the next two chapters, which analyze significant negative and positive outcomes of the Victorian revolution in letter writing.

Chapter 4

Unwanted Missives and the Spread of Vice

"Curious Things," Slander, and Blackmail from *Household Words*
to the Fiction of George Eliot, Charles Dickens,
Wilkie Collins, and Anthony Trollope

> Will clerks write only to their fathers, and girls to their mothers? Will not
> letters of romance or love, intrigue or mischief, increase in at least equal pro-
> portions?
>
> —John Wilson Croker, "Post-Office Reform," 1839

Postal propaganda aligned high postage with vice and corruption and the Penny
Post with goodness and righteousness. Reformist stories highlight families torn
asunder, taxed too heavily to communicate, and poor folk scrambling to find
necessary funds to accept a death notice, only to learn that in the meantime the
missive has been returned to sender. Images of mothers pawning their clothing to pay for a letter, children going without bread for postage, and the death
of poor Rose Maydew in "ONLY A POSTAGE. [A TALE ILLUSTRATIVE OF
THE EFFECTS OF HIGH POSTAGES.]" transformed the unreformed Post
Office into a robber of virtue, basic human needs, and even life itself.[1] Postal
reform stories also offered hope: "'many young persons of both sexes, who
are continually drawn to this metropolis [London] from distant parts of the
kingdom, and are thenceforth cut off from their communication with their
early guardians, might, under different circumstances, be kept from entering
upon vicious courses, to which the temptations are so great, and against which
the restraints, in their case, are so few.'"[2] Such testimonials—which circulated
broadly in diverse sources, including pamphlets by Rowland Hill and W. H.
Ashurst, the writings of Harriet Martineau, articles in *The Post Circular*, and
Henry Cole's "A Report of an Imaginary Scene at Windsor Castle Respecting
the Uniform Penny Postage" (bound into part 13 of Charles Dickens's popular serial *Nicholas Nickleby* [1838–39])—arguably reached "the heart of a large

class of people" (*Administration* 20) who supported the Penny Post for its vision of moral, educational, political, and social reform.

What came of these utopian dreams? Within one year following the Penny Post, the mailing of letters increased 112.4 percent. From this enormous surge in 1841, there was a minor slowdown to an annual letter-mailing increase rate of 105.6 percent until 1850, after which the mailing of letters increased by 62.5 percent each year between 1850 and 1860.[3] "Before the introduction of the Penny Post, most letters were probably sent for business purposes," explains M. J. Daunton in *Royal Mail*; afterward "there was . . . an increase in personal correspondence" (79). The lowering of postage undeniably increased the volume of the post, and the public welcomed both of these developments as blessings, the focus of chapter 5. However, the Penny Post also stimulated unwanted, unsolicited mass mailings, collectively referred to as junk mail and spam today, as well as clandestine and dangerous missives and "mischief," as John Wilson Croker had predicted, publicly exposing arguably preexisting problems and accelerating the spread of vice, not virtue. To quote the terms of an 1844 pamphlet entitled *Administration of the Post Office from the Introduction of Mr. Rowland Hill's Plan of Penny Postage up to the Present Time*, the Penny Post brought neither "the solid comforts of revenue" nor "the luxury of feeling" that spurred this measure into law (22). Postal historians, including Howard Robinson, have thoroughly explored the immediate financial loss and eventual monetary gains the Post Office experienced following reform, effectively answering *Administration*'s revenue argument. What remains compelling is the pamphlet's claim against the "dexterity" with which "the snare of Cheap Postage was spread; that it was represented as a case, not of mere business, but of *feeling*, and won immediate access to the heart of a large class of people" (20).

The Penny Post may have succeeded by making cheap postage a case of feeling, but it did not win the hearts of all people, even as the volume of mail continued to climb. As Pearson Hill points out in *The Post Office of Fifty Years Ago* (1887), in the first five years following Uniform Penny Postage, a disgruntled minority, many of whom opposed Hill's plan in the first place, continued to view it "with the most determined hostility" (21), even after it received Parliamentary approval and the Queen's consent. To anti-Hillites, the Penny Post in its inclusiveness and affordability invited a host of ways to manipulate the weak or unsuspecting through fraud, slander, and blackmail. Some opponents of the measure, such as Croker, a prominent Tory politician, recognized that postal reform would bring about a mix of vice and virtue: "Will clerks write only to their fathers, and girls to their mothers? Will not letters of romance or love, intrigue or mischief, increase in at least equal proportions? Does any rational mind doubt that there will be, on this point of the question, a balance of good and evil?" (532). To other critics, the scales tipped toward evil: the reformed Post Office, by bringing affordable postage to the masses, became a dangerous channel of communication, a mechanism for distributing immorality, and a vehicle for crime, debt, and dishonor.

As Eileen Cleere argues, "although the popular ideology of the Post Office was that it could bring the family together, it constantly threatened to bring the *wrong* family together" (202). While sustaining kinship ties fueled arguments for postal reform, the Penny Post became, as David Henkin explains, "a system that allowed strangers to communicate cheaply throughout the country," a move that "flooded the mails with the sort of correspondence that simultaneously exploited and eroded popular notions of the letter as a form of personal relationship across distance"; from the outset of affordable postage, "users exploited and emphasized the centrifugal, promiscuous, and anonymous features of a network that could bring any two people into direct contact."[4] With a penny postage stamp, pranksters might send insulting missives to persons outside their circle of acquaintance; radical organizations could push their causes by making direct contact with parties unknown to them; schemers could widely distribute circulars promoting scam products; fans might menace celebrities (shades of the paparazzi today); and, on the domestic front, women could go to post offices "to see and be seen" (Henkin 80), to rendezvous with undesirable suitors, or, to use Anthony Trollope's idiom, to "go the wrong side of the post."[5]

Postal reform also engendered less dire problems: some people, of course, overused or abused the post. Dickens illustrates the former in his characterization of ne'er-do-well Mr. Micawber of *David Copperfield* (1850), who sends an "immense number" of letters to people, "often across the table when he has been sitting opposite, and might much more easily have spoken," leading Betsy Trotwood to exclaim of him, "'Letters!' . . . 'I believe he dreams in letters!'" (652). Trollope, who in real life bristled at Rowland Hill, places an increase of superfluous letters squarely on Hill's shoulders in *Can You Forgive Her* (1865), where Mr. Jeffrey Palliser puts down his letter-obsessed spinster cousins, Iphy and Phemy Palliser: "'They don't at all seek people of note as their correspondents. Free communication with all the world is their motto, and Rowland Hill is the god they worship'" (237–38). The creation of the penny stamp came with its own agenda. Designed to improve science, industry, and morality, to curtail riots and unemployment in the workplace, and to spread education through tracts presenting useful knowledge, it also encouraged people not only to mail endless letters à la Micawber and Palliser but to post what Charles Dickens calls "curious things."[6] Key novels of the period (by Trollope, Dickens, George Eliot, and Wilkie Collins), along with narrative paintings, letters, articles, and pamphlets, carry knowledge of such "curious things," of impropriety, slander, fraud, and blackmail—all emerging as outcomes of "free communication," the brainchild of "the god" whom many hailed.

Just as in chapter 3 I feature Becky Sharp's writing desk in *Vanity Fair* (1848) to illuminate issues of Victorian agency, privacy, and deception, throughout this chapter and the next, I analyze nineteenth-century novels and paintings alongside existing period letters to show how authors and artists were aware of and utilizing innovative nineteenth-century technology to exquisite effect.

The railway was a development contemporary with the Penny Post; in fact, by 1847, Post Office contracts speeded the growth of the railway by financing railway companies to carry the mail in all but rural areas. In *Middlemarch* (1872), set in England just before the Reform Bill of 1832, Eliot weaves new developments in medicine, politics, and religion, along with the coming of the railway, into a rich tapestry of British society undergoing momentous change. Committed to presenting history accurately, Eliot sought information in the British Museum to supplement her girlhood memories of these developments.[7] Even minor characters in Eliot's tome, fittingly subtitled "A Study of Provincial Life," talk about the impending railway. The rails are, likewise, the means by which Margaret Oliphant liberates her heroine Janey from a disastrous marriage and, in turn, destroys her in "A Story of a Wedding Tour" (c. 1870). Oliphant's conclusion in the story's penultimate paragraph—that Janey's "tragedy was one of the railway"—confers the onus of agency upon the railway itself: "This was how the train brought back to Janey the man whom the train had separated from her ten years before. The whole tragedy was one of the railway, the noisy carriages, the snorting locomotives" (424). Paddington Station serves as a microcosm of Victorian society in William Powell Frith's 1862 painting *The Railway Station*. Like George Elgar Hicks in *The General Post Office* (1860), Frith crowds the canvas with passengers from all walks of life, including a bride and bridegroom, servants, a criminal, a cabby, detectives, and a Victorian family.

As the century progressed, creative artists continued to use to effect contemporary developments familiar to readers of the time. Bram Stoker, in *Dracula* (1897), empowers his characters with what was then considered "modern technology"—the railway, steamship, and the telegraph—in order to defeat Count Dracula, who, humorously, tries to escape his pursuers via the outdated mode of a sailboat. Novelists and artists coped with change by pointing in their works to then up-to-date information and transportation technologies that excited them and their Victorian audiences alike, even though people today take these same developments for granted or consider them outdated.

VOICES OF CONTENTION

How do we make sense of the emerging opposition to the Penny Post? The vast majority of people welcomed cheap postage and heralded Hill as "Father of the Penny Post" or "King of the Penny Post," as Lyon Playfair called him.[8] In contrast, some objected loudly to Hill and his plan. Did praise for Hill's plan come from those who might be swayed to support it due to an allegiance to Rowland Hill? One often-quoted, leading supporter, Charles Knight, for example, published Hill's famous 1837 pamphlet, *Post Office Reform: Its Importance and Practicability*, as well as an 1844 pamphlet entitled *The State and Prospects of Penny Postage, as Developed in the Evidence Taken before the Postage Committee of 1843*, in which Hill reaffirmed the manifold benefits of the plan (while acknowledging some of its failures) and, accordingly, irritated those who opposed it in the first place.[9] Conversely, some critics objected to Hill's plan because they felt no fondness for Hill or allegiance to the political party that passed the measure. Some were no doubt miffed that they could no longer obtain from their influential friends franks for free carriage of letters. One man writing in Liverpool on the first day of Uniform Penny Postage presented both of these concerns in an extant letter that reads: "It is a great pity that Franking Letters are done away." He goes on to predict the scheme "will answer by and by" and to condemn Hill: "Mr. Hill is a great fool as well as a Mad Man, fit to be hanged or guillotined, with invalid Frost and his wretched party." But even this disgruntled writer, who ostensibly wrote this letter to thank his friend for a gift of a barrel of oysters, admits a benefit of cheap postage: "When one can send a letter for a penny there can be no excuse for being so uncivil as not to acknowledge a Kindness."[10]

The anonymous author of *Administration of the Post Office* calls the Penny Post an "intolerable plague" and goes on to say: "Mr. Hill has fixed the nation with a Penny Postage; and (*exoriare aliquis*) what statesman is likely hereafter to come forward and release us?" (182). In this attack, the evils of the Penny Post take on biblical proportions, and Hill emerges as a false prophet. Even Trollope, while "acknowledging" the boon of the Penny Post, confides in his *Autobiography* (1883), "I was always an anti-Hillite, acknowledging, indeed, the great thing which Sir Rowland Hill had done for the country, but believing him to be entirely unfit to manage men or to arrange labour" (246).

Did Uniform Penny Postage benefit the working class as postal reformers, including Rowland Hill, alleged it would? According to the *Administration of the Post Office*, the poor still wrote infrequently; rather, mercantile firms and bankers greatly profited from the measure: "Thus, where the poor man receives, say eight letters, from his sailor-son, or his daughter in service in the capital, or in some distant town, and thus gains a shilling in the year by cheap postage, let any one consider how much is gained and saved by this Penny Postage in such houses as Loyd [*sic*], Jones, and Co.; Baring Brothers and Co.; Morrison and Co., &c." (196). The anonymous pamphleteer moreover declares another central objection marshaled by opponents of "Hill's plan" (as it was called)—that it transformed the Post Office into "a competitor with the general carrier, by this conveyance of parcels of all descriptions"—ranging from slugs, leeches, mosses, and medicines to game and hazardous substances (104). According to *Administration of the Post Office*, Hill's Penny Post "changed the whole character of the department; it has pretty nearly converted it into a parcel and conveyance delivery company, a public general carrier, a kind of flying bazaar, instead of maintaining its former and permanently honourable position as a board of revenue, and a safe and effective instrument of conducting the correspondence of a great commercial empire" (112). This notion of the post as a flying variety store communicates concern over safety in the mail, a topic relevant to our twenty-first century postal system and the well-being of the general public.

Other voices of contention appear more moderate. The author of "The Post Office," a May 13, 1844, entry that appeared in *McCulloch's Commercial Dictionary*, admits that the old system needed improvement given the "oppressiveness of the old rates of postage" but adds that swiftly adopting the new plan "was rushing blindfold from one extreme, or rather absurdity, to another and endangering a large amount of revenue without any equivalent advantage."[11] The author praises Hill's plan for abolishing franking but argues that in introducing a uniform rate—what he calls a "MISERABLE QUACKERY" (printed in capital letters for emphasis)—it established an unwise fiscal measure, a folly paramount to dropping the duty on sugar to a penny, as sugar, too, "is quite as indispensable to the bulk of people, and especially to the labouring classes, as the writing of letters" (215). Pearson Hill states that "in 1842 the hostility of certain officials to the new reform rose to such a pitch that . . . Sir Robert Peel's Government (then in power) was coerced into putting an end to Sir Rowland Hill's engagement at the Treasury" (29). As Rowland Hill's son, Pearson may well have been biased,[12] but Rowland Hill's 1842 dismissal from the Treasury likely bolstered the opposition that had firmly reared its head five years after the adoption of Uniform Penny Postage, even if Hill's diaries suggest he departed the Treasury because his two-year contract ran out and officials knew sufficiently well how to run the Penny Post without him. However, in 1846, with the rise of Lord John Russell's government, Hill accepted a staff position at the Post Office and, for better or worse, came to be seen not as a reformer from the outside but as a reformer from within. Appointed secretary to the postmaster general of the Post Office in 1846, Hill became secretary to the Post Office in 1854, an office which he held until 1864. Queen Victoria knighted Hill for his work in 1860, and the rhetoric of praise for the Penny Post quickly became encoded in Victorian pamphlets and histories of the post. Nonetheless, dissenting voices warrant investigation; they emphasize how deceptive postal practices grew from a measure designed to bring Britain greater good.

DECEPTIVE POSTAL PRACTICES IN THE WAKE OF REFORM

The notion of a "pathology of information," a term coined by Alexander Welsh in *George Eliot and Blackmail*, is central to understanding Victorians' concerns about forms of vice and immorality ushered in by the Penny Post. Welsh contends that prior to reform, people largely understood the risks associated with the mail, "of submitting their business in writing to hands other than their own" (54). Reform enlarged the scope of the potential risk, requiring of people an unprecedented trust and magnifying their sense of "how invidious its violation must be":

> Rowland Hill and his postmen provided an efficient and greatly expanded service. What is impossible to measure is the influence of this service on modern life. The availability of the penny post probably lent impetus to greater literacy; at the same time, the increased use of the mails and of the telegraph placed a subtle strain on the trust between individuals. As in all uses of writing, the messages are loosed from their origin to be interpreted elsewhere. (54–55)

While democratization of the post encouraged Victorians' optimism as a greater number of them put faith in the Post Office and used it widely, the trust required by the terms of expanded postal service did not prove inviolable. In fact, political scandal greatly shook this trust just a few years after the passing of the Postage Duties Bill: 1844 marked the public discovery of a "spying" room called the "secret" or "inner office" in St. Martin's-le-Grand, where government officials, under the auspices of British Home Secretary James Graham, opened sealed letters written by or to those suspected to be political dissidents. (The practice extended to those writing or receiving letters from abroad.)

Why the outrage? Letter opening was a long-standing practice, dating back to at least the seventeenth century, as William Lewins and Howard Robinson note, respectively, in their postal histories.[13] Prior to the Penny Post, the need to ascertain the number of sheets in a letter to determine postal charges easily justified the candling of letters for various reasons, including suspicion of possible treason or rebellion.[14] By contrast, the letter opening discovered four years after the Penny Post extended nationwide (a measure which essentially made it unnecessary to open a letter) pierced the public's trust in the Post Office and in what had been heralded as a democratic measure. As Lewins notes in *Her Majesty's Mails* (1864), this "branch of Post-office business—previously kept carefully in the dark—... went far to destroy the confidence of the nation in the sanctity of its correspondence" (214). Prepayment gave the public what now appeared to be a false sense of security.[15]

With the revolution in postage, more and more Victorians wrote letters to those whom they did and did not know—letters routinely delivered by hands other than those whom they hired or knew personally. The promise of anonymity, the novelty of long-distance communication, and the affordability of bulk mailings increased letter-based traffic and jammed the bags of letter carriers with many letters that postmen could not easily deliver. Privacy at times had to be sacrificed where some degree of investigation was required—in cases of illegible penmanship or slapdash addressing of letters—to ensure delivery. A poorly addressed letter or one with indecipherable handwriting (perhaps the result of carelessness, haste, or ignorance) typically ended up in the Blind Letter Office or the Dead Letter Office (also called, at times, the Returned Letter Office). There, if it could not be deciphered, the letter had to be opened by a postal official in order to be delivered or returned to sender. In a chapter entitled "Strange Addresses" in *The Royal Mail: Its Curiosities and Romance* (1889), J. Wilson Hyde includes an assortment of curiously addressed letters (for example, "No. 52 Oldham & Bury, London" was supposed to read "No. 52 Aldermanbury, London"), in addition to fifty-seven incorrect spellings for "Ipswich" in letters addressed to the Danish and Norwegian Consul (153–54). Some of these undeliverable letters ended up in the Return Letter Office, which, in its capacity today as the Return Letter Centre, handles about seventy-two million indecipherable items yearly, including the 130 larky art envelopes which Harriet Russell posted in 1998 to challenge Royal Mail.

This problem, which Royal Mail still faces, is rooted in the Victorian era and, specifically, the onset of the Penny Post. In "Valentine's Day at the Post-

Office" (1850), Dickens and Wills graphically describe letters destined for the Dead Letter Office as "whole flocks suddenly struck all of a heap, ready for slaughter; for a ruthless individual stood at a table, with sleeves tucked up and knife in hand, who rapidly cut their throats, dived into their insides, abstracted their contents, and finally skinned them" (7). This image of garroted, butchered letters recalls Eleanor Smyth's description of guillotined missives caught in the sashes of the receiving windows at 6:00 p.m. on opening day of Uniform Penny Postage at St. Martin's-le-Grand. However, Dickens and Wills go on to suggest that violence is done not only to the letter but, metaphorically, to the "throat" of the trusting postal worker and, in turn, to the public in the name of government efficiency. In the words of one letter opener Dickens and Wills describe, "'For every letter we leave behind, . . . we are fined half-a-crown. That's why we turn them inside out'" (*Household Words* 7). As the anti-Graham controversy further revealed to a trusting Victorian public, the "throats" of some letters were also "rapidly cut" because they excited the suspicion of the government and found their way into the secret or inner office.

Other forms of corruption also grew from within the "reformed" Post Office. Lewins attests that lower postage curtailed the illegal transmission of letters in the first three years following the Penny Post: "It was shown beyond all dispute, that the scheme had almost entirely prevented breaches of the law, and that if any illicit correspondence was carried on, it was simply and purely in matters where the question of speed was involved; that the evils, amounting to social prohibitions, so prevalent before the change, had been, for the most part, removed" (198). If Uniform Penny Postage raised the morals of the Victorians using the Post Office, as predicted, it did not necessarily improve the morality of Post Office clerks. Letters could still be purloined or their contents stolen when they were "slit open," turned inside out, and "skinned."

Postal reformers argued that with the Penny Post, letter carriers would no longer be tempted to steal, because candling a letter—which exposed its potentially valuable contents, such as money and jewels—would no longer be required to assess a fee. On the contrary, temptation for clerks to steal actually grew following postal reform, because many more Victorians entrusted valuables to the post and did not always carefully fasten their letters. One opponent of the reformed postal system featured in the *Administration of the Post Office* pamphlet argues that "'a government department should not lead the public to suppose that they afford a security, when *really no security exists*'" (127). *Administration*'s anonymous pamphleteer concurs: "under Mr. Hill's system, . . . a letter posted with money in it might as well be thrown down in the street as to be put into the Post Office. . . . Money orders offered no temptation to clerks and servants; the transmission of jewels, etc., afforded a very dangerous one" (124–25). This same author objects to Hill's plan to establish a cheaper system to register valuables and money because "it holds out an unsafe and immoral mode of dealing with the public; unsafe as to the sender of the registered letter, inasmuch it tempts him to incur a danger by the bribe of a cheap postage; and immoral, as regards to the servants of the Post Office, as it holds out the increased temptation to robbery and subtraction" (127–28). Whereas temptation existed prior to reform, it grew in the context of a rapidly growing postal service, which guaranteed greater anonymity with numerous clerks handling every letter. Moreover, chances grew smaller of finding a thief among an increasing number of clerks in any given post office, making thievery more alluring, especially in light of the cash entrusted to the post. In 1850, for example, an estimated £11,000 in cash alone found its way to the Dead Letter Office of St. Martin's-le-Grand.[16]

The reformed Post Office required a literate public to address a letter correctly (and thus to have an understanding of geography) and to write legibly while simultaneously entrusting a great deal of power to postal clerks and letter carriers. Although sworn to "'honourable secrecy,'" members of the Dead Letter Office were often privy to information they'd rather not have known. As one postman of the period reveals,

"a great deal can be known from the outside of a letter, where there is no disposition to pry into the enclosure. . . . From our long training among the letters of our district, we knew the handwriting of most people so intimately, that no attempt at disguise, however cunningly executed, could succeed with us. We noticed the ominous lawyers' letters addressed to tradesmen whose circumstances were growing embarrassed; and we saw the carefully ill-written direction to the street in Liverpool and London, where some poor fugitive debtor was in hiding. The evangelical curate, who wrote in a disguised hand and under an assumed name to the fascinating public singer, did not deceive us; the young man who posted a circular love-letter to three or four girls the same night, never escaped our notice; the wary maiden, prudently keeping two strings to her bow, unconsciously depended upon our good faith. The public never know how much they owe to official secrecy and official honour, and how rarely this confidence is betrayed. Petty tricks and artifices, small dishonesties, histories of tyranny and suffering, exaggerations and disappointments were thrust upon our notice. As if we were the official confidants of the neighborhood, we were acquainted with the leading events in the lives of most of the inhabitants."[17]

Following the democratization of the Post Office, "communications [were] exposed . . . to agents who have no personal relation to the sender or receiver and hence no personal reason to guard their secrets" (Welsh 58). Delivering the post, letter carriers often could not help but become "official confidants" of those to whom they had no "personal relation."

Describing the evolution of blackmail in *Sexual Blackmail: A Modern History*, Angus McLaren describes how in eighteenth-century England, "the sending of menacing letters—that is, the power of a new, anonymous method of communication—caused disquiet" (12). Welsh's definition of blackmail as "an opportunity afforded to everyone by communication of knowledge at a distance" (58) arguably applies to the posting of menacing letters and other undesirable practices. Clergymen disguising their handwriting, false suitors declaring love to many ladies, debtors on the run from the law, women using pillar boxes to post letters that their families clearly did not sanction—all are examples of such "opportunity afforded to everyone by communication of knowledge at a distance" (Welsh 58). "Petty tricks and artifices, small dishonesties, histories of tyranny and suffering, exaggerations and disappointments" became common knowledge to the letter carrier, who, in turn, became a confidant of secrets, betrayals, deceptions, and other misdemeanors.[18] Anonymity in the postal network also grew, as Daunton points out, because of stamps and pillar boxes: "The popularisation of stamps removed the necessity of visiting a post office or receiving house to prepay the postage in money and also made possible the introduction of road-side pillar boxes in which stamped prepaid letters could be deposited" (40). These developments, in effect, opened the Penny Post to senders who wished to use it as a medium for threats, intimidation, and harassment, outcomes counter to the promise of a postal utopia that Hill and other reformers envisioned.

Insults, Sedition, and Curious Things

In *The British Post Office*, Robinson suggests that cheap postage coupled with the option not to prepay cluttered the post with unwanted and insulting letters. Although only 5 percent of letters traveled unpaid in the 1850s, postal supporters originally hoped that the ultimately unsuccessful 1859 measure mandating prepayment (a "pet reform" which Hill included in his original scheme) "would put a stop to insulting and offensive letters and valentines, as well as to the many advertisements sent by mail" (358, 359). Much of what we call "junk mail" and "spam" today—terms which apply to unsolicited mass mailings and e-mail from organizations, stores, and catalogue companies—has its roots in the Victorian era. In an 1840 article in the *Edinburgh Review*, M. D. Hill (Rowland Hill's brother) speculates on the fate of advertisements with the coming of cheap postage: "It has been objected, that circular letters would become so common, that at length people would be disgusted and refuse to read them, and that consequently they would be discontinued" (571). While this reviewer aptly recognizes that an increase in circulars would "disgust" the Victorian public, this common form of unsolicited advertisement was not discontinued. Au contraire. Although postal reformers advocated the Penny Post on the promise of kinship and connection, "many of the purposes to which the post was put in the first decades of cheap postage had little to do with the desire of separated friends and family to communicate."[19] In the nineteenth century, unsolicited circulars, inquiries, fundraising appeals, propaganda, and business service advertisements, sent to parties whom senders did not know, surpassed the volume of mail sent between those who knew each other (at least for some daily deliveries), initiating a trend increasingly evident in the postal system and in computer-mediated communication today. The twin prospects of anonymity and mass mailing attracted legitimate users as well as schemers. One could solicit strangers through personal ads and send secret letters, as the anonymous author of a January 1867 article in *Blackwood's Magazine* laments: "'the post-office system offers a facility for clandestine correspondence which no respectable father or mother on the European side of the Atlantic would think of without a shudder.'"[20] In turn, the meaning of the post morphed and broadened in the nineteenth century to connote not only kinship and connection across distance but impersonal, offensive, dangerous, anonymous, and promiscuous communication.

The term "circular" in the nineteenth century meant unsolicited printed letters or advertisements with wide distribution. Advertisements for a host of mundane and curious products (clothes, books, leeches); leaflets promoting legitimate social, religious, and political causes; "circular swindles" (which today we call "phishing")—all deluged the mail following postal reform. An extant August 27, 1842, letter from Theo Boast of York lodges a complaint about the quality of the merchandise he received from "Messrs Friedlander & Frankaw of London," a seller of leeches: "Gentlemen, In answer to your circular, you may send me 200 Best Spotted Pond Leeches, *Good Size & Healthy* per post; the last you sent me were not at all *healthy* and *bled a great deal*, which I did *not at all like*, you will oblige me *being particular about this lot*, and oblige."[21] Boast, who ordered an additional 200 leeches in response to this firm's circular, also requests that the seller please send him only healthy, large leeches "per post."

Catalogue companies became a booming Victorian industry. Marshall & Snelgrove, a major Birmingham-based department store chain, employed more than 100 clerks in 1888 just to reply to the 1,000 letters it received on average daily from customers placing orders from its mail order catalogue. In 1900, the Union Postale Universelle published figures showing that only the United States had more letters per head than the United Kingdom. While M. J. Daunton suggests this figure might have given Hill some satisfaction, "Rowland Hill would doubtless have approved neither of the massive traffic generated by the football pools nor the more ribald postcards dispatched from Blackpool" (79–80).

Period advertisements convey to us the social meanings of daily life in the Victorian age. Some advertisers suggest the novelty of prepayment as indicated in an extant advertisement from the *Times* of July 9, 1840, requesting interested parties to reply "by letter, prepaid" about a house to let in South Devon. One extant reply to this advertisement from John Maytby, dated July 14, 1840, inquires about the size of the rooms, the rent, and ends, "Be so good as to mention its exact position, aspect & how near it is to the sea."[22] While a newspaper ad for a house isn't too surprising, one for a wife is another story altogether. "Wife wanted" ads appear in newspapers such as the *Morning Chronicle* (October 24, 1891), a development that anticipates today's personal columns and the premise of some popular reality TV shows (for instance, *Wife Swap*).[23] Businesses and organizations also recognized that they could advertise services (such as insurance) and promote social awareness (the evils of slavery, for example) on Mulreadies (though these were quickly withdrawn in favor of stamp adhesives). An advertisement printed inside an extant Mulready dated May 13, 1841, reveals that dueling was still practiced in 1840s England (see figure 13). The Exeter-based Economic Life Assurance Society includes in its advertisement tables of premiums and information on coverage of "policies on the lives of parties dying by suicide, dueling, or by the hands of justice."[24]

Unwanted mail also took the form of insulting valentines, although the majority of Victorian valentines were about love. Far from being emissaries of love, these cutting valentines lambasted Victorian fashion trends and exposed social pretenses. For example, Dean & Son of Ludgate Hill, London, produced a pair of valentines circa 1860 that deride a dandy and a lady of fashion. The valentine poem for the dandy, inscribed "À Monsieur Chandelle," reads:

In your dandified hat,
From your boot to your glove,
I think I've quite pat,
Drawn your portrait above;
Pray don't take offence,
Nor to anger incline,
In dress show more sense,
You queer Valentine.[25]

The accompanying picture (see figure 14) shows a dandy sporting a red cravat, yellow gloves, a yellow checked vest, a black jacket and pants (made of felt), stylish black leather boots, and an exceedingly tall top hat; what looks like a floral boutonniere (possibly a carnation) has fallen off the card, leaving its

FIGURE 13. Advertising Mulready, May 13, 1841. From the collection of Dr. Adrian Almond.

In your dandified hat,
From your boot to your glove,
I think I've quite pat,
Drawn your portrait above;
Pray don't take offence,
Nor to anger incline,
In dress show more sense,
You queer Valentine.

à Monsieur Chandelle.

FIGURE 14. "À Monsieur Chandelle," c. 1860. © Bath in Time, Bath Central Library.

impression on the suit. The dandy puffs on a cigar, carries a walking stick, swells his chest, and wears an expression of self-satisfaction that augments his "dandified" air.

The coordinating card mocking lady's fashions has a mechanical tab that, if pulled, moves the young lady's lower garment back to reveal the crinoline supporting her enormously wide blue-and-white striped skirt that nearly fills the horizontal space of the valentine. The accompanying poem reads:

> With jacket and hat
> Crinoline and all that
>   No doubt you are pleased with yourself
> But nevertheless,
> With your notions of dress
>   You may find yourself left on the shelf[26]

In an age where marriage was paramount for a woman's economic security and social standing, this poem transmits a harsher social reality than its companion. While the former missive may call the dandy "queer," a term that meant odd in 1860s England, the valentine deriding women's fashion—in its final warning that the wearer may remain "on the shelf"—insults by insinuating that this self-satisfied lady may become a "redundant woman" or spinster, simply because of her poor fashion sense.

Some cutting valentines stand as material memories of the complexities of Victorian courtship. One mid-century specimen sneers at the unwelcome affections of an undesirable suitor: "Don't think yourself so vastly killing / Little men I quite despise / And I never shall be willing / To accept one of your sighs."[27] This missive reveals that, despite women's economic vulnerability, some Victorian ladies preferred poverty to the attentions of an unwanted caller, such as the comical figure depicted in the accompanying drawing: the rotund, "little" man with black coat, top hat, and walking stick looks remarkably similar to the derided dandy, Monsieur Chandelle. Other valentines document and critique Victorian themes of rank and subordination. One valentine of this kind depicts a spoiled and haughty Victorian lady reading a book, oblivious to the labors of her maid, who combs the mistress's long tresses. The accompanying verse reads: "Be gentle Miss, mind what you're at, / And don't a tress displace. / Or when your Mistress finds you out, / You'll surely lose your place. / Who would be a Lady's Maid / To always be in fear / Of bringing up my Lady's rage, / For a few pounds a year."[28] Expressing sympathy for the lady's maid rather than the lady she serves, this valentine transmits a daring social message in a milieu characterized by rigid class stratifications, where rank mattered, and where a lady's maid could so easily "lose her place."

While biting valentines are now rare, other types of unwanted, unsolicited mail common during the Victorian period have endured—particularly bulk mail promoting political causes or candidates and a range of humanitarian efforts. On bulk mail items, a postal official stamped "paid" in red ink, initiating a practice that we now call meter franking or metered mail (James 85). Some Victorian mass mailings, facilitated by the Penny Post, carried polemical intent and transmit knowledge about social activism during the period. Richard Cobden, radical leader and cofounder (with John Bright) of the Anti–Corn Law League, used the Penny Post to create a mini revolution that echoed the reform efforts surrounding the postal service. The Corn Laws, by limiting the import of less costly grains from foreign countries, protected wealthy British landholders. Circulating about 40,000 Anti–Corn Law League tracts, Cobden spread his message far and wide to unknown senders throughout the United Kingdom. Cobden's postal agitations helped bring about repeal of the Corn Laws that protected the high price of British grain from more affordable foreign competition.

Cobden claimed that the Penny Post helped defeat the Corn Laws in 1846 far more swiftly than could have been managed without this revolutionary reform. In an 1843 letter to Rowland Hill, Cobden calls the reformed Post Office "'a terrible engine for upsetting monopoly and corruption: witness our League operations, the *spawn of your penny postage!*'"[29] Ironically, the Penny Post, which Hill promoted in his 1837 pamphlet as a means to promote "the unobstructed circulation of letters and of the many cheap and excellent non-political publications of the present day" (8), actually set in motion Cobden's "unobstructed circulation" of political pamphlets. To Tory John Wilson Croker, these pamphlets perfectly illustrated "'*Sedition made easy*'" (532) and offered concrete evidence of how the Penny Post facilitated rabble-rousing: "the radicals in politics, and the sectarians in religion, have been the warmest advocates—and indeed . . . the only very zealous advocates for this penny post. . . . The reason is obvious; because at present such societies cannot circulate their venom without some kind of machinery and agency" (531). What was polemical venom to a conservative like Croker was a "blessing" to a radical like Cobden, who wrote to tell Hill, "'I, have *blessed you* not a few times in the course of our agitating tour'"; Cobden even declares he felt like "'an emancipated negro— . . . I feel that *you* have done not a little to strike the fetters from my limbs, for without the penny postage we might have had more years of agitation and anxiety.'"[30] The repeal of the Corn Laws, a boon to the working-class and middle-class consumer, was a rabble-rousing measure to the landed gentry, leading anti-Hillites like the anonymous author of *Administration of the Post Office* to complain that following cheap postage, "seditious and irreligious tracts" spread "throughout every nook and corner of the kingdom" (59–60).

The Penny Post laid itself open to overuse and abuse, misuse and manipulation. In "Valentine's Day at the Post-Office," Dickens and Willis include remarks from a "sup-president" of the Post Office that bear directly on the notion of trust. Holding up as evidence artificial flowers and a pair of white satin shoes, this official relays: "'The faith the public have in us is extraordinary. . . . The other day the toe of a similar packet protruded from its very thin casing, and the stamper not being able to stop his hand in time, ornamented it, in vividly blue ink, with the words, 'York, Feb. 1, 1850, D.' You will see by this Parliamentary Return of the articles found in the Dead-Letter Office what curious things are trusted to our care'" (10). The article goes on to list odd mailings that, in addition to blood-sucking leeches, flooded the Victorian Penny Post: portraits and miniatures, samples of corn and hops, silver spoons, an eye-glass, boxes of pills, razors, watches, whistles, sewing materials, nightcaps, and a soldier's discharge. Lewins adds to this remarkable roster an account of undeliverable property in *Her Majesty's Mails*: "Forty thousand letters reach the English returned branch each year containing property of different kinds. Many presents, such as rings, pins, brooches, never reach their destination, and are never sent back to the sender because they are often unaccompanied with any letter. These articles, of course, become the property of the Crown" (276). Undeliverables in Lewins's list also include patent medicines, vegetable seed specimens, tree cuttings, manure, oil, wet mosses, pattern books, fish, game, venison, and turtles (103), although by 1864, when Lewins published his postal history, several Post Office Acts had forbidden the posting of many of these items.

The sundry items that made their way into—but not out of—the Post Office illuminate why some dubbed the Dead Letter Office a "cabinet of curiosities" and the Post Office a "flying bazaar." According to one Post Office official, a Mr. Bokenham, law deeds, jewelry, buttons and buckles, silk, and shoes were "'attended with much inconvenience; they require more space for sorting, and small letters are very apt to get entangled in them.'" Bokenham adds, "'I have seen some of the mail-bags coming up in such a filthy state, that they were scarcely fit to be touched—fish, game, oil, and every kind of article. . . . The stench is so bad in the Office, that sometimes you can scarcely breathe in it.'"[31]

FIGURE 15. "One Penny Trip," by John Leech, c. 1840.

Some things went rotten because the public trusted its "curious" belongings to the Post Office rather than to other carriers. Someone even sent a live snake via the post in 1871—the Post Office at first declined it but then accepted the "'pet who had been out on a visit'" so as not to offend the sensibilities of an "'eccentric gentleman'" who insisted on posting it.[32] Thus, it is not surprising that a host of carelessly wrapped "curious things" found their way into the Dead Letter Office, rather than to the homes of their designated recipients.

Curious mailings naturally became a subject for caricature. Notable is "One Penny Trip," John Leech's cartoon of a woman talking to a Post Office official about posting her young son, whom Leech draws standing up inside a large, open envelope bearing a wax seal (see figure 15). The accompanying caption reads:

"Is this the General Post, Sir?"

"Yes, Mum."

"Then will you just have the goodness to stamp upon my little boy here, and send him off to Gravesend!"

Leech includes in the drawing's left foreground a placard that reads: "ALL SMALL BOYS must be PRE PAID / not accountable for damage."[33] Visible are the heels of another small boy just having been meter stamped and posted through the gaping windows of, presumably, the General Post Office at St. Martin's-le-Grand. Curiously, J. Wilson Hyde confirms in *The Royal Mail* that a boy's best friend—if not the boy himself—*did* get stamped and posted: "Though the tradition referred to of boys being thrown into the letter-box may not have a very sure foundation in fact, it is the case at any rate that a live dog was posted at Lombard Street, and falling into the bag attached to the letter-box, it was not discovered till the contents of the bag were emptied out on a table in the General Post-office" (280). When the express postal system started in the United Kingdom in 1891, it was possible to post things larger than snakes and canines: for a fee, you could post yourself if you did not know how to get to a particular location; an express letter messenger (telegraph boy) would conduct you to your designated address.[34]

Victorians also posted noxious and hazardous substances. We might recall the complaint of the anonymous author of *Administration of the Post Office*: "Is there anything gained by way of expedition in making the Post Office a competitor with the general carrier, by this conveyance of parcels of all descriptions,—and of parcels which, in many cases, the senders lying secret and hid, are not only common nuisances, but very frequently offensive, nauseous, and, in a very high degree, mischievous and dangerous?" (104). There are two key objections here. After 1840, the Post Office was open to the wares of the watchmaker, the banker, the lawyer, the grocer, and the publisher, as well as the crook and the blackmailer. Efforts to create an official parcel post as a division of the Post Office date to a suggestion from Henry Cole in 1839, and Rowland Hill helped to usher in a book post in 1848. The British government's parcel post service did not begin until 1883, however, at which point letter carriers officially became postmen. The advent of this service could be considered a de facto measure since, beginning in 1840, the post came to function as a "general carrier" by conveying things ranging from the "curious" to the irritating and perilous.[35]

The second and far more serious objection cited in *Administration of the Post Office* is the consequence of what Welsh describes as letters "loosed from their origin to be interpreted elsewhere" (55). What was "lying secret and hid" could pose a threat to individuals and national security. Hill's democratization of the post, which provided anonymity and inclusiveness, invited dangerous mailings, encouraging public trust when "really no security exists" (*Administration* 127). Home delivery may have safeguarded privacy by making it unnecessary for people to visit the public space of the Post Office—which, as Hicks depicts, attracted criminal and genteel elements alike—but for those who used the postal network, home delivery simultaneously compromised the privacy and safety of the domestic sphere. Not only impersonal communications arrived through a mail slot in one's front door. Dangerous mailings as well as unsolicited items appeared at recipients' doorsteps or in street-side letter boxes along with personal missives. In response, the government created legislation to protect the postal patron and nation. The Post Office Act of 1870 forbade sending through the post "indecent or obscene prints, paintings, lithographs, engravings, books, or cards," and earlier legislation forbade "sending in letters sharp instruments, knives, scissors, or glass, leeches, game, or fish, gunpowder, lucifer matches 'or anything which is explosive'" (Robinson 369). How effective was this legislation, though? How far removed are Victorian concerns from our twenty-first-century fears surrounding "target mail"—a post-9/11 term describing postings of poisons, deadly viruses, hazmat, and bombs?

Threats and Slander: "Wild fire," Charles Dickens and *Bleak House*, and Anthony Trollope and *Dr. Wortle's School*

The Penny Post without compulsory prepayment made it easy to mail insulting, offensive, threatening, and dangerous letters and packages at no financial burden to the sender. Even the cost of a penny charge was not a deterrent to the criminally minded, as we see in an extant threatening letter (dated March 8, 1862, and signed "Wild fire"), in Dickens's *Bleak House* (1853), and in Trollope's *Dr. Wortle's School* (1880). It was not uncommon for people to post intimidating anonymous letters in order to dissuade someone from following a course of action. "Wild fire" apparently did just that to squelch competition from a new London coffeehouse. Addressed to a Mr. Wesley, this letter (see figure 16) reveals how the Penny Post "opened up space for outside agents to wreak havoc on interpersonal relationships."[36]

> Mr. Wesley What do you think of your Coffee House now we gave you
> a dose and will do it again if you attempt to open it There is no mistake

about it old boy two Coffee Houses is quite enough up here and you nor any one else shall ever open that as a Coffee House

Yours, Wild fire[37]

"Wild fire" admits to being the arsonist who started a small fire in Wesley's newly built but as yet unopened coffeehouse. The envelope, bearing a canceled Penny Red stamp, confirms that the London Post Office of the 1860s was open to an admitted arsonist to "wreak havoc" on an innocent entrepreneur. Even readers living well over a century after this threat was posted can easily imagine the fear it stirred in its recipient, Mr. Wesley, when it arrived at his door. It is not known if Wesley dared to open his new coffeehouse on Stockorchard Street, Holloway, London.

Akin to the anonymous "Wild fire," Dickens and Trollope turn the Penny Post into a vehicle powerful enough to set fire to one's reputation. Publishing *Bleak House* serially between 1853 and 1854, thirteen years after the advent of postal reform, Dickens took advantage of the revolution in letter writing to fuel his complex plot: the Penny Post makes feasible a species of blackmail—slander. Dickens's Lady Dedlock has a skeleton in her closet: the beautiful but haughty wife of Sir Leicester Dedlock, Baronet once loved a Captain Hawdon (believed to have died at sea) and had a daughter out of wedlock (also believed dead). In true Dickensian fashion, both lover and daughter are alive. Intrigue arises when Sir Leicester's lawyer, Mr. Tulkinghorn, discovers Lady Dedlock's secret when she exhibits "animation" (11) on seeing the distinctive handwriting of Hawdon (now a penniless law writer) on law documents that Tulkinghorn brings to Chesney Wold. Tulkinghorn threatens to expose Lady Dedlock to her husband but is murdered before he can see his nefarious plot through to conclusion. While it is well known that *Bleak House* stands, in part, as Dickens's indictment of the ponderous, devouring, and then-unreformed British judiciary, my particular interest in the novel lies in how, after Tulkinghorn's death, the Penny Post facilitates a slander campaign launched by Lady Dedlock's former French maid, Mlle. Hortense, Tulkinghorn's murderess.

Thinking the Penny Post provides her anonymity, Mlle. Hortense floods the post with slanderous letters at a penny each, incriminating Lady Dedlock to divert attention away from herself as a murder suspect.[38] Inspector Bucket "is no great scribe . . . discourages correspondence with himself in others, as being too artless and direct a way of doing delicate business. Further, he often sees damaging letters produced in evidence, and has occasion to reflect that it was a green thing to write them. For these reasons he has very little to do with letters, either as sender or receiver. And yet he has received a round

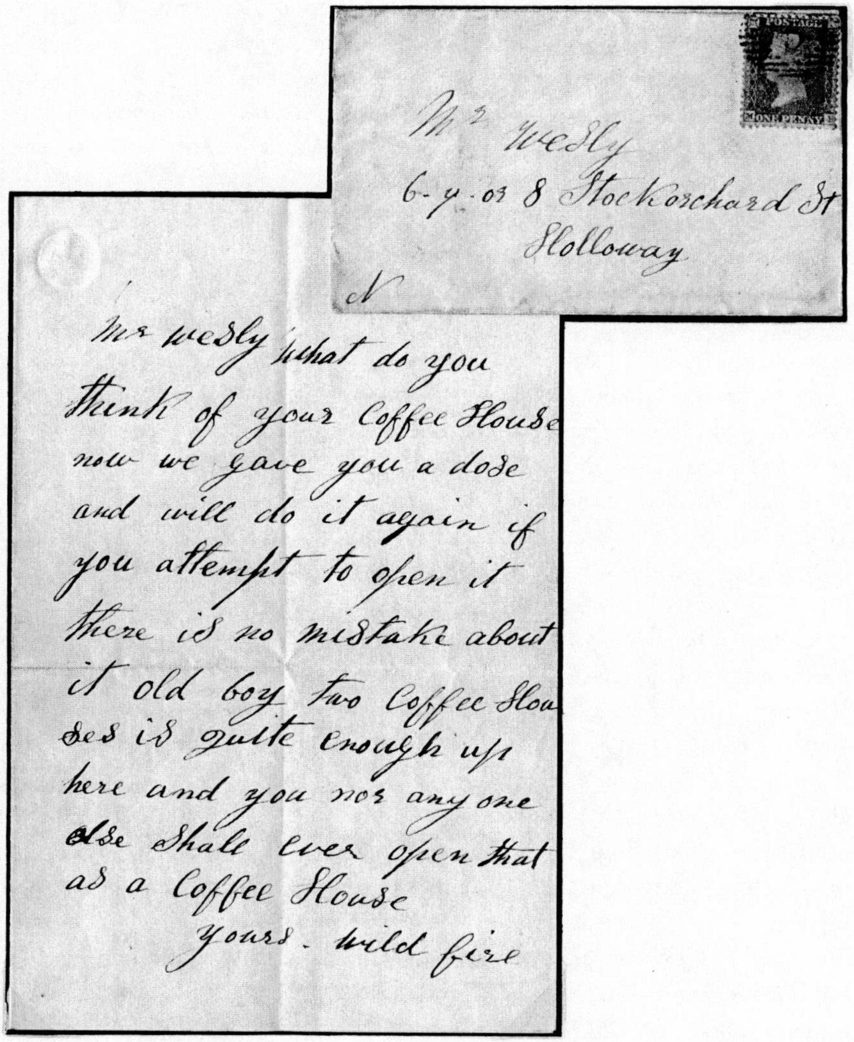

FIGURE 16. "Wild fire" letter, March 8, 1862. From the collection of John Forbes-Nixon.

half-dozen, within the last twenty-four hours" (573). The "round half-dozen" letters Bucket receives "by post" are composed in the same hand and contain the same two words, "boldly written, in each, 'LADY DEDLOCK'" (573). Mlle. Hortense also sends a letter to Sir Leicester Dedlock, which contains three words in it, "'LADY DEDLOCK, MURDERESS.'" According to Bucket, "'These letters have been falling about like a shower of lady-birds'" (594). Suspecting Mlle. Hortense, Bucket directs his wife to spy on her: "'What do you say now to Mrs. Bucket, from her spy-place, having seen them all written by this young woman? What do you say to Mrs. Bucket having, within this half-hour, secured the corresponding ink and paper, fellow half-sheets and what not? What do you say to Mrs. Bucket having watched the posting of 'em every one by this young woman, Sir Leicester Dedlock, Baronet?'" (594). By making postage reasonably priced, the Penny Post even brought letter writing within the means of a dismissed maid, who could afford the "posting of 'em." Damaging letters, which Inspector Bucket proclaims a "green thing to write"(573), in turn, become evidence to condemn Mlle. Hortense, who is found guilty not only of murder but of slander, facilitated by the Penny Post. The centrality of letter-driven criminality in *Bleak House* secures the novel's position as a material memory of the collective social anxiety wrought by postal reform.

In *Dr. Wortle's School,* Trollope shows how a slanderous letter has the power nearly to destroy the reputations of two upstanding members of the clergy, Dr. Wortle and Rev. Peacocke, who run Bowick School for boys and teach there. Rather than unravel a mystery as he does in *Orley Farm* (1862) or *Phineas Redux* (1874), Trollope discloses a marital irregularity in his opening chapters, as Wilkie Collins does in *No Name* (1862), and uses the novel to explore the ramifications of this transgression. In chapter 3 of part 1, entitled "The Mystery," Trollope reveals that, unbeknownst to Dr. Wortle, "Mr. and Mrs. Peacocke were not man and wife" (28). Following their wedding in America, Ferdinand Lefroy—Mrs. Peacocke's estranged first husband, presumed dead—reappears, and the Peacockes discover that Ella is, in essence, a bigamist and that their marriage is not binding. Unable to part forever—which Victorian society (but not Trollope) deems the socially correct action once the irregularity comes to light—the Peacockes travel to Rev. Peacocke's native England, hoping to start life anew. Rev. Peacocke earns a reputation as a brilliant scholar and teacher, but one disgruntled parent, the Honourable Mrs. Staniloup (whom Trollope unflatteringly dubs Old Mother Shipton),[39] insists to the Bishop: "'Don't you think it well you should know something of his life during these five years?'" (25). The past rears its head in the form of Mrs. Peacocke's brother-in-law, who comes to England with blackmail on his mind, and Peacocke, in turn, travels to America to find out if Ella's first husband is now dead, as Wortle suspects. Dr. Wortle allows Ella to remain under his protection (without any official capacity in the school), and this kindness infuriates Mrs. Staniloup, who launches a slander campaign against Dr. Wortle for allowing such moral impropriety to taint Bowick.

In contrast to the epistolary novel of the eighteenth century, which tells a story through letters, the nineteenth-century novel uses letters within the narrative to serve a purpose. Mrs. Staniloup's damning letters, like those of Mlle. Hortense, fly "'like a shower of lady-birds,'" and the resulting smear campaign leaves many parents no alternative but to remove their sons from Wortle's establishment, since "'no boy's soul would any longer be worth looking after if he be left in . . . [Wortle's] hands'" (132). The press fans the scandal (implying Dr. Wortle is eager to have pretty Mrs. Peacocke to himself), and the Bishop warns Wortle of his danger; Wortle, in turn, lambastes the press for slandering his character, and Bowick nearly closes. There is no arrest in this novel as in *Bleak House*, and, ultimately, all comes right for the Peacockes, Dr, Wortle, and Bowick School.[40] Nonetheless, the happy ending does not eclipse Trollope's skillful exposition of the dark side of the Penny Post. The slanderous letter in *Dr. Wortle's School*, its function akin to that in *Bleak House*, becomes a fiery material memory of mischief stemming from the reformed Post Office and its facilitation of a host of unwanted, deceptive, and destructive mailings.

The Rise of Fraud and Blackmail from Daily Life to the Pages of Victorian Fiction

One of the forces powering postal reform was a motivation to curb petty frauds—primarily the sending of letters by illegal means that cheated the Post Office of revenue. The effort to stop this particular con was largely successful. Nonetheless, the Penny Post spawned new types of fraud, the physical artifacts of which—forgeries and falsified documents of various kinds, including letters—serve as material memories of insubordination and deception as they were understood and experienced during the Victorian age. As Hyde observes in *The Royal Mail*, "The Post-office, while it is the willing handmaid to commerce, the vehicle of social intercourse, and the necessary helper in almost every enterprise and occupation, becomes at the same time a ready means for the unscrupulous to carry on a wonderful variety of frauds on the public, and enables a whole army of needy and designing persons to live upon the generous impulses of society" (148).

Hyde's narrative accounts of some of these scams may seem oddly familiar to us: men and women who write the well-to-do to beg assistance on a variety of false pretenses; an elaborate, ingenious scheme to post to wealthy persons letters not actually intended for them in order to exploit their emotions for money. In the latter scheme, a wealthy person receives a letter deliberately addressed to someone else; the letter describes great calamities that have befallen the sender before asking for monetary assistance. One Rev. Mr. Champneys of St. Pancras, London, hoping to help such a letter writer in distress, posted the particulars of the letter in the *Times* and asked for the stated addressee to contact him. Although he did not hear from the addressee, Rev. Champneys received countless letters from people who had likewise received this very same letter, and at once the fraud became clear: "under the guise of a trifling mistake, that of placing a letter in the wrong envelope, a set of dire circumstances were placed before persons who were likely to be kindhearted and generous, in the hope that, though the writer was unknown to them, they might send some money to cheer a poor but respectable family steeped in calamity!" (Hyde 150).

Hyde additionally recounts the particulars of the "confidence trick," another postal scam driven by cheap postage. He tells of an advertisement run in numerous country newspapers allegedly to test the honesty of the Victorian public. In it, an "'elderly bachelor of fortune'" asked people to send him seventeen stamps as a token of confidence, promising to return the stamps along with a present. One lady requested a black silk dress as her reward, while another woman boasted of her interest in dancing the mazourka and going out in "'gay society'" to help the bachelor "'determine the suitability of the present'" (151). Hyde reports that 300–400 letters, each containing seventeen stamps, reached the Dead Letter Office because the advertiser had "'moved on' from the places where he had lived, in consequence of their becoming too warm to hold him" (151).

A notorious Victorian swindler, Joseph Ady similarly seized upon cheap postage as a way to defraud the naïve and gullible by sending vast numbers of unpaid "circular swindles" to strangers during the 1840s and 1850s. In these letters, material memories of deception, Ady promised to give the recipient a great reward if he or she would simply remit a much smaller sum in his name. In an extant unpaid "circular swindle" dated December 22, 1846, Ady claims his high connection to honorable personages and promises "something to your advantage (Value £100.0.0 and upwards) on receipt of 20s by Post Office order on Whitechapel as an Equivalent for his trouble & costs generally."[41] This type of scam was big business on both sides of the Atlantic, given the "anonymity and promiscuity of the mail, which permitted one party to extract money from the other."[42] Profitable scams reached such great proportions that the Post Office in 1848 required the sender, in many cases the swindler, to pay 2d for any unpaid letters that were refused.

Like fraud, blackmail also became a "ready means for the unscrupulous" to prey upon the unsuspecting. Although blackmail long predates the Victorian age, it flourished in the wake of the Penny Post. In Victorian England, blackmail meant payment to secure one's reputation. Typically, a blackmailer sent a letter to a targeted victim to extort money in exchange for guarding a guilty secret. However, as Angus McLaren notes in *Sexual Blackmail*, the term "blackmail" dates to Tudor times when Scottish barons exacted protection money from farmers in the North of England: the term "mail" or "mayle" is the Anglo-Saxon word for "tribute" or "rent." By the eighteenth century, the concept of blackmail in England had evolved, McLaren explains, to include "the sending of menacing letters" in order to exercise the "power of a new, anonymous method of communication" that "caused disquiet" (12). Blackmail, like slander, targets an individual's reputation and, in an era that valued propriety as highly as did the Victorian age, blackmailers traded on the certainty that an individual of means would pay to keep the secrets of his or her past from coming to light. Courts of law in nineteenth-century England heard numerous cases of homosexual blackmail; sodomy was punishable by death through 1836 and remained a criminal offense punishable by ten years' to life imprisonment even after the legal reforms of 1861.

Despite their attachment to propriety and an ideal of domestic sanctity, the Victorian public found stories of illicit activity compelling—a tendency Victorian writers responded to readily, as McLaren points out: "Given the age's preoccupation with protecting family privacy, writers of nineteenth-century romances, mysteries, and melodramas drew on the public's fascination with sexual secrets and mysterious demands" (55). Much Victorian fiction embodies the collective anxieties that of necessity attended the profound social and cultural changes wrought by revolutions in industry and technology, information and communications. Central to representation of such anxiety are stories of blackmail. "Reputational blackmail," according to Welsh, an "unintended result of the information revolution," gave rise to "fictions of blackmail" which, "perhaps better represent the anxieties and displacements at work than the real thing. Far more persons have now imagined or read about blackmail than there are persons who have actually been blackmailed" (29). Sensation writers of the 1860s wove blackmail, espionage, secrets, adultery, impersonations, and murder into a genre that "carried a primary meaning of 'electrical stimulus.' This was fiction that jolted the reader's nerves."[43]

In *No Name*, Wilkie Collins establishes a marital irregularity as the impetus for reputational blackmail. Mrs. Vanstone pays Captain Wragge, whose only address is "Post-office, Bristol," to keep silent in order to secure her secret: she and her husband are not legally married, and her children are, therefore, illegitimate.[44] Mrs. Vanstone confides to her daughters' governess, Miss Garth, that she paid Wragge—son of her mother's first husband (from a previous marriage) and an "incorrigible scoundrel" (22)—"solely from the dread that he would otherwise introduce himself to Mr. Vanstone's notice, and take unblushing advantage of Mr. Vanstone's generosity. Shrinking, naturally, from allowing her husband to be annoyed, and probably cheated as well, by any person, who claimed, however preposterously, a family connection with herself, it had been her practice, for many years past, to assist the captain from her own purse, on the condition that he should never enter the house, and that he should not presume to make any application whatever to Mr. Vanstone" (21–22). A savvy reader of sensation fiction would immediately suspect that Mrs. Vanstone would not repeatedly and regularly "assist" a scapegrace for years simply to keep him from inconveniencing her husband. The post is open to Wragge, who blackmails Mrs. Vanstone, and she, in turn, pays him to keep silent and secures her reputation.

Oscar Wilde—who became all too familiar with the legal consequences of male homosexuality—introduces the subject of reputational blackmail when Dorian Gray threatens to expose the sordid past of a male friend in *The Picture of Dorian Gray* (1891).[45] Wilde, moreover, explores reputational blackmail in greater depth in *An Ideal Husband* (1895), a comedy intertwining honor and political corruption. A seemingly upstanding MP, Sir Robert Chiltern becomes a blackmail victim of the nefarious Mrs. Cheveley, who threatens to expose a damning secret and thus ruin Chiltern's political career and marriage. (The virtuous Lady Chiltern knows nothing of the skeleton in her husband's closet.) Mrs. Cheveley possesses a letter Robert Chiltern wrote to a Baron Arnheim, revealing private government information for which the Baron paid handsomely; Baron Arnheim, in turn, made a fortune, as did Chiltern: "that money gave me exactly what I wanted, power over others. I went into the House immediately. The Baron advised me in finance from time to time. Before five years I had almost trebled my fortune" (27–28). In his characteristically witty satire of upper-crust Victorian society, Wilde reveals the appalling but amusing truth that in order to be a successful blackmailer, one must have an unimpeachable past. Chiltern's friend, Lord Goring, saves Chiltern by threatening to expose Mrs. Cheveley for stealing a brooch that Goring gave to his cousin, Lady Berkshire, and which Mrs. Cheveley lost at the Chilterns' home when she came to blackmail Sir Robert Chiltern.

Blackmail fictions tell us much about the meaning of Victorian propriety: past sins, once exposed, can permanently ruin a reputation. Blackmailers need not remain anonymous,[46] but blackmail works only if the blackmailer does not fear disclosure. What's more, some blackmail fictions work to affirm the status quo and notions of unassailable privilege, reinforcing the rigid class hierarchies of the age as an antidote (however fleeting) to the anxiety—embodied in the figure of the blackmailer—that the high and mighty, with a few strokes of a pen, can be brought down to the dirt. In such cases, blackmail fiction stands as a material memory of imprisoning Victorian class structures, the bitter consequences of insubordination, of stepping out of one's proper social place. At the same time, these fictions reveal the profound unease embodied in the figures of the blackmailer and blackmail itself: the ubiquitous threat posed by vast social and cultural changes to shake everything up—to elevate the low and bring down the high.

A longstanding postal official, Trollope examines how the Penny Post and the omnipresence of the roadside pillar box opened ample opportunities for the slanderer, the mischief maker, and the blackmailer. In *Marion Fay* (1882), Trollope even goes so far as to make the term "Penny Post" a euphemism for blackmail. Dismissed chaplain Mr. Greenwood grows angry that he will lose his post and receive a "beggarly stipend of £200 a year" for thirty years of devoted service to the Marquis of Kingsbury and his family (3: 248). Greenwood, formerly the confidant of the second Lady Kingsbury, knows of her dire plot to dispose of the Marquis's son and heir from his first marriage. Feeling "ill-treated, almost robbed," Greenwood considers trading on this damaging information: "though it might be base to tell her ladyship's secrets, the penny-post was still open to him" (3: 248).

Trollope sows the seeds of blackmail at the start of volume 3: "If the Marquis knew all, and if other people knew all! If it were known how often her ladyship had spoken, and how loud, as to the wished-for removal to a better world of his lordship's eldest son! . . . He had for some days felt her ladyship to be under his thumb, and now it seemed that she had escaped from him" (3: 24). Again resorting to euphemism, Trollope reveals Lady Kingsbury's desire for the "removal" of Lord Hampstead to make way for her own firstborn son to become heir to the Marquis's vast wealth and title. Greenwood possesses potentially damning information: "The whisperings in that up-stairs sitting-room at Trafford had been dreadful . . . ought he not to be paid for holding his tongue?" (3: 249).[47] Greenwood fires off letters to the Marchioness, threatening to reveal to the Marquis their "'confidential discussions'" unless, instead of discarding the chaplain "'like an old glove,'" she sends him a sufficient sum (3: 249). After the third blackmail letter, Lady Kingsbury sends Greenwood a £50 note to silence him. When he returns it in an effort to exact more, Lady Kingsbury shows the blackmail letters to her husband, who, in turn, hands them over to his lawyer. The lawyer warns Greenwood that unless he stops his blackmail, he will be brought before a police magistrate.[48] Even if the Penny Post invites iniquity, the wealthy have the power to foil the blackmailer. Even so, despite partial restoration of the status quo, the novel closes uneasily for Lady Kingsbury; because of the "fears with which Mr. Greenwood had filled her, she had been awed into quiescence" (3: 271). In the face of revolutions large and small, anxieties may be quieted but never entirely put to rest.

While, as Welsh attests, most Victorians never directly experienced blackmail, period fiction made it widely known to them, and titillating blackmail stories, on a par with sensation fiction, abounded in Victorian life. The infamous Branwell Brontë—the only son on whom the illustrious Brontë family pinned its prospects—resorted to alcohol and blackmail to pay his debts following a failed affair with his employer's wife, Mrs. Robinson of Thorp Green. Hired to tutor the Robinson's son, Branwell was dismissed in 1845 after a gardener on the grounds allegedly discovered Branwell and his employer's wife together at the boathouse. According to Brontë biographer Juliet Barker, Branwell "refused to find further employment, blackmailed and stole from his father to obtain money for his drink and drugs, and became violent and unpredictable."[49] Branwell's letters reveal his desperation and readiness to demand money from others after he had "failed to live up to the expectations of his father and sisters. His last letters," Barker notes, "barely coherent pleas for money so that he could avoid being sent to jail for debt, are a sordid illustration of the depths to which this once brilliant and much beloved boy had fallen" (*The Brontës: A Life*, xxi). Branwell's letters about his debts, his promises to pay them, his urgent pleas for money to avoid jail can all be regarded as enfeebled forms of blackmailing. Barker also indicates that Mrs. Robinson continued to send Branwell money periodically, leading us to wonder what exactly she wanted to keep hush.[50] Some critics including Daphne du Maurier suggest the adultery story "had been invented to cover up a far darker crime, hinting that Branwell had been dismissed for sexually abusing or otherwise corrupting the Robinsons' son."[51]

The Penny Post also brought Branwell death threats and scandal. In one letter to Francis Grundy dated October 1845, Branwell revealed that "Three months since, while at home, I received a furious letter from my Employer threat[e]ning to shoot me if I returned from the vacation—and letters from her ladies maid and her physician informed me of the outbreak and threatened proceedings only checked by her [Mrs. Robinson's] firm courage and resolution that come what harm might to her none should come to me."[52] From Branwell Brontë's extant letters to the fiction of Trollope, Collins, Wilde, and Dickens,[53] blackmail stories rekindle the very real anxieties that grew out of the Victorian information revolution, a revolution that in many ways anticipated the host of communications threats—such as Internet scams and pornography, computer viruses and hacking—that plague our current information technologies. Threatening letters sent to Branwell Brontë and Mr. Wesley, the would-be coffeehouse entrepreneur intimidated by "Wild fire," also stand as material memories of one of the profound ironies of postal reform: that dreams of a postal-age utopia engendered by reform and democratization would be ever at risk from darker human forces, given greater room to maneuver by that reform.

Emancipation, Impropriety, and Infidelity by Penny Post

How did the public space of the Post Office and the convenience of the pillar box impact women's emancipation? What were the consequences of anonymous letters communicating knowledge of betrayal from a distance? What kinds of moral irregularities did cheap postage bring to light? The Post Office was not only a civic and administrative institution in the nineteenth century, but also a frequently visited public place, a social space where men and women in town and city alike came in contact with those whom they might not otherwise encounter. Moreover, as Henkin points out, "Post offices were places where adulterous couples could simply run into each other by concealed prearrangement, or where strangers might initiate and develop relationships" (79). In his reading of an 1857 drawing of the New York Post Office printed in *Frank Leslie's Illustrated Newspaper*, Henkin calls attention to how the image shows the post office as a "place of diverse and promiscuous interaction" (71), a depiction which also applies to London's St. Martin's-le-Grand. In Hicks's painting, *The General Post Office, One Minute to Six*, the London Post Office attracts diverse users of the postal network—the young and the old, criminal and Good Samaritan, the working class and the genteel. The scene also recalls Croker's interrogative warning: "Will clerks write only to their fathers, and girls to their mothers? Will not letters of romance or love, intrigue or mischief, increase in at least equal proportions?" (532).

Much as the physical space of the Post Office made promiscuity possible, the openness of the pillar box made it an emissary of mischief. Women, married and single, could now discretely send clandestine letters to their lovers. As accessible as it was to mischief makers, the pillar box was equally as available to morally upright Victorians who felt it their duty to tell a husband of a wife's infidelity, often behind a veil of anonymity. There was a nineteenth-century convention for writing to ladies via their husbands, addressing a letter, for example, to a Mr. F. Brown for Mrs. Brown. This device enabled a husband to open a letter conveying scandalous information about his wife, while the letter sender would have acted aboveboard and according to his or her conscience.[54]

Much Victorian fiction and narrative painting illuminates the almost regulatory role the Penny Post played in circulating the missives that disclosed sexual transgressions and improprieties. Perhaps no author was more aware than Trollope of how freethinking daughters and wives could exploit the reformed Post Office for promiscuous purposes. Prior to the Penny Post, Victorian men of a certain social standing could always receive private letters at their clubs, maintaining discretion and secrecy, but women had no such ready and clandestine ways to exchange letters. (Once a letter arrived, though, they could store it in their locked writing desks.) Whereas in Trollope's early novels, daughters routinely show their letters to their mothers, Trollope's novels of the 1870s and 1880s suggest he increasingly suspected the Penny Post would facilitate what biographer Victoria Glendenning calls "domestic subterfuge": "The pillar box on the corner of the road, as he mentioned more than once, made private correspondences even easier for independent-minded wives and daughters" (372). In *Marion Fay*, Trollope calls upon his early experience as a postal clerk to create a love match between Lady Frances Trafford and a post office clerk in St. Martin's-le-Grand.[55] When Lady Frances's father, the Marquis, and her stepmother, the Marchioness, discover her engagement to George Roden, they immediately remove her to a German chateau at Königsgraaf to break off the match. While Lady Frances resides in Germany, "Mr. George Roden's name was never mentioned by either of the ladies. There was the Post Office, no doubt, and the Post Office was at first left open to her; but there soon came a time in which she was deprived of this consolation. With such a guardian as the Marchioness, it was not likely that free correspondence should be left open to her" (1: 54).

Trollope aligns the reformed Post Office with the notion of "free correspondence." That the reformed postal service remains "open" to Lady Frances marks it as a channel through which an independent-minded daughter can rebel against her parents. Initially, Lady Frances avails herself of the post after openly declaring her love for Roden, but she is not defiant. She acquiesces to her stepmother's threat that "if necessary, the postmistress in the village should be instructed not to send on any letter addressed to George Roden," even though, as Trollope confides, the Marchioness is "not at all thinking that her own instructions would have prevailed with the post-mistress" (1: 114).

Later in this novel, Trollope—who was intimately involved with pillar boxes since he advocated bringing them to Britain from the Continent—utilizes them to effect when Marion Fay, after refusing Lord Hampstead's offer of marriage because of her poor health and his high rank, takes advantage of the pillar box: "As soon as it [the letter] was gone,—dropped irrevocably by her own hand into the pillar letter-box which stood at the corner opposite to the public-house,—she told her father what she had done" (3: 58). Zachary Fay reprimands Marion for being "'flighty and fickle'": why write to a man whom she has refused? Even Marion concurs, "'It was not fitting'" (3: 58). Still, the pillar box and the Penny Post remain open to Marion, just as they are open to Lady Frances and Mr. Greenwood. In this novel, Trollope makes the Penny Post a euphemism not only for blackmail, but for woman's emancipation and impropriety. Additional warning signs, the location of the pillar box next to a drinking establishment and Marion's decision to tell her father *only* after she "irrevocably" drops her letter into the box further evince Trollope's fear that the pillar box promoted women's indiscretions and rejection of parental authority and convention.[56]

Letters are also material proofs of men's improprieties and transgressions, including dueling, eloping, and whoring. An extant anonymous letter dated August 25, 1869, and posted in Wexford, Ireland, challenges its recipient, Mr. Percifull (Percival?), to a duel. The letter is almost as notorious for its lack of punctuation as for its request; dueling was illegal in most countries by the nineteenth century but often practiced in rural Ireland in Victorian times: "Will you be so kind as to meet gentleman which you offended at the ball on the twenty fifth meet him this evening or tomorrow morning at six o'clock he will meet you from one to ten yards distant and do not forget to bring your fancy pistle with you." The volume of letters sent to Gretna Green, a small Scottish border town and center of an illicit marriage trade (sought out by runaway British elopers wishing to marry without publishing bans), informs us of the great number of "irregular marriages" that took place in the nineteenth century. One extant 1885 letter offers a £1 reward for information about the marriage of one Edward Gascoine, Gaskin, or Gascoigne—the variations on the name alone suggest why this man chose to be married in the blacksmith's shop at Gretna Green, which was opened as a visitor attraction in 1887.

An 1842 letter from Edward Wright, a British officer serving in Victorian India, to a Mr. Jonas Paxton of Oxfordshire describes in graphic detail the services and prices of Indian prostitutes. Wright boasts about knowing the Bengalese word for "F——" and describes with some amusement the abundance of prostitutes where he is stationed: "In the slums you receive the polite invitations of a score or two of whores; 'Come my love, vare good bed my house . . . '" Wright's firsthand descriptions give credence to reports of how droves of prostitutes followed British officers of the Honourable East India Company's Army around the subcontinent of British India. Houses of ill fame also operated in England, the subject of an extant letter to W. Bolden Esquire of Lancaster from a tutor at Clare College, Cambridge, dated February 21, 1859. Tutor Arthur Wolfe informs Mr. Bolden that his son "was found yesterday in the middle of the day by one of the Proctors in a house of ill-fame." Though the tutor expresses "no great fault to find with [Bolden's] son in other respects during the past year although by no means so regular or industrious as I could have wished," he reports that Clare College has, nonetheless, decided to suspend the young man for a period of ten months—"what may appear a somewhat severe punishment in order to deter others from an offence of the same nature."[57] We can well imagine how Bolden's son fared during his ten months rustication.

Some letters became confessionals of sorts, where the writer, by listing out his or her transgressions or secrets, might hopefully achieve a sense of distance from them. In *Tess of the D'Urbervilles* (1891), Thomas Hardy explains why Tess chooses the letter as the way to reveal her past to Angel Clare: "Declare the past to him by word of mouth she could not, but there was another way. She sat down and wrote on the four pages of a note-sheet a succinct narrative of those events of three or four years ago, put it into an envelope, and directed it to Clare" (164).[58] For Trollope's *Kept in the Dark* (1882), Sir John Everett Millais created a dramatic illustration of Cecilia Holt writing a letter about her prior history, a missive that she regrettably elects not to post to her intended, Mr. Western: "When the letter was completed, she found it to be one which she could not send. It was as though she were telling him something, on reading which he would have to decide whether their engagement should or should not be continued. . . . It was clear to her that a letter so worded was not fit for the occasion, and she destroyed it" (17). In the Millais illustration (see figure 17), Cecilia sits at a table, sheaves of paper before her, writing about her past liaison with Sir Francis Geraldine, which comes back to haunt her when her former lover maliciously posts a letter to her husband with his version of their broken engagement. Upon receipt of that "fatal letter" (45), Mr. Western writes a letter telling his young wife, "'We have now parted for ever'" (47).[59] In our postmodern age, where we fear paper trails, where an imprudent letter or

FIGURE 17. "When the Letter Was Completed." Illustration by Sir John Everett Millais for Anthony Trollope's *Kept in the Dark*, 1882.

e-mail can have damaging legal consequences, where we shred any evidence that might compromise us in a court of law, we avoid epistolary communication of our indiscretions, a pathway our Victorian ancestors frequently traveled and, at times, "greenly" preferred.

Past and Present, No. 1: A Tale of Marital Infidelity

Augustus Egg's triptych of marital infidelity entitled *Past and Present* (1858) makes a fitting close to this chapter about the rise of unwanted, threatening missives that accompanied reform of the postal service—a reform Hicks so memorably celebrated two years later in *The General Post Office, One Minute to Six*. Egg was not the only painter to employ the device of an incriminating letter in a painting that resembles a cautionary tale. Richard Redgrave includes this icon in his depiction of an unwed daughter's fall in *The Outcast* (1858). According to commentator George Landow, the daughter's impurity is clear in spite of the letter, which ultimately "seems a bit unnecessary . . . since the daughter holds her illegitimate child in her arms—clear enough evidence that she's a fallen woman!"[60] Redgrave's erring daughter looks beseechingly at her stern father, who, after reading the letter of her sad history that lies on the floor close to the open doorway, points both daughter and illegitimate child to the harsh outdoors. Whether the letter image is "unnecessary" in *The Outcast* as Landow asserts or, as T. J. Edelstein concludes, "the final piece of damning evidence" (206), the device wields far greater force in Egg's painting, where it is the means by which the husband discovers his wife's infidelity—the scene depicted in the central canvas in Egg's theatrical and moralizing triptych.

Egg exhibited his narrative paintings with no title, appending only the following comment: "'Aug. 4: Have just heard that B. has been dead more than a fortnight; so his poor children have now lost both their parents. I hear *She* was seen on Friday last, near the Strand, evidently without a place to lay her head—What a fall hers has been!'"[61] The subject of the central or drawing room canvas (see figure 18) is developed by two flanking panels, the panels to which Egg's comment explicitly refers and the events of which presumably unfold several years after the disastrous letter wreaks havoc on a once-happy, prosperous middle-class family. The panel originally exhibited to the left and below the drawing room scene shows the adulterous wife "without a place to lay her head," nursing her illegitimate child beneath the Adelphi Arches and looking into the Thames. Posters on the brick wall behind her are printed with slogans—"Pleasure Excursions to Paris" and "Victims"—which emphasize her miserable situation. The third panel, originally exhibited to the right and below the drawing room scene, shows the couple's daughters, now grown,

FIGURE 18. *Past and Present, No. 1.* First of three panels in a triptych by Augustus Egg, 1858. © Tate, London 2008.

staring at the moon. Miniatures of their irrevocably separated parents appear on either side of an open window. Interestingly, the moon on which the older daughter gazes is the same moon watched by the outcast wife from her shelter beneath the Adelphi Arches.

When Egg exhibited the paintings at the Royal Academy Exhibition of June 1858, the triptych "shocked its audience by animating their deepest fears of family blight" (Auerbach 29). Both the *Leisure Hour* and the *Athenaeum* labeled it a "domestic tragedy" in their respective 1858 reviews. An 1858 review in *Sharpe's London Magazine* even more boldly asserts, "Terrible, true, all of it," and then queries, "but should it ever have been painted? Who can put *that* in his gallery, for honest women to look at? Sure, there is a bound to painted horror."[62] Some contemporary reviewers took the liberty to name the stories the paintings so readily tell. *Sharpe's London Magazine* called it "Faithless Wife," *Athenaeum* titled it "The Adulterous Woman and Her Fate," and Frances Turner Palgrave listed it as "Tale of Terror" in his handbook to the International Exhibition of 1862.[63] While the painting (now on display at the

Tate Britain in the same serial order as when Egg first exhibited it) goes by the name *Past and Present, Nos. 1–3*, some critics today continue to name the individual panels. Nina Auerbach calls the central panel *Misfortune* and the companion panels, respectively, *Despair* and *Prayer* (29). In the same order, Tess Lynch calls them *The Infidelity Discovered, The Wife Abandoned by Her Lover with her Bastard Child*, and *The Abandoned Daughters*.[64]

The central panel—both the most staged and the most symbolically heavy-handed of the three panels—is, likewise, the most pertinent to our discussion of the Penny Post. In it, the image of the letter is ripe with social meaning, focusing on what appears to be the inevitability of discovery of infidelity. The young daughters, curious as to what is unfolding, build on top of a book a house of cards—an emblem of instability that speaks to the fate of the entire family. The author's name, Honoré de Balzac, emblazoned on the spine of the book, alludes to French novels with themes of infidelity—Balzac's own *Cousin Bette* (1846) or perhaps Gustave Flaubert's *Madame Bovary* (1856). This emblem may also allude to the dangers of novel reading by young women— the notion that the romance novel tempted women into dissatisfaction with mundane domestic situations and helped to lead them astray.[65] The paintings on the drawing room walls preach silently but loudly: the wife's miniature appears below a painting of Adam and Eve being expelled from Paradise—an explicit allusion to her own "fall." The wronged husband's miniature lies below a representation of *The Abandoned* (1856), Clarkson Stanfield's highly popular painting of a ship floundering in a stormy sea.[66] These symbols in what Auerbach aptly calls Egg's "cautionary genre-piece" (36), as well as the demeanors of the distraught husband and wife and their innocent children, have captured the most critical attention to date, as this painting forms a piece with other depictions of fallen women and their dire predictions for the woman and her family: "No doubt the Victorian imagination isolated the fallen woman so pitilessly from a social context, preferring to imagine her as destitute and drowned prostitute or errant wife cast beyond the human community, because of her uneasy implications for wives who stayed home" (33).

In the context of *Posting It*, the fateful letter exposing the wife's infidelity is an emissary of Victorian morality. The distressed husband holds the letter that contains evidence of his wife's betrayal. The envelope which once enclosed the incriminating letter lies ripped open, discarded on the floor. With his left foot, the husband stamps upon a miniature portrait of his wife's lover. Edelstein remarks, "The husband, who has just learned of his wife's infidelity in a letter, sits in stunned silence with the fateful missive in his hand" (205). Visual cues that he has only "just" received the letter include the mirror's reflection of an open doorway as if he has only just entered the room; his top hat sitting on the table as if he has only just taken it off; and his umbrella and satchel lying on the floor at the bottom left of the canvas, as if he has just dropped them before staggering to a chair. The distraught look on his face reveals he believes the truthfulness of the incriminating letter. Although the author of the letter remains unknown, we sense the presence of the anonymous "well-wisher," a familiar trope in Victorian fiction.[67]

We can discern a Queen's head in the corner of the red-tinted envelope. The Penny Red stamp (in use in 1858) suggests the letter came via the Penny Post. The red tint of the envelope and stamp aligns the missive with temptation, a suggestion bolstered by the image of the red-skinned apple of Eve's temptation that the fallen wife has been peeling at the very moment her infidelity is discovered. A torn wax seal on the ripped envelope suggests, likewise, the unsealing of her indiscretion. The stunned husband appears frozen as his wife writhes on the floor before him. On both of her wrists, manacle-like bracelets confirm her guilt. The grim set of the husband's face and the woman's prostrate form, her hands clutched in prayer, also corroborate the evidence that has come via the post. The letter transmits knowledge of infidelity, betrayal, and destruction. The wife's sexual transgression will irrevocably destroy this once-happy home, a narrative outcome revealed in the work's companion panels, which invite questions of their own: Does the ostracized wife know her husband is dead? Are the daughters aware their mother and illegitimate sibling are homeless and dying? What will become of the daughters, now "orphaned" and presumably living under the care of a strict guardian? While the wife's infidelity forms the subject of the triptych, the incriminating letter bearing a Penny Red stamp carries the greatest iconographic weight: at once an emblem of Victorian propriety and impropriety, it drives the implacable plot of this visual narrative while prompting a host of difficult questions.

THE MANIFOLD SPAWNS OF PENNY POSTAGE

Negative outcomes of the Victorian revolution in letter writing counter the claims of postal reformers who insisted that with cheap postage, helpful information would fly across the country, young folk would regularly write home to their mothers for advice, daughters would no longer succumb to sexual transgression, vicious criminals would reform, and Britain would become a more upright nation. Material objects, letters, fiction, and art, in their capacity as emissaries of Victorian culture and values and also of its improprieties, reveal that the Penny Post had a dark and dangerous side. It could expose the indiscretions of a soldier, son, daughter, and wife; it could breed dissent in politics and religion; it could inadvertently encourage swindles, frauds, slander, and blackmail; and it was a ready, open route for the passage of insulting and offensive messages. The Penny Post sparked an increase in letter-based traffic and jammed the postal network with a host of curious mailings, spawning types of mail that continue to plague the post today—junk mail, spam, target mail, hazmat, and more. At the same time, many of the postal reformers' predictions and desired improvements also came to fruition, even if the postal-age utopia that reformers envisioned eluded the Victorian age and ages beyond. Alongside the manifold "spawns" of the Penny Post came postal blessings—frequent communications among friends and family members, death notices, health bulletins, travel updates, love epistles, and romantic valentines—bringing us knowledge of the lives and society of the Victorians who sent and received them.

Chapter 5

~

Benefits and Blessings

Letters Home, Friendship, Death Notices, Courtship, and Valentines by Penny Post

Far more important is the opening of the Post Office to hundreds and thousands of these industrious workers than an increase of earnings would be; for the restoration of access to home, which might then be an expensive indulgence, is now a matter of course for all; a benefit enjoyed without hesitation or remorse. . . . And who shall say to how many this privilege has been equivalent to peace of mind—in how many cases to the preservation of innocence and a good name?

—Harriet Martineau, Letter to Thomas Wilde, MP, May 15, 1843

Letter writing soared following postal reform: an estimated 337,500,000 letters passed through the United Kingdom in 1849,[1] nine years after the Penny Post came into effect and six years after Martineau retrospectively blessed the Penny Post for "restoration of access to home . . . for all." Writing in *Household Words* in 1850, Charles Dickens and W. H. Wills cite this statistic along with an interesting anecdote about a visitor to the central Post Office in St. Martin's-le-Grand—a destination not only for Londoners but for tourists, foreign dignitaries, and authors, like Dickens, who came to the General Post Office to witness the amazing amount of correspondence passing through it daily. Dickens's astonished visitor queries a postal official: "'The increase is attributable to the penny system?'" "'Entirely,'" the postal official replies (8). I privilege this anecdote alongside Martineau's view that the Penny Post aided "the preservation of innocence and a good name," because both foreground benefits at the very heart of the Victorian revolution in letter writing.

Dickens pictures "great sheepskin bags of letters tumbling in from the receiving houses." The letters "were *from* all parts of London *to* all parts of London and to the provinces and to the far-off quarters of the globe" (7). In fact, as discussed in chapter 2, many of these far-off lands are represented by ethnic stereotypes on the officially commissioned Mulready stationery. Affordable postage increased citywide and nationwide letter-based traffic, conveying urgent information in an age of rapid industrialization, migratory employment, and emigration.[2] With the creation of the World Postal Union in Bern, Switzerland, on October 9, 1874, cheap postage expanded worldwide, resulting in a relatively flat, cheap international rate and a transnational postal space that linked Britain with most of Europe, Turkey, Egypt, and the United States. Following the formation of this organization, more countries swiftly joined the union.[3]

Writing nearly twenty-five years before the creation of what David Henkin calls this "postal zone without national borders" (178) and ten years after the passing of the Penny Post, Dickens also directs our attention to London mailbags crammed with telltale envelopes headed to local and distant locations: "An acute postman might guess the broad tenour of their contents by their covers:—business letters are in big envelopes, official letters in long ones, and lawyers' letters in none at all; the tinted and lace-bordered mean Valentines, the black-bordered tell of grief, and the radiant with white enamel announce marriage" (7). In Dickensian fashion, these missives announce the best of times— love, success, triumph, and joy—and the worst of times—death, despair, failure, and sorrow. Wishing to "peep" into the contents of these envelopes, William Lewins in *Her Majesty's Mails* (1864) likewise celebrates the diversity of letters "jostling each other quite contentedly" in a postman's mailbag:

> If we could but get a peep, what a much greater variety within! Here, without doubt, are tidings of life and death, hope and despair, success and failure, triumph and defeat, joy and sorrow; letters from friends, and notes from lawyers, appeals from children and stern advice or remonstrance from parents, offers from anxious-hearted young gentlemen, and "first yesses" or refusals from young maidens; letters containing that snug appointment so long promised, and "little bills" with requests for immediate payment, "together with six-and-eightpence." Here are cream-coloured missives, which will doubtless be found to tell of happy consummations, and black-edged envelopes which will still more certainly tell of death and the grave; sober-looking advice-notes, doubtless telling when our "Mr. Puffwell" will "do himself the honour of calling" upon you, and elegant-looking billets in which "shocking business" is never mentioned, are here all jostling each other quite contentedly, and will do so for many hours. (266–67)

Post-1840, Victorians could, "without hesitation or remorse," communicate sober, joyous, and shocking news all for the cost of a penny. Extant lace-trimmed letters spin tales of romance while envelopes with black borders are emissaries of death and grief. Multiple daily postal deliveries brought formal invitations, serious-looking advice notes, marriage proposals, "'first yesses' or refusals," and "happy consummations," such as weddings and births, making connections possible across great distances in an ever-widening postal network. These "great sheepskin bags of letters" traveling in and out of post offices—some of which serve as plot devices in Victorian fiction or telling details in narrative paintings—are material memories of friendship, home, death, love, and courtship and preserve the effect the Penny Post had on Victorian customs and social practices.

QUANTIFYING BLESSINGS? AND THE EVER-WIDENING POSTAL NETWORK

Quickly after Uniform Penny Postage became law, supporters filled their writings with anecdotal praise, establishing postal reform as a moral measure, a social good. It is impossible to quantify how the outcomes of the Penny Post specifically responded to all the promises of those who clamored for it. For example, how well did it serve the poor in addition to members of the middle class and the commercial houses? Nonetheless, it is my contention in this chapter that the rhetoric of affect that powered reform of the postal service and retrospectively blessed its accomplishment was not merely empty rhetoric. Hill, who insists the Penny Post is "Fortunately . . . not a party question," calls it a "powerful engine of civilization": "When it is considered how much the religious, moral, and intellectual progress of the people, would be accelerated by the unobstructed circulation of letters and of the many cheap and excellent non-political publications of the present day, the Post Office assumes the new and important character of a powerful engine of civilization."[4] "The people," an inclusive term, suggests the Penny Post served Victorians across the social classes. Likewise, petitions that clamor for postal reform targeted many allegedly disenfranchised groups: "MOTHERS AND FATHERS that wish to hear from their absent children," friends "who are parted, that wish to write to each other!," emigrants who "do not forget their native homes," merchants and tradesmen needing to increase their businesses, and "MECHANICS AND LABOURERS that wish to learn where good work and high wages are to be had!"[5]

Some of the moral, social, political, and economic dreams pinned on the Penny Post conjure a postal-age utopia that never came to be. However, we cannot deny the egalitarian nature of the reformed Post Office:

> The first thing which will strike an observer placed in such circumstances is, that the Post-office is eminently a democratic establishment, conducted on the most approved *fraternité et égalité* principles. The same sort of variety that marks society here marks the letters; envelopes of all shades and sizes; handwriting of all imaginable kinds, written in all shades of ink, with every description of pen; names the oddest, and names the most ordinary, and patronymics to which no possible exception can be taken. Then to notice the seals. Here is one stamped with the escutcheoned signet of an earl; another where the wax has yielded submissively to the initials of plain John Brown. (Lewins 266)

Lewins, who uses the central refrain of the French Revolution to praise cheap postage, amplifies the idea that revolutionary principles powered reform of the postal service. Uniform Penny Postage ousted the class-based franking system and replaced it with a postal democracy, so letters from the highest earl and the most common man might find their way into the same post, all for the cost of a penny.

Most historians concur that personal letters of advice, affection, friendship, and courtship, although in use prior to the Penny Post, increased following reform, much as postal reformers had predicted.[6] Statistics on the sheer multitude of letters posted after 1840 offer evidence that the reformed Post Office enabled friends, relations, and travelers to reach out to others and stay connected. In the first year following implementation of the Penny Post, letter traffic increased 122.4 percent, slowing only to 105.6 percent growth for the first decade and then to 62.5 percent growth for the second decade (1850–60). M. J. Daunton, who supplies these figures, notes: "Before the introduction of the Penny Post, most letters were probably sent for business purposes and there was subsequently an increase in personal correspondence," although the advent of the telephone eventually led to a decrease in personal letters, which were replaced by telephone calls (79).

In addition, the range and number of cards, letters, notepapers, and envelopes featured in the *Official Descriptive and Illustrated Catalogue* of 1851 offers evidence that eleven years after Uniform Penny Postage, paper and printing companies were booming because Victorians were seemingly taking advantage of postal reform, buying postal products, regularly using their local post offices, and essentially sharing the business of their daily lives. After 1840, one could leave home for business and travel or relocate to far-off places with the confidence that one could stay connected to family and friends whom one might not see or otherwise hear from for weeks, months, years, or ever again.

STAYING CONNECTED VIA THE PENNY POST

Restoring access to home was one blessing of the Penny Post. Staying connected with friends and relatives across an increasingly mobile society—a motto that resonates in our modern world of global telecommunications—was also a central reason why the Victorians believed they needed postal reform. Authors of letter-writing manuals call letters "'the treasured mementoes of the absent, the loved, and lost'" that "'breathed of tender memories and pure affection.'"[7] Letters brought urgent news of life and death to absent relations, reassurance and familiarity to the traveler, and intimacy to spouses and lovers recalling the trace of a writer's hand and his or her lingering scent on the written page. In our age of telecommunications, how often do we phone a friend or relative to hear a reassuring voice, the contemporary equivalent of a familiar written hand? How many times each day do we check our e-mail, use handheld igadgets, or send a text message to stay connected with far-off friends and relations? If we had lived in the Victorian era, every time we wanted to contact friends and family, we would have put pen to paper, not only to share urgent, serious, and important news but insignificant and mundane information.

We still rely on the post for much of our daily living, as David Henkin notes: "Linking distant individuals in a web of regular exchanges and tethering them to networks of institutional power, the postal system fulfills several of the cultural functions attributed to newer media, if at a significantly slower pace" (ix). While "snail mail" aptly describes the slow pace of mail deliveries today (particularly in contrast with instantaneous e-mail communication), to a Victorian time traveler in the twenty-first century, our current postal system would seem quaint. From 1857 until the First World War, central London offered twelve daily deliveries, and suburban areas had six or seven deliveries with service beginning as early as 7:00 a.m. and extending until as late as 8:50 p.m. In the 1850s, Birmingham had three daily deliveries, which expanded to six daily deliveries by 1903—the first at 7:00 a.m. and the last at 6:30 p.m.[8] The Penny Post facilitated a web of exchanges within a major communications network, anticipating newer media that we privilege and herald today.

The dazzling array of writing commodities available after 1840, the focus of chapter 3, also reveals how Victorians regularly wrote to nearby and far-flung friends and relations on a variety of occasions. For example, in the *Official Descriptive and Illustrated Catalogue*, Thomas De La Rue Manufacturers and Proprietors lists a huge selection of "Articles of Stationery": lace letter papers, embossed papers, glazed and colored papers in many colors, hand-colored papers, stationery in fancy packets, "at home" notes, cards embossed in silver and gold for weddings, and message cards—on plain white, tinted, goffered, enameled, and "iridescent papers, the changing colours of which are produced by a thin film of colourless varnish." The diversity of envelopes is equally impressive: the list includes "lace-perforated" and embossed envelopes with matching notepapers in "fancy wrappers," as well as envelopes with seal flaps that are plain, embossed, and adorned (for example, with a cameo design).[9] We can readily imagine some of the Victorians who visited commercial houses, including the establishment of Thomas De La Rue, to select bright-colored papers or unusual stationary for varied epistolary plans: to write a cheery message to a friend who had emigrated to Canada or New Zealand; to post a note to a bedridden relative, as Mulready depicted in his commissioned design; to send a wee note to a friend on vacation, as illustrated by a surviving mid-century missive to "My dear Alice" staying at the Hotel des Bains in Dieppe, France, where the writer opens the letter by declaring it "a novelty writing on this absurdly small paper it is so ridiculous to put it in the post."[10] The color and style of envelopes and papers, ranging from the functional to the ornamental, carries social meaning, suggesting letter writing formed a vital part of both business and leisure, straddling the public and private spheres of Victorian life.

A Golden Age of Letters to Family and Friends

We are poised in an age where e-mails and text messages are rapidly replacing letters. In our "paperless" society of electronic airline tickets and ticketless concert tours, we rely on materials encoded on a hard drive, disc, or flash stick and often do not even print out hard copies of electronic exchanges in order to preserve the environment.[11] The posted letter is now increasingly called "snail mail," "old-fashioned correspondence," even a "dinosaur" in "accounts of global social change" (Henkin ix). The Victorian era appears, in contrast, to be a Golden Age of editions of letters, as Norman Kelvin notes in "Editions of Letters in the Age of the Vanishing Text." Will the genre of traditional letter writing vanish from our daily lives, as Kelvin speculates? Will letter collections become a strictly antiquarian genre? Many leading figures born in the second half of the twentieth century and beyond may leave behind relatively few letters for scholars to collect.

The sheer scope of letter collections by leading Victorian writers and thinkers offers further proof of how regularly Victorians stayed connected with friends and professional associates following establishment of the Penny Post. Even apart from its pragmatic value as a form of communication, letter writing begins to intersect diaristic genres. Such intersections might not have occurred on such a wide scale apart from postal reform. And it is possible, too, that because of these intersections, the letter increasingly becomes in the Victorian era not simply a vehicle of communication but of self-expression—a trend borne out by manufacturers' production of a broad array of papers, inks, seals, and so on. Even though post-1840s Britain did not experience the kind of postal-age utopia of uniformly virtuous young women, low unemployment rates, no labor strikes, unvaryingly well-written books, and endless scientific discoveries, the abundant editions of collected letters indicate that people took pleasure in writing letters and corresponded regularly with friends and family who lived locally and in distant parts of the country and world. In this sense, epistolary contact for the Victorians connoted portable affection. The luxury of self-expression, formerly enjoyed primarily by the affluent, is arguably another one of the fruits of postal reform. On a larger scale, letters from this earlier information revolution, written without publication in view, are unselfconscious sources of cultural history, transmitting information about how real people across social classes viewed the major political, economic, and social developments of their Victorian age.

Florence Nightingale's 1854–1856 correspondence offers a firsthand view of life and conditions during the Crimean War, as do letters of soldiers during that period. An extant letter from Royal Artillery captain John Edward Mitchell to his mother, dated November 28, 1854, includes a sketch and description of the location of guns in Captain Mitchell's unit: "I have headed the letter with an attempt to depict in outline of the position here. The little works marked half up the hills are the guns of positions connected by infantry all entrenched."[12] That the captain is communicating such privileged information via the post suggests that little censorship existed at this point in the Crimean War. To Mitchell's mother, this letter probably held little military strategic interest, serving instead as a "treasured memento" of an absent son and, penned in her son's familiar hand, bringing her reassurance that he was still alive. Dickens's letters from 1859 to 1861 record his response to the start of

FIGURE 19. Hand-drawn "weekly sheet" from George Howell to his brother Josiah, 1842. From the collection of James Grimwood-Taylor.

the American Civil War, a cataclysmic event which also captured the interest of Christina Rossetti and Anthony Trollope, who, like Dickens, had toured America. More mundane, but equally as important, period correspondence gives us access to Victorians' daily lives—including schooling, social occasions, friendships, family ties, and health.[13]

In an existing letter charged 4d and posted on December 19, 1839, during the Uniform Fourpenny Post transition period, W. Dobson, a student in Brixham, wrote to his guardian, Mr. Ashworth of Bolton-le-Moors, requesting advice on which Cambridge college he should attend. While Dobson favors

Trinity, he politely asks his guardian: "What college do you think of choosing for me?" and goes on to report that "The work here is by no means hard, and as Mr. Lyte [his tutor] means to write to you, he can tell you better than I can, what progress I am making."[14] In the 1840s, a talented amateur artist named John Howell sent his brother, Josiah Howell, a weekly comic entitled "SHEET of NEWS"; the letter sheets, filled with poetry, illustrations, and current events, are material memories of brotherly love and friendship. Howell took advantage of the half-ounce penny rate, so he did not have to limit the length of his "sheet." One six-sided, hand-drawn weekly to Josiah, dated "4th/6th June 1842" and charged 1d, features under the salutation a drawing of a hot air balloon above a magnificent sunset (see figure 19) and includes witty cartoons ("ALPHABETICAL ODDITIES," "A NOSEGAY ON NATIVES OUT OF GEORGE'S GARDEN") and puns, such as "Quaint Quill Quibbles" and "A Few Mays in June."[15]

Victorians combined art and writing to create entertaining pictorial letters or "picture letters," as Beatrix Potter called them.[16] Artist and sculptor Edwin Landseer, who designed the lions in Trafalgar Square in central London, includes a drawing of a lion in the salutation of an extant June 18, 1864, letter, where he declines an invitation (a message we might convey today via phone or e-mail) but implores his friend, "do give me another chance" (see figure 20). The picture letter begins with a visual pun on the name of the addressee, Mr. William Lyon, whom Landseer depicts as an actual lion—a kind of play on words that Lewis Carroll made famous in *Alice's Adventures in Wonderland* (1865), where the mouse's "tale" takes the form of an actual "tail" in the printed text.[17] Carroll's biographer, Morton Cohen, describes how

> letter-writing itself was often for him another way of doing something for others, especially for the young girls whose friendship he so ardently cultivated. As he stood at his upright desk, he was often challenged to breathe life and laughter on to the dry leaves of letter paper ranged before him. The result is a stream of letters that Lewis Carroll's fancy alone could create—new self-contained microcosms of Wonderland, vehicles of fun and pleasure that underscore his devotion to others and prove him, in both senses of the phrase, a man of letters. (*Letters* 1: xv)

Most notably, in his letters to his "child friends," as he called them, Carroll provides "fun and pleasure" through pictograms. In his October 5, 1869, letter to Georgina "Ina" Watson, for example, he draws an actual "deer" to stand for "dear"; he sends mirror writing to Margaret "Daisy" Brough in a November

FIGURE 20. Picture letter to Mr. William Lyon from Edwin Landseer, June 18, 1864. From the collection of John Forbes-Nixon.

24, 1883, letter; and he sketches in a letter of January 30, 1868, to Margaret Cunnynghame, including a funny caricature of himself lecturing.[18]

For Potter, who lived a life sheltered by strict and, at times, overbearing parents, picture letters stand as material memories of connection and friendship. Letter writing allowed Potter to stay in touch with those outside her immediate home sphere. Many of her stories in the Peter Rabbit series began as picture letters to the children of her former governess, Annie Carter Moore. The first and most famous of Potter's tales evolved from a picture letter she had written on September 4, 1893, to entertain a sick child; five-year-old Noel Moore was sick in bed, much as Peter Rabbit ends up after overeating lettuces and radishes in Mr. McGregor's garden. Several of Potter's charming picture letters introduce future storybook characters, including Squirrel Nutkin and Little Pig Robinson, while still others preserve her memories of travel and geography and exemplify the burgeoning Victorian interest in naturalism: they brim with sketches of Potter's favorite animals (such as rabbits, frogs, and cats) and of woodlands and lakes she visited on family holidays to Wales and Scotland.[19]

It is curious that Anthony Trollope, who published his own candid *Autobiography* (1883) did not wish his letters to be published (at least according to his son Henry [Harry] Merivale Trollope).[20] That Trollope spent thirty-three years as an officer of the Post Office may have led him to think of letters as a form of communication rather than as a literary genre, even as he, in his role of author, strategically included well-crafted letters in his fiction. To biographer Victoria Glendenning, Trollope's "great letters are in his novels. He did not so much write his characters' letters for them as become his characters as they sat at their writing-tables. He wrote every kind of letter—passionate, treacherous, contrived, manipulative, poisonous, ingenuous, spontaneous, desperate, studied, cute, inhibited, blackmailing, artless, pompous, illiterate, confiding, titillating. Only the illiterate ones fail to convince; Anthony could not 'become' someone who had no command of language at all" (369–70). Comparing his actual letters with those of other prominent writers of his time, Bradford Allen Booth contends that Trollope's "are not weighted with Gray's occasional petulance, Wordsworth's sense of moral responsibility, George Eliot's tension, or Dickens's egoism"; they lack the "ready facility of Stevenson's, the fecund imagination of Thackeray's" (xxi). I feature them in this chapter precisely because their social meaning inheres in being, as it were, a daily "logbook of the busiest man of Victorian letters" (Booth xxi).

Although Trollope did not save incoming correspondence after responding to it, volumes of his letters survive and have been published.[21] Many of Trollope's letters are mundane responses to invitations and thank-you notes. He enjoyed considerable correspondence with other authors—particularly George Henry Lewes and George Eliot, whom he refers to as Mrs. Lewes and greatly admired, and the American journalist Kate Field, whom he calls Kate and to whom he became particularly devoted. Trollope wrote frequently to publisher John Blackwood, with whom he had a firm and trusting relationship. He regularly sent to and received page proofs from Blackwood through the post.[22] Trollope's letters reveal that while charity went against his principles, he did not withhold his generosity in organizing alms for a writer's family in need. Family and home were important to him even if Harry Trollope describes his father's letters to him and his brother as concerned with "'the matter in hand,'" brief and businesslike.[23]

Trollope apparently had difficulty writing a love letter, but he wrote regularly to his wife, Rose, when he traveled. He eagerly awaited her letters, as he expresses in a March 6, 1875, letter written while sailing on the Adriatic: "Pray write & say that you are well & happy—if possible."[24] The longed-for letter written in a loved one's recognizable and comforting hand likely brought Trollope a welcomed touch of familiarity from home and reassurance while he ventured into unfamiliar surroundings. In another letter to Rose dated March 17, 1875, which Trollope wrote once he arrived at the Suez Canal, he again asks how she is managing and urges her to "be happy & enjoy yourself. Tell me every thing of your doings & goings, and of your travelling adventures." This letter—no doubt like many letters of less prominent men and women of Trollope's day—conveys the importance of regular correspondence in an increasingly mobile Victorian society. In this same letter, Trollope also relays a story about a "great misfortune" involving his writing desk:

> You remember my big bottle of ink. When I unlocked my desk I found the bottle smashed in pieces inside the case, which had not been opened, and the ink of course had covered every thing. There were three shirts on top put in to keep things steady. I wish you could see those three shirts, and there were 100 loose cigars. I have not yet tried how cigars, bathed in ink, smoke—but I shall try. Some wretch had pitched the desk down like a ball, and all my beautiful white paper!—However that is now simply black-edged.[25]

We learn a great deal about Trollope from this posted anecdote. We discover the importance of Trollope's writing desk on which he composed his extensive oeuvre. We sense the care he took in selecting stationery in that exclamatory, "all my beautiful white paper!" (After their move to Waltham House, the Trollopes designed their own stationery with their address in Gothic letters and a family crest on the letter and envelope flap.) We also get a rare and private impression of Trollope's personal resilience—a willingness to smoke inky cigars and recycle damaged stationery for an appropriately sad occasion. That Trollope wrote scores of letters like this when he had something of substance to convey and that he relied on regular postings to remain intimately connected with those dearest to him when he traveled find philosophical expression in *Phineas Redux* (1874). In the words of his protagonist, Phineas Finn: "'When there is something palpable to be said, what a blessing is the penny post! To

one's wife, to one's child, one's mistress . . . one's publisher, if there be a volume
ready or money needed . . . a man is able to write'" (23).

Trollope allegedly disdained writing merely to maintain friendships with
those living in faraway places; even so, he kept up a regular correspondence
with Kate Field. However, many Victorians, including poet Christina Rossetti
and the lesser-known poet and writer of children's books, Caroline Gemmer,
took advantage of cheap postage to develop an epistolary friendship while
living at a distance. In "Christina Rossetti and Caroline Gemmer: Friendship
by Royal Mail," Antony Harrison zeroes in on a collection of thirty-two letters
that Christina Rossetti wrote to Gemmer from 1870 to 1893. Regrettably, the
extant correspondence remains one-sided; Rossetti apparently destroyed all
letters from Gemmer along with the greater part of her incoming post. From
their first meeting in 1865 and their brief time as neighbors attending Christ
Church on Albany Street from 1865 to 1867, they sustained a strong friendship
nearly exclusively by Royal Mail. Their correspondence is, at once, evidence
of companionship and a material record of daily life that documents both
major and minor issues and activities of the Victorian age, evidence of how
the letter as artifact reveals much about the letter writer and his or her times.
Their epistolary topics include horticulture (Rossetti and Gemmer were fond
of flowers); family health (bulletins not only about their own health but that
of Christina's sister, Maria, for example, and of her brother William Michael's
son, who died very young); sisters-in-law (Lucy Madox Brown Rossetti, William Michael Rossetti's wife, and Elizabeth Siddal, Dante Gabriel Rossetti's
wife); popular cures of the day, such as galvanism (a medical treatment using
electricity to stimulate muscles and nerves); antivivisection activism (Gemmer apparently introduced Christina to the movement); Gemmer's children;
the American Civil War; the rise of Louis Napoleon (Napoleon III) after the
coup of December 2, 1851; their respective writings (Christina's *Speaking Like-
nesses* [1874], *Goblin Market* [1862], and *Sing Song* [1872] and Gemmer's poem
"Little 'Fairy'; or 'Love me, Love my Dog'" published in issue 10 of *The Animal World: An Advocate of Humanity* in 1879); book publishers (Macmillan);
reading preferences (Coventry Patmore, Robert Browning, and others); and
the art of Christina's brother, Pre-Raphaelite painter Dante Gabriel Rossetti.
Christina, who admits "a general satisfaction" when her eye "lighted on [Gem-
mer's] familiar handwriting waiting for me at the breakfast table," routinely
signed her letters to Mrs. Gemmer as "Affectionately yours" and used other
endearing lines suggesting their close friendship, such as "May my letter find
you pretty well, & not displease you, & leave me snug in my nook for your

friendship."[26] Collectively, their correspondence is an emblem of Victorian friendship, a hallmark of shared participation in a widening postal network.

Such intimate epistolary friendships were common throughout the period and carry knowledge of same-sex intimacy as well as personal aspirations, daily living, and current events. Charlotte Brontë maintained two such long-term epistolary friendships with school friends Ellen (Nell) Nussey and Mary Taylor, who emigrated to Wellington, New Zealand. Charlotte wrote to Ellen about her domestic life but expressed her literary aspirations to Mary Taylor in far-off New Zealand, as Mary shared Charlotte's ambition to write. For example, Mary Taylor wrote to Charlotte on July 24, 1848, praising the force and credible characterization of *Jane Eyre* (1847): "About a month since I received and read *Jane Eyre*. It seemed to me incredible that you had actually written a book. Such events did not happen while I was in England. I begin to believe in your existence much as I do in Mr. Rochester's. In a believing mood I don't doubt either of them. . . . Your novel surprised me by being so perfect as a work of art" (Barker, *The Brontës: A Life* 200). Although Taylor presumably destroyed Charlotte's letters when she emigrated to New Zealand, Charlotte's many letters to Ellen Nussey survive. Brontë's husband, Arthur Bell Nicholls, was wary of Charlotte's regular correspondence with Nussey, requiring Charlotte to exact a promise that Ellen burn their correspondence—a promise that Ellen happily did not keep since these letters illuminate the life of a largely reclusive author. Charlotte tells Nell in a letter dated October 20, 1854, that "Arthur says such letters as mine never ought to be kept—they are dangerous as lucifer matches"; in a letter written on November 7, 1854, Charlotte adds that "it is not '*old' friends* he mistrusts, but the chances of war—the accidental passing of letters into hands and under eyes for which they were never written" (Barker, *The Brontës: A Life* 394, 395). Imagine Nicholls's horror if he were to travel through time into the twenty-first century to behold Juliet Barker's edition of Charlotte's letters passing "into hands and under eyes for which they were never written."

Mourning by the Post

Of the tales of hardship that helped to usher in postal reform, many centered on having the means to accept a death notice, which, following the passing of the Postage Duties Bill, could be posted for only a penny. "'With respect to the poor, it was amazing how little they knew of their friends at a distance—they hardly ever corresponded,'" according to a report appearing in an 1839 issue of *The Post Circular*; the article goes on to offer an anecdote of a servant in Yorkshire who received a black-edged missive stating his sister had died (the servant did not even know she had been ill) as a prime example of "a great many instances of work-people, who never heard of their distant relations but when they died."[27] M. D. Hill's touching anecdote of a poor man not being able to accept a death notice for lack of funds appears in his 1840 *Edinburgh Review* article, "Post-Office Reform": "It would be easy to fill pages with instances of pain and misery which result from there being no post-office for the poor" (554). Among other tales of "pain and suffering" included in this article is a secondhand story relayed by a needle manufacturer, who tells of a poor man who did not know of a relative's death for six to eight months because he could not pay the postage (554).

The idea of the poor not knowing of a loved one's death for over half a year because of an inability to pay high postage was a scenario that touched the heartstrings of many a Victorian. High child mortality rates, epidemics, and poor sanitation made death—and particularly early death—an integral part of Victorian life. Charlotte Brontë was the only one of six siblings to live beyond the age of thirty. People commonly died in their homes, and relatives prepared their bodies. Elaborate funeral processions were frequent sights on city streets. Victorians lived in an age concerned with the rituals and religious significance of death and dying, as emotion-laden death scenes in fiction by Dickens and Gaskell quintessentially immortalize. Victoria's forty-year widowhood and wearing of mourning weeds from the time of Prince Albert's death in 1861 until her own in 1901 likely made mourning rituals popular not only among the wealthy, but among the middle and lower classes, who imitated the actions of the upper reaches. Customs, appearance, even spectacle form part of the process of Victorian grieving. The Victorians marked loss with postmortem photography (posing the dead to look alive or peaceful), keepsake mementos (a photograph of the deceased or a lock of hair, sometimes made into hair jewelry, to honor the dead), as well as extravagant funerals. Men and particularly women wore intricate mourning dress and jewelry for prescribed periods of time. They hired coaches draped in black velvet and ostrich feathers to transport the body of the deceased. In *Oliver Twist* (1838), Dickens grants young orphan Oliver such "'an expression of melancholy in his face'" that the undertaker, Mr. Sowerby, has him play the part of a mute and walk along the mourning coach for children's burials to create "'a most superb effect'" (28–29). There were strict rules on mourning etiquette—what one wore, how long one wore it, what one did and did not do, and—of relevance to *Posting It*—how one communicated the news of death. Death notices on black-edged stationery informed family and friends of a loss of a loved one, and mourners used black-edged letters and envelopes during a prescribed mourning period.

These widespread missives, which mark the high death rate among adults and children, carry memories of ritual and religion in the Victorian age.

Some death notices brought tidings of inheritance as well as loss. In *Jane Eyre*, Jane learns of the death of her Uncle Eyre and her inheritance of £20,000 in the same letter. Two death notices frame the opening chapters of Dickens's *Nicholas Nickleby* (1839), the very serial which helped to usher in postal reform because savvy postal reformers bound into its monthly numbers Cole's skit scripting Queen Victoria's approval of Uniform Penny Postage before it actually came to be. In chapter 1, "there came, one morning, by the general post, a black-bordered letter to inform" Mr. Godfrey Nickleby "how his uncle, Mr. Ralph Nickleby, was dead, and had left him the bulk of his little property, amounting in all to five thousand pounds sterling" (2). This notice brings a windfall to Mr. Godfrey Nickleby, whose slim income of £60 to £80 a year cannot support a wife and two sons (Ralph the elder and Nicholas the younger). A second death notice in chapter 3 brings a more sober reality: after Nicholas Nickleby (Godfrey's son) loses his money by speculation and dies, his widow and two children (Nicholas and Kate) fall on "hard times," so they, in turn, send a mourning letter to their rich, miserly uncle, Ralph Nickleby, hoping he will come to their aid. Dickens takes pains to describe the look of this letter: "Post-mark, Strand, black wax, black border, woman's hand, C. N. in the corner" (17). Ralph Nickleby aptly surmises on seeing the black wax, black border, and initials on the cover, "'I shouldn't be surprised if my brother were dead'" (17).

Dickens's reference to the black-bordered letter in both instances signals how the Victorians presented and perceived death by post. The black border, an emissary of loss and grieving, says much about Victorian culture: as the society grew more mobile and friends and family lived at a distance, one commonly learned of the passing of friends and family via letters; a black-bordered letter offered a way to gently prepare the letter recipient for news of the grave that might be difficult to bear. Likewise, in *Vanity Fair* (1848), Thackeray announces old Sir Pitt's death to the Rawdon Crawley household simply by noting that "This letter, with a huge black border and seal, was accordingly dispatched by Sir Pitt Crawley to his brother the colonel, in London" (517). Thackeray includes an illustration of Becky Sharp gleefully anticipating her "great expectations": "She took up the black-edged missive, and having read it, she jumped up from the chair, crying 'Hurray!' and waving the note round her head" (517). More typically, "black-bordered" missives "tell of grief," as Dickens and Wills relay in their discussion of envelopes in *Household Words*.

FIGURE 21. *The Poor Teacher,* by Richard Redgrave, 1844. Courtesy of V&A Images/ Victoria and Albert Museum, London.

The mourning letter came to be encased in a mourning envelope following Uniform Penny Postage. Richard Redgrave's *The Poor Teacher* (1844), sometimes called *The Governess*, features a pale young woman dressed in black, holding a black-edged letter in her hand (see figure 21). The setting appears to be a schoolroom. Two girls, pupils, play outdoors on the sunlit terrace pictured in the far right background of the canvas. Inside the darkened schoolroom, a third pupil sits in her chair, book in lap, gazing out the open doors onto the sunlit scene as if she has been kept inside to learn her lessons. Among his contemporaries, Redgrave was known for creating paintings with a social purpose. *The Poor Teacher* represents the plight of unmarried women in Victorian England at a time when, due to emigration, illness, and war, there was a surplus of women—a situation generally referred to as the "woman problem." Forced to eke out a living on their own, many unmarried middle-class and impoverished women sought employment as governesses—a marginalized position in a home not one's own.

The central figure in Redgrave's painting, a sad but pretty young woman, holds loosely in her hand a black-edged missive. Like many narrative paintings of the period, this one provides details to help the viewer unlock the mystery of the governess's situation. Helene Roberts, in her analysis of this and other Victorian narrative paintings, directs us to some of these clues: "The viewer must be able actually to read the title of the sheet music on the piano for it might hold the key to the message of the painting. Or the black border of the crumpled letter might be the necessary detail to bring a tear to the viewer's eye" (46–48). Entitled "Home Sweet Home," the sheet music suggests that the death announcement comes from the governess's own home. Someone in her family has died, and like the young pupil who is kept by her schoolwork from the sunshine world of her happier companions, the governess, far from her family and working in a stranger's house, occupies a dark room in the world. Cast downward, her eyes appear to hold back tears. Her quiet manner contrasts with the mirth of the girls laughing in the sunshine. Is the letter from a beloved sibling? Does it convey news about the death of a parent? Is the death unexpected? Despite what the painted details reveal, what remains untold of her story emphasizes the young woman's obscurity.

Not surprisingly, the 2004 Penguin Classics paperback edition of Anne Brontë's governess novel, *Agnes Grey* (1847), displays this very Redgrave image on its cover, forecasting Agnes's fears about the approaching death of her beloved clergyman father. Becoming a governess following her father's reversal of fortune, Agnes receives two letters in chapter 18, "Mirth and Mourning," telling of her father's poor health and impending death. Rather than wait to receive a black-edged letter, much like the one the governess holds in *The Poor Teacher*, Agnes gets permission from her employer, Mrs. Murray, to leave Horton Lodge to travel home to the family parsonage. She arrives home only to learn her clergyman father is "'Dead!' That was the reply I had anticipated; but the shock seemed none the less tremendous" (211).

The Brontës themselves were no strangers to death. The eldest two of the six Brontë children, Maria and Elizabeth, died at Cowan Bridge School. Charlotte fictionalized Cowan Bridge as Lowood Institution in *Jane Eyre*, casting her sister Elizabeth as the fictional Helen Burns, who dies in Jane's arms. Their mother, Maria Branwell Brontë, died in 1821, leaving behind their clergyman father and four surviving children when Anne, the youngest, was just a year old. As young women, Charlotte and Emily hurried home from Brussels when they received an urgent letter that their surrogate mother, Aunt Branwell (their mother's sister), was dying; Aunt Branwell died before they reached Haworth.

Charlotte wrote letters to her friends about the heart-wrenching deaths of her three remaining siblings—Branwell, Emily, and Anne—and poems to mark Emily's and Anne's deaths.[28] On October 2, 1848, Charlotte expresses the devastating loss of Branwell to her trusted friend William Smith Williams, a reader at her publisher, Smith, Elder & Co., who believed in Charlotte's literary talent and became her close confidante: "I do not weep from a sense of bereavement—there is no prop withdrawn, no consolation torn away, no dear companion lost—but for the wreck of talent, the ruin of promise, the untimely dreary extinction of what might have been a burning and a shining light. . . . My poor Father naturally thought more of his only Son than of his daughters, and much and long as he had suffered on his account— he cried out for the loss like David for that of Absalom—my Son! My Son! And refused at first to be comforted" (209). Only three months later, Charlotte again wrote to William Smith Williams on December 20, 1848, about the agony of losing Emily:

> When I wrote in such haste to Dr. Epps, disease was making rapid strides, nor has it lingered since, the gallopping consumption has merited its name—neither physician nor medicine are needed now. Tuesday night and morning saw the last hours, the last agonies, proudly endured till the end. Yesterday Emily Jane Brontë died in the arms of those who loved her. . . . The last three months—ever since my brother's Death seem to us like a long, terrible dream. (216)

Given the flood of grief Charlotte and her father experienced, and the "long, terrible dream" of loss that continued as Charlotte proceeded to lose her sister Anne but five months later on May 28, 1849, we can imagine why the appearance of a letter—the sight of which alerted those living at a distance to the death of one very dear—mattered much to the Victorians and why the ability to receive a death notice following Penny Postage was a much-anticipated blessing.

Victorians used black-edged stationery throughout the entire mourning period, not just for actual death notices. Christina Rossetti used black-bordered stationery in a May 1877 letter to Caroline Gemmer, a full six months after the death of Christina's sister, Maria Rossetti, from cancer on November 24, 1876. Another of Christina's black-bordered letters to Gemmer, dated January 26, 1883, relays the loss of her beloved nephew Michael, the youngest son of William Michael and his wife, Lucy, which had occurred just two days before: "Death has again been among us; & my poor brother and sister have lost their youngest of all, little Michael. He had just turned a year and a half old, & could not get thro' his hard teething. Poor William & Lucy & nurse & I watched the little life ebb without (we trust) consciousness: he looked so beautifully pure

& peaceful afterwards, laid out with flowers."[29] Christina's observation that "Death has *again* been among us" (my emphasis) suggests that she may have been thinking of the earlier loss of her talented brother Dante Gabriel Rossetti, who had died the year before on April 8, 1882. The use of black-bordered stationery for up to a year following the death of a close relative indicates the elaborate and formal mourning customs of the Victorian age. Victorian mourning letters, like Rossetti's, of which there are many surviving examples, reveal the reserved and ordered Victorian response to the prevalence of death. The black-edged letter is a formal signal of loss that permits the writer to announce his or her despair without the disorderly or disruptive articulation of private emotions.

George Elgar Hicks tells a similar story of death's ubiquity in his 1863 narrative painting *Woman's Mission: Companion of Manhood* (see figure 22). This canvas forms the central panel of a triptych that depicts the ideal Victorian woman's roles as loving mother to her child (*Guide to Childhood*), devoted wife to her husband (*Companion of Manhood*), and caring daughter to her aged father (*Comfort of Old Age*). Hicks's triptych, which pictorially conscripts one woman's entire life to three relational roles (that is, she exists only in her relation to man), pays homage to the Victorian cult of woman as domestic angel, a presence mitigating between men in their public, worldly roles and a spiritual domain accessible primarily through domestic harmony and feminine sympathy. In the words of leading Victorian advice writer Sarah Stickney Ellis, "'The love of woman appears to have been created solely to minister; that of man, to be ministered unto.'"[30] An 1863 reviewer of Hicks's painting zeroes in on the husband's distress and his wife's ministering efforts: "'In the second [panel], we see a wife in the act of giving solace to her husband under a severe blow of affliction.'"[31] Standing upright next to the mantel, the husband covers his face with his right hand to hide his tears while his devoted wife attempts to console him. As if to represent the popular Victorian axiom, "he is still the oak, she the vine," the wife clings to her husband even as she comforts him.[32]

Though the central figures in *Companion of Manhood* are the grieving husband and his helpmeet, Hicks surrounds them with strategic details that form an iconography of domestic order, signaling a good wife's ordering of the Victorian home. Among these details, as Elaine Shefer points out, are those "stressing order and arrangement . . . the table to the woman's right, upon whose spotless white cloth fine English china has been ceremoniously laid and the day's mail carefully set" (8–9). The handsomely furnished room, the serving table with its ample cloth, the china tea set and silver tea service, the flowers set on the mantel in an elegant vase, and the comfortable hearth—the

FIGURE 22. *Woman's Mission: Companion of Manhood,* by George Elgar Hicks, 1863. © Tate, London 2008.

metaphoric heart of a Victorian home—are visual testaments of this devoted wife's homemaking skills.

Similarly expressive of domestic order is the arrangement of the morning post on the tea table. (That this is the morning mail is suggested by the husband's wearing red bedroom slippers.) Hicks took pains to carefully render the Penny Red stamps on the envelopes, revealing that the morning mail has come via Penny Post. The only item out of place in this orderly domestic scene is the torn mourning envelope, a black "X" printed across its reverse side, lying on the bearskin rug not far from what appears to be the husband's chair. By showing a torn, crinkled envelope flap, Hicks suggests the husband's urgency in opening the notice and a retrospective narrative action where, in his grief and shock, he has probably stumbled to the mantle from his seat at the tea table, dropping the envelope and clutching the black-edged death notice in his left hand. By 1863 when Hicks painted this canvas, Victorians commonly used envelopes to enclose their letters (over twenty years had passed since a letter weighing up to a half ounce could travel across England for a penny). The black edging on the envelope makes it an emissary of the loss the letter contains.

Hicks leaves to the viewer's imagination the identity of the letter writer and of the deceased. The portraits Hicks depicts above the mantelpiece—a place where Victorians often displayed pictures of family members—suggest that the letter may announce the death of one of the husband's relatives.[33] By the depth of the husband's grief—an angst that matches what Charlotte Brontë describes of her father's weeping for Branwell, his only son—we can surmise that the husband is reading of the death of one very dear to him, perhaps an aged parent or a beloved sister. Hicks's painting iconographically represents the centrality of the death notice to the Victorian grieving process, a centrality similarly expressed in a surviving black-edged missive written between 1860 and 1870 by Charlotte Barker to her son Ted:

My dear Ted

You will see by the enclosed what has happened The poor soul never spoke after you left remained insensible and died at 10 minutes to seven last night the very time she was taken for death on Wednesday night

John staid at home yesterday & watched with me and well he did or I never could have borne up Fortunately her eyes were closed and insensible but towards the last what with the hakin [?] and suffocation it was awful I felt the last beat of her pulse & told John h[er] struggle and all over

I helped lay her out and never shed a tear cannot make it out but expect to feel it by and bye

John is very since gone to the undertaker and order mourning for me Boofeelor most kind The coffin is to be in their parlour I have just been to look at the remains her poor nails are turned her mouth was dreadful blood is oozing all day God save that Lollie may never be called upon to witness what I did Away I regret not knowing what she was suffering from before tho' I have done my duty Take care of yourself

Your Affectionate Mother[34]

Despite the lack of punctuation in this mourning letter, posted at Bath, Charlotte Barker vividly describes the death at home of one who appears to have been her beloved daughter. The death is arduous and ugly, a far cry from Christina Rossetti's description of her beloved nephew looking "beautifully pure & peaceful afterwards, laid out with flowers." Barker's letter conveys intimate knowledge of Victorian death rituals. A mother does her "duty" in caring personally for the "poor soul" in her final hours, laying out the body herself and writing immediately to her son to convey news of the grave. The fact that black-edged missives appear not only among surviving correspondence but as a central trope in the art and literature of the period indicates that the letter is a key part of Victorian mourning rituals. That it becomes central, even iconographic, in this way may be attributable to postal reform.

The Penny Post and Changing Rules of Courtship and Conjugal Happiness

The notion of a love letter as a treasured keepsake existed long before the Penny Post increased traffic of portable tokens of affection. Likewise, a suitor's ability to compose a well-written letter established his character. Many an impatient lover, unable to secure a private interview with a loved one, adopted "the agency of a *billet-doux* in declaring his passion."[35] Jane Austen—who received a verbal proposal of marriage from Harris Bigg-Wither in December 1802, which she accepted and then declined the next morning—recognizes in *Emma* (1815) how many suitors unburdened their hearts in written marriage proposals. Mr. Robert Martin's letter to Emma Woodhouse's bosom friend Harriet Smith "contained a direct proposal of marriage" that far surpasses Emma's expectations of the epistolary skills of a country farmer and ultimately raises her opinion of him: "'Yes, indeed, a very good letter, . . . so good a letter, Harriet, that every thing considered, I think one of his sisters must have helped him. I can hardly imagine the young man whom I saw talking with you the other day could express himself so well, if left quite to his own powers, and yet it is not the style of a woman. . . . No doubt he is a sensible man, and I suppose may have a natural talent . . . when he takes a pen in hand, his thoughts naturally find proper words" (50–51).[36] In *Bleak House* (1853), Dickens conversely equates pitiable epistolary skills with a gentleman's poor character. Richard Carstone, who attempts and quits three professions in quick succession, proves even more unworthy of his cousin and fiancée, angelic Ada Clare, because, when apart from her, "he soon failed in his letter-writing" (182). Although Charlotte Brontë tells Ellen Nussey in December 1852 that Arthur Bell Nicholls proposed to her in person—"he made me for the first time feel what it costs a man to declare affection where he doubts response"—on her father's insistence, she penned "a distinct refusal" to which Nicholls replied by letter, revealing his passion. As she tells Nussey: "That he cared something for me— and wanted me to care for him—I have long suspected—but I did not know the degree or strength of his feelings" (Barker, *The Brontës: A Life* 357–58). As Brontë's "dear readers" well know, Charlotte eventually married Nicholls on June 29, 1854.

The increase in letters of love and affection post-1840 undeniably shaped the meaning of the post as a vehicle for intimacy in Victorian culture. The Penny Post upped expectations for frequency and length of letters during courtship and marriage. In *Wives and Daughters* (1866)—set in England before the 1832 Reform Bill when postage was determined by number of sheets and enclosures and the distance a letter actually traveled—Elizabeth Gaskell correlates contentment in marriage with the number of letters Dr. Gibson's second wife writes her husband while away from Hollingford. Two gossipy spinster sisters, the Miss Brownings, calculate:

> Now two letters during the week of her absence showed what was in those days considered a very proper amount of conjugal affection. Yet not too much—at elevenpence halfpenny postage. A third letter would have been extravagant. Sister looked to sister with an approving nod as Molly named the second letter, which arrived in Hollingford the very day before Mrs. Gibson was to return. They had settled between them- selves that two letters would show the right amount of good feeling and proper understanding in the Gibson family: more would have been ex- travagant; only one would have been a mere matter of duty. (440–41)

Gaskell repeats the word "extravagant" to illustrate that the high cost of post- age before the coming of the Penny Post in 1840 necessitated prudence: even if a couple "really got on together" (440), to write thrice during a week at "elev- enpence halfpenny postage" would exceed good taste. To write a spouse only once a week seemed little more than the obligatory fulfillment of a contractual duty, but writing twice a week was considered "a very proper amount of con- jugal affection." These standards changed following Uniform Penny Postage. For example, while visiting London in 1882, Trollope wrote his wife, Rose, who was staying in Harting, four times over a period of eight days (October 3–Oc- tober 11, 1882). Although the epistles are brief and controlled, as was Trollope's style of letter writing in general, he addresses Rose as "Dearest Love" and signs his letters "Your own."[37]

A popular Victorian poem, written around 1840 and attributed to James Beaton, flatly credits the increase in love letters to Rowland Hill and the coming of the Penny Post:

> Something I want to write upon, to scare away each vapour—
> The "Penny Postage" shall I try? Why, yes, I'll write on paper.
> The great invention, Rowland Hill, each person loudly hails;
> The females are all full of it, and so are all the mails . . .
> The letters in St. Valentine so vastly will amount,
> Postmen may judge them by the lot, they won't have time to count;
> They must bring round spades and measures, to poor love-sick souls
> Deliver them by bushels, the same as they do coals.
> As billet-doux will so augment, the mails will be too small,
> So omnibuses they must use, or they can't carry all;
> And ladies pleasure will evince, instead of any fuss,
> To have their lovers' letters all delivered with a 'bus![38]

While Beaton seizes upon the Penny Post as an opportunity for jest, substance underpins the humor. Epistolary traffic of billets-doux and romantic valentines post-1840 could well have been delivered by the bushel. It was not uncommon for lovers to post letters daily, as Trollope illustrates in *Marion Fay* (1882). Marion may refuse Lord Hampstead's offer of marriage because of his high station and her poor health, but she writes him every day and savors Hampstead's billet-doux: "She read the letter a dozen times, pressing it to her lips and to her bosom" (3: 52).[39] Here we see the clichéd notions of love letters that filled countless letter-writing manuals of the day: the billet-doux becomes a treasured object to be kissed in place of the absent beloved.

With mail now costing only a penny, what were the ramifications if a suitor sent unwelcome letters to a lady or if one's fiancé became an infrequent or absent correspondent? In two of his novels, Trollope, not surprisingly, considers both cases to show how Victorian letters at times were emissaries of impropriety and betrayal. In *Barchester Towers* (1857), the pretty, wealthy widow Eleanor Bold arouses the worst fears of her relatives merely in accepting letters from the odious Rev. Slope. Eleanor's sister, Susan Grantly, tells her: "'I must say it's rather singular . . . that a young lady in your position should receive a letter from an unmarried gentleman of which she will not tell the contents, and which she is ashamed to show to her sister'" (2: 11). On Dr. Grantly's insistence, Eleanor shares one of Slope's letters, which reads "in almost every respect [like] the letter of a declared lover; it seemed to corroborate his worst suspicions; and the fact of Eleanor's showing it to him was all but tantamount to a declaration on her part, that it was her pleasure to receive love-letters from Mr. Slope" (2: 18). Trollope acutely conveys that a young widow's mere acceptance of a few letters from an unmarried gentleman could excite suspicion in the days of the Penny Post.

In *The Claverings* (1867), Trollope features a delinquent letter writer: Harry Clavering. When "another post came without any letter from Harry, poor Florence's heart sank low in her bosom" (271–72). Absence coupled with inconstancy in letter writing were hot topics in Victorian writing manuals, confirming the social gravity of the situation Florence Burton faces. (*A New Letter-Writer, for the Use of Gentlemen* [1868], for example, includes a letter template, "Complaining of Not Receiving a Letter" [73–74], that demonstrates how a man whose fiancée has failed to write him recently goes about making a polite protest.) Initially, Harry is "most constant with his letters" to Florence Burton, who is known to "boast of them as being perfect in their way" (233) and to declare she could "'live upon letters'" (34). Since a letter's length was a barometer of Victorian affection, Florence initially finds herself in an "ecstasy of delight," for Harry writes such "a long and very affectionate letter to his own Flo, . . . that, as a love-letter, it was perfect" (146). Soon after, he writes her a "stupid, short letter, in which he declared that he was very busy, and that his head ached. In a postscript he told her he was going to see Lady Ongar that evening" (147). Then Harry stops writing Florence altogether—"What could he say to her that would not be false?" (224)—leading his sister Fanny to suspect that "things were not altogether right" between them (233).

Harry finds himself essentially engaged to two women: Florence is good, middle class, and unpretentious; Lady Ongar, his first love, is beautiful, wealthy, and now a widow. If Harry concludes in exasperation, "'Women expect such a lot of letter-writing!'" (233), he also admits that in respecting his fiancée Florence, "'I have been remiss, I know'" (233). Mr. Burton takes some convincing, but agrees that Florence should travel to London to stay with her brother to determine the state of her love affair with Harry:

> "It would look as if we were all afraid," said Mr. Burton, "and after all what does it come to?—a young gentleman does not write to his sweetheart for two or three weeks. I used to think myself the best lover in the world, if I wrote once a month."
> "There was no penny post then, Mr. Burton," [replied Mrs. Burton].
> "And I often wish there was none now," said Mr. Burton. (273)

In *The Claverings*, published more than two decades after the coming of the Penny Post, Trollope correlates infrequent billets-doux with romantic betrayal. A young woman could be considered "ill treated" if her sweetheart neglected to write her for just a few weeks, although prior to the Penny Post, writing one's fiancée once a month was considered more-than-sufficient proof of attachment. Trollope understood how Victorian letter-writing manuals were meant to help sweethearts navigate the romantic vicissitudes of inconstancy and absence, and several of the fictional letters in *The Claverings* resemble those modeled in manuals of the day. In a letter strongly resembling "From a Lady to a Gentleman accusing him of Inconstancy and demanding the return of her Letters" (*Wide World Letter Writer* [n.d.]), Florence Burton asks Mrs. Clavering to return Harry's letters and trinkets to him, noting: "'your son is more warmly attached to another lady than he is to me, and under those circumstances, for his sake as well as for mine, it is necessary that we should part'" (422–23). All comes right with Harry and Florence in the end: Harry realizes his follies and posts Lady Ongar a letter similar to "A Gentleman desirous of discontinuing his Addresses" from *A New Letter-Writer*.

The Victorian revolution in letter writing more often empowered the sweetheart than her beau and required Victorian gentlemen to "Be cautious about letter-writing" (173), as Billy Pringle's wise Mamma warns him in Robert Surtees's, *"Ask Mamma"; or, The Richest Commoner in England* (1858).[40]

> "Be cautious too about letter-writing. There is no real privacy about love-letters, any more than there is about the flags and banners of a regiment, though they occasionally furl and cover them up. The love-letters are a woman's flags and banners, her trophies of success, and the more flowery they are, the more likely to be shown, and to aid in enlightening a Christmas tea-party. Then the girls' Mammas read them, their sisters read them, their maids read them, and ultimately, perhaps, a boisterous energetic barrister reads them to an exasperated jury, some of whose daughters may have suffered from similar effusions themselves." (173)

Where private love letters become public "flags and banners" of affection, "trophies of success," they have the potential to be as "dangerous as lucifer matches," to recall Charlotte Brontë's words to Ellen Nussey. Surtees's novel reminds us of Nicholls's deepest fear about letters—the "accidental passing of letters into hands and eyes for which they were never written," including the hands and eyes of domineering mothers, gossipy sisters, nosy maids, and willing barristers (Barker, *The Brontës: A Life* 395). Did the risk of a private letter's becoming public lead Trollope to conclude, via the Platonic musings of his protagonist Harry Clavering, "confessions . . . may be less difficult to make with pen and ink than with spoken words, but . . . when so made are more degrading. The word that is written is a thing capable of permanent life, and lives frequently to the confusion of its parent. A man should make his confessions always by word of mouth if it be possible" (439–40).

Despite the risks of written pledges, period novels, nonetheless, suggest the Victorians' penchant for confessing love, proposing, and breaking off relations by post. Victorian letter-writing manuals—rich in material memories of collegiality, friendship, love, and courtship—likewise reveal an emerging etiquette for properly proposing and breaking off engagements. For example, *The Wide World Letter Writer* contains a section on "Letters of Love" with sample letters including "Letter from a Gentleman to a Lady Offering her his hand," "Favourable Reply to the foregoing," "From a Gentleman to a Lady, Confessing Change of Sentiment," "From a Lady to a Gentleman Desiring Release from an Engagement," and "From a Gentleman to a Lady Seeking to Renew a Ruptured Engagement." The introduction to this section advises that "Love letters written in sincerity and faith need but little guidance from the heart of the writer. The true lover will find the words he seeks flow easily from his pen, and probably the eyes resting next upon them will not criticize very severely. . . . A lady's letter should be always dignified. . . . Be sure that your betrothed will respect you more for a quiet, affectionate dignity in writing, than if you put too much of the most sacred of all feelings upon paper" (130). The model letters demonstrate the tonal and rhetorical attributes the manual recommends—sincerity and fidelity for men, reserve for women—and in so doing convey much information about Victorian propriety. A gentleman offering a lady his hand writes of his sincere love: "Has the deep, faithful love that I feel for you any response in your heart? . . . If you will be my wife, it will be the pride of my life to try to shield you from all sorrow, and to give you all the happiness that a tender, loving husband can bestow upon his first and only love" (131). Ideally, the lady replies favorably with "affectionate dignity": "Your kind and manly letter opens my eyes to the fact that what I believe to be only a warm friendship is a stronger feeling. I see that it would be a pain to me to lose your visits and presence, and that such love as you promise your wife would make me very happy" (131).

Likewise, Rev. Cooke's *Universal Letter Writer* (c. 1850) includes a section "On Love, Courtship, & Marriage," modeling how, by letter, a man can declare love like a gentleman and a woman can accept or reject an offer with dignity, modesty, and restraint—all important Victorian virtues.[41] In Eliot's *Middlemarch* (1872), letters exchanged by Edward Casaubon and Dorothea Brooke exemplify the masculine and feminine modes of romantic communication promoted in letter-writing manuals of the day. Casaubon proposes to Dorothea with the sincere affection of the true gentleman: "To be accepted by you as your husband and the earthly guardian of your welfare, I should regard as the highest of providential gifts. In return I can at least offer you an affection hitherto unwasted, and the faithful consecration of a life which, however short in the sequel, has no backward pages whereon, if you choose to turn them, you will find records such as might justly cause you either bitterness or shame" (67).[42] Dorothea, who "trembled" reading the letter, immediately replies with grace and gentility characteristic of a true lady: "I am very grateful to you for loving me, and thinking me worthy to be your wife. I can look forward to no better happiness than that which would be one with yours" (68). In *Bleak House*, Dickens even goes so far as to have Mr. John Jarndyce, Esther Summerson's guardian, write a genteel and sincere proposal of marriage to Esther, although they live in the same house. Of the letter, Esther remarks: "It was so impressive in its love for me, and in the unselfish caution it gave me, and the consideration it showed me in every word, that my eyes were too often blinded to read much at a time. But I read it through three times, before I laid it down. I had thought beforehand that I knew its purport, and I did. It asked me, would I be the mistress of Bleak House" (488–89).[43]

A written marriage proposal also carried legal meaning: it could hold a gentleman accountable in a court of law. Trollope was keenly aware of the legal possibilities for the "permanent life" of letters. In *Kept in the Dark* (1882), Trollope includes a coy marriage proposal from Sir Francis Geraldine to Francesca Altifiorla: "'Don't you think that you and I know each other well enough to make a match of it?'" (67). Sir Francis has second thoughts when Francesca asks to think it over, and he responds rather brusquely: "'All right. See you soon. Ever yours, F. G.'" (74). More important than the proposal is the commentary that follows it:

> Such was the entire response which Miss Altifiorla received from her now declared lover. Sir Francis had told himself that he hated the bother of writing love-letters. But in truth there was with him also an idea that it might be as well that he should not commit himself to declarations that were in their nature very strong. It was not that he absolutely thought of any possible future event in which his letters might be used against him, but there was present to him a feeling that the least said might be the soonest mended. (74)

After Francesca accepts him, Sir Francis complains, "'There is no end to her letters'" (88)—and he, in return, sends "but two answers to six letters, and each answer had been conveyed in about three lines. There had been no expressions from him of confiding love nor any pressing demands for an immediate marriage. They had all been commenced without even naming her, and had been finished by the simple signature of his initials" (86).

Confident that Francesca "'hasn't got a word of my writing to show,—not a word that would go for anything with a jury'" (87), Sir Francis jilts her via the post, turning not to a model letter himself but to his friend, Captain McCollop, who writes a letter similar to *Wide World Letter Writer*'s "From a Gentleman to a Lady, Confessing Change of Sentiment." The exemplar reads in part, "I will not attempt to excuse myself, for I deserve your anger, but I will only say that I was myself deceived in my own feelings" (137). Sir Francis takes the blame for a change of sentiment, though his second sentence lacks the elegance of the epistolary model: "'I think that I am bound in honour without a moment's delay to make you aware of the condition of my mind in regard to marriage. I ain't quite sure but what I shall be better without it altogether.' . . . 'I think that perhaps I may have expressed myself badly so as to warrant you in understanding more than I have meant. If so, I am sure the fault has been mine, and I am very sorry for it'" (88). Despite Miss Altifiorla's fury in losing her suitor's wealth and affection, she recognizes that even as "She took out every scrap of letter that she had received from the man, and read each scrap with the greatest care. . . . she doubted whether she could depend upon it in a court of law" (89). Why does Sir Francis keep his letters coy, "wickedly crafty," vague, and short (89)? He is aware of the legal power a billet-doux carried in a Victorian court of law.

The Victorian Valentine Tradition

Today Valentine's Day is largely a commercial affair associated with the buying and giving of cards, chocolates, and flowers, but in the nineteenth century, it was primarily "a postal holiday," and, as historian David Henkin explains, "a compelling symbol of the forms of social interaction made possible by an affordable mail system" (149).[44] The exchange of Valentine's Day cards long predates the Victorian era. Legend has it that the tradition began when the Duc d'Orléans, imprisoned in the Tower of London, mailed his fiancée a romantic missive on February 14, 1415. Valentine's Day gift giving (of personal items, such as garters, stockings, and gloves) became quite popular in the seventeenth century, and by the mid-eighteenth century, handmade love tokens often took the form of love knots, gloves, and puzzle purses, which, when opened, revealed a love message inside. Although printed papers with Valentine's Day themes, poems, and pictorial scenes grew in popularity in the early nineteenth century, "the British postal system," as art historian Debra

Mancoff points out, "stood in the way of heartfelt intentions" (27). Of course, the Penny Post changed that: "When uniform postal rates for the entire United Kingdom were established in 1840, the English Valentine card tradition began in earnest."[45] The establishment of a "single, prepaid rate throughout the country for a half-ounce letter," notes Debra Mancoff, "both increased the cards' popularity and led to the design of elaborate envelopes, making the package as appealing as its contents" (46).

Dickens describes with flourish an influx of valentines arriving in St. Martin's-le-Grand on Valentine's Day in 1850, ten years after the coming of the Penny Post: "The sacrifices to the fane of St. Valentine—consisting of hearts, darts, Cupid peeping out of paper-roses, Hymen embowered in hot-pressed embossing, swains in very blue coats and nymphs in very opaque muslin, coarse caricatures and tender verses—caused an augmentation to the revenue on this anniversary equal to about 70,000 missives; 123,000 being the usual daily average for district and 'byes' during the month of February" (*Household Words* 8). Roughly 200,000 letters passed through the General Post Office in London on February 14, 1850, even if letter carriers did not "Deliver them by bushels, the same as they do coals," as Beaton humorously mused in his poem on the postal hubbub. Beaton's images of "bushels" of valentines and "scribbling elves" illustrate how thoroughly the Penny Post made Valentine's Day a commercial venture, stimulating business for printers and stationers: "And lots of paper will be used by every scribbling elf, / That each should be a paper manufacturer himself."[46]

Sweethearts still send each other valentines, but, as Emma Bradford explains in *Roses are Red: Love and Scorn in Victorian Valentines*, "the Golden Age of the Valentine card was the Victorian era" (1).[47] Statistics substantiate this claim: in 1841, just one year after Uniform Penny Postage, Victorians sent more than 400,000 valentines throughout England; by 1871, three times that number passed through the London post alone (Mancoff 46). Howard Robinson gives a slightly higher estimate, noting that around 1870, "One of the lucrative sources of postal revenue . . . was the valentine—the day of picture post cards had not yet come. The valentines at the time numbered annually a million and a third for London only" (369). Premier London stationery shops, including Dobbs and Company, George Meek, and Joseph Mansell, designed their own popular lines of valentine cards adorned with lace, silk, ribbon, and cut-paper flowers and leaves. Though some of the Valentine's Day posts included the biting valentines described in chapter 4, the vast majority of Victorian valentines were emissaries of love—adorned with cupids, hearts, darts, and "tender verses." Still others carried messages of friendship, parental affection, and gentle humor (for example, urging a bachelor to marry). Stationers created novelty valentines, which sometimes took the form of telegrams (from "Loveland") or of banknotes (from the "Bank of True Love"). Behind all of these, however, both ready-made and hand-crafted valentines, lie stories of ardent passion, shy or secret love, warm affection, pleading, jealousy, imagined happiness, and feared rejection. Through words and symbols, Victorian valentines, in turn, "still rekindle today the fresh message of love, scorn or affection which they first carried through the Victorian penny post" (Bradford 1).

While today we usually purchase a ready-made valentine at a shop and post it, Victorians often bought materials at a stationer's shop and assembled their own valentines. To some, a romantic valentine was an artistic creation, as Judith Holder suggests in *Sweethearts and Valentines*: "one might purchase the blank card, a paper lace frame, a picture or pictures, and a verse or motto, then glue all these together to produce one's own specially designed valentine. It is particularly romantic to think of young Victorian gentlemen, who would rarely lift a finger in practical matters such as sewing or cooking, spending hours with scissors and paste assembling these valentines" (7). Stationer's shops offered Victorian men and women a wide array of materials for creating original valentines: colored and gilt cards, lace frames, cupids and hearts made out of paper, bows and ribbons, and appliqués made of lace, feather, shell, and gold and silver foil. Stationers also sold printed verses and mottoes that could be added to a design.

While some Valentine's Day cards came ready-made with design and verse, still others had a designated blank space for the writer to supply his or her own verses, as Thomas Hardy illustrates in *Far from the Madding Crowd* (1874). As a lark, Bathsheba Everdene sends a valentine she intended for a field hand's child to Farmer Boldwood, a sober bachelor and owner of a neighboring farm. Hardy describes how "Bathsheba took from her desk a gorgeously illuminated and embossed design in post-octavo, which had been bought on the previous market-day at the chief stationer's in Casterbridge. In the centre was a small oval enclosure; this was left blank, that the sender might insert tender words more appropriate to the special occasion than any generalities by a printer could possibly be" (86). Bathsheba's maid, Liddy, supplies some pat sentimental lines for her to inscribe on the valentine: "'The rose is red, / The violet blue, / Carnation's sweet, / And so are you'" (86). Just as Bathsheba prints the verses and concludes, "'Yes, that shall be it. It just suits itself to a chubby-faced child like him'" (86), Liddy convinces her to send the valentine anonymously to Boldwood as a practical joke.

Bathsheba randomly chooses a seal that reads "'MARRY ME'" and posts it, setting in motion with one frivolous act the fatal series of events—including insanity and murder—that will ultimately follow from the intense love that erupts in Boldwood once he recognizes the valentine's handwriting and discerns the identity of the sender. In an age when marriage was sacrosanct, Boldwood's powerful, sincere response to Bathsheba's paper prank reveals the degree to which a romantic valentine was considered an emissary of love and marriage, a point Gaskell also intimates in her story "Mr. Harrison's Confessions" (1851). Playing a joke on his friend Dr. Frank Harrison, an eligible bachelor new in town, Jack Marshland sends a "most passionate valentine" (258) to one of Dr. Harrison's patients, Miss Caroline Tomkinson, expertly imitating Harrison's handwriting. This leads the townspeople of Duncombe to upbraid Harrison when he denies any intention to marry her. In Gaskell's as in Hardy's day, "a time," as Mancoff explains, "of regulated courtship and restrained emotions, the valentine had genuine power. . . . According to the rules of Victorian romance, a valentine was 'love's messenger,' the most sincere communication from heart to heart" (7). Even the reserved Boldwood would likely have known that, in the Victorian age, valentines "offered the one exception to the rule of feminine discretion: a woman could not declare her love verbally, but she could send a valentine" (Mancoff 37).[48] To Boldwood, the valentine connotes more than the touch of the sender: he imagines a woman's hand writing out these sentimental lines; he sees a "misty shape" and wonders if her lips—"red or pale, plumped or creased?—had curved . . . to a certain expression as the pen went on" (89).

Concealment of the sender's identity added to the allure of romantic valentines, which shaped postal contact as portable intimacy. We cannot underestimate how the posting of romantic and insulting missives depended on anonymous collection and distribution of the mail. Secret admirers could declare love anonymously and disguise their handwriting. Since senders and receivers of valentines were typically members of the same community, anonymous senders had to take care to conceal their penmanship, as Hardy's Bathsheba forgets to do. In addition, a prankster might imitate another's hand, as Gaskell's Marshland intentionally does. However, even disguised handwriting could be deciphered and identities exposed. Worse, a prankster could cause matrimonial conflicts by sending a "flaming valentine" as a practical joke. (The Victorian "flaming valentine"—a name based on Cupid's flaming torch—is a passionate declaration of love.) Returning for a moment to "Mr. Harrison's Confessions," that the entire town of Duncombe assumes Dr. Harrison's positive engagement with Miss Tompkinson from a passionate valentine; that this presumption nearly foils his plan to marry his true love, Sophy Hutton (the vicar's daughter); that the erring prankster must write a letter confessing his hoax "'with a deeply penitent heart'" (268)—these elements in Gaskell's plot demonstrate the social weight the valentine carried in Victorian England.

Victorian Valentine Collections

Over 200 flower- and cliché-filled valentines from the Bath Central Library and the Frank Staff Collection of the Bath Postal Museum transmit a visual iconography of Victorian love. These ready-made, personalized, and hand-crafted valentines reveal much about Victorian aesthetics and sensibilities surrounding the new moral attitude of love that burgeoned in 1830, accompanying the end of the reign of the rakish George IV. Flowers, churches, angels, lovebirds, bird's nests, cupids, flaming torches, bows, butterflies, arrows, musical instruments, hearts, and wedding rings are all common Victorian icons of romantic love. So are "hearts and darts" (129), which Gaskell places on the valentine that Mary Barton receives from her secret admirer, Jem Wilson, in *Mary Barton* (1848). Many period valentines feature clichéd printed messages, such as "Constant and True," "Be for ever mine," "Thine forever," "Remember Me," and "Ever Affectionate," aligning romantic love with constancy and lasting affection, as well as with monogamy. In addition to using lace, feathers, fabric, shell, and metallic foils in their handmade valentines, Victorians also used intricate cutouts, fine fabrics (like silk, tulle, and netting), bows and ribbons, small bits of mirror, grasses and ferns, seashells, seeds, mother of pearl, fabric flowers and leaves, appliqués of fruits, and scents—materials that appeal to the senses and that illustrate the age's budding interest in naturalism. Some cards appear stitched or embroidered, in which case the valentine becomes an example of genteel domestic art. Popular mechanical valentines opened to reveal a hidden message or could be moved (a man nods his head, a woman beckons with her hand, and in bawdy valentines, a figure shows her ankle or petticoat). Intricate cobweb or beehive designs (also called flower cage valentines) transformed the ordinary valentine into a work of fine art.

The two most ubiquitous Victorian valentine icons are flowers and churches (or church spires). The Victorians were well versed in the sentiments and values that different types of flowers represented, and Victorian illustrator Kate Greenaway's 1884 *Language of Flowers* provides a charming example. Today, we still associate roses with love, but "in the demure Victorian age, secret passions could . . . best be expressed in the form of a bouquet, each plant of which possessed hidden meaning" (Holder 8). Placing images of specific kinds of flowers on a romantic valentine offered a way to personalize a missive

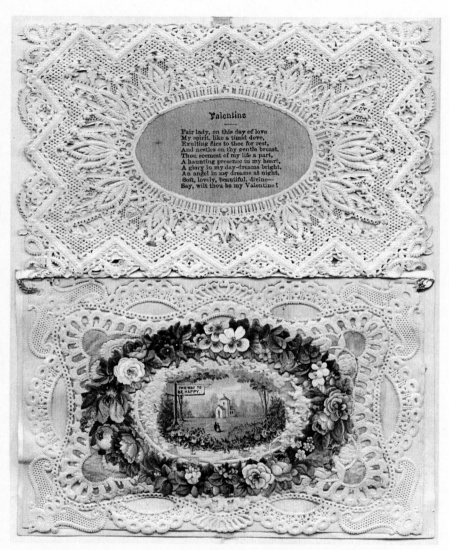

FIGURE 23. "Valentine," c. 1860. © Bath in Time, Bath Central Library.

or express love without words. According to Greenaway's glossary, the three flowers Bathsheba includes in her valentine poem—red rose, blue violet, and carnation—mean "love" (55), "faithfulness" (51), and, depending on the color of the carnation, either "Alas! for my poor heart" (deep red carnation) (48) or "Woman's love" (pink carnation) (33). No wonder Boldwood is entranced. Other flowers commonly found on period valentines include pansies for "thoughts" (32), lilies of the valley for "return of happiness" (27), bluebells for "constancy" (10), forget-me-nots for "true love" (18), daisies for "innocence" (15), and white lilies for "purity and sweetness" (27).

The church or church steeple, the second most popular icon on romantic Victorian valentines, signifies fidelity in love and honorable intentions and helps impart to these missives their strong and recognized associations of sincerity, devotion, and marriage plans. This was an age when engagements often lasted for years. A couple could not marry until a man was financially secure, so a fiancé, by choosing a card with a church image, could assure his betrothed of his unfailing love. For those not yet engaged, the image of a church, even when it appeared only as a spire in the background of a romantic scene, offered a way for a suitor, particularly a shy one, to inform his sweetheart of his true and honorable intentions. Many cards show a happy couple strolling down a lane filled with brightly colored flowers, their destination a wedding chapel (see figure 23). The church also commonly appears on valentines with military or nautical themes (see figure 24) to inform a loved one that if she will only wait for her lover's return from his long absence in the army or navy, her patience, a supreme Victorian virtue, will be rewarded.

Adorned with pink ribbon and titled simply "Valentine," the card shown in figure 23 offers a good example of the Victorian valentine handmade from various store-bought parts—romantic scene, floral wreath, lace paper, and printed verse—and demonstrates the iconographic marriage of flowers and churches characteristic of many romantic valentines of the period.[49] When the card is opened, its upper inside face shows a verse, printed in black on pink satin:

Fair lady, on this day of love
My spirit, like a timid dove,
Exulting flies to thee for rest,
And nestles on thy gentle breast.
Thou seemest of my life a part,
A haunting presence in my heart,
A glory in my day-dreams bright,

An angel in my dreams at night,
Soft, lovely, beautiful, divine—
Say, wilt thou be my Valentine!

In these lines chosen by a Victorian gentleman for his "fair lady," romantic love appears in an earnest religious context. The lover is represented as a dove, a common ecclesiastical image and the form the Holy Spirit assumes descending to earth. In a Victorian context, the dove also means peace and divinity. Likewise, the lady in this verse is likened to a "divine" or celestial angel. Nurturing her dove/love on her "gentle breast," she embodies the Victorian ideal of woman as "angel in the house," a sweet and selfless companion of manhood (as Hicks depicts in *Woman's Mission* in figure 22), approaching the divine on earth. In the lozenge-shaped scene on the lower inside face of the card, a happy couple walks arm in arm to a church. To make the message perfectly clear, a road sign on the couple's path reads, "THE WAY TO BE HAPPY." The church appears in a pastoral setting, one that came to be seen as an escape from the increasingly industrialized Victorian world. Some of the colorful flowers in the wreath encircling the scene carry readily identifiable meanings. Using Greenaway's *Language of Flowers* again, the blue forget-me-nots signify "true love" (18), the cabbage roses stand as "ambassadors of love" (48), the iris refers to "a message" (23), and ivy means "fidelity" and "marriage" (23): taken together, the flowers in the wreath reinforce the matrimonial theme the image of the church conveys.

Elaborate rhyming verses on romantic valentines frequently mention Hymen, one of the Greek gods of song associated with matrimony and weddings, particularly the wedding hymn, also referred to as the hymeneal or bridal song. Some novelty valentines were configured as checks or banknotes allegedly drawn on the "Temple of Hymen" or the "Bank of True Love."[50] In late eighteenth-century London, the Temple of Hymen proved to be a popular and lucrative establishment run by Dr. James Graham, which "featured many strange and mysterious wonders the very touching or seeing of which could be guaranteed to ease young lovers' paths to happiness."[51] Verses to Hymen coupled with icons of the wedding ring and the church infuse the valentines on which they appear with Victorian notions of love as necessarily involving fidelity, constancy, duty, affection, and marriage. Hymen forms the central motif in the verse accompanying the hand-colored, military-themed valentine shown in figure 24, where a red-coated soldier stands beneath a banner emblazoned with "LOVE & DUTY" in large, block letters.[52] Romantic valentines like "LOVE & DUTY" may appear cloying to those with modern-day

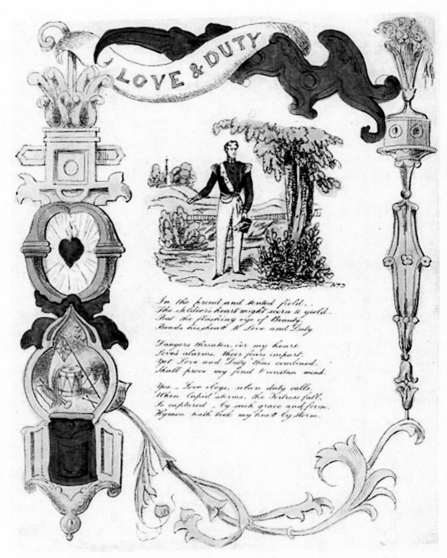

FIGURE 24. "Love & Duty." Undated Victorian valentine from the Frank Staff Collection. Image used with permission of Bath Postal Museum.

sensibilities, but to Victorian men and women, each telling visual detail and textual cue spoke clearly of romantic love. The poem conveys the soldier's twin passions—he will remain faithful to his true love as he dutifully serves his country: "Yes—Love obeys, when duty calls / When Cupid storms, the Fortress fall, / So captured—by such grace and form / Hymen hath took my heart by storm." The heart depicted on the side of the valentine is presumably the soldier's heart, and the church spire in the background—an assurance that marriage will reward a virtuous heart—makes clear this is the very altar where Hymen will lead the soldier-suitor and his true love.

Also popular during the Victorian period were comic valentines, which foreground a relationship between courtship and humor. Different from insulting valentines, comic missives display a broadly smiling, Horatian style of satire and often targeted the bachelor. For example, one mechanical valentine designed by Dean & Sons around 1850 features a bachelor in a dressing gown furiously attempting to sew a button onto his pants.[53] The corresponding verses read, "For a Bachelors troubles who should care / He ought to get married they all declare. / If a button come off, he must sit up in bed, / And make a sad bungle with needle and thread. / But if he'd take courage and also a wife, / He'd find 'twas the happiest day of his life." When the viewer pulls the mechanical tab, the bachelor nods his head in agreement.

While cards of this kind tease a bachelor to take a wife, others pleasantly point at navigating the lands and waters leading to a married state. Among the comic strain of Victorian novelty valentines, so-called maps of matrimony were popular. Shown in figure 25, "A MAP of MATRIMONY" transforms the pitfalls of Victorian courtship and marital blessings into regions, lakes, and mountains on an actual map. In addition to plotting the "Strait of Flirtation" and the "Isle of Jealousy," located off the "Bay of Courtship," the map labels "Engagement Bay" as an area of "Dangerous Navigation" and places the "Quicksands of Censure" alongside it. While it might be desirable to enter into marriage, the way there, as this and topographical valentines like it make clear, often proved hard to navigate. Poking fun at the law profession, the "cartographer" labeled the high peaks "Mountains of Delay Inhabited by lawyers." The derisive placement of the "Land of Spinsters" at the upper left-hand edge of the map gives concrete form to an unmarried or redundant woman's marginality in Victorian society. Not surprisingly, the "Road to Content" leads to the "Port of Hymen" under the jurisdiction of the Greek god of matrimony and, if a couple can steer clear of dangerous waters, the affianced may actually arrive in the "Region of Rejoicing."[54]

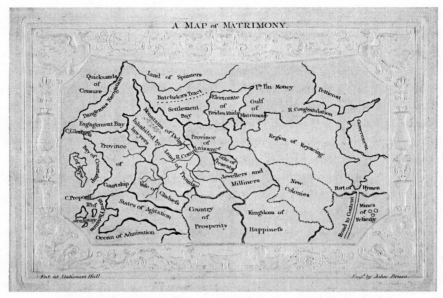

FIGURE 25. "A Map of Matrimony," c. 1860. © Bath in Time, Bath Central Library.

Other valentines tease about the responsibilities of impending fatherhood. One of these in a series of valentines entitled "A PEEP THROUGH THE WEDDING RING" shows a man and a woman standing together inside a flower-festooned wedding ring. His arm encircles her shoulders as she pins a flower on his lapel. Beneath them, sitting on a cushion of clouds, three angels read a book called "LOVE." The accompanying humorous verse is written from the woman's point of view: "I think you love me, it is true / And well, perhaps it may be, / But if we're married, say will you, / Object to nurse the baby."[55] This, like the other humorous valentines featured here, is a representative rather than an isolated example. In 1842, *Punch* published a whole series of comic valentines, attesting to their popularity. The twelve full-page designs by leading Victorian illustrators, such as Hablot Knight Browne (Phiz), Alfred Crowquil, John Leech, and Kenny Meadows, were created specifically for "distressed lovers" and "PERSONS ABOUT TO MARRY" and thus to enter the "Temple of Love," presided over by Cupid. Valentines titled "The Speculative Mama," "The Man About Town," "The Literary Gentleman," "The Pet Parson," "The Medical Student," "The Politician," and "The Milliner" are all caricature illustrations, a style still in vogue in the 1840s. Characters are represented as types of humanity, with exaggerated facial features and accompanied by traditional and exemplifying props. The literary gent poised to write sensation fiction about burglary and murder is depicted among smaller images of books, a writing desk, a skull, and a gallows circle. The politician who pores simultaneously over five newspapers is surrounded by the busts of famous political leaders and philosophers, including Napoleon, Caesar, and Confucius.

Arguably, the funniest valentine in "Punch's Valentines!" is "The Speculative Mama," drawn as a formidable figure not unlike Surtees's Emma Pringle in *"Ask Mama,"* who cautions son Billy about the dangers of writing billets-doux. Kenny Meadows comically depicts the "Speculative Mama" as a sour-faced dowager with expansive skirts, a ridiculous-looking feathered headpiece, and gloved arms folded across an enormous bosom. Written as a rhyming letter to a mother of seven daughters, the missive points to the economic realities of Victorian marriage. The suitor is a bachelor, roughly age 48, who makes only £600 a year and confesses he is so eager to enter into marriage that "At the feet of your daughters my fortune I fling, / And will wed any one of the seven." While the bachelor does not like daughter number two's hair color and requests a discount if he marries daughter number four, who squints and is rather plain, he concludes:

> An answer, *per post*, saying how you decide,
>   Will "lull my fond bosom's fierce flame,"
> For I'm dying to know which fair girl is my bride,
>   In case some one asks me her name.
> From your own early feelings you truly can guess,
>   What a fervid affection is mine;
> So to one of the seven I fondly confess
>   Until death I'm her own VALENTINE. (63)

How fitting that the fervent suitor awaits confirmation of his "own valentine" via the Penny Post, the very mechanism that allowed valentines—among other postal blessings of friendship, counsel, and courtship—to flourish in the Victorian age.

THE MANIFOLD BLESSINGS OF THE PENNY POST

Writing in 1864, William Lewins concludes part 1 of *Her Majesty's Mails* with an optimistic summation of the reformed postal service: "The past ten years have been years of great, gradual, and unexampled improvement. Nor is there anything but progress and advancement in prospect. . . . the Post-office is an institution capable of infinite extension and growth" (246–47). Progress and advancement made the Penny Post an inclusive, affordable, and accessible network that facilitated regular and frequent social exchanges, a trademark of the Victorian revolution in letter writing. As the Post Office continued to grow, some of the marvelous predictions of postal reformers seemingly came true. As we explored in chapter 4, the Penny Post may well have invited in curious, extraneous, and dangerous missives and "constantly threatened," as Cleere explains, "to bring the *wrong* family together" (202). At the same time, however, it did bring the *right* people together—parents and children, consumers and commercial houses, authors and publishers, mourners and friends, spouses and romantic partners.

To the Victorians, the contents of a postman's mail bag appears to have been what today we might call a "mixed bag": "'the thoughts of rogues, lovers, bankers, lawyers, clergymen, and shopkeepers; the loves and griefs, the weal and woes, of the town and country lie side by side, and for a few hours at least will enjoy the most complete and secret companionship.'"[56] The Penny Post carried the active and immediate "loves and griefs" of townsfolk and city dwellers alike. If it facilitated mass mailings of radical organizations and allowed solicitors, pranksters, fans, fundraisers, and scam artists to communicate with strangers, the Penny Post—as reformers advocated—also increased opportunities for friends, relations, consumers, clergy, spouses, and lovers to communicate at a distance and, in the case of Valentine's Day, for secret admirers to send romantic missives anonymously in one's hometown. Following the advent of cheap postage, which Martineau heralds in her 1843 letter to Sir Thomas Wilde as "a benefit enjoyed without hesitation or remorse" (46), Victorians regularly wrote letters of business, friendship, advice, mourning, and love—manifold blessings of the Penny Post.

Conclusion

Looking Forward from the Victorian Revolution in Letter Writing to Information Technologies Today

Of all the wild and visionary schemes which I have ever heard or read of, it [the Penny Post] is the most extravagant.

—Lord Lichfield, *Mirror of Parliament*, June 15, 1837

Twenty years after Uniform Penny Postage, George Elgar Hicks exhibited a scene from contemporary life at the Royal Academy Summer Exhibition that pictorially anticipated a claim William Lewins made four years later in *Her Majesty's Mails* (1864): "the Post-office is an institution capable of infinite extension and growth" (247). Depicting a diverse group of Londoners rushing to make the last posting at St. Martin's-le-Grand, *The General Post Office, One Minute to Six* (1860) features the Penny Post as a symbol of Victorian progress and, to recall Rowland Hill's words, "an engine of civilization"—despite opposition crystallized in Lord Lichfield's 1837 pronouncement that the Penny Post plan was not only "wild" but "extravagant." I return to Hicks's painting, introduced in chapter 2, to focus on four clusters of relevant details and figures on the left half of the canvas that carry economic, social, and political meaning: letters bearing Penny Red and Two Pence Blue postage stamps; a lost child and four patrons, hurrying to make the last post of the day; a pickpocket reaching into the pocket of an unsuspecting patron; and a policeman, arresting the pickpocket (see figure 26). These four interrelated images, which I will treat in turn, not only recall Victorian culture and society, they illuminate how the Penny Post served as a point of origin for inventive technologies of the late twentieth and twenty-first centuries.

Letters displaying Penny Red (1d) and Two Pence Blue stamps (2d) in Hicks's painting bring to mind the opening of the Penny Post and signal innovation. Prepaid stamps and stationery revolutionized the mail network in a

FIGURE 26. Detail from *The General Post Office, One Minute to Six,* by George Elgar Hicks, 1860. © Museum of London.

postal age, linking individuals across the United Kingdom in a web of regular and frequent exchanges by post. Letters weighing up to half an ounce could travel anywhere in Britain for a penny. The democratic measure that enabled this system toppled class-based franking along with the practice of charging postage by number of sheets and enclosures and distance traveled that resulted in the high fees due on delivery that the middle and lower classes often could not afford.

Next, we turn to Hicks's figure of the lost child on the brink of tears, gazing with scared eyes at a kindly man in a black top hat who has come to her aid. She is the first in a cluster of five figures, arranged from left to right in the front foreground of the canvas, that form a kind of tableau of anxious Post Office patrons—all of them looking earnestly toward the Post Office window that lies somewhere outside the picture plane. After the figure of the lost child, beginning just under the raised arm of her kind helper, we see a nervous errand boy holding two stacks of letters stamped with 1d and 2d stamps. Hicks has painted him with a fixed gaze and set jaw suggestive of tension and urgency. He appears to be worried about whether or not he will get these letters, presumably from the business employing him, to the window on time. Behind the errand boy, a young woman, probably in her late teens, leans forward in a red cloak. Her wide, stunned eyes and parted lips (suggestive of breathlessness, even panic) register urgency and distress. She is succeeded by the figure of a well-dressed lady in a brown gown, dark tartan shawl, and off-white bonnet, who inclines toward the window counter, rushing to get her 2d letter into the last daily post. Finally, we see a little girl in a red plaid dress and brown cape and hat, holding a letter with a Penny Red stamp, who gazes uneasily in the direction of the counter. Taken singly, but especially regarded as a group or tableau, these figures evoke the bewilderment and anxiety that many Victorians experienced following the legislation of cheap postage as they rushed every day among chaotic, mixed crowds to make the last daily post.

Behind and to the left of the lost child, we see another cluster of figures: a boy pickpocket, his intended victim—an unsuspecting genteel woman in pale lilac–gray dress and a pink bonnet—and a tall, bearded policemen whose arm reaches forward to intervene in the crime. Together, the three figures retell one of the main narratives that accompanied the coming of the Penny Post—that it brought the innocent and unsuspecting into dangerous contact with criminal elements in society.

The figure of the blue-uniformed policeman, who appears to be stopping the pickpocket mid-theft, stands as an emblem of the law and brings to mind the groups of policemen who marshaled crowds on opening day of the Penny Post in St. Martin's-le-Grand. The insignia "A29," visible on the policeman's collar, designates his division and exact number in a London police squad. By using this exact detail in his depiction of the policeman, Hicks affirms both the authority and legitimacy of the law. This detail, coupled with the immediacy of the policeman's represented action—we see him *in the act* of stopping a crime (quite literally extending the arm of the law)—also suggests the precision and immediacy involved in policing in general. Among the few completely upright figures in Hicks's painting, the policeman has a pillar-like attitude that brings a kind of reassuring order to the chaos and welter of humanity Hicks portrays.

The ideas suggested by these figures—by precisely depicted Penny Reds and Two Penny Blues on the soon-to-be-posted envelopes (innovation), by the apprehensive patrons (confusion and anxiety in response to something radical and new), by the pickpocket and his victim (the potential for crime), and by the interposing policeman (law and order)—not only comprise the principal elements involved in the story of the Victorian revolution in letter writing. Together, they anticipate the excitement, challenges, and dangers of information technologies today.

INNOVATION FROM THE VICTORIAN POST TO CYBERSPACE

The Victorian inventions of the stamp and prepaid stationery anticipate our desire to stay connected with friends and family, as well as our present fascination with progress in the field of communications. As Eileen Cleere advances in *Avuncularism*, "Indeed, the Victorian ideology of kinship as frequent communication is not far removed from our late twentieth-century belief that kinship is *tele*communication" (203–4). David Henkin concurs with this view: "A postal network that became popular during the middle of the nineteenth century laid the cultural foundation for the experiences of interconnectedness that are the hallmarks of the brave new world of telecommunications" (ix). To people who regularly surf the Web or send e-mails and text messages—hallmarks of modern communication—stamps and postal stationery seem commonplace or even quaint. To the Victorians, these inventions, along with the telegraph and telephone, were among the greatest innovations of their time.

With an affordable postal network in place, Victorians leaving home no longer "bore" what Harriet Martineau called "the depth of silence" (*History* 2: 425). Martineau suggested to her Victorian public that life before the Penny Post was similar to that during the time of the Crusaders, when husbands and sons went to war, knowing it might be months or years before they heard from their loved ones again: "till a dozen years ago, it did not occur to many of us how like this was the fate of the largest classes in our own country" (*History* 2: 425). With letters traveling cheaply and swiftly by rail and, in time, by ship, Victorians who left home for employment, to serve their country, or to emigrate to New Zealand, Canada, or America no longer had to endure "the depth of silence" or lose contact with their circle of family and friends.[1]

Kinship ties still motivate information technologies in our global, digital information age. Parents parting with children who will study abroad for a semester or husbands and wives going to war in foreign countries now know that their loved ones are only an e-mail, text message, or phone call away. Peer-to-peer Internet telephony networks allow for inexpensive voice and video conferencing across the world. Communications technologies today have inherited from an earlier communications network the ability to transcend boundaries of time and space. Writing about nineteenth-century America in *The Postal Age*, Henkin lauds the coming of cheap postage as a time "when a critical mass of Americans began reorganizing their perceptions of time, space, and community around the existence of the post" (3). Howard Rhein-gold in *The Virtual Community* uses compellingly similar vocabulary to de-scribe computer-mediated communication (CMC), such as computer confer-encing, "as a tool for using the communication capacities of the networks to build social relationships across barriers of space and time" (7).

Cutting-edge technologies attract us beyond the desire to stay connected. Just as Victorians in record numbers rushed to attend the Great Exhibition of 1851 to marvel over Edwin Hill and Warren De La Rue's envelope-folding ma-chine and other innovations, just as the early Victorians clamored to the Post Office on January 10, 1840, to be among the first to post a letter for a penny and cheer for Rowland Hill, today we stand in line, or even camp out overnight, to be the first to purchase new technology to facilitate instant communication. In *The Virtual Community*, Rheingold pinpoints the human desire for what is up-to-the-minute and life changing: "these new media attract colonies of enthusiasts because CMC enables people to do things with each other in new ways, and to do altogether new kinds of things—just as telegraphs, telephones, and televisions did" (6). New technologies, which enable people to do "new kinds of things," in turn, bolster the economy by fostering business—a reality Hicks represents in *The General Post Office* in the figures of errand boys post-ing letters and workers sorting newspapers.

As fans of material progress, we continue to look forward to and purchase new products, including Web-controlled consumer gadgets for information processing and "smart machines" and related technologies guided by artifi-cial intelligence.[2] A caption in one of Dave Whamond's recent *Reality Check* cartoons reads: "I've got an iphone, an ipod, iphoto, and an ibook . . . Now I just have to get an ilife."[3] Arguably, this spirit of revolution in commercial progress dates to an earlier information revolution in the Victorian era, which witnessed an enormous rise in literacy, a widespread dissemination of infor-mation, and what William Lewins characterized as an "infinite extension and growth" in communications (247). Has the "i" prefix merely replaced the "penny" prefix, which dominated the Victorian information industry, as in *The Penny Magazine* (1832–45), *The Penny Illustrated Paper* (1861–1913), as well as Penny Dreadfuls and other Penny Part serials?[4]

Many of our current innovations in communication now sacrosanct to mo-bile professionals—the laptop and, most importantly, access to the Internet—arguably have extended rather than replaced the Victorian invention of the Penny Post by inviting in an even wider range of readers, writers, and speakers. The telegraph and telephone swiftly followed the Penny Post, illustrating how new inventions often stand alongside and, in time, gain precedence over what we come to see as old-fashioned or commonplace. Most sizeable English towns offered electric telegraph service by 1857, and the Post Office incorporated the telegraph in 1869.[5] Noting parallels between the telegraph and the Internet, Tom Standage advances in *The Victorian Internet* that during Queen Victoria's reign, long before the advent of our information superhighway, the telegraph was dubbed the "highway of thought" because it allowed people to transmit messages from one telegraphic apparatus to another almost instantly across countries, continents, and oceans.[6] The paths e-mail messages take in traveling through cyberspace from mail server to mail server recall the journeys of telegraph messages that operators spelled out in Morse code along wires from telegraph to telegraph. As Standage observes, "Although it has now faded from view, the telegraph lives on within communications technologies that have subsequently built upon its foundations: the telephone, the fax machine, and, more recently, the Internet. And, ironically, it is the Internet—despite being considered as a quintessentially modern means of communication—that has the most in common with its telegraphic ancestor" (205).

While Standage singles out the telegraph as the predecessor of cutting-edge online technology, calling it the Victorian forerunner of the Internet and the "mother of all networks," arguably the latter epithet belongs to an even earlier information network—the Penny Post. While today we occupy a world of global communications, an electronic frontier populated by "virtual communities," the Penny Post—empowered by Ralph Allen's organized system of cross posts (1720), John Palmer's mail coaches (1784), and nationwide railway service (c. 1847)—is the engine that first made it possible to stay connected with family and friends despite their travels and emigrations. The formation of the World Postal Union in 1874, an outcome of the International Postal Congress held in Bern, Switzerland, that same year, led to a postal network that overcame national boundaries in enabling the British to correspond with most of Europe, Turkey, Egypt, and the United States for a relatively uniform and cheap international rate. More countries swiftly joined this union, renamed the Universal Postal Union in 1878, which established a model for global communications—a hallmark of computer-mediated communication today. The Internet inherits from the Penny Post and the Universal Postal Union a model of opportunity: the chance to communicate with people living in other countries long before meeting them and to interact and conduct business virtually with people one may never meet in person.

Technology is always upgrading itself and making once-heralded innovations outmoded, quaint, less desirable, or obsolete. Following swiftly on the heels of communication by telegraph and Penny Post, the first telephone exchange in London occurred in 1879, with the Post Office acquiring telephone service in 1882.[7] By the late 1880s, the telephone was flourishing as the telegraph was waning, its heyday over by the end of Queen Victoria's reign. This pattern, where new inventions in telecommunications stand alongside the old as they replace them, remains ongoing. The fax machine of the 1980s offered nearly instantaneous transfer of copies via the telephone network. Due to problems in quality and proprietary format of faxes, e-mail has become the primary mode of electronic transmission of documents with faxing assuming a peripheral position. Landlines still have a place in telecommunications, but the 1980s launched commercial cellular networks, and the 1990s witnessed the rise of mobile phones (as well as a miniaturization of them). In addition to the voice function of the standard telephone, mobiles allow a full range of services, including Short Message Service (SMS) and Multimedia Messaging Service (MMS).[8] People now rely on mobile technologies to conduct business from any location, including trains, planes, and cars, and to reach out to friends and family in the midst of any away from a landline activity, including exercising, shopping, or traveling. As the mobile phone gains primacy in the twenty-first century for talking and texting, people are electing to drop landline service altogether, keeping mobile service as their sole means of phone communication.

The laptop computer, made commercially available in 1981, builds upon its nineteenth-century precursor, the Victorian writing desk. As I note in chapter 3, there were more writing desks in the Victorian period than ever before. In addition to rising literacy rates, desk production soared because the Penny Post made letter writing affordable across the social classes. Moreover, the grand display of writing products at the Great Exhibition of 1851 actually increased middle-class demand for these commodities, leading to the mass production of affordable, commercially-made desks for the populace.[9]

The portable desk, which developed out of the medieval lectern, gave way to the table desk, the briefcase, and the twentieth-century laptop, forging a connection between epistolary space and cyberspace. In fact, a writing desk might aptly be called a Victorian laptop.[10] The Victorians found their writing desks indispensable for storing writing materials (pens, papers, stamps, wafers, seals, sealing wax, ink, et cetera) as well as their valuables (including money and jewelry), business papers and vital documents (such as passports and wills), and private correspondence (such as love letters). Lap desks were secure because of their key locks. Their portability made them handy in the days before electricity and heating, and their small size proved convenient for travel. Likewise, in our increasingly mobile, global world, a wide range of pro-

fessionals, as well as students, view mobile devices, including laptop computers, as indispensable for generating and developing information that is secure
and portable. These devices conveniently allow us to save and analyze data, to
write, compose, create, design, record, and store. Victorians locked their writing desks with keys and often stowed information in hidden or secret drawers.
In the case of our contemporary, password-protected laptops, a password is
equivalent to a key. And though portable digital devices do not have actual
"secret drawers," they *do* use "virtual" drawers for security: individuals can
devise elaborate filing systems to make sure information remains safe even in
the event that someone gains access to their passwords.

The laptop is but one twentieth-century communications innovation with
its prototype in the Victorian postal age. Victorians' collect-on-delivery letters
are comparable to today's collect phone calls. The term "return of post" that
Victorian letter writers could use to direct receivers to send responses by the
next earliest daily mail anticipates the "return receipt requested" option some
people select to ensure an e-mail is received. Speed of communication was as
important to the Victorian information revolution as it is to current communications technologies. Developments in railways and steamships speeded the
delivery of the post. Telegraphs and telephones, which came under the jurisdiction of the Post Office, brought increased cash flow to Post Office revenues
and, in turn, made for an improved postal system. Similarly, e-mail and text
messaging have created new ways of conducting business, particularly online
sales, while advancing speed of communication. Conversely, just as letters got
lost during the Victorian age—moldering in fire hydrants mistaken for post
boxes, "stolen" from post boxes by birds using the boxes for nesting purposes,
or dropped during treacherous deliveries (one circa 1887 missive found its
way into a block of ice on the Thames off Deptford)[11]—e-mails go astray in
cyberspace: lost in transit, some e-mail never finds its way to its destination,
while other messages are delayed or incorrectly tagged as spam. What was
once anticipation of a billet-doux has transformed into waiting for a phone
call, for an e-mail—the premise of the 1998 romantic comedy *You've Got Mail*,
starring Tom Hanks and Meg Ryan—and most recently, for text messages.

The Penny Post established a postal network that the Universal Postal
Union expanded into a "postal zone without national borders" (Henkin 173)
so that people could affordably interact with others they did and did not know
despite geographical boundaries. Communication became more regular, distance surmountable, and the world somehow smaller. The Victorian inventions of the postage stamp and prepaid stationery, followed by the telegraph
and the telephone, shrank the world, which continues to grow smaller daily

as we usher in more cutting-edge technologies, such as global mobile phones, teleconferencing, Wi-Fi, and social networking sites.[12] We pay bills online, buy consumer products, send text messages across the globe, receive electronic bank statements, take correspondence courses, send announcements and invitations, make friends, and meet potential mates through online dating services. Communications companies promote electronic multitasking via one-bill systems for local and long distance phone and high speed Internet services, making it all the easier to stay connected.[13]

Daily the possibilities for communication in virtual communities grow:

> People in virtual communities use words on screens to exchange pleasantries and argue, engage in intellectual discourse, conduct commerce, exchange knowledge, share emotional support, make plans, brainstorm, gossip, feud, fall in love, find friends and lose them, play games, flirt, create a little high art and a lot if idle talk. People in virtual communities do just about everything people do in real life, but we leave our bodies behind. You can't kiss anybody and nobody can punch you in the nose, but a lot can happen within those boundaries. (Rheingold 3)

Just as the Victorians heralded the coming of the Penny Post and, in turn, the telegraph for improvements in education, commerce, and kinship, today we turn to the Internet for business, romance, friendship, entertainment, education, and global understanding. The possibilities for the Web are boundless because, as is common with any technological revolution, the Web itself is undergoing constant transformation.

As Timothy O'Reilly observes in an online article, following the "bursting of the dot-com bubble in the Fall of 2001 . . . the web was more important than ever, with exciting new applications and sites popping up with surprising regularity" (1). Companies that survived this collapse and thrived did so because, according to O'Reilly, they are part of Web 2.0, a term O'Reilly coined in 2005 to describe the next generation of Web technology. Web 2.0 is a service more than a product: it is a "platform" like Web 1.0, but it collectively harnesses intelligence through hyperlinking and enables social interaction among users during their online experiences. Companies like Amazon.com and eBay that leverage Web 2.0 technologies grow organically from the collective activity of their users, who become participants and codevelopers: that is, users can create, publish, and manage content provided by sharers, and the technology itself benefits by aggregating the input of its countless virtual users.[14] Looking forward from the days when Victorians rushed to get a stamped letter into the post by 6:00 p.m. to today, when people rush to be the first to use "i" products and "leave their bodies behind" to enter cyberspace—a conceptual world where people interact through computer-mediated technologies—we can only imagine what the future has in store for communications.

FROM BEWILDERMENT AND ANXIETY AT ST. MARTIN'S-LE-GRAND TO TECHNO-ANXIETY

While many people embrace new technology with an excitement and absorption that we inherited from our Victorian predecessors, others approach these inventions with bewilderment—a sentiment embodied in the figure of the little girl lost in the commotion of closing time at St. Martin's-le-Grand in Hicks's *The General Post Office*. Her body language and facial expression— like those of the four equally nervous patrons arranged in the painting to her right—display the anxiety many Victorians must have experienced post-1840 in entering a public space where people of many types, classes, and ages commingled in one common locale to get their letters into the last post before closing time. The nineteenth century offered frequent and speedy postal deliveries, widely facilitated by the railway by 1847. The Post Office maintained schedules to ensure swift and timely deliveries and, as a result, devised a scheme of fees for late letters. The designation "Too late" on Margaret Hale's long-awaited letter from her fugitive brother, Frederick, stating he is safely out of England in Elizabeth Gaskell's *North and South* (1855), means, as Gaskell's narrator surmises, Frederick likely "trusted" his letter "to some careless waiter, who had forgotten to post it" (260). It might be more accurate to say that the waiter failed to post the letter in time for the last dispatch of the day, which is why it would have been marked "too late." This designation on a letter also speaks to the promptness of postal deliveries in the Victorian age, leading to the frenzy at one minute to closing time that Hicks illustrates on canvas.

This sense of anxiety over technology and change seems endemic to how humans respond to any revolution in industry and communications. Linda Simon makes this very point in her book about the coming of electricity in nineteenth-century America. Called *Dark Light*, it is fittingly subtitled *Electricity and Anxiety from the Telegraph to the X-Ray*: "Like our nineteenth-century forebears, we feel, at times, overwhelmed, powerless, and exhausted. In part those feelings stem from the media's thrilled or ominous—but always hyperbolic—reporting about the new. In part our concerns are generated by confusion about whom to trust when experts disagree, sometimes violently, about how technologies might affect us, our children, the world" (299). Simon's words aptly apply to the coming of the Penny Post. In addition to the frenzy of patrons rushing to make the last posting, emotional anxiety arose because Victorians disagreed, "sometimes violently," about the outcomes of Uniform Penny Postage, much as media experts today vehemently express opposing views about the Internet, creating confusion and fear of the new. Consider, for example, rival views of two respected Victorians featured in this book—journalist, historian, and author, Harriet Martineau, and Tory states-man and regular contributor to the *Quarterly Review*, John Wilson Croker. To Martineau, prior to this measure, "hundreds of thousands of apprentices, of shopmen, of governesses, of domestic servants, were cut off from family relations as if seas or deserts lay between them and home" (*History* 2: 426). By contrast, in ominous words, Croker warns of pernicious "spawns" of the Penny Post: "Will clerks write only to their fathers, and girls to their mothers? Will not letters of romance or love, intrigue or mischief, increase in at least equal proportions?" (532). In Martineau's eyes, postal reform is a social and moral good; in Croker's, it is a harbinger of immorality.

Likewise, opposing views of the Internet flood the media today. Many ex-perts, including Howard Rheingold and David Weinberger, see both sides of computer-mediated communication, each offering reasons for optimism and caution. For Rheinghold, "because of its potential influence on so many peo-ple's beliefs and perceptions, the future of the Net is connected to the future of community, democracy, education, science, and intellectual life—some of the human institutions people hold most dear, whether or not they know or care about the future of computer technology" (6). Weinberger cautions, on the other hand, that "the distancelessness of the Web is just the most obvious of the disconnects between it and the real world." He compares the Web to a "new world that we're just beginning to inhabit" but cites one important differ-ence: "The Web . . . has no geography, no landscape. It has no distance. It has nothing natural in it. . . . We don't yet even know how to talk about a place that has no soil, no boundaries, no near, no far" (6, 8–9). Does the "disconnect" between virtual and real life temper, or perhaps even undermine, the benefits for humanity linked to computer-mediated communication?

To this Web-driven informational plenitude, whether it bodes well or ill, we can compare the flurry of activity in St. Martin's-le-Grand one minute before closing time. Hicks represents a human commotion so urgent that it not only seems to have distracted the unwitting pickpocket victim and distressed any number of nervous Post Office patrons, but it also inundates the viewer with synesthetic stimuli—sights, sounds, smells, gestures, motions—that approxi-mate the information overload techno-wary computer users experience on a daily basis. I cite one important difference in the location of anxiety. Hicks locates signals of apprehension largely in the faces of the younger figures in his work: a lost child, a pair of errand boys, several girls and young women—all urgently gathered to post their letters. Called upon to similarly portray apprehension among Internet users, we would likely depict senior citizens. Undeniably, computer phobia exists among some young people, but by and large, how many adults turn to their tech-savvy children and grandchildren—members of the Net generation who have grown up with the Internet and mobile phones— to ask for advice on how to set up e-mail accounts or input friends' numbers into a mobile phone? A recent survey by the Pew Internet and American Life Project reveals that 15 percent of those polled who are age 60 and older do not have a mobile phone or access to the Internet. Of the 85 percent of Americans who use the Internet and mobile phones, only 10 percent take advantage of all the features and benefits mobile phones offer. Moreover, of the 49 percent of Americans who describe themselves as "occasional" tech gadget users and the 20 percent who describe themselves as "middle-of-the-road," 11 percent of the former group and 10 percent of the latter group find electronic communication "annoying" or "intrusive" and describe information overload as a "hassle."[15] While undeniably many seniors use mobile phones and some embrace the Internet, the terms Simon uses to describe the Victorian response to the advent of electrification—"overwhelmed, powerless, and exhausted"—also aptly describe how a large segment of our present-day "techno-wary" population has responded to computer technology since its inception. This response is tinged with mistrust not unlike that of the Victorians who experienced the increased accessibility of people and businesses to each other via the Penny Post as an invasion of privacy and domestic sanctity.[16]

Computer technology has become an increasingly intricate, vital part of our daily lives. Library catalogues are online, schools use programs to report student grades, e-mail has replaced interoffice communication, and businesses and academic institutions continue to embrace technology for academic, administrative, and financial matters. As computer networks link homes, businesses, organizations, schools, and academic institutions, people, young and old, who do not use or cannot afford new technology will feel increasingly left behind in our quest for more efficient and effective communication. Computer-mediated communication has thus given rise to a syndrome researchers define as "computer anxiety." Psychologists L. D. Rosen and M. M. Weil have identified three levels of computer anxiety, also called technophobia: the uncomfortable user, who is slightly anxious; the cognitive technophobe, who seems calm on the outside but fears hitting the wrong button and is self-conscious about lack of knowledge; and the anxious technophobe, who demonstrates physical symptoms of panic when using the computer.[17]

While some people avoid the computer because of "computer anxiety," others face their techno fears by taking courses to familiarize themselves with the computer and thereby reduce their anxiety. Local libraries and continuing education programs offer courses to introduce novices of all ages to technology, typically for a small fee. Among the older set, computer-supported social networking, which provides access to children and grandchildren, becomes increasingly attractive. As a Verizon Wireless spokeswoman concludes, "'you can't discount the older-than-25 crowd.'"[18] More and more we define ourselves in relation to an increasingly virtual world, an idea informing books and articles in major publications ranging from *Science News* to *Business Week*, the *New York Times*, and *abcnews.com*.[19] As more elementary and middle school–age children grow up with technology and use it to text their friends, check their e-mail, make friends on Facebook, or download episodes of their favorite TV shows onto their mobile phones; as today's Net Gen youth become the parents and seniors of the future, computer anxiety will become a fear of the past, as did the once-potent fears surrounding the advent of electricity and prepaid postage. Still, the bewilderment Hicks represents in the faces of the anxious Post Office patrons in his 1860 painting of St. Martin's-le-Grand has an enduring relevance for information technology: the fear of computers will likely shift to inventions in communications not even dreamed of today.

"GO[ING] THE WRONG SIDE OF THE POST" AND THE INTERNET

Criminal mischief, symbolized by the pickpocket in Hicks's painting, quite obviously enters into our experience of current information technology, where it takes the form of junk mail, scams, phishing, viruses, and target mail—problems that arguably stem from the rise of the Victorian Penny Post almost 170 years ago. As I explored in chapter 1, postal crime long predated the coming of the Penny Post. In fact, postal reformers, including Rowland Hill, Henry Cole, and Harriet Martineau, seized on numerous ruses people devised to avoid paying postage as reasons why the post needed reform in the first place. Some senders took advantage of the payment on delivery option, deliberately mailing out blank letters, for which receivers refused to pay: the letter itself signaled that its sender was well. A casualty of this ruse, Samuel Taylor Coleridge tried in 1822 to play Good Samaritan in the Lake District by paying a shilling for a poor woman to receive what turned out to be a blank letter.[20]

When Rowland Hill traveled the Lake District in 1823 (these were the days when MPs had free franking privileges), he admittedly practiced a mild form of postal evasion then widely used with newspapers. To save his family the expense of receiving his mail but still convey information about his well-being, Hill sent home old newspapers, each franked with the name of a member of Parliament. To signal ill health, he used the name of a conservative Tory; the name of a liberal signaled Hill's vigor and wellness (Hill and Hill 1: 240).

People often seize upon new technologies as a way to make big money—legally or illegally. Following postal reform, the practice of candling that Hill and others tied to Post Office crime was no longer needed to determine the cost of a letter. As a result, more people trusted sending money and valuables through the post, which, critics of the Penny Post argued, sorely tempted postal employees to commit theft.[21] Likewise, as Standage points out in *The Victorian Internet*, just as reform-era "scam artists found crooked ways to make money by manipulating the transmission of stock prices and the results of horse races using the telegraph," their twentieth- and twenty-first-century "counterparts have used the Internet to set up fake 'shop fronts' purporting to be legitimate providers of financial services, before disappearing with the money handed over by would-be investors" and "hackers have broken into improperly secured computers and made off with lists of credit card numbers" (208). Evidently, the temptation to evade laws, reap huge profits on new products, and manipulate the naïve (hence the enduring term, "caveat emptor") is a human tendency in all eras. Today, as in the Victorian age, innovation opens opportunities for criminal activity in both real and virtual worlds.

In addition to the fake shop fronts and hacking with which we sometimes must contend, legitimate and illegitimate solicitations of money by businesses, social action networks, and environmental and political groups spam and jam both our e-mail and regular mailboxes. So do advertisements, by the hundreds, for clothes, books, catalogues, magazines, vitamins, so-called male enhancement products, weight loss solutions, miracle cures of various kinds, and so on. These unsolicited, often unwanted, missives continue to increase and show no sign of abating. Web 2.0 supports "open source software" that is architecturally designed to encourage participation from sharers and users, keeping the Web "open" to participation by the honorable and the dishonorable alike. This very terminology of "openness" recalls Victorian opposition to the Penny Post on account of its being open to blackmailers, swindlers, seducers, independent-minded women, and organizations that flooded the mail with circulars to repeal the Corn Laws, to promote a host of products (such as patent medicines, seed catalogues, pattern books), and to practice fraud on unsuspecting customers. Returning to Croker's remark from his 1839 *Quarterly Review* commentary, political radicals and religious sectarians zealously supported the Penny Post, because they benefited from the opportunities it provided to push their causes. In his view, the Penny Post was "'*Sedition made easy*'" (532).

Today, communications-based troublemaking often takes the form of frauds and scams that steal or misuse our financial information. Many spam offers are actually cyberscams that involve "phishing"—where one user claims falsely to be the representative of a legitimate company (like eBay, AOL, or PayPal) in order to "pickpocket" his or her contact's private information, including account passwords, credit card numbers, social security numbers, and so on. Such cyberscams are a form of identity theft and often involve hackers' attempts to gain access to user accounts in order to utilize them for criminal purposes. In a virtual context, cyberscamming, hacking, and identity theft are curiously akin to mail-driven Victorian slander and blackmail—phenomena that took off following the Penny Post. Just as they did during the Victorian era, such dangerous forms of communication target and, in some cases, trade upon or harm the reputations of victims today, who may be as naïve and unsuspecting as the pickpocket's victim in Hicks's vivid portrait of Victorian life. In acting illegally, users who violate network security are, to recall Trollope's idiom from *The Claverings* (1867), "'go[ing] the wrong side of the post'" (178).

The rise of what many Victorians called "curious mailings" also traces to the advent of the Penny Post. In *Household Words* (1850), Dickens and Wills include a conversation with a postal official, who observes, "'of the articles found in the Dead-Letter Office what curious things are trusted to our care'" (10). In fact, commentators and authors of the period often use the term "curiosities" to describe the items channeled through Britain's post offices.[22] J. Wilson Hyde devoted an entire book, *The Royal Mail: Its Curiosities and Romance* (1889), to recounting the anecdotes and odd lore of the British postal system. In a critique of Uniform Penny Postage published in *Administration of the Post Office* (1844), four years after Hill's plan went into effect, the anonymous author argues that postal reform "changed the whole character of the department; it has pretty nearly converted it into a parcel and conveyance delivery company, a public general carrier, a kind of flying bazaar, instead of maintaining its former and permanently honourable position as a board of revenue, and a safe and effective instrument of conducting the correspondence of a great commercial empire" (112).

The rush of curious mailings in the Victorian period following postal reform—plant specimens and tree cuttings, slugs, leeches, samples of corn and hops, manure, wet mosses, et cetera—undeniably has a counterpart in our age of computer-mediated communication: online shopping. Even more than major online stores like Amazon.com, eBay is a shopping and auction Web site that comprises "the collective activity of all of its users" and "grows organically in response to user activity" (O'Reilly 2). In that sense, eBay might aptly be called a "flying bazaar," where with the click of a button we can purchase clothing, jewelry, furniture, and a whole range of curiosities: water that Elvis Presley allegedly sipped during a concert in North Carolina in 1977; a grilled cheese sandwich bearing an image resembling the Virgin Mary; a single cornflake; and the city of Bridgeville, California, sold three times since 2002. In fact, the weird and fascinating items we buy and sell on eBay have garnered substantial media attention, both serious and silly: a CNBC documentary entitled *The eBay Effect: Inside a Worldwide Obsession* that first aired on June 29, 2005; a host of novelty books including, most recently, Christopher Cihlar's 2006 *The Grilled Cheese Madonna and 99 Other of the Weirdest, Wackiest, Most Famous eBay Auctions Ever*; and a 2003 song called "eBay"—Weird Al Yankovic's parody of the Backstreet Boys hit "I Want It That Way"—where the narrator describes all the crazy items he bids on or buys at eBay, including a PEZ dispenser, a pet rock, vintage tube socks, and William Shatner's discarded toupee.[23]

In addition to junk mail and solicitations, which arguably originated in a postal network that rapidly expanded with the Penny Post, the Internet likewise provides ready opportunities for academic fraud, plagiarism, and worse. People can skim online summaries of a novel rather than read the actual book. Prewritten documents are available for sale at a host of Web sites, where a student can purchase an essay or a research paper rather than write it him- or herself.[24] Just as people in the nineteenth century met via telegraph networks, today people can meet in online chat rooms, forming relationships in such "virtual" spaces without ever actually seeing or talking to each other in person. Stories of Internet affairs fill the media. Online predators cloak themselves in the anonymity of the Internet in order to lure victims. The Internet allows anyone who has such an inclination to become a master of disguise.

Facebook, Inc., a social networking site begun in 2004, offers security settings that, for the most part, protect users from sexual predators and stalkers. But the online hangout has grown so rapidly and, in turn, become so profitable, that critics complain Facebook's safeguards are inadequate. In 2007, investigators posing on the site as 12- to 14-year-olds received sexual solicitations from other users—an occurrence that indicates big gaps in company security measures.[25] Alibi Network, a Chicago-based company, offers a twist on Internet self-disguise: for a fee, it provides convincing excuses or lies for those in need. A simple lie might cost only $75.00, while an elaborate lie can cost thousands. Founded in 2005, Alibi fabricates itineraries for bogus conferences, generates fake airline receipts, and creates "virtual hotels," complete with addresses and telephone numbers of where the errant party is supposed to be (actors answer the phones and direct calls to the client's cell phone). As a journalist who profiled the company points out, Alibi "assumes many of its clients are using the service for the purpose of committing adultery. Not exactly uplifting news. But, hey, if Alibi's site is the worst thing you can find on the Internet, then you're not looking that hard" (Tucker 18). With Web 2.0 programs, which invite user involvement to shape them, the possibilities for posing and scamming seem boundless.

Disturbing parallels exist between the Penny Post and cyberspace, because crime and danger inevitably accompany innovation. The unsavory and even criminal activity tied to the Internet's vast distribution of information characterizes both the Victorian Penny Post and the telegraph that succeeded it. With the arrival of the Penny Post, as Lewins notes in *Her Majesty's Mails*, people undermined public safety by sending not only curious but dangerous things through the mail. The poisons and medical wastes that traveled via Penny Post anticipate the hazardous mailings and computer viruses that wreak havoc on both snail mail and cyberspace communications today. As I asked in chapter 4, how different are Victorian concerns over the posting of things the anonymous author of *Administration of the Post Office* calls "frequently offensive, nauseous, and, in a very high degree, mischievous and dangerous" (104) from our current fears about what postal officials today call "target mail"—a term which includes leaking packages, poisons, deadly viruses, hazmat, and bombs? Since the terrorist attacks of September 11, 2001, we fear such mail. We live in an age of anthrax scares and post office bombings. Computer viruses are arguably cyberspace equivalents of noxious, poisonous parcels sent via the Victorian post. Just as actual viruses replicate inside their host, computer viruses can replicate themselves inside the memory, storage, and network systems of a computer and thus harm it in several ways—by deleting files, damaging programs, or depositing "bugs" that cause programs to crash. Viruses can be spread from one computer to another when they share USB (Universal Serial Bus) drives. They can also spread from one computer to an entire computer network via infected software. Akin to viruses, computer worms spread without a host, and e-mail attachments, seemingly harmless files, can become deadly when executed.

The ease with which information can be circulated today—via cable and satellite television, phone lines, and the Internet—intersects its ability to intrude upon and clutter our lives. Our sense of information overload is not unlike what the Victorians experienced post-1840 when unsolicited mail began to enter their private homes on a regular basis. Today, of course, we receive only one daily post—a far cry from the six to twelve deliveries that major urban post offices provided customers during the mid- to late Victorian period. Even so, nonstop phone solicitations from businesses, charities, and social and political organizations intrude upon our daily lives and harass us.

In one of his last works of fiction, *Marion Fay* (1882), Trollope presents the Penny Post as a euphemism for blackmail (3: 248). Though blackmail still occurs, we are perhaps less familiar with that crime than we are with other unsavory elements that enter our lives via regular mail, telephony, electronic messaging systems of various kinds, and the Internet. Phone and e-mail solicitors try to catch the weak and unsuspecting by offering sham offers, "get rich quick" schemes, and phony services calculated to gain access to private homes. We readily associate the Internet with scam artists, identity thieves, hackers, and sexual deviants, all of whom are in no short supply in cyberspace. Looking forward from the Victorian age, we recognize that while the main routes of con-artistry have largely switched from the post to telecommunications and cyberspace, the principle of exploiting the unknowing and innocent continues to thrive today.[26]

LAW AND ORDER FROM THE POST OFFICE TO CYBERSPACE

In *The General Post Office*, Hicks portrays a pickpocket at his work. The thief's surprised face turns toward a policeman, who appears to have just intercepted him with a white-gloved hand. Henry Cole indicates the stabilizing role of the police in St. Martin's-le-Grand in an 1840 article published in *Westminster Review*: "The great hall was nearly filled with spectators, marshalled in a line by the police, to watch the crowds pressing, scuffling and fighting to get first to the window."[27] Hicks's lady in lilac, perhaps conversing with her friend about the latest dress pattern or her hopes of receiving a letter from an admirer, appears unaware that a pickpocket has targeted her as a victim. But the officer is primed to police the crowd and stop crime before it occurs.

While the policeman in Hicks's painting is a traditional figure of law and order, and one clearly associated in his work with the Victorian post, we, too, have policing agencies and security measures that protect our communications. Pickpocketing still exists, of course, in the way Hicks, Dickens, and Cruikshank knew it. (Recall how, in *Oliver Twist* [1838], innocent Oliver gets blamed for stealing Mr. Brownlow's handkerchief, which Cruikshank, in his illustration of the scene, shows the Artful Dodger plucking from the gentleman's pocket.)[28] Beyond its traditional identity as a form of petty theft, however, pickpocketing can also be understood as a metaphor for the assorted shams, scams, cons, and identity thefts that are regularly carried out through our twenty-first-century communications channels.

What are some of the agencies and measures that strive to protect present-day communications? How do we safeguard ourselves from unwanted callers, cyber-pickpocketers, and hackers? Caller ID, first marketed in the 1980s, displays the phone number and, often, the name of the calling party, allowing the receiver to filter calls and thus protect him- or herself from telemarketers and a host of both legal and illegal solicitations. Finding and marketing ways to combat identity theft is big business for venture capital firms, credit agencies, and investors. Both new and established companies extend diverse solutions to this problem on large and small scales, from Fortune 500 companies to individual consumers.[29] With spam mail at epidemic levels and e-mail users receiving hundreds of spam messages daily, software companies have developed antispam software to protect personal home computers, as well as computer networks at businesses and academic institutions.[30] Because junk e-mail continues to get through and legitimate e-mail messages sometimes get tagged and deleted as spam, software companies are constantly working to refine and develop new types of spam blockers. Just as spam mail has engendered antispam products, computer viruses have led to the creation of antivirus softwares. Available since about 1988, antivirus programs provide Internet security for homes, academic and other institutions, and businesses.[31] Such software offers detection and blocking of viruses, worms, and spyware (programs that allow others to see into your computer), while the software companies issue regular, automatic program updates to ensure the latest detection and blocking of new viruses.

To apply the theme of law and order from Hicks's *The General Post Office* to the Internet, antivirus software might aptly be called the "cyberspace police." Just as the Victorian police apprehended criminals, who devised ever-new ways to rob or harass the innocent, weak, or unsuspecting, the companies and programmers creating software to "police" computer-mediated communication have to keep up with ingenious hackers and schemers. While the exact crimes and crime-prevention methods have changed since Hicks's policeman apprehended his pickpocket on canvas, the desire to "'go the wrong side of the post'" and, in turn, the need to create innovative policing technologies to arrest it, endure.

*   *   *

At the beginning of this chapter, I emphasized four groups of figures in Hicks's painting and the themes they convey: the Penny Reds and Two Pence Blues (innovation); apprehensive post office patrons (anxiety and bewilderment); the pickpocket and his victim (crime); the interposing policeman (law and order). Born out of and informing the Victorian revolution in letter writing, these themes also suggest lessons applicable to how we interact with new technologies in our digital age. Hicks recognized that members of his Victorian public wanted to get what each felt was an important communication to St. Martin's-le-Grand before 6:00 p.m. so that they would not have to pay the extra late fee required if they missed the ordinary closing. Closing time generated crowds, and crowds, in turn, created anxiety and bewilderment. The thief would not have been at St. Martin's-le-Grand were there not so many pockets in one place to pick. (The post office crowds that captured Hicks's imagination similarly intrigued Smyth, Cole, Dickens, and other eminent Victorians.) Likewise, our innovations in i-technology have generated real crowds of both techno-savvy users, who embrace new products, and techno-wary users, who feel anxious, left behind, and vulnerable. Hackers and scam artists wouldn't spend so much time in virtual worlds, nor would we require the ongoing services of programmers to intercept and counteract digital misdeeds, were there not so many people eagerly taking advantage of new technologies or rushing to profit, legally and illegally, from the online networks and Web sites whose number and extent continue to increase without abatement.

A Victorian time traveler to the twenty-first century would probably be surprised to find people talking into small rectangles pressed tightly to their ears, staring at or moving print around on flat glass screens, or punching numbers into handheld devices. While mobile phones, personal computers, and igadgets would seem improbable to the Victorian, who mainly communicated by post, technological innovation per se—the anxieties and temptations attending it and the need to regulate the errant tendencies surrounding it— would seem uncannily familiar. Just as they did during the Victorian age, new communications technologies still entrance and bewilder us, attract criminals as well as Good Samaritans, and engender all kinds of regulatory and protective devices and agencies. Taken together, these century-spanning parallels appear to beg the question: along with our passion for progress, have we inherited a concomitant obsession with the complications and challenges that revolutionary change inevitably brings? If we stop a moment to gaze at our high-tech world through Victorian spectacles, we can see it as the unfolding of a Victorian legacy that has shaped and continues to shape our ever-changing communications technologies today.

POSTSCRIPT

The past ten years have been years of great, gradual, and unexampled improvement. Nor is there anything but progress and advancement in prospect. Never at any time in its history were the authorities more alive to the fact that the Post-office is an institution capable of infinite extension and growth . . .

William Lewins, *Her Majesty's Mails*, 1864

'She won't go the wrong side of the post.'

Anthony Trollope, *The Claverings*, 1867

Is there anything gained by way of expedition in making the Post Office a competitor with the general carrier, by this conveyance of parcels of all descriptions,—and of parcels which, in many cases, the senders lying secret and hid, are not only common nuisances, but very frequently offensive, nauseous, and, in a very high degree, mischievous and dangerous?

Administration of the Post Office, 1844

The Post-office, while it is the willing handmaid to commerce, the vehicle of social intercourse, and the necessary helper in almost every enterprise and occupation, becomes at the same time a ready means for the unscrupulous to carry on a wonderful variety of frauds on the public, and enables a whole army of needy and designing persons to live upon the generous impulses of society.

J. Wilson Hyde, *The Royal Mail: Its Curiosities and Romance*, 1889

. . . the Post Office assumes the new and important character of a powerful engine of civilization.

Rowland Hill, *Post Office Reform: Its Importance and Practicability*, 1837

What a mass of tradesmen's patterns and samples, of trade circulars, of bills and small sums of money, of music and books, of seeds and flowers, of small merchandize and friendly gifts, of curious specimens passing among men of science, of bulletins of health to satisfy anxious hearts, is everyday sent abroad over the land—and now spreading over wide oceans and across continents, through Rowland Hill's discovery of a way to throw down the old barriers, and break through the ancient silence!

Harriet Martineau, *The History of England*, 1850

In each of these Victorian commendations, if we substitute "Internet" for the words or concept of "Post Office" or "post," we discover a startling modernity.

Notes

INTRODUCTION

1. See "Letter arrives eight years late," *BBC News*, and "Was It *Really* Lost in the Mail?" *CBS News*, which states: "Some of these long-lost letters probably really were stuck in a mail chute or behind a piece of postal processing machinery—but not all."

2. See "Letter arrives eight years late." See "Greetings from 1956" for incidents of long-lost US letters.

3. "2,500 post offices face closure," *BBC News*, and "2,500 more post offices to close," *BBC News*. Demonstrations proved unsuccessful in, for example, Lacock, UK, where locals and public figures recently protested the closure of the local post office. One prominent protestor was Dame Judi Dench, who recently filmed *Cranford* in Lacock. The determination to close the post office came in March 2008. See "Post office loses battle," by Scott McPherson, in *Wiltshire Gazette & Herald*, March 20, 2008.

4. By 1857, most large English towns were connected by telegraph service, and we can date the first telephone exchange in London to 1879; see Pool, *What Jane Austen Ate*, 152, and "Key Dates" and the online exhibition Victorian Innovation at the British Postal Museum & Archive Web site.

5. Henkin, *The Postal Age*, 80, 64. Though Henkin's observations pertain to the nineteenth-century Unites States Post Office, they apply equally well to post offices in Victorian Britain.

6. For more information, see Robinson, *British Post Office*, 403. (I capitalize Post Office throughout this book to signal its identity as one of Britain's largest and most important bureaucratic institutions.)

7. See C. R. Perry, *Victorian Post Office*, 19.

8. C. R. Perry, *Victorian Post Office*, discusses changes in nineteenth-century communications technologies at length. The British Post Office's takeover of the telephone occurred in 1912. Of course, telegraphs are now obsolete, and while landlines are in decline, mobile phone use is booming globally.

9. See "2,500 more post offices to close," *BBC News*.

10. In "Community impact of PO closures," *BBC News*, a 68-year-old woman comments on using her post office for post, finance, information, and socializing: "'a lot of elderly come to visit and use it too.'"

11. "2,500 post offices face closure," *BBC News*.

12. Breen's cartoon appeared in the Life section of the *Saratogian*, July 10, 2008.

13. See "Key Dates" and the online exhibition Victorian Innovation at the British Postal Museum & Archive Web site. In 1846, London-based mail coach service essentially ended, although horses still carried post in rural areas.

14. Though Henkin's point refers specifically to the American postal system, it also applies to the British Penny Post, which got going sooner.

15. For more on these points and a fuller quotation from Cole, see Asa Briggs, *Victorian Things*, 327, 333.

16. Zurich issued the 6 Rappen and 4 Rappen on March 1, 1843; Geneva released the Double Geneva on October 1, 1843. The Canton of Basel issued the Basel Dove on July 1, 1845. Brazil produced the Bull's Eye stamp on August 1, 1843, and on July 1, 1847, the United States issued 5- and 10-cent stamps featuring, respectively, Benjamin Franklin on a red-brown stamp and George Washington on a black stamp.

17. In the growing area of Victorian material culture studies, I include Valerie Steele's groundbreaking 2001 work, *The Corset: A Cultural History*; conferences, such as "Victorian Materialities," North American Victorian Studies Association (NAVSA), October 10–13, 2007, University of Victoria, Canada; and a forthcoming collection, *Material Possessions: The Objects and Textures of Everyday Life in Imperial Britain*, edited by Dr. Deidre McMahon and Dr. Janet Myers.

18. Briggs titles chapter 1 of *Victorian Things*, "Things as Emissaries"—a term he attributes to T. S. Eliot. An epigraph to this chapter from Eliot's 1947 *Notes Toward the Definition of Culture* reads, "Even the humblest material artefact [*sic*] which is the product and symbol of a particular civilization, is an emissary of the culture out of which it comes" (11).

19. Later in Victoria's reign, certain British dominions and colonies (e.g. India and Canada) used an older effigy of Victoria on stamps.

20. I recommend Humphreys's "Dickens's Use of Letters in *Bleak House.*"

21. See *Letters of Lewis Carroll*, ed. Cohen; *Letters of Anthony Trollope*, ed. Booth; and *Letters and Private Papers of William Makepeace Thackeray*, ed. Ray.

22. See Barker, ed., *The Brontës: A Life*. Richard Redgrave illustrates the effect of receiving a mourning letter in his 1844 painting, *The Poor Teacher*. See figure 21. A color reproduction of this work is available on the *Victorian Web*, <http://www.victorianweb.org/painting/redgrave/paintings/2.html>.

23. See Shields, *Jane Austen*, 19. Francis Austen saved this letter, which was found among his papers after his death.

24. This black-edged notice is item A.L. 349 in the Autograph Letters Collection, Bath Central Library, Bath, UK.

25. See Barker, ed., *The Brontës: A Life*, 46–48.

26. This letter comes from the private collection of John Forbes-Nixon.

27. For more on the specific inequities of the pre-reform British postal system, see Smyth, *Sir Rowland Hill*, 42, and Staff, *Penny Post*, 72.

28. Rowland Hill's nephew, George Birkbeck Hill, edited his uncle's two-volume memoir after his death. I cite it throughout my book as Hill and Hill 1 or 2.

29. See "Post Office Reform," 34. Hill states that this information comes from a "highly respectable merchant and manufacturer of Birmingham."

30. The first pamphlet, which appeared early in January 1837, was marked "Private and confidential" and printed by William Clowes and Sons. Critics suggest that there may have been several editions; see Muir, *Postal Reform*, 42.

31. Jane Austen is more fully quoted in Shields, *Jane Austen*, 145.

32. Due to overwhelming objection, compulsory prepayment never passed, and letters can still be sent unpaid and charged double postage upon delivery; see Robinson, *British Post Office*, 360.

33. James, *Sir Rowland Hill*, 5; James covers much of the same ground as Lewins. Feminist biblical historians redeem Vashti, the banished queen.

34. Posts relaying messages in tandem began in antiquity. For more examples, see Robinson, *British Post Office*, 3.

35. Qtd. in James, *Sir Rowland Hill*, 6; Lewins also discusses Cyrus in *Her Majesty's Mails*, 4–5.

36. See Robinson, *British Post Office*, 3; Robinson notes that private citizens often directed slaves to carry messages for them or dispatched missives via itinerants and other travelers.

37. Fresh riders stationed at twenty-mile intervals carried mail for distances up to 100 miles a day. Trade and exploration made royal messengers important, leading Henry VIII to create a "Master of the Posts" (Lewins 20). Though, according to Robinson, "a definite postal service took shape" at this time (3), England was still behind other European nations. Under Elizabeth I, ordinary citizens could use the Queen's Post, but cost was high, and royal mail took priority (see James, *Sir Rowland Hill*, 9). Unofficial letter carriers existed but were regarded as a potential source of treason under Henry VIII, Elizabeth I, and Stuart rule. To prevent spying, a 1591 law decreed that only official letter carriers could transport mail leaving England. Since the government did not regularly enforce the law, merchants and private messengers continued illegal carriage of letters for a fee.

38. Robinson aptly calls early seventeenth-century postal history "a confusing record" (36). Muir qualifies the accomplishment of Charles I in setting up a public running post by calling it "less a service than a new source of revenue" (11).

39. Dockwra's partner, Robert Murray, claimed he originated the Penny Post, which may be true (see Muir, *Postal Reform*, 14). After Murray's arrest for political reasons, Dockwra laid out an efficient postal system, dividing urban areas into districts (see Staff, *Penny Post*, 39–40).

40. Muir (*Postal Reform*, 14, 182) attributes this argument to E. S. Gladstone, author of *Great Britain's First Postage Stamps*.

41. Qtd. in Robinson, 207. In 1773, Dublin began a Penny Post. In 1793, the British government took over a successful private Penny Post that Peter Williamson started in Edinburgh in 1773 or 1774. The 1790s witnessed successful penny posts in Birmingham, Bristol, and Manchester.

42. For discussion of the bye-road and cross-post-road systems, I recommend Robinson, *British Post Office*, 101–5, and Staff, *Penny Post*, 62. Allen (who made his fortune in the Bath limestone quarries) became mayor of Bath in 1742 and dramatically increased postal service across England in the first half of the eighteenth century.

43. Robinson, *British Post Office*, vii. Palmer, son of a Bath theater proprietor, became a Bath theater licensee.

44. Wymer, *Social Reformers*, 13, notes some of the surprising parcels covered by the franking system.

45. See also the advice under "General Hints" in the introduction to *Wide World Letter Writer*, xxv.

46. The Bray example comes from the philatelic collection of John Forbes-Nixon. Harriet Russell includes seventy-five of the 130 illustrated envelopes she posted in 1998 in *Envelopes: A Puzzling Journey Through the Royal Mail*.

47. Qtd. in Muir, 31–32.

48. Rowland and his brother Arthur wrote about Hazelwood, which established the Hills as educational reformers. Rowland and his brother Matthew were founding members of the Society for the Diffusion of Useful Knowledge, initiated by Henry Brougham and publisher Charles Knight.

49. Lewins in *Her Majesty's Mails*, 19, notes that this instruction dates to the reign of Edward II. In New Zealand, Post Haste Couriers Ltd. specializes in express delivery and takes its name from this saying.

50. As I note in my methodology, Henkin advances a similar argument in relation to Victorian America. I apply some of his terms to Victorian Britain, where the postal age began earlier.

51. The use of stamped paper for communications apparently began in Italy in the 1820s, where it was short lived.

CHAPTER 1. WHY THE VICTORIANS NEEDED A REVOLUTION IN LETTER WRITING

Author's note: For the full letter excerpted in the chapter 1 epigraph, see F. G. Kenyon's edition of Elizabeth Barrett Browning's *Letters*, 1: 141–42.

1. I refer the reader to Daunton, *Royal Mail*, 7.

2. The term "postman" replaced "letter carrier" in 1883 with the creation of a Parcel Post. See Daunton, *Royal Mail*, 59.

3. This chapter considers several authors' versions of this story, including James in *Sir Rowland Hill*; Hey in *Rowland Hill*; Martineau in *History of England*; and Smyth in *Sir Rowland Hill*.

4. "Touching anecdotes" and egregious examples of postal fraud form part of the lengthy appendix of Hill's *Post Office Reform*, where an important vignette involving Samuel Taylor Coleridge also appears.

5. For English census information, see "Key Dates in the Sociological History and Development of Great Britain," <http://www.thepotteries.org/dates/census.htm>. The 1801 census showed Britain's population as 8.3 million.

6. For more on the petition drive of the Mercantile Committee on Postage, see Staff, *Penny Post*, 83.

7. Hooper also published W. H. Ashurst's 142-page postal reform pamphlet.

8. This story appears in both the English (2: 114) and the American (200) editions of Coleridge's *Letters*, both published in 1836.

9. Cleere in *Avuncularism*, 179, erroneously identifies the players as a barmaid and her

brother and incorrectly references Hill and Hill, *Life of Sir Rowland Hill* (2: 239). The story actually appears in Hill and Hill 1: 239, and it is essentially the same version as Coleridge's— the parties are a mother and a son—although Hill calls the "carter" a "letter-carrier." In *Sir Rowland Hill*, Smyth, in a footnote (60), indicates many versions of the story that turn the absent son into a father or husband. In *History of England*, Martineau, like Smyth, calls the deliverer a "postman" (1: 425). I am grateful to Robert Johnson, a philatelist in Bristol, UK, for supplying distinctions among the terms "carter," "letter carrier," and "postman."

10. See Hill and Hill, 1: 239, where the actual story and Martineau's apocryphal version are both mentioned in an extended note.

11. This version of the story also appears in Rowland Hill's memoir; see Hill and Hill 1: 239.

12. Robinson refers to French and Spanish postal histories that embellish the tale. See *British Post Office*, 264, n. 24.

13. Postal evasion is apparently not exclusive to Britain. Twentieth-century Italian post offices used to cover postcards with paper sleeves so that the messages could not be read until postage due was paid.

14. I refer the reader to the complete anecdote at the *Glassine Surfer* Web site: <http://www.glassinesurfer.com/stamp_collecting/gsrowlandhill.shtml>.

15. Some critics suggest there were five editions—two came out in either February or March of 1837. See Muir, *Postal Reform*, 42.

16. Hill includes Burdett's name in both versions of the tale.

17. Daunton reproduces Tenniel's cartoon in *Royal Mail*, 4.

18. Letter 133018 in the British Library's Fletcher Collection. In this letter, the writer asks the recipient not to beat a hunting dog, Mungo, for losing a pheasant.

19. Reported in *The Post Circular* 7 (Friday, May 11, 1838), 37–38.

20. Martineau published *History of England* in 1849–50 in two volumes. A revised one-volume edition appeared from George Bell and Sons in 1877–78. In this later version, Martineau still incorrectly maintains that the story is about a brother and sister.

21. These prices seem considerably higher than those Hughes and Bentley record in their histories of daily life in Regency and Victorian England.

22. Since Somerset is in southwest England and a deputy lieutenant could be considered a magistrate, this could conceivably be a version of the same tale.

23. See Hibbert, *Daily Life in Victorian England*, 72.

24. Likewise, Rowland Hill at age eight ran to the pawnshop to raise postage. This skit is commonly referred to as "Queen Victoria and the Uniform Penny Postage—A Scene at Windsor Castle" in texts including Fryer and Akerman's.

25. In *Avuncularism*, Cleere situates "the unreformed Post Office and the pawnshop as points on the same continuum of family demoralization" (172).

26. The word "connection" and variations of it appear in the advertising logos for many telecommunications companies. Wi-Fi Zone, a global nonprofit alliance for wireless communication, uses this very language: "WI-ZONE Helps Travelers Stay Connected Around the World." BT-FON of BT, the premier fixed-line telecommunications and broadband Internet provider in the UK, offers the opportunity to be "part of the world's largest Wi-Fi Community" and "allows its members to connect for free in thousands of places around the

UK and the world." Phone companies promise customers they can "stay connected when it matters most" via affordable services, including digital cellular phone and nationwide walkie-talkie services. In 2005, Motorola and Nextel announced that the Motorola i760 "helps individuals stay connected when it matters most." Also see Cleere, *Avuncularism*, 203–4, on MCI's Friends and Family Plan.

27. See Martineau's "Letter to Sir Thomas Wilde, M.P." (hereafter cited as "Letter to TW") in Pearson Hill's *Post Office of Fifty Years Ago*, 44.

28. For remarks on rural isolation in respect to the post, see *The Post Circular* 14 (June 28, 1839), 63.

29. Qtd. in Pearson Hill, *Post Office of Fifty Years Ago*, 46. Pearson Hill reprints Martineau's full letter along with Sir Rowland Hill's pamphlet for Penny Postage.

30. See Hughes, *Writer's Guide to Everyday Life*, 154. Twenty shillings made up a GBP (Great Britain Pound or Pound Sterling). Presumably, these figures represent costs in a major city, where a professional would gain employment. To place postage costs of Rowland Hill's time in today's terms, a 50-gram letter (about 1.7 ounces) would have cost 6d in 1840 or 2.4p in today's money. Although this figure does not account for recent inflation, the cost of a 50-gram first class UK inland letter is no more expensive in 2009 than it was in 1840 (depending on what historic inflation index is used).

31. See, for example, *The Post Circular* 10 (Thursday, March 28, 1839); *The Post Circular* 11 (Wednesday, April 17, 1839); and *The Post Circular* 12 (Tuesday, April 30, 1839). Some variations occur.

32. This message first appeared in *Spectator*, along with other endorsements of cheap postage, and was later reprinted in *The Post Circular* 11 (Wednesday, April 17, 1839).

33. The placard is the size of four 11 × 17 inch sheets.

34. Consider also Lord John Russell's June 21, 1848, parliamentary address to the House of Commons: "I was about to allude to the reduction of postage in a parenthesis with other measures, but I really think that, viewed as a great social change, nothing more beneficial has taken place in later times (Hear, hear). When you contemplate the enormous increase which has taken place in correspondence, you may estimate the number of persons who were deprived of the benefit of communicating with their friends and of offering the interchange of domestic affections" (reprinted in Hill and Hill, 2: 98).

35. Qtd. in M. D. Hill, "Post-Office Reform," 557.

36. See Altick, *English Common Reader*, 169–72, for statistics from the 1840 *Second Annual Report of the Registrar General*. The later figures come from G. R. Porter, *Progress of the Nation*, 147.

37. This report is partially reprinted in Cleere, *Avuncularism*, 187.

38. This letter is partially reprinted in Cleere, *Avuncularism*, 187.

39. Qtd. in Ashurst pamphlet, 69.

40. See, for example, Martineau, *History of England*, 2: 436.

41. See, respectively, *The Post Circular* 14 (June 28, 1839), 61, and *The Post Circular* 7 (May 11, 1838), 38.

42. Qtd. in Lewins, *Her Majesty's Mails*, 201.

43. Qtd. in Pearson Hill, *Post Office of Fifty Years Ago*, 38–40.

44. See *The Post Circular* 1 (Wednesday, March, 14, 1838), 1.

45. Amazingly, some of these specimens have survived. A sample is housed with the

Cole Papers at the National Art Library Victoria and Albert Museum. Cole also indicates he included a specimen in a pocket of volume 2 of *Fifty Years of Public Work*.

46. Cole's skit is reprinted in Fryer and Akerman, *Reform of the Post Office in the Victorian Era*, 2: 742–45. The authors suggest Cole may have created it to be performed by amateur theatrical groups. Critics variously refer to it as a play and a playlet and under different titles.

47. All excerpts from the play cited in this and the following paragraph appear in Fryer and Akerman, 2: 742–45.

48. Lichfield also memorably states that with Penny Postage, "'The walls of the Post Office would burst'" (see H. W. Hill, *Rowland Hill*, 13). Maberly likewise called Hill's scheme, among other things, "'utterly fallacious'" (qtd. in Robinson, *British Post Office*, 287).

49. Qtd. in Muir, *Postal Reform*, 104.

50. For full discussion of the playlet's creation and distribution, see Fryer and Akerman, 1: xl–xli and 2: 742.

51. Qtd. in Staff, *Penny Post*, 82.

52. Qtd. in Fryer and Akerman, 1: xli.

53. For more information on actual postal rates, see Muir, *Postal Reform*, 69.

54. Qtd. in *The Post Circular* 11 (Wednesday, April 17, 1839), 54.

CHAPTER 2. SIGNED, SEALED, DELIVERED

1. See Hill and Hill *Life*, 1: 391, and Wymer, *Social Reformers*, 23. Hill hoped that not less than 100,000 letters would be dispatched on January 10, 1840.

2. According to E. B. Evans (*Mulready Envelope* 5), Philbrick and Westoby in their 1881 *Postage and Telegraph Stamps of Great Britain* suggest that the real genius behind the drawing was Queen Victoria herself, with possible assistance from Prince Albert. This conjecture is stuff of legend, but the rumor had made its way into the *Morning Herald* in May 1840, and Mulready felt called upon to publicly deny it (see Muir, *Postal Reform*, 177–78).

3. "Our Address," qtd. in King and Plunkett, *Victorian Print Media*, 385.

4. Qtd. in Hey, *Rowland Hill*, 72. Variations of this scene appear in Smyth, *Sir Rowland Hill*, 163; Wymer, *Social Reformers*, 23; and Hill and Hill, *Life* 1: 391.

5. Smyth describes opening day of the Uniform Penny Post in detail in *Sir Rowland Hill*, 162.

6. Sir Rowland Hill included journal entries throughout his memoir.

7. Smyth does not mention whether she was at St. Martin's-le-Grand or was reporting information gleaned secondhand. If she was present on the occasion, she would have been about nine years old.

8. See *Letters*, 1: 141–42. Three Glorious Days (also called the July Revolution of 1830) took place from July 26 to July 29 and resulted in France's constitutional monarchy. Louis-Philippe, the Duc d'Orléans, successfully overthrew his cousin, King Charles I.

9. Staff (*Penny Post* 90–91) attributes this description to Cole, citing the May 1840 *Westminster Review*. Muir, on the other hand, calls it an anonymous contribution to the February 1840 issue of that journal (see *Postal Reform*, 108–9).

10. Qtd. in Muir 111.

11. From the Uniform Postage Act (also called the Postage Duties Bill), qtd. in Muir, *Postal Reform*, 78.

12. According to Muir (*Postal Reform* 63), Hill was to work for the Treasury for two years

to arrange for the reduction of postal rates to a uniform penny, but his work was challenging because he had no "direct control" over Post Office operations.

13. Recall that in Cole's skit (see chapter 1), Queen Victoria bemoans Baring's irregular postings.

14. Muir cites this date in *Postal Reform*, 78. Other scholars give other dates, including September 6, 1840.

15. Treasury Commission, qtd. in Briggs, *Victorian Things*, 338.

16. For more on these design submissions, including illustrations, see Muir, *Postal Reform*, 81.

17. While some artists sent anonymous submissions to the competition, others included their names or used initials or pen names.

18. Although there were other considerations involved in deciding a winner, Muir considers these four of the "greatest importance" (*Postal Reform* 79).

19. For details on the Treasury competition, see chapters 6 and 7 in Muir, *Postal Reform*.

20. According to Muir, "it is sometimes reported that Mulready claimed" not to have received payment on this date (*Postal Reform* 121); an entry in Cole's diary, however, records Mulready's receipt of payment for his design on June 17, 1840.

21. See Muir, *Postal Reform*, 150: Perkins, Bacon & Petch—originally a printer of banknotes—commissioned Henry Corbould to create the stamp based on the Queen's head from Wyon's City Medal. He received payment of £12.

22. Qtd. in Rigo de Righi, *Story of the Penny Black*, 25.

23. John Forbes-Nixon, a philatelist from Bristol, UK, notes that Mulreadies commonly carried commercial advertisements from stores and companies of various kinds or conveyed social messages, such as appeals to end slavery, from various public and philanthropic organizations.

24. Mulready is buried in Kensal Green Cemetery, London.

25. Qtd. in Rigo de Righi, *Story of the Penny Black*, 27.

26. Qtd. in Muir, *Postal Reform*, 121.

27. Qtd. in Lowe, *British Postage Stamp*, 83.

28. The gender of the older child is ambiguous, but the dress on the younger child identifies her as a girl.

29. Martineau, "Letter to TW," qtd. in Pearson Hill, *Post Office of Fifty Years Ago*, 47.

30. Initially, Mulready drew cherubic messengers, but in discussions with Cole and John Thompson, the engraver, Mulready changed them to angels and removed from the bottom of the design a steamboat chugging across an aqueduct; see Muir, *Postal Reform*, 121.

31. In *Mulready Envelope* (3), Evans suggests the figure is a Laplander in a sleigh. Reindeer herding, along with hunting and fishing, remain traditional activities of Laplanders, also called the Sami people. Northern locales with reindeer populations include Northern Russia, Scandinavia, Greenland, and Canada. Bristol philatelist Robert Johnson suggests that Canada is probably the land that Mulready chose to depict, given that much of the region was under British imperial control between 1763 and 1867.

32. By way of comparison, take a look at period journals such as the *Illustrated London News* of 1851 to view the representation of "far-off" nations participating in the Great Exhibition.

33. Evans (*Mulready Envelope* 3–4) suggests the scribe in the left foreground of the envelope could be a Turk or a Persian. He also resembles one of the many scribes in Indian market towns that Rudyard Kipling memorably depicts in *Kim* (1901).

34. Today we question the arguments by which the British government justified its expansionist agenda in India: that the natives needed the civilizing force of British rule; that certain of the country's religious practices were so abhorrent that the British were morally obligated to outlaw them for the country's own good; that India was so despotic that it required a reliable system of British governance. This "ethic of improvement" dominated Britain's social policy until the brutal Indian Rebellion of 1857–58, which was, in turn, entirely crushed, leading Victoria, in the final stage of the British Raj, to consider ways to improve the well-being of her Indian subjects.

35. Though Britain banned opium use at home, opium was a major profit-making monopoly of the British East India Company, which found a ready market in China, disregarding China's ban on its use. The growing opium trade led to long disputes and eventually to war.

36. Mulready's representation offers a nineteenth-century British point of view of the First Opium War with China. A mandarin in 1840 would scarcely have considered that the British were engaging in "friendly . . . commercial intercourse" with his country, Mulready's stated intention.

37. While West's painting portrays seventeenth-century America as a place of liberal tolerance (where Indians live peaceably with Europeans), his iconography also emblematizes British imperial power. (Under royal charter, Penn had come to America to create a colony, having been given land by King Charles II as payment for an outstanding debt the Crown owed Penn's father.) In the context of Penn's mission, West's iconography points to the beginning of a European colonization of America that brought upon the Indians proselytizing, disease, war, displacement, and removal, sanctioned by the 1830 Indian Removal Act.

38. Fiction offers many examples of British landholders in the West Indies. Austen describes one such absentee planter in *Mansfield Park* (1814): Sir Thomas Bertram makes his fortune in Antigua. In *Jane Eyre* (1847) Charlotte Brontë uses Bertha Mason's fortune as the reason why Rochester travels to Jamaica expressly to marry her and hence take possession of her property and money. In *Vanity Fair* (1848), Thackeray saddles Miss Schwarz with a fortune of £200,000 from her father—a British slave owner living in the fictitious Cannibal Islands—and makes her prey for fortune hunters.

39. British planters faced bankruptcy after 1840 because they lost their free labor. Many blacks left the plantations to establish free villages. The abolition of the Corn Laws in 1846, enabled by cheap postage, led to the dissolution of preferential duties for colonial sugar between 1846 and 1854. There were riots in the West Indies, among which the Eyre controversy of Jamaica (1865–1874) was the most notable and bloody.

40. Qtd. in Briggs, *Victorian Things*, 343.

41. See Rigo de Righi, *Story of the Penny Black*, 30.

42. A special machine had to be created to destroy the large quantity of extra stock, as it proved impossible to burn them under secure conditions. See Muir, *Postal Reform*, 180.

43. Despite the public reaction to Mulready's design, it is interesting to consider how closely it met most of the criteria established by the Treasury competition. Though some critics did not find the design convenient for public use because of its limited address space,

the design's intricacy likely made it secure from forgery, while the easily recognizable icons may well have facilitated the checking of the design. No objections seem to have been raised as to the expense of its production or circulation.

44. Cole's *Fifty Years of Public Work* was published over forty years after postage reform.

45. Muir offered this explanation during a meeting at the British Postal Museum & Archive on Friday, November 10, 2006.

46. These reactions of the press appear in Muir, *Postal Reform*, 176, 177.

47. Qtd. in Hill and Hill, *Life*, 1: 394. Though Hill doesn't name the paper, he does use as a heading to his excerpt the column title "Money Market and City Intelligence." From this, we can trace the article to *The Tablet*, a paper founded in 1840 by John Lukas and still published today. Its first edition, which appeared on Saturday, May 16, 1840, is reproduced online by the Tablet Publishing Company, <http://www.thetablet.co.uk/1840/>.

48. Qtd. in Muir, *Postal Reform*, 175. The reviewer is likely referring to the Vagrancy Act of 1824, amended in 1838, just two years before the Mulreadies went on sale.

49. Qtd. in Hill and Hill, *Life*, 1: 394.

50. Qtd. in Hill and Hill, *Life*, 1: 394.

51. For the entire poem, see Evans, *Mulready Envelope*, 35–36.

52. Qtd. in Muir, *Postal Reform*, 176–77.

53. Victoria dismisses Lord Brougham, the Duke of Wellington, Lord Melbourne, Lord John Russell, and Mr. Spring Rice. See Evans, *Mulready Envelope*, 86.

54. This signature appears on at least the first five caricatures in the series.

55. While Phiz caricatured the Mulready, George Cruikshank never did. See Evans, *Mulready Envelope*, 44, 107.

56. Postmarks to indicate prepayment and stamps used as tickets date to earlier times; James Chalmers, among others, lays claim to the invention of the adhesive postage stamp. See Briggs, *Victorian Things*, 337.

57. Qtd. in Rigo de Righi, *Story of the Penny Black*, 23.

58. The brownish-red stamp remained in use until 1879. The cancellation on the red stamp was a Maltese cross in black ink.

59. See Rigo de Righi, 7–16.

60. I refer the reader to the following Web site on Wyon: http://users.bigpond.com/cruzi/Coins/Grading/Engravers.htm#WilliamWyon.

61. While the 2s od piece (or florin) was first produced in 1848, its production for general circulation began in 1849. Decimalization of UK currency was a social and political subject from 1824.

62. See Muir, *Postal Reform*, 144, on the enduring use of Wyon's bust design.

63. For more of Cheverton's views, see Briggs, *Victorian Things*, 339.

64. For more on Halévy, see Briggs, *Victorian Things*, 339.

65. Comical lines accompany this *Punch* caricature of the Penny Black as well as the following caption in caps: "A PROOF BEFORE LETTERS" (166).

66. Qtd. in Williams and Williams, *Postage Stamp*, 19.

67. Qtd. in Muir, *Postal Reform*, 180.

68. Interpretations of British and French stamp language vary. William Cochrane's "The

Language of Stamps" explains a stamp placed upside down in the top left corner meant "I love you." "Le Langage de Timbres" provides meanings associated with various positions. For example, a stamp placed horizontally in the top center of an envelope (postage amount facing down) meant "je pense à vous," or "I think of you."

69. Qtd. in Briggs, *Victorian Things*, 355.

70. The omission of "Britain" continues even now on domestic British stamps.

71. Altick offers this percentage in *English Common Reader*, 172. It means that 97 percent of those aged 16–25 who married could sign the marriage register. Thus, many older illiterates lived beside members of an increasingly more literate younger population.

72. For more information on numbers of daily deliveries and pillar box collections, see Daunton, *Royal Mail*, 47.

73. For this interesting Victorian commentary, see Bruce Rosen's blog, *Victorian History*. Rosen (professor emeritus, University of Tasmania) locates the quotation in the *Times* of May 8, 1861, 5. Several editions of the *Times* were published daily; this was issue 23927, and the letter appeared in column F.

74. For facts on the expansion of the Post Office, I recommend C. R. Perry, *Victorian Post Office*.

75. In Hardy's 1891 *Tess of the D'Urbervilles*, a mail carriage kills the family horse, Prince, when Tess falls asleep driving the family hives to market early one fateful morning.

76. Daunton, *Royal Mail*, 5, fully critiques Hill.

77. Qtd. in Bills, 550.

78. Trained at the Royal Academy, Hicks consciously emulated William Powell Frith, who specialized in narrative paintings of daily Victorian activities.

79. Qtd. in Bills 550.

CHAPTER 3. "WHY IS A RAVEN . . . ?"

1. See "Pillar Boxes," 1.

2. Hill took credit for the pillar box, but Robinson concludes, "If Rowland Hill did have the idea in 1840, it was not acted upon for over a decade" (333–34).

3. After standardization in 1859 and until 1874, pillar boxes in the UK were generally bronze green. However, in 1874, red became the standard color for pillar boxes, first in London and then gradually throughout the UK.

4. See "Pillar Boxes," 1, 2.

5. Pillar box design changed over the years and in the twentieth century branched into special boxes for airmail and metered mail.

6. Qtd. in Henkin, *The Postal Age*, n. 56, 197.

7. Quoted in Muir, *Postal Reform*, 117. Martineau's discussion of the doorway adaptations Victorians made to receive mail at home also appears in Hill and Hill, 1: 390.

8. Qtd. in Muir, *Postal Reform*, 117. Londonderry's complaint also appears in Hill and Hill, *Life*, 2: 90–91.

9. Captain James Cook sailed for New Zealand and the South Seas from Whitby. This notice comes from the private collection of John Forbes-Nixon.

10. Robert Johnson, a philatelist from Bristol, UK, graciously provided the Iona and Duran examples.

11. In 1875, Burritt was alive to see the formation of the Universal Postal Union, guaranteeing a uniform rate of 2½d per half ounce to member countries, irrespective of distance. For more information, see Staff, *Penny Post*, 125.

12. A reproduction and discussion of this envelope appears both in Evans, *Mulready Envelope*, 190, and Lowe, *British Postage Stamp*, 94.

13. The Victorian Peace Society envelope is reproduced in Lowe, *Postage Stamp*, 95. The mid-Victorian period was a time of wars, and hence, also a time of antiwar activity. By 1850, the British were involved in the First Opium War with China (1839–42), the first and second Sikh Wars (1845–46 and 1848–49), the First Afghan War (1838–42), the Battle of Blood River in South Africa (1838), and the Second Xhosa War (1846).

14. Evans in *Mulready Envelope* (217–21) is thorough in his discussion of temperance envelope designs but does not provide dates for them.

15. See *Mulready Envelope*, 176–81. Evans provides commentary about and reproduces two examples from the Akermans's Comic Envelopes series.

16. Letter #201, Autograph Letters collection, Bath Central Library. The letter begins, "You have already, my thanks, but not my <u>due</u> thanks for your very kind present."

17. For more on commemorative and celebratory designs, see Evans, *Mulready Envelope*, 180–83, and Lowe, *British Postage Stamp*, 90–94.

18. Charles Lamb preferred to write a "naked note," one which "Whitechapel people exchange with no sweet degrees of envelope," qtd. in Briggs, *Victorian Things*, 362.

19. Henchard prevents his daughter's marriage, tells her biological father she is dead, and falls back into a state of drunkenness, impoverishment, and disillusionment.

20. Austen's nephew notes in 1870 that "her paper was sure to take the right folds, and her sealing-wax to drop in the right place." Qtd. in Pool, *What Jane Austen Ate*, 152.

21. In *Villette* (1853), Lucy Snowe realizes an envelope does not guarantee security: she buries her treasured letters from Dr. John to keep them safe from Mme Beck. Monsieur Paul helps Lucy secure lodging outside the Pensionnat de Demoiselles to ensure "'the safe transmission of letters,'" because in the Pensionnat, located in the Rue Fossette, letters "'become liable to misapplication—perhaps abuse'" (584).

22. These sayings come from the archives of the Bath Postal Museum in Bath, UK. I had the opportunity to view these ephemera in November 2006. The museum maintains an excellent Web site, where many of their collections are now reproduced digitally. <http://www.bathpostalmuseum.co.uk/index.html>.

23. Qtd. in Robinson, *British Post Office*, 343.

24. *Punch* cartoon, "Paul Pry at the Post Office," reproduced in Robinson, *British Post Office*, 342.

25. See Harris, *Portable Writing Desks*, 24.

26. Qtd. in Briggs, *Victorian Things*, 350.

27. Qtd. in Briggs, *Victorian Things*, 351.

28. Today, "Dear Abby" prints a booklet entitled *How to Write Letters for all Occasions* that fits into a business envelope.

29. See Altick, *English Common Reader*, 170. Also, Harris estimates that 60 percent or more of the British population was literate in 1850; see *Portable Writing Desks*, 22.

30. Although the book is undated, its inscription is October 13, 1902.

31. This example comes from the private collection of James Grimwood-Taylor.

32. See "Lewis Carroll Related Postage Stamps," <http://lewiscarrollsociety.org.uk/pages/inspired/stamps.htm>.

33. The following Web site offers responses from famous people, such as Aldous Huxley: <http://www.straightdope.com/classics/a5_266.html>.

34. In particular, the Great Exhibition of 1851 is considered a response to the triumphant French Industrial Exposition of 1844.

35. "The Great Exhibition" entry, *Wikipedia*, <http://en.wikipedia.org/wiki/Great_Exhibition>.

36. Letter qtd. in Barker, *The Brontës: A Life*, 324.

37. Jones and Stallybrass offer some interesting insights on Marx's theory of commodity fetishism in *Renaissance Clothing*, 7–9. See Berlin, "The Original Text of Karl Marx," for observations on Marx in London, 1.

38. Qtd. in the introduction to *Great Exhibition of the Works of Industry of all Nations, 1851. Official Descriptive and Illustrated Catalogue* (hereafter *ODIC*), 1: 3, 4.

39. Robert Ellis, "Preface," *ODIC*, 1: v.

40. Briggs (*Victorian Things* 183) gives machinery used in the creation of steel pens in Birmingham as an example.

41. Class 17 is described in section 3, *ODIC*, 2: 536.

42. See Harris, *Portable Writing Desks*, 27.

43. Entry #41, sec. 3, class 17, *ODIC*, 2: 539.

44. Entry #41, sec. 3, class 17, *ODIC*, 2: 540.

45. Entry #32, sec. 3, class 17, *ODIC*, 2: 539.

46. Entry #42, sec. 3, class 17, *ODIC*, 2: 540.

47. Entry #93, sec. 3, class 17, *ODIC*, 2: 543.

48. Entry #144, sec. 3, class 17, *ODIC*, 2: 546.

49. See Briggs, *Victorian Things*, 182–83. Briggs includes discussion of several Birmingham manufacturers who pioneered the steel pen.

50. Entry #694, sec. 3, class 22, *ODIC*, 2: 667.

51. For more on pens, see Briggs, *Victorian Things*, 184–86.

52. Entry #690, sec. 3, class 22, *ODIC*, 2: 667.

53. Entry #76, Thomas De La Rue & Co., sec. 3, class 17, *ODIC*, 2: 542.

54. See Briggs, *Victorian Things*, 64. Briggs gives the number as sixty envelopes a minute, higher than Thomas De La Rue's estimate.

55. In *Story of the Penny Black*, 25, Rigo de Righi notes 2,500 envelopes per hour but provides no source.

56. See "Envelope-making machines," part of the British Postal Museum and Archive's online exhibition Victorian Innovation, <http://www.postalheritage.org.uk/exhibitions/onlineexhibitions/victorianinnovation>. The envelope was not invented by the British; it likely dates to the Ottoman Empire. Following the *ODIC* and Hill and Hill, I call this invention an envelope-folding machine.

57. The British Postal Museum and Archive estimates that by 1855, 93 percent of all mail was sent in envelopes. See "Envelopes: the Mulready design," part of the British Postal Museum and Archive's online exhibition Victorian Innovation, <http://www.postalheritage. org.uk/exhibitions/onlineexhibitions/victorianinnovation>.

58. References to writing desks to safeguard a "purse of Duckets" appear in Shakespeare's *A Comedy of Errors*. See Harris, *Portable Writing Desks*, 10–11, for a complete history.

59. The *Catalogue* also records such innovations: see "Ladies' writing-table, with drawers, on an entirely new principle," entry #289, Mrs. Creasor of Euston Square, sec. 3, class 26, "Furnitures, Upholstery, Paper Hangings," *ODIC*, 2: 757.

60. See Harris, *Portable Writing Desks*, 5–9. More common are the second and third types of desks, which have room for storage and a writing slope.

61. Entry #144, sec. 3, class 17, *ODIC*, 2: 546.

62. This estimate comes from Harris, *Portable Writing Desks*, 18.

63. Also in *Phineas Finn*, Lady Laura Kennedy, on separating from her husband, asks to take only her writing desk and clothes.

64. Trollope designed his traveling desk while working as surveyor for the Post Office. It was destroyed during a trip to America in the 1860s.

65. I refer the interested reader to Trollope, *Autobiography*, 154, 317.

66. Writing desks were extremely popular among many male and female writers, such as Alexander Pope; see Harris, *Portable Writing Desks*, 15. For more on Austen's writing desk, see Shields, *Jane Austen*, 45, 71, 103, 121.

67. Austen letter qtd. in Harris, *Portable Writing Desks*, 17.

68. See the frontispiece to Harris, *Portable Writing Desks*, for a picture and description of Charlotte Brontë's writing desk.

69. "Furniture, Upholstery, and Paper Hangings" includes entries up to #536, but the entries are not presented consecutively and several hundred are ultimately missing, though some entries appear in an appendix.

70. Entry #134, sec. 3, class 26, "Furnitures, Upholstery, Paper Hangings," *ODIC*, 2: 743.

71. Entry #285, sec. 3, class 26, *ODIC*, 2: 756.

72. Entry #285, sec. 3, class 26, *ODIC*, 2: 756.

73. See, respectively, entry #205, Robert William Herring & Sons; entry #343, Henry Strugnell; and entry #79, John J. Mechi (class 26, "Furnitures, Upholstery, Paper Hangings," *ODIC*, 2: 751, 758, 739).

74. See, respectively, entry #205, Robert William Herring & Sons, entry #136, McCallum & Hodson, and entry #138, Richard Turley, sec. 3, class 26, *ODIC*, 2: 751, 743.

75. Desks arguably show what the male manufacturer anticipated the female consumer wanted in her parlor or bedchamber.

76. Entry #136, sec. 3, class 26, *ODIC*, 2: 743.

77. Entry #200, sec. 3, class 26, *ODIC*, 2: 751.

78. Entry #70, sec. 3, class 26, *ODIC*, 2: 734.

79. Bracketed commentary by W.C.A. following entry #131, sec. 3, class 26, *ODIC*, 2: 742.

80. Entry #70, sec. 3, class 26, *ODIC*, 2: 734. Another remark by W.C.A. on inlaying pearl in high quality papier-mâché follows an entry by McCallum & Hodson, a well-regarded Birmingham firm; see Entry 136, sec. 3, class 26, *ODIC*, 2: 743.

81. See sec. 3, class 26, *ODIC*, 2: 748. The remark is probably by R. E. and follows the Jennens & Bettride entry #187, on that same page.

82. An illustration accompanying the Jennens & Bettride entry features many exquisite papier-mâché products.

83. There are several reasons for the decline of the portable writing desk in the late Victorian period. More widespread lighting and heating of homes undercut the utility of a portable over a fixed writing desk, and changes in travel patterns—people now traveled more often and on shorter trips—made it unnecessary to carry so much furniture along. The writing desk gave way to the stationery desk and to the briefcase, which appears in the form of a leather writing case or dispatch box in catalogues as early as the 1850s; see Harris, *Portable Writing Desks*, 31–32.

84. I refer the reader to Sutherland's introduction to the Oxford edition of *Vanity Fair*, viii–ix. All references are to this edition.

85. See "'What is the Use of a Book?' Becky Sharp as Revolutionary Reader in William Makepeace Thackeray's *Vanity Fair*" in Golden, *Images of the Woman Reader*, 202–24.

86. They include George Osborne, Rawdon Crawley, William Dobbin, Sir Pitt the younger, Amelia Sedley, Becky Sharp, Miss Barbara Pinkerton (shown writing a letter at her desk), Lady Steyne, and Miss Briggs.

87. Before Becky departs as governess at Queen's Crawley, Amelia "ransacked all her drawers, cupboards, reticules, and gimcrack boxes—passed in review all her gowns, fichus, tags, bobbins, laces, silk stockings, and fallals, selecting this thing and that and the other, to make a little heap for Rebecca" (75). Or, Amelia gives Becky "the white cornelian and the turquoise rings and a sweet sprigged muslin, which was too small for her now" (22), and perhaps also the desk?

88. Briggs, living with Becky upon Miss Crawley's death, gives her inheritance to Becky, who uses it for her own profit.

89. At one point, Thackeray refers to Becky's desk as a "box"—"that very box which Rawdon Crawley had ransacked in his furious hunt for Becky's concealed money" (860). "Writing box" and "box" are among the many Victorian synonyms for writing desk; see Harris, *Portable Writing Desks*, 4.

90. The illustration of Becky seated at her "box" suggests that it is large enough to house a miniature painting, like that of Jos on the elephant.

91. Presumably, George writes the note asking Becky to run away with him on his own writing desk, the note that she, in turn, transfers to the desk "which she had had from Amelia ever so many years ago" (864).

CHAPTER 4. UNWANTED MISSIVES AND THE SPREAD OF VICE

1. No story is more dramatically a case of "feeling" than "ONLY A POSTAGE," published in the *Brighton Herald* and reprinted in *The Post Circular* 12 (Tuesday, April 30, 1839), 60.

2. Mr. Porter, Statistical Department, Board of Trade, qtd. in Hill, *Post Office Reform*, 93.

3. These figures are cited by Daunton, *Royal Mail*, 79.

4. While Henkin makes these points about American postal culture in the wake of

cheap postage, they similarly apply to the British Post Office, which initiated reforms, such as the postage stamp, that America swiftly followed; see *The Postal Age*, 171, 169, 153.

5. Trollope, *The Claverings*, 178. This idiom is part of an extended racing metaphor likening women to fillies. I concur with Cleere's interpretation that Trollope uses it to signal a reformed postal system's invitation to women to morally stray. For more on the public space of the post office, see Henkin, 80. Henkin's discussion of this point in *The Postal Age* informs my thinking.

6. This term comes from Dickens and Wills' 1850 *Household Words* article, "Valentine's Day at the Post-Office" (6–12), the whole of which I highly recommend.

7. See Mason, "Middlemarch and History," 417–31.

8. Qtd. in Briggs, *Victorian Things*, 347. Lyon Playfair (1818–98) was a Scottish parliamentarian and scientist.

9. This opposition comes through strongly in *Administration of the Post Office*, 2–4. Also see Lewins, *Her Majesty's Mails*, 198.

10. This letter comes from the collection of James Grimwood-Taylor.

11. This quotation is on p. 213 in *Administration of the Post Office*, which reprints the entire entry, 212–18.

12. Most of the early writings on Rowland Hill were authored by his relatives, who we might expect had a natural partiality. For a more objective account, see Daunton, *Royal Mail*, 3–34.

13. See Robinson, *British Post Office*, for a discussion of longstanding practices of letter opening and the 1844 scandal, 119–25, 337–52.

14. See my introduction for an explanation of this and other now-outdated postal terms.

15. Home Secretary Graham took the blame for the intrusive measure, leading *Punch* to cast him as "Paul Pry at the Post Office" (1844); see Robinson, *British Post Office*, 342.

16. For more discussion of the valuables that ended up in the Dead Letter Office, see Dickens, "Valentine's Day at the Post-Office," 10.

17. Qtd. in Lewins, *Her Majesty's Mails*, 299–300.

18. Postal worker, qtd. in Lewins, *Her Majesty's Mails*, 300.

19. Henkin, *The Postal Age*, 153. The author also examines here how unsolicited mail during this period exceeded mail between friends and acquaintances.

20. Qtd. in Henkin, *The Postal Age*, 63.

21. From the private collection of John Forbes-Nixon, this letter of complaint about unhealthy leeches includes the postscript, "I have lost a great many."

22. This letter comes from the collection of Dr. Adrian Almond.

23. Dr. Adrian Almond has four replies in his collection to this advertisement, all dating to 1821—well before Penny Postage.

24. From the collection of Dr. Adrian Almond. Although outlawed in nineteenth-century England, duels were still performed surreptitiously and illegally, until they faded out by the early twentieth century.

25. Valentine Cards collection, #268, Bath Central Library.

26. Valentine Cards collection, #104, Bath Central Library.

27. Valentine Cards collection, #223, Bath Central Library.

28. Valentine Cards collection, #201, Bath Central Library.

29. Cobden letter qtd. in Hill and Hill, *Life*, 1: 478.

30. Cobden letters qtd. in Hill and Hill, *Life*, 1: 477–78 and 2:31.

31. Bokenham's evidence appears in *Administration of the Post Office*, 133. The anonymous author uses it to support the complaint that by stepping into the business of general delivery, the Post Office abrogated its traditional and honorable role in British civic life and created a host of problems.

32. For the complete anecdote, see Robinson, *British Post Office*, 369.

33. After an extensive search, I have not been able to verify where this cartoon originally appeared. I have reproduced it from Alan James, *Sir Rowland Hill and the Post Office*, 54, which does not list the source. The image also appears as the frontispiece to Frank Staff's *Penny Post*. Although Staff also does not list the source, he notes in his caption, "A comical cartoon by John Leech inspired by the introduction of uniform penny postage." Staff includes the word "just" in the final sentence of the cartoon caption, as does A. G. Rigo de Righi, who includes this cartoon as the frontispiece to his *Story of the Penny Black*. Like Staff, Rigo de Righi identifies Leech but no source.

34. I am grateful to Robert Johnson for this information and other philatelic curiosities.

35. Robinson (*British Post Office* 59, 328, 410) discusses some of these items curious and perilous.

36. Cleere, *Avuncularism*, 199. Cleere goes on to illuminate this point with an analysis of mischievous mailing in Anthony Trollope's novel *John Caldigate* (1879); a letter of blackmail and forgery sent from Australia (where Caldigate temporarily emigrates) masquerades as proof of bigamy until an honest postal clerk, who is an authority on postage stamps, proves the damning colonial letter to be a forgery.

37. This letter comes from the collection of John Forbes-Nixon.

38. Many characters in *Bleak House* have reason to want Tulkinghorn dead: Captain George (in custody) owes him money; Lady Dedlock lives in fear of his threatened disclosures. Mlle. Hortense kills Tulkinghorn because he reneges on his promise to help her find work in return for clinching Lady Dedlock's connection to the deceased Nemo.

39. Old Mother Shipton (c. 1488–1561) was an English prophetess and witch.

40. Rev. Peacocke finds proof of Ferdinand Lefroy's death, and Dr. Wortle legally marries the Peacockes. The school flourishes (many pupils return), the Peacockes have children, and even Dr. Wortle's daughter marries well.

41. This "circular swindle" is from the collection of James Grimwood-Taylor.

42. Henkin, *The Postal Age*, 157. Henkin details numerous Victorian American "circular swindles."

43. See Sutherland's introduction to Collins's riveting sensation novel *The Woman in White*, xiii.

44. Collins, who himself fathered three illegitimate children, explored through fiction the notion of illegitimacy and the absurdity of English law respecting children born to unmarried parents.

45. See McLaren, *Sexual Blackmail*, 18, for a discussion of how fictional references to homosexual blackmail begin to appear in novels after 1885, including *The Picture of Dorian Gray* and Stevenson's *Dr. Jekyll and Mr. Hyde* (1886). Could Dr. Jekyll be a victim of Mr. Hyde's homosexual blackmail for an indiscretion of his youth?

46. Dickens fills *Bleak House* with many hopeful blackmailers, such as Mr. Smallweed and Mrs. Snagsby, eager to trade on Lady Dedlock's secret from her past.

47. Cleere (203) discusses how the Penny Post becomes a euphemism for blackmail; though brief, her analysis is convincing.

48. Greenwood writes to the Marchioness, Lady Kingsbury, "'I have not as yet been driven to open out my sad case to any one but yourself. Do not force me to it,—for the sake of those darling children for whose welfare I have ever been so anxious" (3: 251).

49. See Barker's preface to *The Brontës: Selected Poems*, xxxiv.

50. See the following letters in Barker, *The Brontës: A Life*: Branwell to Francis Grundy, Haworth, October 1845, for his own account of the affair with Mrs. Robinson, 136; Branwell to John Brown, sexton of Haworth, undated, 192; and Branwell to J. B. Leyland, Haworth, June 22, 1848, for a description of Branwell's desperation, 191–92.

51. Lucasta Miller, *Brontë Myth*, 85; Miller cites Daphne du Maurier's *Infernal World of Branwell Brontë* (1960) as one source.

52. Barker, *The Brontës: A Life*, 137.

53. While women are usually the victims of slander and blackmail in Victorian fiction, in *Middlemarch* Eliot creates a male victim in Nicholas Bulstrode. Worse, Dr. Tertius Lydgate indirectly becomes associated with Bulstrode's deception since Bulstrode hires him to care for Raffles.

54. I am grateful to Robert Johnson of Bristol, UK, for reminding me of this convention.

55. Trollope eventually discloses that George Roden is really the son of an Italian nobleman and entitled to be called Duca di Crinola.

56. Trollope is not unique in his suspicions. In *Villette*, Charlotte Brontë uses the post as a narrative means to facilitate a clandestine romance between Polly Home and Dr. John Bretton.

57. The India and dueling letters come from the collection of James Grimwood-Taylor. The ill-fame and Gretna Green letters belong to the collection of Dr. Adrian Almond. Officer Wright states: "I know the Bengalese for two things; 'Give me a light' and 'Fuck want.' 'Jig-a-jig' is a most expressive word and that signified (I need hardly say) 'Fuck.'"

58. Tess slides the letter under Angel's door, but, by an act of fate, it wedges under the carpet, and she retrieves it. Likewise, Lady Dedlock, who reveals her history to Esther Summerson in a letter, requests Esther destroy the missive. In *David Copperfield*, Little Em'ly writes Ham Peggotty of her transgression: she "will be never to come back, unless he brings me back a lady" (383).

59. Commonly, an outsider writes an incriminatory letter to disclose the immorality of an erring wife or daughter. In Catherine Gaskell's "Lizzie Leigh," Lizzie's "father had had his letter to his daughter returned by her mistress in Manchester, telling him that Lizzie had left her service some time—and why" (254).

60. See Landow's commentary on Redgrave's painting at the Victorian Web, <http://www.victorianweb.org/painting/redgrave/paintings/4.html>.

61. Qtd. in Auerbach, "Rise of the Fallen Woman," 29; Auerbach goes on to discuss the significance of Egg's phrasing in the context of Victorian sympathy and punity.

62. The reviews that Edelstein excerpts in his article include "A Morning with Pictures,"

from *Leisure Hour* 7 (September 1858), 556; "Royal Academy," from *Athenaeum* (May 1, 1858), 566; and "Fine Arts," from *Sharpe's London Magazine* 12 (May 31, 1858), 333.

63. For contemporary responses to Egg's triptych and an analysis of them, see Edelstein, 202-12.

64. See Lynch's article on composition and color in Egg's work at the *Victorian Web*, <http://www.victorianweb.org/painting/egg/paintings/lynch1.html>.

65. For those interested in the Victorian concerns over young women's novel reading, I recommend my book *Images of the Woman Reader in Victorian British and American Fiction*.

66. According to Edelstein, 205, this painting was displayed at the Royal Academy just two years in advance of Egg's triptych.

67. Not all were quick to accept the truth of anonymous missives. In *Marion Fay*, the Marquis declares, "'I don't believe a word of it,' . . . 'There is nothing so wicked as anonymous letters'" (2: 120). Hardy uses an anonymous letter in *Tess*: Marion and Izz write Angel of Tess's trouble and sign it "From Two Well-wishers" (292).

CHAPTER 5. BENEFITS AND BLESSINGS

1. Glendenning gives a figure of nearly 329 million letters in 1849 in *Anthony Trollope*, 193.

2. The American philanthropist Elihu Burritt led a campaign for Ocean Penny Postage in the 1850s. Overseas postage remained high after the 1840 measure for Uniform Penny Postage. Until 1858, it cost 8d, for example, to send a half-ounce letter to the United States. However, those in the military stationed abroad were still entitled to pay only 1d postage for a half-ounce letter home, as was the case prior to the 1840 reform.

3. Today, all United Nations members belong to the Universal Postal Union (UPU), which remains an important organization for worldwide postal exchanges. The United Nations plays an advisory role to the UPU, which has 191 member countries and is based in Bern, Switzerland.

4. Rowland Hill, *Post Office Reform*, iv, 8. Hill frequently used the phrase "Fortunately this is not a party question," and other reformers repeated it.

5. This petition appears in many editions of *The Post Circular* as a separate sheet. See, for example, issue 11 (Wednesday, April 17, 1839), 55.

6. See, for example, James, *Sir Rowland Hill*, 94-95, and Lewins, *Her Majesty's Mails*, 246-48. Birthday and greeting cards date to this period, including the Christmas card, which Henry Cole designed and published in 1843. The rise of the greeting card deserves separate study. The postcard, which originated in Austria in 1869, proved enormously popular when it came to England in 1870; 75 million postcards sold that year. Postcards were first prestamped white cards costing half a penny; the Post Office then allowed stamps to be affixed to cards with pictures (see James, *Sir Rowland Hill*, 85-86).

7. These references come from two period manuals—*Carrie Carleton's Popular Letter Writer* (7-8) and Hubert Howe Bancroft's *California Inner Pocula* (278)—cited in Henkin, *The Postal Age*, 100.

8. For additional delivery statistics, see Daunton, *Royal Mail*, 47.

9. See volume 2, entry #76, sec. 3, class 17, 542.

10. This letter comes from the philatelic collection of John Forbes-Nixon. Interestingly, the cost to post this tiny note was 3d rather than 1d, because cross-channel carriage to France was considered overseas posting.

11. In the summer of 2007, pop star Fergie had a ticketless concert tour, sponsored by Verizon Wireless, where admission was verified via phone message (see Fran Golden, "Sit right down").

12. This letter, in the collection of philatelist John Forbes-Nixon, arrived in London marked with a fancy 3 strike, indicating the letter was unpaid and cost three pence.

13. See Kelvin, "Editions of Letters," 590–93. Kelvin gives interesting examples from published letter collections of Charles Dickens, Thomas and Jane Carlyle, and Florence Nightingale, among others, to demonstrate the many current events, domestic activities, and professional responsibilities the Victorians documented.

14. Letter from the collection of Dr. Adrian Almond. As explained in chapter 1, there was a short transition to the new postage system with letters uniformly charged 4d from December 5, 1839, to January 10, 1840; this fourpenny rate applied to letters sent outside of London, while letters within the London area under ½ ounce cost 1d if prepaid and 2d if not prepaid.

15. "SHEET of NEWS" letter from the philatelic collection of James Grimwood-Taylor.

16. Besides Beatrix Potter, many Victorian author-illustrators—including Lewis Carroll, William Thackeray, Dante Gabriel Rossetti, and Edward Lear—wrote and drew interchangeably in their letters.

17. The Landseer letter is from the collection of Mr. John Forbes-Nixon.

18. These appear in volume 1 of Cohen's two-volume edition of *Letters of Lewis Carroll*, 141–45, 516–17, and 112–13, respectively.

19. See Linder, *History of the Writings*, 7–41.

20. In his introduction to *The Letters of Anthony Trollope*, Booth notes, "It was characteristic of Trollope to depreciate his talent. . . . he never sought to equate himself with the more distinguished men of his age" (xviii).

21. In *Anthony Trollope*, Glendenning likewise suggests "his letters were written to inform rather than to charm. . . . The majority of them are 'business' letters, even when the recipients were his friends" (368).

22. Prior to reform, publishers often delayed or declined to send final page proofs due to cost. See, for example, Trollope's letter of May 24, 1835, to Richard Bentley, lamenting how "The Printers send the sheets very irregularly; in fact for the last month I believe they have not sent any" (1) and his mention of sending back page proofs in "To Austen Henry Layard," November 9, 1867, in Booth, *Letters of Anthony Trollope*, 210.

23. Qtd. in Glendenning, 368. Glendenning speculates that Trollope rigorously maintained an objective epistolary stance, because he guarded his deepest emotions; she suggests that in this respect Trollope was akin to his character George Western in *Kept in the Dark*, a man who loves his estranged wife, Cecilia, but finds his "manliness" precludes his expressing his emotions in a letter.

24. In Booth, *Letters of Anthony Trollope*, 337.

25. In Booth, *Letters of Anthony Trollope*, 339–40.

26. These excerpts are respectively from Rossetti's letters of February 4, 1870, and January 26, 1875, both qtd. in Harrison, 239.

27. Manchester Town Council report, *The Post Circular* 14 (Friday, June 28, 1839), 63.

28. The letters Charlotte wrote of her siblings' untimely deaths were likely edged in black, although editor Juliet Barker regrettably does not provide this descriptive detail in *The Brontës: A Life*.

29. Excerpted in Harrison, "Christina Rossetti and Caroline Gemmer," 243.

30. From *The Wives of England* (1844), qtd. in Roberts, "Marriage, Redundancy or Sin," 48.

31. See "Fine Arts Exhibition," *Art Journal* (1863), 111, qtd. in Shefer, "Woman's Mission," 8.

32. Roberts makes this point in "Marriage, Redundancy or Sin," 48.

33. See Roberts, "Marriage, Redundancy or Sin," especially 48. For the appointment of Victorian homes, see Flanders, *Inside the Victorian Home*.

34. A.L. 2929, Autograph Letters Collection, Bath Central Library, Bath, UK. The English in this letter is irregular, and the text is unpunctuated. I place "[?]" next to the word "hakin" to indicate that I cannot decipher it easily. The references to "suffocation" and "blood" describe something similar to consumption, so "hakin" may be a vernacular or erroneous form of "hacking."

35. *Webster's Ready-Made Love Letters*, 16. On the same page, this combination etiquette and writing manual recommends a verbal proposal but cautions that an impatient lover who is never left alone with his sweetheart often has "unburdened his heart of its secret through the medium of a letter."

36. In *Pride and Prejudice*, Darcy feels compelled to write a very long letter to Elizabeth Bennet to clear his character: "This, Madam, is a faithful narrative of every event in which we have been concerned together" (252).

37. Booth, *Letters of Anthony Trollope*, 901–2. Trollope wrote three times to his wife in March 1875: on the 4th, the 6th, and again on the 10th. In his March 6 letter, Trollope writes, "I hope I shall find a letter tomorrow." Apparently Rose wrote her husband often, as Trollope frequently refers to her letters and urges her to write.

38. The complete poem appears in Hyde, *Royal Mail*, 288–89. Victorian fiction also illustrates the increased traffic of love letters in the post-reform era. In Trollope's *Can You Forgive Her* (1865), proposals of marriage, acceptance, and rejection fly to and fro via the Penny Post.

39. In *Villette* (1853), Lucy Snowe longs for a letter from Dr. John and, when it arrives, stores her "untasted treasure" in a locked writing case, contemplating "'Will it be cool?—Will it be kind?'" (319, 324).

40. In *Avuncularism*, Cleere uses this example from Surtees to suggest that the Penny Post "was often represented as the downfall of masculine autonomy" (198).

41. For gentlemen's model letters, see 130–51; for ladies' model letters, see 65–108.

42. Dorothea's uncle, Mr. Brooke, delivers this letter in person.

43. Esther replies in person: "I put my two arms round his neck and kissed him; and he said was this the mistress of Bleak House; and I said yes" (492).

44. Though Henkin is concerned with Valentine's Day in Victorian America, his insights apply equally well to Victorian Britain.

45. Qtd. in the online exhibition A Flowering of Affection: Victorian Valentine Cards at the Lilly Library, "The first modern Valentine cards," <http://www.indiana.edu/~liblilly/valentines/valentine1.html>.

46. Qtd. in Hyde, *Royal Mail*, 289.

47. The pages in Bradford's forty-page compilation of Victorian valentines are unnumbered. The page references given in my text are based on counting.

48. Once Gabriel Oak identifies Bathsheba's handwriting for him, Boldwood proposes to Bathsheba, who admits that sending the valentine was a "wanton thing which no woman of self respect should have done" (114).

49. Item #253, Valentine Collection, Special Collections, Bath Central Library, Bath, UK.

50. "Bank of True Love" valentines appear in the Frank Staff Collection, Bath Postal Museum, <http://www.bathpostalmuseum.co.uk/digitalcollections/25_valentines/index.html>, and in the Valentine Cards collection, Bath Central Library.

51. For further discussion of Dr. James Graham's character and the popularity of his establishment called the Temple of Hymen, see Holder, *Sweethearts and Valentines*, 24.

52. Valentine 1993-08-29, Frank Staff Collection, Bath Postal Museum, Bath, UK.

53. Item #203, Valentine Collection, Special Collections, Bath Central Library, Bath, UK.

54. Item #279, Valentine Collection, Special Collections, Bath Central Library, Bath, UK.

55. Item #202, Valentine Collection, Special Collections, Bath Central Library, Bath, UK.

56. Qtd. in Lewins, *Her Majesty's Mails*, 297. Here Lewins presents not the thoughts of a specific person but what he surmises would be the thoughts of a general postmaster.

CONCLUSION

Author's note: Lord Lichfield's remark appears in Henry Cole's 1838 postal reform playlet, "A Report of an Imaginary Scene at Windsor Castle Respecting the Uniform Penny Postage." The full text of Cole's playlet is reproduced in Fryer and Akerman, 2: 742–45.

1. See "The Campaign for Ocean Penny Postage" in Staff, *Penny Post*, 105–25. Even prior to postal reform, soldiers and sailors were entitled to penny postage.

2. Smart technology and robotics remain controversial. See Teller, "Smart Machines and Why We Fear Them."

3. Whamond's cartoon appeared in the Life section of the *Saratogian*, September 25, 2007.

4. The Penny Parts that started up in the 1830s were popular serial stories printed in booklet form (cheaper than other forms of serialization) and comprised mainly of rewritten or reprinted versions of older Gothic tales in addition to contemporary adventure stories. They primarily appealed to the working classes. Beginning in the 1850s, Penny Dreadfuls were lurid tales marketed to teenage boys.

5. Trollope features the telegraph in *The Claverings* (1867) as the means by which news of the death of Lady Ongar's husband in Italy and her imminent return home is communicated. That the telegraph took some time to catch on is represented in Gaskell's *North and South* (1855), where one of the characters laments not "having sooner thought of the electric telegraph" (250) to notify London authorities of a passenger traveling on a train from Liverpool to London.

6. In addition to chapter 12, "The Legacy of the Telegraph" (esp. 205–11), see his prefatory discussion comparing the Victorian telegraph to the Internet (vii–ix).

7. See Daniel Pool's brief but informative chapter "Mail" in *What Jane Austen Ate*, 150–52.

8. SMS offers text messaging, e-mail, and packet switching, while MMS supports the sending and receiving of photos and videos.

9. For descriptions and pictures of a range of Victorian writing desks, see Harris, *Portable Writing Desks*, 22–23.

10. It is also known as a writing box, writing slope, writing case, portable desk, traveling desk, or lap desk (as well as simply a case, box, or desk).

11. In his 1889 *Royal Mail*, Hyde provides many entertaining anecdotes about mail gone missing, including an alleged robbery of a letter by a family of tomtits (small birds) that took possession of a letter box in Cheshire (this scene is charmingly illustrated) and the story of the frozen letter. See especially 211 and 215.

12. Wi-Fi means wireless interface of laptops and other mobile computing devices. MySpace and Facebook are popular social networking applications.

13. Online dating services include eHarmony, Perfect Match, and Great Expectations (fittingly Victorian). Verizon Wireless offers a one-bill system.

14. "What Is Web 2.0" is an excellent article, though O'Reilly does not offer a succinct definition of the term. I culled this definition from ideas in the article.

15. See Tahmincioglu's one-page commentary, "Adults often 'techno-wary,'" available online at <http://www.usaweekend.com/07_issues/070722/070722coping.html>.

16. We might recall Welsh's discussion of the social impact of postal reform in *George Eliot and Blackmail*: "the increased use of the mails and of the telegraph placed a subtle strain on the trust between individuals. . . . messages are loosed from their origin to be interpreted elsewhere. They arrive as interruptions to other routines or excitements" (55).

17. Qtd. in Orr, "Computer Anxiety."

18. Brenda Raney, qtd. in Tahmincioglu.

19. See chapter 3, "Psychology + Technology: Defining Identity in a Virtual World," in Kress and Winkle, *NextText*. This chapter includes essays previously published in newspapers, journals, and online resources that explore the impact of computer and related technologies upon the way students today think.

20. This anecdote appears in *Letters* 2: 114 and in the one-volume *Letters, Conversations, and Recollections of S. T. Coleridge*, 200.

21. For further discussion of post-reform postal crime, see, for example, *Administration of the Post Office*, 124–25, 127.

22. In *History of England*, 2: 426, Martineau uses the similar phrase, "curious specimens," to describe the mailings "passing between men of science."

23. I recommend the entry on eBay offered at *Wikipedia*, <http://en.wikipedia.org/wiki/EBay>, which also provides a link to Weird Al Yankovic's song.

24. Popular sites of this kind include Sparknotes, A1Essays.com, BuyPapers.com, and AcademicTermPapers.com. See also Stevenson, "Adventures in Cheating."

25. Andrew Cuomo spearheaded this investigation. See Gormley, "Cuomo Warns Popular Web Site."

26. Cleere makes a similar point at the end of chapter 5 of *Avuncularism* (203–4), arguing that Hill's Penny Post forecasts modern and postmodern communications technologies, as well as the dangers contingent upon them.

27. For more of Cole's *Westminster Review* description of the Penny Post's opening day, see Muir, *Postal Reform*, 108–11.

28. Cruikshank captures this scene in "Oliver Amazed at the Dodger's Mode of 'Going to Work,'" one of the twenty-four illustrations to *Oliver Twist*.

29. See Stone, "In ID Theft," for the names of new companies combating this problem—Debix, LifeLock, TrustedId—along with established credit companies, such as Equifax and TransUnion.

30. Plug-in antispam programs protect PCs. Stand-alone and server-side spam filters scan e-mail for potential triggers, e.g. phrases or formatting styles. Catchy titles of Internet security software programs with informative Web sites include "SurfControl," "Cloudmark Desktop," "Mailwasher," and "Spam-Firewall."

31. Top-rated antivirus software companies include Norton AntiVirus, Shield Deluxe, AVG Anti-Spyware, and BitDefender.

Bibliography

Adams, Cecil. "Why Is a Raven Like a Writing Desk?" *The Straight Dope*, April 18, 1997. <http://www.straightdope.com/classics/a5_266.html>, accessed December 15, 2007.

Administration of the Post Office from the Introduction of Mr. Rowland Hill's Plan of Penny Postage up to the Present Time. London: Hatchard, 1844.

Allam, David. *The Social and Economic Importance of Postal Reform in 1840*. London: Harry Hayes Philatelic Pamphlets, 1976.

Altick, Richard. *The English Common Reader: The Social History of the Mass Reading Public, 1800–1900*. Chicago: University of Chicago Press, 1957.

Arnstein, Walter N. "Victoria, Queen of England." *Victorian Britain: An Encyclopedia*. Ed. Sally Mitchell. New York: Garland, 1988. 835–37.

Ashurst, W. H. *Facts and Reasons in Support of Mr. Rowland Hill's Plan for a Universal Penny Postage*. London: Henry Hooper, 1838.

Auerbach, Nina. "The Rise of the Fallen Woman." *Nineteenth-Century Fiction* 35.1 (June 1980): 29–52.

Austen, Jane. *Emma*. 1815. Oxford: Oxford University Press, 1988.

———. *Lady Susan*. 1871. Ed. R. W. Chapman. London: Schocken Books, 1984.

———. *Mansfield Park*. 1814. Ed. Margaret Drabble. New York: Signet, 1996.

———. *Persuasion*. 1818. Ed. Gillian Beer. London: Penguin, 2003.

———. *Pride and Prejudice*. 1813. Pref. George Saintsbury. Illus. Hugh Thomson. New York: Dover, 2005.

———. *Sense and Sensibility*. 1811. Ed. Tony Tanner. London: Penguin, 1986.

Autograph Letters Collection. Special Collections. Bath Central Library, Bath, England.

Balzac, Honoré de. *Cousin Bette*. 1846. Introd. David Bellos. Trans. Sylvia Raphael. Oxford: Oxford University Press, 1998.

Barker, Juliet R. V., ed., *The Brontës: A Life in Letters*. New York: Overlook Press, 2002.

———, ed. *The Brontës: Selected Poems*. London: Dent, 1993.

Benjamin, Walter. "The Work of Art in the Age of Mechanical Reproduction." *Illuminations*. Ed. Hannah Arendt. Trans. Harry Zohn. New York: Schocken Books, 1969. 217–51.

Bentley, Nicholas. *The Victorian Scene, 1837–1901*. London: Jarrold, 1968.

Berlin, Isaiah. "The Original Text of *Karl Marx*." Posted April 17, 2006. *Isaiah Berlin Virtual Library*. Isaiah Berlin Library Trust. <http://berlin.wolf.ox.ac.uk/published_works/km/uncut/pdfs/marx1uncut.pdf>, accessed June 26, 2008.

Bills, Mark. "The General Post Office: One Minute to Six." *Burlington Magazine*, September 2002: 550–56.

Booth, Bradford Allen, ed. *The Letters of Anthony Trollope.* London: Oxford University Press, 1951.

Braddon, Mary Elizabeth. *Lady Audley's Secret.* 1862. Ed. David Skilton. New York: Oxford University Press, 1998.

Bradford, Emma, comp. *Roses are Red: Love and Scorn in Victorian Valentines.* London: Albion Press, 1986.

Breen, Steve. *Grand Avenue* (comic strip). *Saratogian* (Saratoga Springs, N.Y.), July 10, 2008. Available online at *Comics.com*. <http://comics.com/grand_avenue/?DateAfter=2008-07-10&DateBefore=2008-07-10&Order=d.DateStrip+DESC>.

Briggs, Asa. *Victorian Things.* Chicago: University of Chicago Press, 1989.

Brontë, Anne. *Agnes Grey.* 1847. Ed. Angeline Goreau. New York: Penguin, 2004.

Brontë, Charlotte. *Jane Eyre.* 1847. Ed. Richard J. Dunn. Norton Critical Editions. 3rd ed. New York: Norton, 2001.

———. *Villette.* 1853. Ed. Mark Lilly. Introd. Tony Tanner. New York: Penguin, 1985.

Brontë, Emily. *Wuthering Heights.* 1847. Ed. Linda H. Peterson. Boston: St. Martin's, 1992.

Brooks, Peter. *Reading for the Plot.* Cambridge, Mass.: Harvard University Press, 1984.

Browning, Elizabeth Barrett. *The Letters of Elizabeth Barrett Browning.* 2 vols. Ed. F. G. Kenyon. New York: Macmillan, 1897. Teddington, Middlesex, UK: Echo Library, 2007.

Bulwer-Lytton, Edward. *Eugene Aram.* 1832. Philadelphia: Lippincott, 1891.

Burney, Fanny. *Evelina, or The History of a Young Lady's Entrance into the World.* 1778. London: T. Lowndes, 1779.

Carroll, Lewis. *Alice's Adventures in Wonderland.* 1865. Illus. John Tenniel. London: Macmillan, 1866. New York: Knopf, 1984.

———. *The Annotated Alice: Alice's Adventures in Wonderland* and *Through the Looking-Glass.* Ed. Martin Gardner. Illus. John Tenniel. New York: New American Library, 1960.

———. *Eight or Nine Wise Words About Letter-Writing.* 1890. Delray Beach, Fla.: Levenger Press, 1999.

Cleere, Eileen. *Avuncularism: Capitalism, Patriarchy, and Nineteenth-Century English Culture.* Stanford: Stanford University Press, 2004.

Cochrane, William. "The Language of Stamps." *Philatelic Database,* June 4, 2008. <http://www.philatelicdatabase.com/nostalgia/the-language-of-stamps/>.

Cohen, Deborah. *Household Gods: The British and Their Possessions.* New Haven: Yale University Press, 2006.

Cohen, Morton N. *Lewis Carroll: A Biography.* New York: Knopf, 1995.

———, ed. *The Selected Letters of Lewis Carroll.* New York: Pantheon Books, 1978.

Cohen, Morton N., ed., assisted by Roger Lancelyn Green. *The Letters of Lewis Carroll.* 2 vols. New York: Oxford University Press, 1979.

Cole, Henry. *Fifty Years of Public Work.* 2 vols. London: George Bell, 1884.

———. "A Report of an Imaginary Scene at Windsor Castle Respecting the Uniform Penny Postage." 1838. In Fryer and Akerman, *Reform of the Post Office,* 2: 742–45.

Coleridge, Samuel Taylor. *Letters, Conversations, and Recollections of S. T. Coleridge.* 2 vols. London: Moxon, 1836.

———. *Letters, Conversations, and Recollections of S. T. Coleridge.* New York: Harper, 1836.

Collins, Wilkie. *The Moonstone.* 1868. New York: Dover, 2002.

———. *No Name.* 1862. Ed. Mark Ford. London: Penguin, 1994.

———. *The Woman in White.* 1860. Ed. John Sutherland. Oxford: Oxford University Press, 1996.

"Community impact of PO closures," *BBC News,* December 9, 2006. <http://news.bbc.co.uk/1/hi/uk/6165035.stm>, accessed December 9, 2007.

Companion to the Writing Desk; or, How to address, begin, and end letters. London: R. Hardwicke, 1861.

Cooke, Rev. T. *The Universal Letter Writer; or New Art of Polite Correspondence.* 1771? London: Milner and Company, c. 1850.

Croker, John Wilson. "Post-Office Reform." *Quarterly Review* 64.128 (October 1839): 513–74.

Cruikshank, George. *The Bottle. In Eight Plates by George Cruikshank.* London: David Bogue, 1847.

———. *The Drunkard's Children. A Sequel to the Bottle. In Eight Plates by George Cruikshank.* London: David Bogue, 1848.

Daunton, M. J. *Royal Mail: The Post Office Since 1840.* London: Athlone Press, 1985.

de Vries, Lloyd. "Was It *Really* Lost in the Mail?" *CBS News.com,* October 20, 2002. <http://www.cbsnews.com/stories/2002/10/15/national/main525701.shtml?source=search_story>, accessed August 15, 2008.

Dickens, Charles. *Bleak House.* 1853. Illus. Hablot Knight Browne. London: Chapman & Hall, 1892.

———. *David Copperfield.* 1850. Ed. Jerome H. Buckley. Illus. Hablot Knight Browne. New York: Norton, 1990.

———. *Nicholas Nickleby.* 1839. Illus. Hablot Knight Browne. New York: Penguin, 1999.

———. *Oliver Twist.* 1838. Ed. Kathleen Tillotson. Illus. George Cruikshank. New York: Oxford University Press, 1982.

———. *Sketches by Boz.* 1836. Ed. Dennis Walder. Illus. George Cruikshank. New York: Penguin, 1996.

Dickens, Charles, and W. H. Wills. "Valentine's Day at the Post-Office." *Household Words: A Weekly Journal,* March 30, 1850: 6–12.

Disraeli, Benjamin. *Endymion.* New York: D. Appleton, 1880.

Edelstein, T. J. "Augustus Egg's Triptych: A Narrative of Victorian Adultery." *Burlington Magazine,* April 1983: 202–12.

Eliot, George. *Adam Bede.* 1859. Ed. Stephen Gill. New York: Penguin, 1988.

———. *Middlemarch.* 1872. Ed. W. J. Harvey. New York: Penguin, 1976.

———. *The Mill on the Floss.* 1860. Ed. Gordon S. Haight. New York: Oxford University Press, 1980.

Evans, E. B. *The Mulready Envelope and its Caricatures.* London: Stanley Gibbons, 1891.

"The Exhibitions of 1860." *Fraser's Magazine,* June 1860: 878.

Favret, Mary. *Romantic Correspondence: Women, Politics, and the Fiction of Letters.* Cambridge: Cambridge University Press, 1994.

"The first modern Valentine cards." A Flowering of Affection: Victorian Valentine Cards at the Lilly Library. Online exhibition. <http://www.indiana.edu/~liblilly/valentines/valentine.html>, accessed May 29, 2007.

Flanders, Judith. *Inside the Victorian Home: A Portrait of Domestic Life in Victorian England*. New York: Norton, 2004.

Flaubert, Gustave. *Madame Bovary*. 1857. Ed. Leo Bersani. Trans. Lowell Bair. New York: Bantam, 1989.

Fletcher Collection. Philatelic Collections. British Library, London, England.

Frank Staff Collection. Valentines. *Bath Postal Museum Digital Collections*, Bath, England. <http://www.bathpostalmuseum.co.uk/digitalcollections/25_valentines/index.html>.

Fryer, Gavin, and Clive Akerman, eds. Fwd. Asa Briggs. *The Reform of the Post Office in the Victorian Era and Its Impact on Economic and Social Activity: Documentary History 1837 to 1864 Based on Sir Rowland Hill's Journal and Ancillary Papers*. 2 vols. London: Royal Philatelic Society, 2000.

Gaskell, Elizabeth. "Lizzie Leigh." *Nineteenth-Century Stories by Women: An Anthology*. Ed. Glennis Stephenson. Peterborough, Ontario: Broadview Press, 1993. 249–83.

——. *Mary Barton*. 1848. Ed. Edgar Wright. New York: Oxford University Press, 1998.

——. "Mr. Harrison's Confessions." 1851. *Cranford and Other Stories*. London: Wordsworth, 2006.

——. *North and South*. 1855. Ed. Alan Shelston. New York: Norton, 1995.

——. *Ruth*. 1853. Ed. Alan Shelston. Oxford: Oxford University Press, 1989.

——. *Wives and Daughters*. 1866. Ed. Pam Morris. New York: Penguin, 1996.

Glendenning, Victoria. *Anthony Trollope*. New York: Knopf, 1993.

Goethe, Johann Wolfgang von. *The Sorrows of Young Werther*. 1774. London: Scholartis, 1929.

Golden, Catherine J. *Images of the Woman Reader in Victorian British and American Fiction*. Gainesville, Fla.: University Press of Florida, 2003.

Golden, Fran. "Sit right down and write someone a letter." *Saratogian*, August 19, 2007: 1C.

Gormley, Michael. "Cuomo Warns Popular Web Site," *Saratogian*, October 1, 2007: 1A+.

Gotland, Bob, and Dick Armstrong. "Returned Letter Wrappers." *Journal of the GB Philatelic Society* 43.4 (July/August 2005): 91–96.

"The Great Exhibition." *Wikipedia*. <http://en.wikipedia.org/wiki/Great_Exhibition>, accessed August 21, 2008.

Great Exhibition of the Works of Industry of all Nations, 1851. Official Descriptive and Illustrated Catalogue. By Authority of the Royal Commission. In Three Volumes. London: Spicer Brothers, 1851.

Greenaway, Kate. *Language of Flowers*. London: Routledge, 1884.

"Greetings from 1956." *Saratogian*, April 15, 2006: 3C.

Hardy, Thomas. *Far from the Madding Crowd*. 1874. New York: Bantam, 1974.

——. *The Mayor of Casterbridge*. 1886. New York: Signet, 1962.

——. *Tess of the D'Urbervilles*. 1891. Ed. Scott Elledge. 3rd ed. New York: Norton, 1991.

Harris, David. *Portable Writing Desks*. Buckinghamshire, UK: Shire, 2001.

Harrison, Antony H. "Christina Rossetti and Caroline Gemmer: Friendship by Royal Mail." *Victorians Institute Journal* 24 (1996): 225–46.

Henkin, David. *The Postal Age: The Emergence of Modern Communications in Nineteenth-Century America.* Chicago: University of Chicago Press, 2006.

Hey, Colin. *Rowland Hill: Genius and Benefactor 1795–1879.* London: Quiller Press, 1989.

Hibbert, Christopher. *Daily Life in Victorian England.* New York: American Heritage, 1975.

Hill, H. W. *Rowland Hill and the Fight for the Penny Post.* London: Warne, 1940.

Hill, M. D. "Post-Office Reform." *Edinburgh Review* 80 (January 1840): 545–73.

Hill, Pearson. *The Post Office of Fifty Years Ago.* London: Cassell, 1887.

Hill, Rowland. *Post Office Reform: Its Importance and Practicability.* 2nd edition. London: Charles Knight, 1837.

———. *The State and Prospects of Penny Postage, as Developed in the Evidence Taken before the Postage Committee of 1843.* London: Charles Knight, 1843.

Hill, Rowland, and George Birkbeck Hill. *The Life of Sir Rowland Hill.* 2 vols. London: De La Rue, 1880.

Holder, Judith. *Sweethearts and Valentines.* New York: A & W, 1980.

"Horiginal Obserwations." *Punch, or, The London Charivari* 3.69 (November 5, 1842): 166.

Houghton, Walter. The Victorian Frame of Mind. New Haven: Yale University Press, 1957.

Hughes, Kristine. *The Writer's Guide to Everyday Life in Regency and Victorian England from 1811–1901.* Cincinnati, Ohio: Writer's Digest Books, 1998.

Humphreys, Camilla. "Dickens's Use of Letters in *Bleak House.*" *Dickens Quarterly* 6.2 (June 1989): 53–60.

Hyde, J. Wilson. *The Royal Mail: Its Curiosities and Romance.* London: Simpkin, 1889.

James, Alan. *Sir Rowland Hill and the Post Office.* Then and There Series. London: Longman, 1972.

John, Richard. *Spreading the News.* Cambridge, Mass.: Harvard University Press, 1995.

Jones, Ann Rosalind, and Peter Stallybrass. *Renaissance Clothing and the Materials of Memory.* Cambridge: Cambridge University Press, 2000.

Kandaouroff, Prince Dimitry. *Postmarks, Cards and Covers: Collecting Postal History.* New York: Larouse, 1973.

Kelvin, Norman. "Editions of Letters in the Age of the Vanishing Text." *Victorian Literature and Culture* 27.2 (1999): 589–600.

"Key Dates." British Postal Museum & Archive. <http://www.postalheritage.org.uk/history/keydates/?searchterm=key%20dates>, accessed January 26, 2009.

"Key Dates in the Sociological History and Development of Great Britain." Educational Resources. *thepotteries.org.* <http://www.thepotteries.org/dates/census.htm>, accessed December 15, 2007.

King, Andrew, and John Plunkett, eds. *Victorian Print Media: A Reader.* New York: Oxford University Press, 2005.

Kipling, Rudyard. *Kim.* London: Macmillan, 1901.

Kress, Anne, and Suellyn Winkle, comps. *NextText: Making Connections Across and Beyond the Disciplines.* New York: St. Martin's, 2007.

Kriegel, Lara. *Grand Designs: Labor, Empire, and the Museum in Victorian Culture.* Durham, N.C.: Duke University Press, 2007.

Kucich, John. *Repression in Victorian Fiction*. Berkeley: University of California Press, 1988.

Laclos, Pierre Choderlos de. *Les liaisons dangereuses*. 1782. Trans. and ed. Douglas Parmée. Introd. David Coward. New York: Oxford University Press, 1995.

Landow, George. "Richard Redgrave." *Victorian Web*. <http://www.victorianweb.org/painting/redgrave/paintings/4.html>, accessed December 15, 2007.

"Language of Flowers." *Victorian Bazaar*. <http://victorianbazaar.com/meanings.html>, accessed December 15, 2007.

"Le langage des timbres." *Mag'Timbre*. <http://timbreposte.free.fr/mag-timbre/langage-des-timbres.html>.

"Letter arrives eight years late." *BBC News*, August 4, 2005. <http://news.bbc.co.uk/1/hi/england/wear/4744591.stm>, accessed December 7, 2007.

Lewins, William. *Her Majesty's Mails: A History of the Post Office and an Industrial Account of Its Present Condition*. 1864. 2nd ed. London: Sampson Low, Son, and Marston, 1865.

"Lewis Carroll Related Postage Stamps." *Lewis Carroll Society*. <http://lewiscarrollsociety.org.uk/pages/inspired/stamps.htm>, accessed January 26, 2008.

Linder, Leslie, ed. *The History of the Writings of Beatrix Potter*. London: Warne, 1979.

Lowe, Robson. *The British Postage Stamp of the Nineteenth Century*. London: National Postal Museum, 1968.

Lynch, Tess. "Composition and Color in Egg's *Past and Present*." *Victorian Web*. <http://www.victorianweb.org/painting/egg/paintings/lynch1.html>, accessed December 15, 2007.

Macaulay, Thomas Babington. "Southey's Colloquies." *Critical and Historical Essays, Contributed to the Edinburgh Review*. London: Longman, 1861. 97–120.

Mancoff, Debra N. *Love's Messenger: Tokens of Affection in the Victorian Age*. Chicago: Art Institute of Chicago, 1997.

Martineau, Harriet. *The History of England During the Thirty Years' Peace*. 2 vols. London: Charles Knight, 1850.

———. "Letter to Sir Thomas Wilde, M.P." In *The Post Office of Fifty Years Ago*, by Pearson Hill. London: Cassell, 1887. 44–48.

Mason, Michael York. "Middlemarch and History." *Nineteenth-Century Fiction* 25.4 (March 1971): 417–31.

McLaren, Angus. *Sexual Blackmail: A Modern History*. Cambridge, Mass.: Harvard University Press, 2002.

McPherson, Scott. "Post office loses battle." *Wiltshire Gazette & Herald*, March 20, 2008. <http://www.gazetteandherald.co.uk/news/headlines/display.var.2135631.0.post_office_loses_battle.php>, accessed July 4, 2008.

Meisel, Martin. *Realizations: Narrative, Pictorial, and Theatrical Arts in the Nineteenth Century*. Princeton: Princeton University Press, 1983.

Miller, Lucasta. *The Brontë Myth*. New York: Anchor Books, 2005.

Muir, Douglas. *Postal Reform and the Penny Black: A New Appreciation*. London: National Postal Museum, 1990.

A New Letter-Writer, for the Use of Gentlemen. Philadelphia: Porter & Coates, 1868.

O'Keefe, Donna. "Public Ridicules Mulready Envelope." *Linn's Stamp News*, November 5, 1979: 66.

Oliphant, Margaret. "A Story of a Wedding Tour." *Nineteenth-Century Stories by Women: An Anthology*. Ed. Glennis Stephenson. Peterborough, Ontario: Broadview Press, 1993. 403–27.

O'Reilly, Timothy. "What Is Web 2.0: Design Patterns and Business Models for the Next Generation of Software." *O'Reilly*, September 30, 2005. <http://www.oreillynet.com/pub/a/oreilly/tim/news/2005/09/30/what-is-web-20.html>, accessed November 29, 2007.

Orr, Linda V. "Computer Anxiety." Paper written for Communication 499, University of Southern Maine. <http://www.usm.maine.edu/~com/lindap~1.htm>, accessed December 10, 2007.

Patmore, Coventry. *The Angel in the House*. 1854–63. London: Dutton, 1876.

Perry, C. R. *The Victorian Post Office: The Growth of a Bureaucracy*. Suffolk, UK: Boydell Press, 1992.

Perry, Ruth. *Women, Letters, and the Novel*. New York: AMS Press, 1980.

Philbrick, Frederick, and William Westoby. *Postage and Telegraph Stamps of Great Britain*. London: Sampson Low, Marston, Searle & Rivington, 1881.

"Pillar Boxes." Archive Information Sheet. British Postal Museum & Archive. <http://postalheritage.org.uk/history/downloads/BPMA%20Royal%20Mail%20Archive%20Info%20Sheet%20Pillar%20Boxes%20UPDATED%20March%202009.pdf/>.

Pool, Daniel. *What Jane Austen Ate and Charles Dickens Knew*. New York: Simon and Schuster, 1993.

Poole, John. *Paul Pry: A Comedy in Three Acts*. 1825. New York: E. M. Murden, 1827.

Porter, G. R. *The Progress of the Nation*. London: Murray, 1847.

The Post Circular. Or, Weekly Advocate for a Cheap, Swift, and Sure Postage. Ed. Henry Cole. No. 1. Wednesday, March, 14, 1838.

The Post Circular. Or, Weekly Advocate for a Cheap, Swift, and Sure Postage. Ed. Henry Cole. No. 2. Wednesday, March 21, 1838.

The Post Circular. Or, Weekly Advocate for a Cheap, Swift, and Sure Postage. Ed. Henry Cole. No. 3. Wednesday, March 28, 1838.

The Post Circular. Or, Advocate for a Cheap, Swift, and Sure Postage. Ed. Henry Cole. No. 4. Thursday, April 5, 1838.

The Post Circular. Or, Advocate for a Cheap, Swift, and Sure Postage. Ed. Henry Cole. No. 5. Tuesday, April 24, 1838.

The Post Circular. Or, Advocate for a Cheap, Swift, and Sure Postage. Ed. Henry Cole. No. 6. Friday, May 4, 1838.

The Post Circular. Or, Advocate for a Cheap, Swift, and Sure Postage. Ed. Henry Cole. No. 7. Friday, May 11, 1838.

The Post Circular. Or, Advocate for a Cheap, Swift, and Sure Postage. Ed. Henry Cole. No 8. Friday, May 25, 1838.

The Post Circular. Or, Advocate for a Cheap, Swift, and Sure Postage. Ed. Henry Cole. No. 9. Thursday, July 5, 1838.

The Post Circular. Or, Advocate for a Cheap, Swift, and Sure Postage. Ed. Henry Cole. No. 10. Thursday, March 28, 1839.

The Post Circular. Or, Advocate for a Cheap, Swift, and Sure Postage. Ed. Henry Cole. No. 11. Wednesday, April 17, 1839.

The Post Circular. Or, Advocate for a Cheap, Swift, and Sure Postage. Ed. Henry Cole. No. 12. Tuesday, April 30, 1839.

The Post Circular. Or, Advocate for a Cheap, Swift, and Sure Postage. Ed. Henry Cole. No. 13. Monday, June 24, 1839.

The Post Circular. Or, Advocate for a Cheap, Swift, and Sure Postage. Ed. Henry Cole. No. 14. Friday, June 28, 1839.

The Post Circular. Or, Advocate for a Cheap, Swift, and Sure Postage. Ed. Henry Cole. No. 15. Friday, October 11, 1839.

The Post Circular. Or, Advocate for a Cheap, Swift, and Sure Postage. Ed. Henry Cole. No. 16. Wednesday, November 20, 1839.

Pratchett, Terry. *Going Postal: A Novel of Discworld.* New York: Harper Collins, 2004.

"Punch on the Queen's Head." *Punch, or, The London Charivari* 3.69 (November 5, 1842): 201.

"Punch's Valentines!" *Punch, or, The London Charivari* 2.31 (February 12, 1842):62–74.

Ray, Gordon N. *The Letters and Private Papers of William Makepeace Thackeray.* 4 vols. Cambridge, Mass.: Harvard University Press, 1946.

Rheingold, Howard. *The Virtual Community: Homesteading on the Electronic Frontier.* Reading, Mass.: Addison-Wesley, 1993.

Richardson, Samuel. *Clarissa, or The History of a Young Lady.* 1748. Ed. Angus Ross. New York: Penguin, 1985.

———. *Pamela, or Virtue Rewarded.* 1740. Introd. George Saintsbury. London: Dent, 1914.

Rigo de Righi, A. G. *The Story of the Penny Black and Its Contemporaries.* London: National Postal Museum, 1980.

Roberts, Helene. "Marriage, Redundancy or Sin: The Painter's View of Women in the First Twenty-Five Years of Victoria's Reign." *Suffer and Be Still: Women in the Victorian Age.* Ed. Martha Vicinus. Bloomington: Indiana University Press, 1972. 45–76.

Robinson, Howard. *The British Post Office: A History.* Princeton: Princeton University Press, 1948.

Rosen, Bruce. *Victorian History.* Blog. <http://vichist.blogspot.com/2006_10_01_archive. html>, accessed December 15, 2007.

"The Royal Academy." *Punch, or, The London Charivari* 38.988 (June 16, 1860): 246.

Russell, Harriet. *Envelopes: A Puzzling Journey Through the Royal Mail.* New York: Random House, 2005.

Shefer, Elaine. "Woman's Mission." *Woman's Art Journal* 7.1 (Spring–Summer 1986): 8–12.

Shields, Carol. *Jane Austen.* New York: Penguin, 2001.

Simon, Linda. *Dark Light: Electricity and Anxiety from the Telegraph to the X-Ray.* Orlando: Harcourt, 2004.

"Sir Rowland Hill and The Penny Black." *Glassine Surfer.* <http://www.glassinesurfer.com/ stamp_collecting/gsrowlandhill.shtml>, accessed December 15, 2007.

Smyth, Eleanor C. *Sir Rowland Hill: The Story of a Great Reform Told By His Daughter.* London: T. Fisher Unwin, 1907.

Staff, Frank. *The Penny Post 1680–1918*. Cambridge, UK: Lutterworth Press, 1964.

Standage, Tom. *The Victorian Internet*. New York: Walker, 1998.

Steele, Valerie. *The Corset: A Cultural History*. New Haven: Yale University Press, 2001.

Stephens, Frederick George. "Royal Academy." *Athenaeum*, May 19, 1860: 688.

Stevenson, Robert Louis. *The Strange Case of Dr. Jekyll and Mr. Hyde*. 1886. Illus. Mervyn Peake. London: Dent, 1974.

———. *Treasure Island*. 1883. New York: Signet, 1998.

Stevenson, Seth. "Adventures in Cheating: A Guide to Buying Term Papers Online." *Slate*, December 11, 2001. <http://www.slate.com/?id=2059540>, accessed November 11, 2007.

Stoker, Bram. *Dracula*. 1897. Ed. Nina Auerbach and David J. Skal. New York: Norton, 1996.

Stone, Brad. "In ID Theft, Some Victims See Opportunity." *New York Times*, November 16, 2007. <http://www.nytimes.com/2007/11/16/business/16venture.html?r=1&>, accessed December 10, 2007.

Surtees, Robert. *"Ask Mama"; or, The Richest Commoner in England*. London: Bradbury & Evans, 1858.

Sutherland, John. "Introduction." *The Woman in White*. By Wilkie Collins. Oxford: Oxford University Press, 1996. vii–xxiii.

Tahmincioglu, Eve. "Adults often 'techno-wary.'" *USA Weekend*, July 20–22, 2007: 13.

Teller, Astro. "Smart Machines and Why We Fear Them." *New York Times on the Web*, March 21, 1997. <http://www.cs.cmu.edu/~astro/nytimes.html>, accessed November 30, 2007.

Thackeray, William Makepeace. *Vanity Fair: A Novel without a Hero*. 1848. Illus. W. M. Thackeray. 3 vols. New York: Scribner's, 1903.

———. *Vanity Fair: A Novel without a Hero*. Ed. John Sutherland. Illus. W. M. Thackeray. Oxford: Oxford University Press, 1983.

Trollope, Anthony. *Autobiography*. 1883. New York: Dodd, Mead, 1916.

———. *Barchester Towers*. 1857. Ed. John Sutherland. Oxford: Oxford University Press, 1996.

———. *Can You Forgive Her*. 1865. Ed. Andrew Swarbrick. Introd. Kate Flint. Illus. Lynton Lamb. Oxford: Oxford University Press, 1991.

———. *The Claverings*. 1867. Ed. David Skilton. Oxford: Oxford University Press, 1991.

———. *Dr. Wortle's School*. 1880. Ed. John Halperin. Oxford: Oxford University Press, 1984.

———. *He Knew He Was Right*. 1869. Ed. John Sutherland. Oxford: Oxford University Press, 1996.

———. *Kept in the Dark*. 1882. Illus. John Everett Millais. New York: Dover, 1978.

———. *Marion Fay*. 1882. New York: Penguin, 1993.

———. *Orley Farm*. 1862. Illus. John Everett Millais. New York: Dover, 1981.

———. *Phineas Finn*. 1869. Ed. Jacques Berthoud. Illus. T.L.B. Huskinson. New York: Oxford University Press, 1991.

———. *Phineas Redux*. 1874. Ed. John C. Whale. Illus. T.L.B. Huskinson. New York: Oxford University Press, 2009.

————. *The Warden.* 1855. Introd. David Skilton. Illus. Edward Ardizzone. Oxford: Oxford University Press, 1998.

Tucker, Reed. "Are You for Real." *USA Weekend*, September 21–23, 2007: 18.

"2,500 more post offices to close." *BBC News*, May 17, 2007. <http://news.bbc.co.uk/2/hi/uk_news/politics/6664109.stm>, accessed December 10, 2007.

"2,500 post offices face closure." *BBC News*, December 14, 2006. <http://news.bbc.co.uk/1/hi/uk/6176929.stm>, accessed December 10, 2007.

Valentine Cards. Special Collections. Bath Central Library, Bath, England.

Victorian Innovation. Online exhibition. British Postal Museum & Archive. <http://www.postalheritage.org.uk/exhibitions/onlineexhibitions/victorianinnovation/victorian innovation/?searchterm=Victorian%20Innovation>, accessed November 1, 2007.

Watt, George. *The Fallen Woman in the Nineteenth-Century English Novel.* London: Croom Helm, 1984. Totowa, N.J.: Barnes & Noble, 1984.

Webster's Ready-Made Love Letters. New York: De Witt, 1873.

Weinberger, David. *Small Pieces Loosely Joined (A Unified Theory of the Web).* Cambridge, Mass.: Perseus, 2002.

Weintraub, Stanley. *Victoria: An Intimate Biography.* New York: Dutton, 1987.

Welsh, Alexander. *George Eliot and Blackmail.* Cambridge, Mass.: Harvard University Press, 1985.

Whamond, Dave. *Reality Check* (comic strip). *Saratogian* (Saratoga Springs, N.Y.), September 25, 2007. Available online at *Comics.com.* <http://comics.com/reality_check/?DateAfter=2007-09-25&DateBefore=2007-09-25&Order=d.DateStrip+DESC &PerPage=1&Search=&x=45&y=8>.

"What is the Harm of Novel-Reading?" *The Wesleyan-Methodist Magazine*, October 1855: 932–34.

The Wide World Letter Writer: Letters With Answers. London: Milner, n.d.

Wilde, Oscar. *The Picture of Dorian Gray.* 1891. Ed. Richard Ellmann. New York: Bantam, 1982.

————. *An Ideal Husband.* 1895. New York: Dover, 2000.

"William Wyon." *Bits and Pieces.* Articles on the history of coins. <http://www.users.bigpond.com/cruzi/Coins/Grading/Engravers.htm#WilliamWyon>, accessed December 15, 2007.

Williams, L. N., and M. Williams. *The Postage Stamp: Its History and Recognition.* London: Penguin, 1956.

Wilson, A. N. *The Victorians.* New York: Norton, 2003.

Wymer, Norman. *Social Reformers.* Oxford: Oxford University Press, 1955.

Index

Catherine J. Golden is professor of English at Skidmore College. She has published widely on Victorian illustrated fiction and British and American women writers. She is author of *Images of the Woman Reader in Victorian British and American Fiction* (UPF 2003) and editor of five books, including, most recently, *Charlotte Perkins Gilman's* The Yellow Wall-Paper: *A Source-book and Critical Edition* (2004) and *Book Illustrated: Text, Image, and Culture 1770–1930* (2000).